The Ruins of Allegory

Paradise Lost and the

Metamorphosis of Epic Convention

Catherine Gimelli Martin

Duke University Press   Durham and London

1998

© 1998 Duke University Press

All rights reserved

Printed in the United States of America

on acid-free paper ∞

Typeset in Adobe Caslon by Keystone Typesetting, Inc.

Library of Congress Cataloging-in-Publication

Data appear on the last printed

page of this book.

For Michael Fixler,

"magnanimous to correspond"

". . . he who would not be frustrate of his hope to write well hereafter in laudable things, ought him selfe to bee a true Poem, that is, a composition, and patterne of the best and honourablest things; not presuming to sing high praises of heroick men, or famous Cities, unlesse he have in himselfe the experience and the practice of all that which is praise-worthy."

JOHN MILTON, An Apology

Contents

Preface

Like every work of its kind, this one has antecedents to which neither I nor this preface can fully do justice, although they can at least be named. First in order of time there are Robert Peters and the late Diane Dickinson and, at the University of California, Santa Cruz, Harry Berger Jr., to whose influence over a great many years I owe whatever small skill I have in dealing with the rich ambiguities of the poetic text. Then there are George Amis and Angus Fletcher, who helped shape the original parameters of this project, and, in particular, Hayden White, to whom I owe not only a general refinement of my rhetorical and theoretical concerns but also sincere gratitude for his quasi-"heroic" faith in this project and in my work generally. Later, in the world of Milton and seventeenth-century studies I have been fortunate to encounter scholars who have either encouraged or specifically critiqued the various versions and successive drafts of my manuscript. In the former group I would express my appreciation first to Mary Ann Radzinowicz, Stella Revard, Joan Bennett, Ted-Larry Pebworth, and Claude Summers, in the latter to Marshall Grossman, John Shawcross, and Gordon Teskey. Along with these, I owe an enormous technical debt to my computer expert and colleague William O'Donnell and to the University of Memphis for numerous semester and summer grants.

However, most of all I must thank a belated but far from insignificant contributor to this project. When, after the first draft of my complete book manuscript was accepted by the Duke University Press, I submitted an article to *Milton Studies* on the "reformed" and scientifically "prophetic" aspects of Milton's Chaos, it was critiqued by an enormously learned and at first anonymous reader who afterward asked to correspond with me on the subject of chaos theory. He has since become a dear friend, close collaborater, and postgraduate course rolled into one. Because the incommensurable scholarly debts that I have since incurred to Michael Fixler and his enormously hospitable family can by no means be repaid in any other way, this book is dedicated to him. Nevertheless, at least symbolically this dedication is meant to include the hospitality and resources generously extended by Charlotte Fixler during the final revision of this manuscript. To my own family it goes without saying that my debts are equally enormous; their exemplary standing and waiting, *almost* always with "no fear lest dinner cool," has been virtually prelapsarian. This book, then, is also for them—for Richard, Justin, Matthew, and Jessamyn—as well as for the rest of my extended family in scholarship and its friendly persuasions.

Acknowledgments

Portions of chapter 2 are based on "'Boundless the Deep': Milton, Pascal, and the Theology of Relative Space," which appeared in *ELH* 63 (1996): 45–78, here reprinted with the permission of the Johns Hopkins University Press. Two separate and shorter versions of chapter 4 are contained in two articles: "'Pregnant Causes Mixt': The Wages of Sin and the Laws of Entropy in Milton's Chaos," which appeared in *Arenas of Conflict: Milton and the Unfettered Mind*, ed. Kristin McColgan and Charles Durham (Selinsgrove, Pa.: Susquehanna University Press, 1997), here reprinted with the permission of the Associated University Presses; and "Fire, Ice, and Epic Entropy: The Physics and Metaphysics of Milton's Reformed Chaos," which appeared in *Milton Studies*, vol. 35, ed. Albert C. Labriola (Pittsburgh: Pittsburgh University Press, 1998), here reprinted with the permission of the University of Pittsburgh Press. Finally, the first half of chapter 6 was first published as "Demystifying Disguises: Adam, Eve, and the Subject of Desire," in *Renaissance Discourses of Desire*, ed. Claude Summers and Ted-Larry Pebworth (Columbia: University of Missouri Press, 1993), here reprinted with the permission of the University of Missouri Press; and the second half as "Ithuriel's Spear: Purity, Danger, and Allegory at the Gates of Eden," in *Studies in English Literature, 1500–1900* 33, no. 1 (Winter 1993): 167–90, here reprinted with the permission of *Studies in English Literature, 1500–1900*.

Introduction

It might be said that civilization can only have its epic poets in advance. Just as a man cannot report his own death when it happens, but only foresee it and describe it as something lying in the future. So . . . if you want to see an epic description of a whole culture, you will have to look at the works . . . composed when the end of this culture could only be foreseen . . . [whence] it's not to be wondered at that it should only be written in the obscure language of prophecy, comprehensible to very few indeed.

LUDWIG WITTGENSTEIN, *Culture and Value*

1

Philosophers have been telling us for the better part of our century that "the end of this culture" to which Wittgenstein refers, the culture of modernity, has been upon us ever since the skeptical quest for certainty—beginning with Descartes—paradoxically turned up as its only certainty the uncertainty of certainty itself. Acceptance of this paradox, if not all of its ramifications, may well be the defining premise of the postmodern, which in theoretical terms foregrounds the uncertainty of certainty as inherent in the self-referential domain wherein language about language describes itself. This ironic, self-reflexive, or metalinguistic character of all writing is now considered the constitutive condition of its powers as well as of its inherent limitations, with the result that limitations in language have actually begun to define the limitations of philosophy itself. But philosophy of course can know no terminus ad quem, no more than the ongoing activity of the human mind can be said to define the limits of a culture; only by going beyond postmodern celebrations of uncertainty to a way of building on uncertainty itself—as quite probably the creative ground of all meaning—can we choose to consider the aptness of Wittgenstein's remark to *Paradise Lost*.

In a number of respects, its aptness would seem wholly uncontroversial since Milton's epic has long been considered an "obscure prophecy" not only of the "fall" of Christian culture from its pinnacle in the Renaissance but also of the demise of the heroic conventions that it had inherited from the classical past. Yet this standard view also precludes the epic's poetic potential to foresee the demise of post-Cartesian culture since this interpretation regards it as the culmination of the privileged Renaissance mode, not as a vision of the demise of the mode that would succeed it. This received view also substantially accords with Marx's memorable image of Milton "spinning" the fibers of his poem from some wellspring of innate and acquired materials, like the silkworm constructing the cocoon of a common culture that was about to evolve into an altogether different phase, that of alienated value and commodity exchange.[1] Although this argument has some undeniable merits, the current study attempts to weave its supporting strands into a fabric of an ultimately antithetical shape—one in which Milton's epic represents a society already in the process of rupturing and giving birth, as by a great "divorcing command the world first rose out of Chaos,"[2] to a completely mutated form of existence. This cataclysmic or disjunctive view of literary evolution therefore entails a detailed examination of the cultural and aesthetic conditions that turn *Paradise Lost* into a completely different kind of apotheosis, one far more in harmony with Walter Benjamin's thesis that seventeenth-century allegories are to "the realm of thoughts, what ruins are in the realm of things"[3]—a baroque rupture with normative allegory.

Benjamin's alternative perspective on this traditional mode also supports Wittgenstein's account of the "tragic" loss of certain or determinate meaning occurring with the onset of modernity in the seventeenth century. Yet, now, as then, the absence of linguistic certitude leaves behind not merely chaotic "noise" but (as in modern information theory) an instability that through reiterative or poetic redundancy provides the ground of all meaningful communication. In beginning to contemplate "what the laws are of a true *Epic* poem," Milton seems early to have foreseen this latest chapter of linguistic history in asserting that poetry intuitively and communicatively supersedes logic and rhetoric, as at once "more simple, sensuous, and passionate" than either (*CPW*, 2:402–3). Thus, in both Miltonic and post-Wittgensteinian theory, maximum clarity actually equals minimum communication, much like maximum noise, for (as Claude

Shannon has shown) truly "meaningful" or content-bearing communication fuses allusive obscurity with the clarity of transparently referential or redundant language.[4] From this perspective, the purely referential project of logical positivism, the linguistic "calculus" that Russell, Whitehead, and the early Wittgenstein sought to develop, was inherently doomed to failure, which again makes the latter's remark a peculiarly apt description of Milton's epic project. When the project of fashioning a purely referential language began in the seventeenth century along with that of Cartesian philosophy, Descartes believed that his "clear and distinct" ideas could banish the "evil genius" of obscurity from rational discourse. In response, Milton's epic directly addresses the problem of evil in terms that make poetic obscurity an inevitable aspect even of the unfallen language that his *Art of Logic* asserts we retain. Yet, precisely because he does respond to this new paradigm, neither his great epic nor *Paradise Regained* can completely banish the evil genius of the Cartesian philosopher who had come to dominate the age. Instead, he appears in the guise of Satan, who expects these "clear and distinct" first principles to justify his epic existence:

> We know no times when we were not as now;
> Know none before us, self-begot, self-rais'd
> By our own quick'ning power. . . .[5]

Ironically, Satan's self-creation from Lucifer also makes him right, or at least in part. Yet, by reframing these assertions as satanic illusions, *Paradise Lost* foresees the coming *eschaton* to which Wittgenstein alludes in secular terms, a moment that Milton's poetic account of the Fall could prophesy only obscurely: the downfall of the Cartesian certitude then triumphant. But the quasi-satanic specter of Descartes is never conclusively defeated since this shadowy Achillean figure, like Galileo's explicit presence, supplies the continuing rivalry in the epic contest between the poet-protagonist and his contemporary Hectors, the fellow visionaries of a disputed future. And in the background is another burning Troy that all alike must leave behind, the "ruined" cultural catalogs of classical Christian or Realist allegory. This context supplies the distant backdrop of Milton's heroic poem, much as the problems inherent in our current understanding of the certainty of uncertainty provide its foreground. For its valuable survey of that background, or of the transition to late Reformation or baroque allegory generally, Benjamin's study of this "tragic" mode of cultural elegy is particularly relevant here. In these transitional baroque records of rupture, as in Milton, the truth of prophecy is never numinously "present," not even in the figural and linguistic gaps that typically (as in both Dante and Spenser) point toward a completion in things just beyond the realm of poetic thought.[6] Thus, like the current study, Benjamin's theory begins with the old scholastic relation of "words, things, and thought" that had triangulated the whole realm of meaning (where "thoughts" were to "things" as "words" were to both) and its rupture in the seventeenth century. Yet, since this triangulation of correspondences is always inherently unstable, we take Benjamin to mean in part that any extended analogy—which allegory assuredly is—breaks down internally, when it is pushed too far, or externally, when its conceptual foundation is eroded.

The analogy of allegory depends on a secure assurance that the complexity of the world can be subsumed within the intelligibility of a figural and/or diagrammatic relation of parts. In a divinely or-dained world, allegory is hieratic insofar as it reflects a ceremonial or ritual "ascent" to a vision of this wholeness. In the seventeenth cen-tury, this integration is vitiated not by any generalized loss of faith in the wholeness of the world or even in its ultimate divinity but by a scientific realism that demanded that its autonomous parts be vir-tualized (or real-ized) according to naturalistic rather than hieratic or initiatory schemas. Milton is typical of baroque artists in that he responds to the restrictions imposed by the new scientific order by cultivating a form of allegorical equivocity that allows the parts of his cosmos to be configured both as organic and as immanently numi-nous remnants of a divine hierarchy. Thus, "What if earth / Be but the shadow of heaven?" also means, What if it is not? an equivoca-tion that allows the figure ceaselessly to oscillate between both poles of meaning, which, in terms of information theory, means that it attracts enriched possibilities of meaningfulness. Yet, at the same time, it also means that allegorical certitudes have begun to break down into the ironic mode of baroque meta-allegory.

Thus, like baroque allegory generally, *Paradise Lost* not only "ruins" but "gathers up" in order to mourn the hieratic remnants of its own fragmentation. Benjamin traces the origins of this process to early seventeenth-century works like Shakespeare's *Hamlet*, which opens with the hero facing the ghost of chivalric culture, the father in whose shadow he stands. Such works are repetitively purgatorial rather than redemptive, framing their reflections on the ruins of their Elsinores through the elaborately interlocking architectonics that we describe as metatheatrical: plays within plays within plays. Much the same structure can be found in the nondramatistic *trauerspiel* or "tragic play" of late Reformation lyric and epic modes, which, as in Milton's "Lycidas" and *Comus* as well as *Paradise Lost,* exhibit a highly self-reflexive or meta-allegorical form. The convoluted architectonics of works so enmeshed in the circularity of self-reference is thus parallel to that discussed in Michel Foucault's famous analysis of Velasquez's *Las meninas,* which creates multidimensional mirrors so mutually intensifying as to become ultimately "ruinous."[7]

Yet, like the form of referentiality we find in Hamlet's play within plays, Milton's epic "interplay" paradoxically becomes a more realistic record of loss precisely to the degree that its staging is explicitly recognized as artificial. Just as the audience of *Hamlet* watching the audience watching the old-fashioned ritual drama *The Mousetrap* is temporarily removed from both immediate contexts to observe the hero/director observing Claudius, its own intimate involvement with these multiple frameworks also allows the spectators more immediately to engage with the backstage realities of Hamlet's dilemma. This same trompe l'oeil or baroque form of realism surrounds the reader watching God watching Satan observing Adam admiring Eve, a process that thoroughly implicates him or her, if not in Satan's morally suspect voyeurism, then at least in the problems of value inherent in any purely inward or internal sense of worth that, through Satan, threatens the reader's perception of paradise and its God with his competing perspective. This apparent disparity between subjective and objective perspectives additionally underlies the problems of value that exercised Wittgenstein, problems that inevitably confront any culture that grounds its certitudes on such "transparent" or "literal" concepts as Cartesian "clear and distinct ideas" or on the Reformers' similarly "distinct idea" of the "spirit within."

The irony here, then, is that this rationalist age of renewed certitude in philosophy, science, and religion is actually the beginning of a greater age of doubt that prophetic poets like Milton (as well as anti-Cartesian philosophers like Pascal) could begin to foresee in advance. Yet, like most prophetic moments, it begins by looking backward, by mourning the lost certitudes and assured transcendence of the old closed universe, which could project its metamorphoses onto the still point just beyond the finite world. But, since they also look forward, such visionary thinkers also project a limited recovery of these assurances onto the infinite plane of the boundless universe. If, then, there is no strict Miltonic equivalent to Pascal's famous meditation on how the universal "double infinities" find their absent, incommensurable center in his hidden God, the young, like the mature, poet similarly mourns the absent body of "virgin Truth" whose thousand remnants have been infinitely scattered. Yet, in this famous passage from *Areopagitica,* he also imagines her ruins being reassembled, not just in the infinite climax of the Second Coming, but in the ever-growing light of that "combust" space wherein "the opposite motion of [planetary] orbs bring them to such a place in the firmament, where they may be seen evning or morning" (*CPW,* 2:549). Thus even now these partially ruined remnants of Truth are not *lacking* in all the numinous significance traditionally associated with pagan myth, which, as here, "translated" the natural sacramentalism of the *priscii theologiae* into Christian symbols; but, as its central myth testifies, these ancient "dying god" motifs are ceaselessly reborn only to die again in new form. Nevertheless, since Milton's Isis can never recover the body of Osiris entire, most certainly not by any initiation into the "holy rites" of truth classically signified by normative allegory, here, as in his "Nativity Ode," they are placed under meta-allegorical erasure, victims of the baroque impulse to recapitulate the original ruin wherein the pagan gods died and were resurrected as the abstract virtues and powers of Christianity.[8]

An obvious impetus to this process is the Reformation's rejection of the "whorish attire" of such pagan figures, particularly after they have been identified (as in the *Animadversions*) with the suspect sacramentalism of the *"Popish* Masse" (*CPW,* 1:687). Yet, as previously, this reforming impulse produces not an utter rejection but a self-conscious, Isis-like "sifting" of inherited symbols and tropes, an activity intensified in the late Reformation phase when Christianity itself began its decay from its original historical/hermeneutical synthesis into the more violent dissent over symbolic forms exemplified in Milton's *Animadversions.* Later it would decay even further into a sort of literary biblical supply house for the kind of satiric epic "fable" that Dryden or Pope might write, although their ironic employment of the traditional psychomachia is already apparent in Milton's War in Heaven. Yet, in Milton's still pre–mock heroic phase, the gods do not merely die; they are ironically/organically reborn once again as fallen angels locked "In dubious Battle on the Plains of Heav'n" (*PL,* 1.104). Thereafter revived as demons who finally deteriorate into pagan idols, these end up having an eerily contemporary ring, not just by coming to rest in "the *Celtic* . . . Isles" (1.521) inhabited by the poet, but more specifically by being led by Moloch, Belial, and Mammon, easily identified as post-Restoration, protocapitalist deities of war, luxury, and greed. In making this historical process explicit, the epic thereby opens the possibly interminable prospect of the death and renewal of all cultural personifications, as if the symbolic creatures of Scripture itself might have only a contingent, relative, and renewable value in relation to humanly accommodated truth. In self-reflexively critiquing such personifications, the meta-allegory of *Paradise Lost* formally and semantically explores the limitations of standard intentional as well as traditional sacramental meaning by metatheatrically redoubling its already doubled identity as fictive/literal truth. In the process, it also proleptically foreshadows the mysterious dynamism inherent in uncertainty itself, a potential that seemed to be foreclosed both by Cartesian thought and by the more "certain" allegorical tradition then drawing to a close.

However, before returning to this foreground, it will be necessary to examine the background of Milton's epic critique more closely, especially since it has so often been confused with the theodicy that he simultaneously undertakes.[9] Although it has important antecedents in Prudentius and Pseudo-Dionysius, the mainline tradition of Christian epic-allegory (including the Christianization of Virgil) stems chiefly from Augustine's Platonic conception of the disparity between the city of God and the city of Man. Because the former is eternal and the latter ephemeral, works based on this schema trace the progress of the soul upward from flesh to spirit, from earth to heaven, from shadowy types or images to truth. Both their plot and their conception of language are thus ultimately based on the ancient myths of purgation and return that form the central sacramental belief system of Christianity and that similarly calls for an upwardly intensifying structure of symbolic progress on the ladder leading to the inner sanctum of divine mystery. Although the final book of *Paradise Lost* alludes to this standard ascent, it does so in characteristically critical Reformation terms. Having outgrown the "imposition of strict Laws" and ceremonies, the believer is to enter into the current dispensation of "free / Acceptance of large Grace" freed from "servile fear" (*PL,* 12.303–5). Even more significantly, this obliquely self-referential, individualistic, and antiprelatical conception of grace is placed in the context of the epic's final descent into the wilderness of the world, the city of Man.[10]

Here, Adam and Eve shed some "natural tears" (*PL,* 12.645), for, in the very real sense of which Milton is aware, the standard allegorical ascent is more "natural" insofar as it addresses our longing not just for Eden but for some more concrete diagrammatic or "logical" map to its point of return. However iconically dense, opaque, or conventional ritual symbols may be, they at least have the virtue of conveying assurances that Milton's "paradise within" must refuse. And along with this refusal is lost that translucence that illuminates even the most mysterious of poetic veils, the clear light produced by a far stricter segregation of the sacred from the profane, of the impure from the pure, than Milton's epic affords. The far more dubious encounters of meta-allegory are thus more "natural" only according to a quite different conception of human life, one largely stripped of transcendence and plunged into the secular indeterminacy associated with modern conceptions of naturalistic mimesis.

Thus, in keeping with Adam's "natural tears," no aspect of Milton's epic—most especially *not* the enigmatic finale of his War in Heaven—provides any ultimate segregation or victory of good over evil. Instead, we find, not only an ambiguous and largely inward sense of how evil may be overcome, but also the sense that evil is merely that form of depravity inimical to life. Hence, even Satan—as critics uncomfortable with the baroque have notoriously objected—exhibits a highly psychologistic, even humanly sympathetic struggle between virtue and vice. This conception is utterly inconsistent, not only with the Dantean devil frozen in sin, but also with the Scholastic schematism and sacramentalism of allegory's normative mode. Rather, in harmony with the empirically based natural theology favored by progressive seventeenth-century divines, Milton's theodicy must then confront the problems inherent in its "scientistic" premises, which attempt to command the same consensual agreement as the objectively clear and distinct data of Cartesian reason. For, like the new science itself, this theology tends to create a rationalized deity little capable of dispensing grace, much less of explaining the classic questions surrounding the original "contamination" that all Christian epic-allegory, but particularly Milton's postrevolutionary epic, confronts: the reason for the origin and continuation of evil.

Earlier, this problem more than any other caused the allegorical Christian godhead to remain inscrutable and indecipherable, a three-personed deity conveniently subdivided into the competing qualities of justice (the Father), mercy or love (the Son), and wisdom or grace (the Spirit), a schema that Milton early toyed with and later rejected. While some of this mystery persists in the relation between his Father and Son, the unitary will of the former remains far too clear and the mercy of the latter far too shadowy to achieve a comparably Dantean resolution.[11] Instead, Milton's monistic, naturalistic universe, where there is no ultimate segregation between earth and heaven (*PL,* 5.469–79), seems to demand a godhead of the same order—which is precisely what Milton's enigmatic Almighty later announces he is: a "boundless deep" everywhere and nowhere in nature (7.168–73). The result is a "solution" to the problem of evil that Benjamin would consider classically baroque: one that combines the deity's unsatisfying "self-defense" in book 3 with an enigmatic displacement of his goodness downward rather than upward, into the depths of the creation itself. As Benjamin suggests, this semi-naturalistic solution is rooted in the structure of Reformation theology, although in Milton's case far more in Calvin than in the gloomier Luther behind Benjamin's *trauerspiels.*

Just as Calvin argues that the "skillful ordering of the universe is for us a sort of mirror in which we can contemplate God, who is otherwise invisible," so in Milton's obliquely self-organizing continuum (one that conducts creation's natural ascent, not that of an immaterial soul), the reader finds the opaque footprints of the "track Divine" (*PL,* 11.354) chiefly in natural signs. This track provides the primary testament to God's mercy, love, and freedom, the final and highest quality of divinity that Milton's theology of grace appends to the *imago dei* as reflected in Adam (8.440)—but one that further obscures this "sort of mirror." Fusing the "discursive" logic of natural theology (in this case, that of the newly awakened or "natural" Adam) with the intuitive logic of his "sudden apprehension," the human *imago dei* uncertainly fuses Cartesian reason with the apprehension of angels and the mysterious "supplement" of divine grace (8.353–54, 5.487–90). Thus, in contrast to both the deistic First Cause and the revealed deity, Milton's God baroquely multiplies his images—first through this discursive/intuitive logic, then through his audible word and visibly "transfused" Son (which tend to be enigmatically self-canceling [6.681–82, 719–21]), and finally through the clear/obscure "light . . . giv'n us . . . to discover onward things more remote from out knowledge" (*CPW,* 2:550). In this sense, Milton considerably overgoes Calvin, who laments that, without the scriptural book of knowledge to read "through" the creation, its "burning lamps" "can of themselves in no way lead us into the right path. Surely they strike some sparks, but before their fuller light shines forth these are smothered."[12]

Precisely because Milton's far more paradoxical God is at once active and passive in words and things, not utterly transcendent like Dante's *or* Calvin's, his presence is suffused throughout an organic continuum whose track divine conserves all the indeterminacy and not a little of the natural magic that in normative allegory had been exclusively reserved for the godhead and his magical agents or "daemons." These agents are the virtues who in the classical Christian mode counter the darker magic transfused through the satanic vices associated with corrupt matter, which is mythically allied with the origin of evil.[13] Yet, in *Paradise Lost,* where matter is allied with good, the naturalistic continuum itself provides the allegorical substrate that will be infused with a series of magical personae who sporadically erupt in order to remind the reader of the immanent judgment of divine law and grace. The cumulative effect of a meta-allegorical epic in which even Sin and Death naturalistically undergo birth, life, and death is thus not simply to rupture Christian tradition but also to "reform" it through a penetrating critique of the traditionally mystified relations between words, things, and thought—a critique that, in being pushed to its limits, reveals a new ground of meaning beneath both rationalist and mystical forms of certitude.

2

One early result of this critique is the synthesis of rationalized pastoral allegory with self-referential prophetic typology such as one finds in "Lycidas" and *Comus,* whose baroque pictorial analogues extend from Velasquez's halls of mirrors to Rembrandt's chiaroscuro. What all these works have in common is a tendency to displace onto obscurities of "style" such issues as the conflict between meaning and indeterminate meaningfulness, which, once settled, introduce Dryden's neoclassical domestication of Miltonic verse in heroic couplets. In either case, the important thing is that these differences in style provide metaphoric indices to the more important differences in the period "decorum" of linguistic usage and its underlying assumptions. Such differences clearly heighten the ability of Milton's epic to speak to us now about the ruin of allegory since they are rooted in calculated indeterminacies of grammar, meter, and allusiveness: in a word, in the meta-allegorical impulse to explore the meaning of meaning. Yet this very comparison addresses one of the primary issues surrounding the problem of defining Miltonic allegory, which stems from the way in which baroque allegory was later submerged in the far less conflicted rationalism of the neoclassical mode. Initiated in the same period by Dryden and the other "sons" of Ben Jonson, this seismic shift also creates the conditions that have made the literal levels of Milton's great argument—its ethical, logical, political, and theological design—far better documented and debated than its stylistic ones. One especially unfortunate result of this essentially neoclassical critical tradition has been the repression or effacement of the existence of allegory in a work that, by any modest estimate of its "fantastic" episodes, is largely governed by that mode.[14]

Yet this occlusion is also predictable, given that neoclassical aesthetic criteria were canonized by the first professional literary criticism in England, which flourished immediately after Milton's death in the era of the other classicizing Johnson, Samuel himself. His prescriptive neoclassical devaluation of Miltonic allegory has been further canonized by the fact that both this aesthetic (which would limit allegory to "naturalistic" symbols used for emphasis or ornament) and its otherwise antithetical counterpart in Romantic theory are alike antiallegorical. Their theoretical differences thus all but disappear on this central mimetic issue since, although Romanticism favors the fantastic, like neoclassicism it privileges naturalistic ambiguity over what Coleridge mistakenly understood as the excessively clear or rationalistic tropes of normative allegory. Thus, Coleridge ironically completes the effacement of allegory in *Paradise Lost,* largely because he locates in Milton the origin of his own "esemplastic" symbolism, which, if organicist in form, actually remains allegorical in content. Owing to these well-documented aesthetic confusions, regardless of which tradition Milton's critics inherit or what synthesis they attempt, the general consensus has been either to condemn his extended, fantastic, and/or "irrational" excursions altogether (as Johnson did) or symbolically to "contain" or misrepresent these allegorical forms of surrealism (as Coleridge did), long after the surreal and the fantastic had themselves come back into vogue. Here, the ultimate historical irony seems to be that, while T. S. Eliot's and the Leavisite's antienthusiastical and antirevolutionary bias has long been recognized as subverting a proper appreciation of Milton's poetics, their objectivist standards are still being applied to an epic-allegory designed to resist the purely rational calculus that Milton himself scorned.[15]

There is also, however, an additional historical irony in that Milton's aesthetics reflect the tendency of his period to privilege the allegorical emblem over the symbolic impresa, a position that actually inverts the values of Romantic theory, which in the form of synecdoche or overdetermined analogy glorified the impresa or symbol. Although in the seventeenth century this trope was often regarded as too condensed or mysterious, like most of the Romantics Coleridge and Wordsworth wanted a quasi-Cartesian yet also quasi-mystical return to the "plain language of men," a language that would privilege symbolic concretion as an access to greater clarity but would also mysteriously evade the rationalist conventions they regarded as inimical to poetry. The failure of this project has been recently demonstrated in a number of powerful critiques, which show that it produced only a rationally mystified version of the normative allegorical icon, without restoring its transcendental aura.[16] Nevertheless, Romanticism's affinity for its own form of baroque mystification left behind a strong legacy in the aesthetic evaluation of Milton. Following the inherently contradictory standards of this tradition, but also more explicitly exploiting its internal ironies and ambiguities, the New Critics would thus definitively argue that the poem was saved by its own inconsistencies—that is, saved from a faulty allegorical (or, in much the same sense, theological) design that was either self-canceling or otherwise self-subsumed into the purely satanic dimensions into which a Blake or an Empson would cast it. The result has been to reinforce the unexamined cliché that Milton's poetic practice is either neoclassically or Romantically "antiallegorical" when it in fact provides the foundation for the obscure and immanent allegory that Coleridge in practice employed not only in "The Rime of the Ancient Mariner" but in the bulk of his work. Thus, by almost any definition, the aesthetics that he applied to Milton cannot be confined to the symbolic mode—as it has been by nearly all the latter's critics, who generally follow some version of the neoclassical and/or Romantic critical tradition.[17]

Rather than neoclassically "emptying" Milton's poem of its allegorical content or subsuming it in the self-canceling ironies of neo-Romantic critics, the current study thus attempts to restore these resonances by redrawing the limits of both metaphor and analogy in ways better able to discriminate between "merely" symbolic and fully allegorical meaning. As a first step in this direction, it will be necessary to bury another barely examined cliché—that, since serious allegory ceases to be written during Milton's period, he could not have seriously considered writing one. For baroque allegory vigorously flourishes in the seventeenth century, where, if it is marginally impoverished, it is also empowered by the decline of the old sacrificial, sacramental, and ceremonial worldview conserved by the Renaissance.[18] Within that decline, allegory does not so much degenerate as explode into manifold forms, some more successful than others. These would include such diverse examples as its trivialization in the court masque and, later, the mock epic; the transformation of the sick self into an allegorical microcosm of the sick or decaying macrocosm in Donne's *Anniversaries* and *Devotions upon Emergent Occasions;* the addled allegories of Francis Quarles; the lugubrious philosophical melancholy of Henry More's retreating Platonism; and (by far the most interesting) the equivocal architectonics of Marvell's "Upon Appleton House." In other words, what distinguishes Milton's *Paradise Lost* as an allegorically dominated epic success is not its singularity in preserving the mode or even its baroque form, which, as we have seen, seems to originate in Shakespeare's later middle period. Rather, it is Milton's far greater penetration into the grounds of a new synthesis of vitalistic physics and organic metaphysics that would conserve divine immanence within the largely secular grounds of the new scientific universe.

Before proceeding, however, we will also need to qualify Benjamin's terms, for, in addition to mourning the normative mode's lost unities, baroque allegory also seems capable of endowing the *providential* undecidability of the language and nature of things with a semirenewed form of immanence. Although this recuperation is not without its nostalgic yearning for the statically numinous (as Benjamin stresses), the positive or "comic" impulse within its Reformist religiosity can also take "tragically" ruined Christian tropes and at least partially restore their original and fecund ambiguity, which is also to say, their metaphoricity. For, like his allegory itself, the equivocity of Milton's tropes is relative rather than absolute, to a degree best gauged by its distance from the Platonically Realist and dualist conventions that he at once inherits and metamorphically transmutes. When after his early poetry Milton seems to have abandoned the philosophical underpinnings of the older occulted substances that were thought to underlie Realism's semitransparent medium, the "veils" or "shells" interposed between eternal and ephemeral reality (respectively, the Real and the accidental realms of being), he yet appears to have abandoned the concatenative associationalism of the old triadic relation of words, things, and thought only reluctantly. Just as reluctantly, he gradually surrendered the authoritative ability of the old science to string out huge implicative chains or networks of connectivity. In this respect, his early work may be linked to a characteristic mid-seventeenth-century or transitional style, which still hovered between Cartesian objectivism and the vestigial Neoplatonism of the Cambridge school.

Later, without rejecting Cartesianism's claims or "retreating" into the closed, concentric "shells" of the earlier Renaissance cosmos, the late Milton assimilated the bipolar valence of baroque chiaroscuro to the older providential conception of God's and the poet's work as a *concordia discors,* some of whose unresolvable dissonances derive from the incertitudes implicit in Cartesian skepticism itself. But, in the seventeenth century, such harmonic discord is still generally referable (either explicitly or implicitly) to the old notion of a world harmony derived from Pythagorus: the discovery that the tetrachord of musical harmony and the tetractys of classical geometry and arithmetic, respectively, unify its temporal and spatial dimensions. Yet, for progressives like Milton, it was rapidly being reassimilated to the contemporary revival of atomism. Thus, like Lucretius's *De rerum natura,* his mature epic traces the idea of universal concord to a primal "swerve" in atomic flux, a generative entropos or in turning arising within his ambiguously male and female Chaos, the rough equivalents of the Mars and Venus principles in Lucretius. These interlocking analogies help explain not only the continuing predominance of mythical allusion in his monistic epic (a practice more generally shunned or repressed by other Independent theologians) but also why they remain so much more playfully metaphoric than in Spenser or Dante.[19] While these epic "concatenations" are hardly the same as the Pythagorean harmonic chains of Milton's second Prolusion, they are still represented as the enigmatic links that Homer represents suspending earth from heaven—which Satan later observes but does not "see" in approaching the created world, unaware of the obscure and by now meta-allegorical significance to which he is blinded. As a result, these enigmas now represent the *problem* of a metaphoric vision whose clarity is obscured for all but the deity, who alone comprehends how to "value right / The good before him," without perverting "best things / To worst abuse, or to thir meanest use" (*PL,* 4.202–4).

This metaphoricity must then be distinguished from the mysticism of normative allegory, simply because it exhibits none of the aversion to words and their displacement onto discardable symbols that characterizes the mode. Instead, the opaque "free play" of Milton's signifiers can be traced to the pressure he places on an unfallen language to unriddle enigmas that meta-allegorically intensify signs until, like the Cartesian "objects" of Wittgenstein's investigations, they break down into self-referential "meaningfulness"—the multiply ambiguous language games embedded in the Latin roots on which Milton so often plays. This interplay suggests, not that the Miltonic metaphor has no symbolic/allegorical pretensions, but simply that there is no way that such a poetic catalog of its culture can be made fully consistent with itself since, in itself, it embodies the paradox that its attempt to assert linguistic certainty within its own language must inevitably become circular and therefore break down.[20] Ultimately demonstrating only the certainty of uncertainty itself, the poem thus takes shape not only in the ruins of a philosophical and political revolution but also in the ruins of a form of literary allegory rooted in a barely veiled plenum of linguistically and physically sacred or absolute meaning.

Thus, rather than asking to be read according to Cartesian or neoclassical standards of consistency, the poem instead asks how its nearly self-concealing inconsistencies can be used to adumbrate the logical dilemmas of both the old and the new poetic order. For these dilemmas also structure the outlines of the divine plan, the mysterious conjunction of God's concealed (intuitive or organic) with his revealed (discursive or logical) will (*CPW,* 2:292, 295). Where these inconsistencies somehow harmonize, the chief task would then seem to be to tune in to their implicativeness, keeping in mind that such clear/obscure "dissonances" evoke some unity of being capable of mediating between the older visionary order of things and the information-theoretic one that it seems "prophetically" to anticipate and that does not therefore ultimately recognize Cartesian distinctions between subject/object, inside/outside, or even sign/signified except in their contextual, metareferential senses. In looking backward and forward, the baroque style thus paradoxically anticipates the breakdown or ruin that latterly has overtaken the Cartesian "certitudes" on which modernity was founded by revaluing the uncertain function of signs in relation to presumptive truth, just as it allegorically "ruins" the cosmic "book" wherein it was once imagined that God's design could more or less transparently be read.

The self-reflexive, processural, or meta-allegorical ambiguity thereby "metamorphosed" in *Paradise Lost* then also suggests a longing for the historically particular and/or "concretely" numinous that is one of the chief hallmarks of the baroque, although it hardly produces the iconic form of mystical particularity that we find in Dante. Moving relentlessly backward and forward in time, the chief axis of Milton's vision, like that of other baroque artists, turns on an internally intensified, ultimately iconoclastic mythopoetics. The highly paradoxical structure of this poetics seems also to have prompted Andrew Marvell's fear that Milton would Samson-like "amaze" the entire edifice of Christian allegory, thereby "ruin[ing] . . . / The sacred Truths to Fable, and Old Song" ("On Paradise Lost," lines 6– 8).²¹ Such trepidations are more than amply justified on more than one score: not only does Milton's technique tacitly implode the whole system of Neoplatonic figuration in which Marvell's pastorals had taken half-ironic refuge, but it also ultimately brought the long tradition of Christian epic to a close. Yet, in directly confronting the problem of symbolic form, Milton's poem also achieves a Samson-like vindication, leaving in its wake a truly tragicomic genre of prophetic cultural elegy. In the process, it encyclopedically records the resurrection of both an allegorical and a paradoxically self-ironizing artifact. Thus, like Milton's Samson, it "lives" chiefly in the concrete self-renewals of human time, in the phoenix-like reincarnations of that "self-begotten bird" that later, in the Romantic image,

Revives, reflourishes, then vigorous most
When most unactive deem'd,
And though her body die, her fame survives,
A secular bird ages of lives.
(*SA*, lines 1704–7)

So, in *Paradise Lost*, language is ironically reborn out of language, historical meaning out of its own condition of incipient meaningful-

ness, process itself taking precedence over form within its own reso-
nating possibility as a species of self-reflexive meaningfulness.

3

Conventionally, however, like irony, metaphor is considered incom-
patible with allegory, which Gordon Teskey has described as oscillat-
ing between a "project of reference and a project of capture." In other
words, allegory's originating impetus lies somewhere between the
loosely extended analogy (its conventional definition) and forcible
identity (Teskey's allelophagy), both of which compete with the still
looser, more generative associations of metaphor and the dissocia-
tions of irony.[22] Yet, while this distinction adequately describes the
linguistic tensions of normative allegory, it also leaves out of the
account the more radically mixed allegorical mode described by
Angus Fletcher, where the chaotic generativeness of irony prevails:
"Because irony seems to collapse the multileveled segregations of
allegory . . . , it has been called 'antiallegorical.' . . . [Yet] since
irony still involves an otherness of meaning, however tenuous and
shifty . . . we might call ironies 'collapsed allegories,' or perhaps,
'condensed allegories.' They show no diminishing, only a confusion,
of the semantic and syntactic processes of double or multiple-leveled
polysemy."[23] This polysemously ironic form remains properly alle-
gorical both in Northrop Frye's generic sense and in Fletcher's modal
sense, although both scholars provide ultimately different schemas of
literary anatomy. Thus, unlike Frye, Fletcher views allegory as oper-
ative in texts spanning a wide range of genres, not as a relatively
exclusive or self-conscious narrative "kind"; hence, any text can be
defined as allegorical so long as it ideologically encodes its values
through a repetitive, ritual, and/or magical "realism" inherently op-
posed to "true" mimesis. Yet, remarkably, although these two defini-
tions of *allegory* are usually incompatible (as Teskey also stresses),
some version of both applies to the symbolic practices at work in
Paradise Lost. Not only are its metaphors "tenuous and shifty" as in
Fletcher's intermediate or ironic allegorical mode, but, as Frye stipu-
lates, its meaningfulness is consistently generated through the ex-
plicit interventions and "instructions" of the narrative voice.[24]

   Yet, even were that not the case, Milton's symbolic poetics could be
described as allegorical on other grounds—not least of which is that

he immediately and unambiguously pronounces that his epic is de-
signed as a theodicy. The opening invocation then "instructs" its
readers to match its form with an underlying content, thereby stress-
ing the notion of an internal "splitting" between two levels of mean-
ing, literal and figurative, which is common to all definitions of the
allegorical genre or mode. However condensed these levels may be-
come during the Reformation, this division still conserves a broad
potential for pluriform "meaningfulness," including some version of
the traditional redoubling into the traditional fourfold schema of
allegorical representation: literal, typological (historical), moral, and
anagogical (eschatological). Thus, once we get beyond Reformation
polemics (whose anti-allegorism is often taken too literally), it seems
relatively clear that allegorical arguments or "Ideas" rarely ever re-
quired the presence of each level in every figure or even every epi-
sode, merely the presence of a "double plot" that organizes and
directs the second or symbolic level of its principal actions. In
William Empson's view, this extended symbolism can be regarded as
allegorical so long as these "two levels of being correspond to each
other in detail . . . [and] there is some underlying reality, something
in the nature of things, which makes this happen."[25]

In dividing reality into literal and figurative planes, *Paradise Lost*
then makes its underlying meaning "happen" by reconnecting its
literal images and events with the ambiguously lower and higher
reality that Milton saw in "the Apocalyps of Saint *John*," which he
thought projected "the majestick image of a high and stately Trag-
edy" (*CPW,* 1:815) "soaring" "to a Prophetick pitch in types, and
Allegories" (*Animadversions, CPW,* 1:714). This classical metalinguis-
tic approach to the figurative meaning of Scripture, as revealed in
types and allegories continued to supply the basis of the multiply
coordinated or "modal" senses of the way Christians read not only
John's Revelation but also their own secular literature and much
classical literature as well. Considered in detail, these schemas are
variable and often confusing, the fourfold hermeneutical method of
Aquinas differing from that of Dante, even though he was directly
influenced by it. Here, however, we are concerned chiefly with the
most common terms, in which all secondary, extraliteral senses are
generally labeled *allegorical,* although these often also embrace ana-
gogy (the last things) and typology (specific symbolic anticipations
and/or fulfillments of earlier and later events in Christian history).

Although typological "literalism" in the interpretation of historical events becomes especially important in the Reformation and, more notoriously, the revolutionary periods, we should thus beware the common argument that its figuration becomes antiallegorical on at least two grounds: (1) In practice, the distinction between all three secondary levels of meaning, but particularly the distinction between allegory and typology, not only overlaps, but often fuses, as a number of commentators have shown. (2) If Milton privileges either trope, then it is actually the allegorical sense, where "more is meant than meets the ear" ("Il Penseroso," line 120).[26] Types, on the other hand, seemed to him more suspect than allegories, simply because they represent no more than the historically concrete or "outward signe or symbol of admission . . . [while] it is the *inward* calling of God that makes a Minister" (*CPW,* 1:715; emphasis added). Here, the "signe or symbol of admission" of course refers to the key Protestant concept of vocation, not to an Anglican anointing, although both figures are essentially typological insofar as they refer back to the principle historical "type" of baptism, itself prefigured by the Israelite passage through the Red Sea. Thus, as his reference to the Revelation of Saint John suggests, Milton generally accepts the differences between types and allegories as ultimate continuities, as a means whereby the literal/symbolic level of historical recurrences (types) can be "sublated" into the higher and more inward, if also more dramatic, figural vision of allegories.[27] Hence, here, much as in the famous passage in Galatians (a favorite among the Reformers) where Hagar represents the concubinage of the old law or covenant and Sarah the spouse of the promise or new covenant, typology is merely the symbolic vehicle wherein Christian allegoresis imposes its meanings on the details of literal history. No wonder, then, that a religion based on an allegorized rereading of a historical and prophetic text can never wholly distinguish between literal and figural, much less typical and allegorical: these confusions and/or conflations are the lifeblood of its being, of a Word whose primary Word is not a sign but a Son.

Thus, ironically, as Reformation exegesis was becoming more historically concrete, it was also becoming more figural, simply because, by the seventeenth century, not only Dante's sacramental realities but even his literal nature had begun to disappear. Throughout the century, not just the concentric structure of his sacred universe but even the actual existence of his hell and purgatory were becoming far more metaphoric. Of course, for these very reasons, the Protestant poet does place more emphasis on the temporal fulfillments of his fictive representations (both in his own time and in that of the reader), although that displacement hardly renders his poetry more *restrictively* concrete, as the strand of criticism descending from Erich Auerbach's influential "Figura" would maintain.[28] Instead, Protestant prophetic poetry displays a notable lack of that graphic quality that Dante assigns the "fulfillments" attending the sinners of his hell and purgatory as a direct consequence of the Reformers' far more skeptical relation toward outward signs or "seals" of sin or salvation, which, like the sacrament itself, no longer serve as special conduits of grace. These disjunctions collaterally drive their more vigorous efforts to fuse Old Testament "types" with New Testament antitypes, although such efforts regularly lead to the proliferation of polysemously and ambiguously "antitypical" symbols that we find in the remarkable epic similes and catalogs of Milton's hell.

These expansive adaptations should thus be understood as a sort of compensation for the rupture of other forms of continuity, much like the compulsive use of biblical analogy in the historical and exegetical sermonizing of the period. This same interpretive drive toward synthetic particulars also characterizes its poetic use of allegory and typology, which interchangeably fuse inner meanings with outward signs. Since neither level of meaning can be concretely isolated in what a contemporary exegete refers to as their "transaction," Reformed figuration's most undisputed divergence from its past lies in the polysemous sense of inwardness exemplified in Milton, one that ultimately produces a more personal and therefore ambiguous sense of the fulfillments of biblical truth than any conveyed by a more outwardly oriented sacramentalism.[29] In this more positive sense, then, Eliot's controversial critique of Milton was at least partly right: in its very temporality, Milton's Protestant baroque mode is far less sensuous or physically concrete than either high Anglican or Counter-Reformation poetics, especially in contrast with the latter's sacramental fixation on Christ's nativity and Passion. Yet the radical Protestant baroque is also far more temporally and philosophically imaginative and in that respect far more deeply responsive to the ambiguities and obscurities of inner vision.

In sum, where signs had once signified in terms of the old Scholastic triad of words, things, and thought, now the historical understanding not only of signs but of their relation to the "things" of the universe was taking on the entirely new spatiotemporal configuration that Thomas Kuhn describes as the paradigm shift by which modernity was born.[30] Implicit in this shift was a kind of a priori consideration analogous to the a priori intuitive apprehensions of time and space by which Kant later described the transcendental or framing functions of the mind. The Cartesians had effectively destroyed the old symbolic schematizations of space and time in all their concatenative confluence in order to clear the ground for new principles of order (as yet undiscovered) by which a newly binary relation of words and things could be forged into sharp and serviceable distinctness of thought, the third term that until very recently was all but exiled from explicit consideration.[31] Milton preserved the basic outline of this new schematization by incorporating its altered values into the space/time structure of *Paradise Lost.* Yet he also preserved a space for thought by allegorizing the "vertical" stance of the poet in a space still descending from and through God. As in most baroque art, this vertical axis is undercut by the horizontal vector of an immanently evolving matter interactively creating the highly mutable basis of secular and salvation history.

The poem essentially enacts the paradox of the "immanent" representability of this matter through a species of discontinuous allegory centered on the poet's own shifting self-representation. Wrapped in the "virtuality" of the singing robes he first donned in declaring his epic ambitions (*CPW,* 1:808), the symbol of his inspirational access to an *ad extra* grace, Milton is within its world what his God is in his, a knower and foreknower of his work's outward and hidden codes: the external revelation of its laws and the inwardness of its concealed or providential will. This focus centering on the will waiting on the emergent immanence of its "free" enactors, including himself, provides the similitude that, analogically extended, serves as the governing allegory of Milton's poem. But, like any analogy, it is a representation that cannot be pushed too far for exactitude or consistency, either by the poet or by us—no more than we can push into exact identity the poem's cognate ontological analogy so impressively framed in the inexact interrogative, "What if Earth / Be but the shadow of Heaven. . . ?"[32]

History, then, emerges from the story of the Fall, but here as an emergent pattern of meaningfulness that will be able to survive the secularization of its fable precisely because, in metanarrative terms, "the ruins of our first parents" (*CPW,* 2:366–67) become those of allegory—the uncertain symbolic register embracing at once the Fall's effect on the poet in his poem, on his story, and on the unpredictabilities of our responses. Underlying this transposition are the constraining conditions whereby all indeterminate, to say nothing of determinate, meaning must negotiate the hazards of poeticized history. For example, nowhere does the poem as *concordia discors* more deeply resound to the tension of its calculated indeterminacies than where it opens the possibility of its own reduction qua form to the mere overdeterminations of its poetic structure. Yet this is also where the paradigm shift informing it becomes most dramatic, where, in confronting the occluded potential of a restrictive formalism, it takes on the prophetic status of the first major work to exemplify the newly triumphant aspect of a temporally, spatially, and linguistically relativistic universe. In this way, the old allegorical correspondences and their concatenations are infinitistically reborn and redeemed in ways that make them accessible to the still more mimetic narrativization of the novel.[33]

Ironically, then, this epic confrontation with a seemingly dead or dying allegorical formalism (a fourfold structure "justified" by its ability to adumbrate a now exploded world picture) also accounts for the poem's resonance with a global dimension that would otherwise have remain closed. In its ability to critique the instability of any totalizing representation of a culture that would privilege the clarity and distinctness of determinate sense, it exalts the indeterminacy of human freedom and signification as the only valid ground of meaning. The conceptual dilemma thereby created is avoided by shifting meaning from level to level of possibility in ways anticipated, although hardly contained, within the older fourfold hermeneutical ascent of allegory and inspiration. Like Vico and after him Marx (particularly as revived by Fredric Jameson), Milton was of course aware of the hermeneutical schema of textual levels by which Raphael suggests that the book of the universe may still be Edenically read.[34] Yet, instead of directly historicizing this archaic fourfold system as closed, Milton hinges it to the unpredictabilities of personal consciousness mediating narrative choice in his four invocations. In self-reflexively coordinating the traditional invocational registers of the poem's musical and narrative "keys," he thus revises the mystical "descent to light" into a descent from eternity into time. This means that the poet and his readers descend not into a fully secular but into an uncertain providential history, which as the domain of typology is traditionally the lowest and most literal level of its fourfold schema— but, in this new metamorphosis, also its highest.[35]

Technically, of course, the highest level of the poem remains the classically "anagogic" level of assured divine love, the universal height to which the first invocation aspires but that it fails to attain, except in the "historical particular" dimension (as Hegel might call it) of the "upright heart and pure." To justify God's ways to man from this grounding height/depth of fallen signs and history, the poet must therefore reenact an Adamic descent that ascends, not as a medievalized "fortunate fall," but as the reemergence of the evolving covenant of "spirit and truth" that opens and closes the poem (*PL*, 1:17–18, 12.533). Descending from this anagogic or ultimate level into the concrete typological dimension that throughout books 1 and 2 intimates the proleptically revealed or Apollonian design of history (the domain of the fallen "romance" of Satan, Sin, and Death on the plains of hell and Chaos), the poet then takes us through the sterile void of false theology and philosophy in his limbo or Paradise of Fools. This realm's inversion of Dante's epic schema might seem merely a parody of the Italian poet's sacramental structure, did it not herald the poem's subsequent descent into the moral or Dionysian level of "self-authored" history (3.122). Introduced by its central, "Orphic" invocation at the exact turning point of the epic, here the concrete, Dionysian expression of divine love forecast in the proleptic redemption of book 3 emerges in the vitalistic creation episodes of book 7. These in turn give way to an exploration of Adam's struggle for personal and erotic self-realization in book 8 (which at once reflects and recapitulates the experience of Eve), culminating in the final, Tellurian invocation of book 9. By specifying its "earthy" departure from all earlier epic-allegorical canons here, this fourth and final descent/ascent into the literal domain of fallen history also revives the Dionysian level that thematically connects the whole.

In this descending progression, the poem thus sums up Adam's evolution through allegory's "shadowy types to Truth" (*PL*, 12.303), which is not a truth beyond signs or types but one organically contextualized, concretized, and finally meta-allegorically "ploughed back into the soil" of human experience.[36] Hence, this last and primal phase of Milton's epic process also projects the ascending/descending spirals of material history that must remain forever incomplete, a process whose paradoxes parallel the Romantic attempt to regain lost transcendental auras while rejecting eternity, "whose end no eye can reach" (12.556).[37] From this perspective, *Paradise Lost* contains one of the most complex epic catalogs ever written, the shadowy, semierased history of the transition from one great epoch to another, the new paradigm whose poem this is. More than a transition, the great phase change that history undergoes in this interval is a metamorphosis from a narrow or closed conception of providential time into a freely evolving model responsive to the uncertainties of human understanding. Thus, only by "long choosing and beginning late" was its poet able to compose a new synthesis of God's universal design based on the new material monism that had latterly come to dominate the philosophy of his period. In this epoch, the old signatures "translating" the macrocosmic/microcosmic correspondences between the eternal and immutable macrocosmos and the imperfect, temporal sphere of Spenser's "Mutabilitie Cantos" or Dante's *Divine Comedy* have been collapsed into one single "ring of fire" so that "In the Beginning" both "the Heav'ns and Earth / Rose out of *Chaos*" (1.9–10). Here, then, we encounter the new unities of the nominalist universe, in which there are no more immutable essences (as Milton similarly concludes in his *Christian Doctrine*), only human words and chaotic things, whose interaction produces the characteristic natural magic of the baroque.

4

This final accommodation represents the poem's most fully Protestant transformation of both Christian allegory and Cartesian discourse. The sign is now at once means and end of the quest, not a "disposable" means to an end as in the bulk of the Christian epic-allegorical tradition. Whereas allegory's traditional role is to point toward eternal stasis, baroque allegory embraces linguistic modulation as the only mediation consistent with the uncertainties of temporal revelation. Yet, if Edward Craig is right in describing Cartesianism as the empirical reinvention of the old "similarity thesis" relation between the subjective and divine or ultimate truth, then the foreground of Milton's prophetic vision alternatively envisions its replacement with the equally ancient "agency theory" implicit in an alternate version of the Platonic tradition—the idea of the demiurgic or self-creating subject variously exploited by atomism and Gnosticism.[38] Thus, in addition to the philosophical and theological revolutions in which it participates, *Paradise Lost* forecasts the enormous tropological shift in which a form of "self-fashioning" based on

Spenserian similitudes is replaced with the ideal of the self-enacting metaphor. Paralleling Shakespeare's metatheatrical technique in a more systematic, epic form, the poetic process thereby created features successively intensifying self-virtualizations that progressively build toward Milton's final and most polemical invocation, where he announces that his great argument is "Not less but more Heroic than the wrath / Of stern *Achilles* on his Foe pursu'd" (*PL,* 9.14–15). Yet how can the poetic voice make itself the "pattern" of such a "heroic" argument, particularly when confronted by the enormous gap between his subject and its Homeric referent? This "sad task" (9.13) is made more difficult still by his distance from the more immediate tradition of epic convention:

> Since first this Subject for Heroic Song
> Pleas'd me long choosing and beginning late
> Not sedulous by Nature to indite
> Wars, hitherto the only Argument
> Heroic deem'd, chief maistry to dissect
> With long and tedious havoc fabl'd Knights
> In Battles feign'd: the better fortitude
> Of Patience and Heroic Martyrdom
> Unsung . . .
> . . . .
> Not that which justly gives Heroic name
> To Person or to Poem. Mee of these
> Nor skill'd nor studious, higher Argument
> Remains, sufficient of itself to raise
> That name, unless an age too late, or cold
> Climate, or Years damp my intended wing
> Deprest; and much they may, if all be mine,
> Not Hers who brings it nightly to my Ear.
> (9.25–33, 40–47)

Like Hamlet's, the poet's alienation from recent chivalric convention is translated into an apparent alienation both in space (more northerly or "cold / Climate") and in time ("an age too late," perhaps including his own damper "years"). Even more significantly, the poet fears that he is too personally, politically, and culturally out of tune for his "prophetic pitch" any longer to be heard by his countrymen, unless heavenly inspiration intervenes.

These self-dramatized incertitudes explain the fundamental restructuring of the epic muse, no longer Beatrice, Clio, or even Urania herself, whose "meaning not the Name" he calls on in the invocation to book 7. Yet, this central epic displacement also signals the radically new theory that keys the poem's inspirational and hence meta-allegorical structure. Although its verse seems "easy" and "unpre-meditated," it may in fact miss its mark, may not be "sufficient . . . to raise / That name" to the heroic height toward which he aspires. These highly introspective, self-questioning, and ironizing concerns, then, project a radically different sense of interiority than that ideal-ized by the older, essentially oral, and communal tradition of rhetoric and poetics. Rather than a self-confident or "full" sense of presence, the sense of self to which Milton's *Apology* first gave expression (as indicated by the epigraph to this study as a whole) demands both a new "ethos of composition" and a new sense of the "true poem" that such a self would write. That neither are fully formed or stable "artifacts" is indicated throughout Milton's sonnets as well as his epic, which like his politics reflect a patient waiting on the "emergent revelations" of a history whose subjects have become no mere sub-jects but "Authors to themselves in all / Both what they judge and what they choose; for so / [God] form'd them free, and free they must remain" (*PL*, 3.122–24).[39]

That such selves require a new form of heroism as well as a new martyrdom (which, as in Milton's case, includes the extreme inward-ness produced by the loss of external eyesight and liberty) is also projected by epic invocations where darkness, danger, and solitude (*PL*, 7.26–27) become the very grounds of a new insight into how the entire universe itself arose from Chaos (7.218–27), the dark realm whose incertitudes stochastically "magnify his works, the more we know" (7.97). Such self-intensifying scrutiny is hardly that of Achilles, much less of Spenser's Guyon, the closest "type" on which this poetic antitype might seem to have been modeled (*CPW*, 2:516). Yet even this apparently close correspondence is actually remote since only the prophetic poet himself completes the type who would augment, if not wholly displace, his own putative heroes, Adam and his heavenly alter ego, the anointed Son of God. In intellectual-historical terms, this "event" is coterminous with the rupture that this study explores: the process by which the idealized human subject (here the self-reflexive poet) becomes a godlike agent of time. No longer a mere similitude or reflection of the *imago dei* as he is in both classical Christian and Cartesian thought, the poet as microcosmic

man is theomorphically created "magnanimous to correspond with
Heav'n" (*PL,* 7.511; *CPW,* 1:892), with the result that he alone models
both the beginning and the end of an unsung culture that only in a
profoundly new, existential sense can "justly give . . . Heroic name /
To Person or to Poem."

This same context provides the framework of a redemptive history
that proceeds as naturalistically as Satan's slow decay. Everywhere, as
in this archetypal instance—archetypal since Satan does provide the
initial "answer" to the poet's insistent demand that his muse "say first
what cause" initiated the Fall—such questions begin and end in
allegory, although they are intermediately displaced onto more mi-
metic episodes before finally being "condensed" into meta-allegori-
cal tableaus. Thus, the lapse traceable to Satan is first displaced onto
Milton's allegory of Sin and Death, which is thereafter displaced
onto and disintegrated into epic scenes that enact the meaning of
temptation and sin in the framework of God's natural creation. But,
once the apple has been tasted by our Grand Parents, the whole
process is repeated in a highly illusionistic allegory where it is re-
petitively retasted by all the demons on all the indefinitely replicated
apple trees of hell. Since a careful reader knows that, for Milton,
repetition is a form of sin, the successful reading of such scenes
demands a far more internalized dialectic than the relatively external
process of symbolic displacement that normally creates that upward
spirals of conventional Christian allegory.

Thus, *Paradise Lost* demands the constant forward and "back scan-
ning" that has caused Walter Ong to identify it as the first fully
"literate" epic, that is, the first to depart from the concrete hier-
archies characteristic of the oral life world, which is also the old
sacramental life world to which Spenser still belongs.[40] Stripped of
this ritual magic, the poem's allegorical machinery can no longer
"confine" even overtly allegorical personae like Sin and Death,
whose sting can no longer simply be purged in a ritual House of
Holinesse. Instead, both reader and poet must experience the psy-
chological effects of a sin against which they can never be externally
inoculated. Yet, since chaotic matter itself is not innately corrupt but
merely mutable in ways that include its capacity to "swallow" Sin and
Death (*PL,* 10.635–39), for both subjects and objects perversion or
redemption now means permitting corrupt matter to die of the same
virtually natural causes that lead others to life. By allowing chaos to
"come again" in the newly ambivalent sense that allows the subjective

will to engender either life or death from its inscrutably mixed "roots," not through external veils or seals, chaos itself is reordered but never ruined.

In order to analyze the processes at work in Milton's progressive "ruin of allegory," I have structured the following chapters to reflect its descending structure and the ways in which it inverts the traditional allegorical ascent. The first chapter discusses the broader outlines of his theological and epistemological divergences from the old sacral worldview inscribed in traditional Christian allegory. The second explores the framework of the greatly expanded cosmos on which his poem's narrative allegory is projected, the universe in the process of being discovered (as his allusions to Galileo remind us) by the new science. The third then relates these macrocosmic alterations to the greatly expanded naturalism of his microcosmic emblems, the signs, similitudes, and allegorical insignia of his epic machinery. This discussion in turn leads to the fourth chapter's discussion of the naturalistic form of causality that replaces the traditionally magical causality of allegorical personae, which is followed by an analysis of the poem's most definitively baroque design, its meta-allegorical re-presentation of an ironically "naturalized" psychomachia. Through this self-referential War in Heaven and the vitalistic creation episodes that follow, chapter 6 then modulates into the episodes that are not only its counterpart but in some sense its antithesis: the disordering yet also reordering contiguities of Adam and Eve's sexual love and its simultaneously metaphoric and metonymic need of "touch." From their pre- and postlapsarian perspectives, it then considers some ramifications of Milton's baroque epic-allegorical technique: not only how it transforms the relation between the human genders, but also how it transforms the human understanding of history and its hermeneutics (chap. 7) and of divine accommodation (conclusion).

In the latter, the poem's broader theological and metaphysical, as opposed to its more narrowly Puritan, dimension is explored by comparing its ideological framework to the views of Pascal, Milton's Jansenist contemporary, who in many ways similarly mediates between Cartesian rationalism and the newly "ruined" forms of ritual allegory and theodicy. This final extension is intended to suggest a synthetic answer to this work's overriding question: What could the idea of *ruin* have meant to a Milton who literally takes the "ruin" of humanity to have been effected by its first parents? The answer would have to be an "irreparability," unless the individual, each a second Adam or Eve, again literally becomes an agent endowed by his or her power of re-creating the pattern and composition, that is, the "type" of that poem of true history, the patterned composition that defines a culture's image of itself—the metamorphic form that only the prophetic poet could see in advance. Here I conclude that Milton's meta-allegorical response to the transitional character of the period bears a significant resemblance to the antidualistic rationalism analogously evident in Pascal, whose sense of the disparity of the human condition parallels Milton's struggle to accommodate it to an infinite and incomprehensible, although still providential, God, the rationally knowable "Author" of a material universe mysteriously governed at all levels by his obscurely revealed "law." Like Pascal, Milton knows that reason can open this space to knowledge but that it cannot fill it with new positivities. Thus, unlike the redemptive models employed by either Augustine, Aquinas, or Calvin, and contrary to the binary models of human figuration that both Weber and Foucault regard as exclusively dominating the age, those employed by Milton and Pascal envision fallen modern man earning an imaginative "paradise within," not by opposing heaven and earth, but by intuitively uniting them through the introspective leap of a soul en route to becoming something far closer to an ambivalent Freudian psyche than a discursive Cartesian subject.

By virtue of such philosophical and linguistic revisions, the poem as meta-allegory escapes the limitations of allegory as a diagrammatic analogy whose elaborations tend toward mystification, which is what happens when the poem is read only as a first-order allegory within a dualistic world system. For Benjamin, as for us, the realm of thought is historical, and, insofar as it is limited to the improbable or "surreal" extensions of the closed analogies implicit in its originating similitude, any specific allegory fails the test of historicizing the actual. For, in the very act of encoding the abstract ideals of a culture, the aims of allegory necessarily exceed the mimetic range of the probable. In the process, its analogies, like its referents, become entangled, not only with the systemization of cultural values, but also with their contradictions. For this reason alone, any insistence that Milton's epic-allegory should have a consistent, that is, a determinate or certain as against an indeterminate or uncertain, sense would seem to misunderstand its construction, which by definition cannot be univocal even in meta-allegorical terms—the terms that explicitly address these contradictions. From this perspective it seems ironic that the literary criticism most overtly concerned with this indeterminacy has tended to reinscribe it within a less than appropriate allegorical context: not within the immanent, ambiguous, meta-referential, and thus virtually mimetic mode that Benjamin identifies with the baroque "return" to the original mode of Homeric myth, but within the transcendental, self-canceling, and hence mystically "numinous" mode better associated with Augustine, Dante, or Spenser.

"Dark with Excessive Bright"

Milton's Metamorphosis of Allegory

1

Somehow one imagines Milton valuing the experience of writing *Paradise Lost* more than the contemplation of it as finished product. At least there remain in the poem, as some of its most attractive features, the traces of that experience. Even if the work as a whole cannot all have been spirit quickened, the inspirational convention that Milton so powerfully deployed preserves within its considerable formal and substantive presence something of the reality of that *ad extra* or poetic grace in principle communicated through the effect both of the text and its prose "supplement," Milton's frequent prose animadversions on poetry. Thus, in theory as in practice, the result is a poetics bearing witness to what was contemporarily understood as the impressed or infused "motions" of the aroused spirit and, within them, the obscure presence of the God whose apparent but not actual absence from history constituted the essence of what most needed Milton's justification. The accessing of such presence as experiential motion or form of emergent revelation by which the phenomenal mediates the noumenal thus suffuses all his epic's related linguistic "formalisms," the interrelated practices of meditation, prayer, preaching, and poetry.[1] In memorializing this power of presence language must raid the inarticulate, for, if the poem were only the textual memorial of an extinguished poetic experience, it would be as much a dead letter as Scripture read without the enlightening Spirit.

Here, I mainly rehearse these "archaic" presuppositions in order to recover something important about Milton's material monism—of which more will be said—and its practical weighing of compositional or transactional "process" over product, the process in itself bearing that trace of spiritualizing presence that in several central senses is ultimately both the poem's final subject and its own self-characterization. This processural model also uniquely illuminates the characteristic Miltonic view, both early and late, of the poet as type of the self-perfecting soul everywhere seeking traces of "the track divine," spiritual motifs that remain continuous from the early letters to Diodati to the final books of *Paradise Lost*. It also illuminates why these traces cannot be found in the blinding eruptions of all-effacing (in)comprehension that characterize Dante's ritually static visions of the divine order but emerge here in the vitalistic transactions that metaphorically frame poetic experience. Owing to its theology of emergent Spirit, the inspirational structure of the poem becomes its only image of ascent or descent, itself a succession of the invocational and vocational stances that will allow the poet to become the image or pattern of his true poem. In memorializing the very quest he conducts, the poem's allegorical structure is then self-reflexively destabilized in ways further intensified by its multiple time schemes, which prevent its mythos or narrative form from becoming a Dantean icon of its own poetic process. Instead, the poem's thematization of its own enactment stands as a species of framing assumption that vitalistically inscribes its justifying conception in a perpetual motion no longer conducive to any iconic devices whatsoever.

In choosing to write "a prophetic and mythic narrative" in the comprehensive epic mode, Milton marks his intention to catalog these spiritual changes in the context that will most readily foreground them. Insofar as the hero of his epic-allegory is no longer an Achilles or an Odysseus but the poet himself, he announces his intention to sing the song of himself as an archetypal Protestant individual, the "type" or model of the yet "unsung" (*PL*, 9.31–33) culture Phoenix-like arising from the ashes of the Renaissance but also proleptically descending into its own secular ruin.[2] Yet, within as well as beyond these innovations, Milton's epic aim remains relatively continuous with that of more traditional allegorists: to instill his own ethos in his readers, which, as the epigraph to this work suggests, now means to make oneself, along with one's art, "a true Poem, that is, a composition, and patterne of the best and honourablest things" (*An Apology*, *CPW*, 1:890). What is altered, then, is the sense that after the Copernican and Cartesian revolutions, there can no longer be quite the same "sanction for a 'cosmic poetry'" that existed before it; or, at least, there clearly can no longer be the same easy translation of the eternal "design" of the supralunar sphere into the abstract moral "meaning" of its sublunar narrative level. Not only can the universe no longer be conceived as a set of concentric circles reflecting each other's "meaning" in a tightly ascending hierarchy of metaphysical truth, but words themselves can no longer be unproblematically translated into emblematic "things." In fact, metaphysics itself has become suspect, not only in the discourse of the Cartesian cogito, but also in the Protestant discourse of the Word, where the Spirit alone authorizes the "true" word much as the Cartesian cogito authorizes all its *ergo sums*. No similar problematic exists in the allegories of a Dante or a Spenser, who can begin their revelatory "process of speech" without the skeptical equivocations of a Raphael or the disputative interventions of a narrative voice. Although a guide or an interpreter is often necessary at the more critical junctures of their respective hermeneutical journeys, the primary "work" of correspondence in these early allegories is effected by emblematic *kosmoi* that more or less spontaneously force "the reader into an extreme consciousness of difference in status" between the world of appearances and its ultimate realities.[3]

In *Paradise Lost*, the reader instead confronts a celebration of the unified Galilean cosmos of space and time. Rather than lamenting the cosmic disruption of traditional hierarchies in the fashion of Donne's *Anniversaries*, Milton transforms them into the new terms of a monism whose single "ring of fire" emanates from God's "increate" essence (*PL*, 3.6), the all-encompassing light "palpably" imparting it holistic vision even to the blind. The unitary force of this "sovran vital Lamp" (3.22) blends physical with spiritual vision in ways that make the old system of allegorical segregations and correspondences not only unnecessary but potentially idolatrous since microcosmic man is now connected with the macrocosmic universe by all the thoughts "that voluntary move / Harmonious numbers" (3.37–38), not merely by the static "forms" whose passive contemplation once connected him to God. This ideal domain, rather than Milton's natural "Book of knowledge fair" (3.47), had formerly provided the ultimate province of allegory: the celestial reaches beyond the moon and, finally, beyond all human space and time, which became most ideally "Real" in ceasing to exist, in subsuming the particular in the universal. In Milton's epic, universal light translates only into particular vision, which seems to be why his third invocation makes such a point of his blindness: even from the perspective of the "Universal blanc" in which he is immersed, the poet can summon "Celestial Light" to

Shine inward, and the mind through all her powers
Irradiate, there plant eyes, all mist from thence
Purge and disperse, that I may see and tell
Of things invisible to mortal sight.
(3.48, 51–55)

If not precisely identical with the "universal blank" of philosophi-
cal doubt from which Descartes generates the particular conditions
of his rational universe, this situation provides a suggestive parallel.
Milton's "things invisible" are not truly "blanks" to be filled in by the
normative allegorical reader's imagination of mysterious transcen-
dence but the abstract outlines of the "clear and distinct" conditions
circumscribing necessity, reason, choice, free will, and knowledge.
These conditions emerge in the relatively mimetic heavenly dialogue
introduced by the invocation, an accommodation of divine law
guided in one sense by the poet's newly "planted" eyes but in another
by the abstract logic of any inner eye whose unfettered reason might
infer the principles at work in freely allowing Satan loose on earth.
Far from being wholly beyond "mortal sight," this logic is compared
to the kind of intensification produced by Galileo's telescope, which,
had it been invented, could have transmitted the scope and meaning
of these heavenly scenes. While such observation is not necessarily
neutral—a point emphasized by the different appropriations of the
sun's "sharp'n'd . . . visual ray" by Uriel and Satan (*PL*, 3.613–22)—its
uses remain equally available to all. Not even Satan's gaze is more
internally darkened than the deceived archangel's since their reason
operates within the domain of a monistic "celestial light" that can be
clouded either by false internal distortions or by mistaken external
impressions, such as those "implanted" by Satan's disguise. As the
source of perfect reason and light God alone sees through all misper-
ceptions, although here even he is subject to the light of his own
humanly comprehensible, rational laws, which are so far from being
transcendently ineffable or inscrutable that they are pronounced by
the deity himself.

Paradise Lost thus registers the profoundly naturalized perspec-
tives of baroque space and time that accompany the period's rapid
philosophical revision of the older and far more mystical relations
between universal and particular, subject and object. The variability
of its "boundless" universe (7.168–69) thus far exceeds that associ-
ated with earlier conceptions of infinity derived from the concept's

inventor, Nicholas of Cusa. According to Nicholas, the "veritable" man of the infinite universe becomes subjectively capable of ascending to the objects of divine vision only by freeing himself from the accidental or the particular, a freedom that requires a regimen of Christ-like self-abnegation or "emptying." By disciplining itself in the contemplation of ascending "essences," the human intellect ultimately achieves the passive or "clear" condition that allows it to receive the power of infinite knowledge, which then "fills" it with the power to affect all nature. Yet, as Gordon Worth O'Brien observes, this epistemological model inherently makes the enlightened soul little more than a successful *"patient"* on the cosmic wheel." Although this Neoplatonic schema is later expanded to allow the microcosmic "patient" to become an active agent in the cosmic scheme, its privileging of universals persists, along with its conception of "first matter" as the merely passive receptacle of universal essences or forms, which "imprint" the mysterious receptacle or *chora* of Plato's *Timaeus.* Gradually, however, natural philosophy's evolution from alchemy to modern chemistry produces an active notion of substance that parallels the interactive notion of agents, until both no longer merely reflect God's originating "Idea" but, through human thought and experimentation, participate in the divine.[4] In the seventeenth century, this evolution is greatly accelerated by the revival both of atomism and of elements formerly latent in Christian theology, which together produce late Reformation culture's tendency to replace Scholastic and/ or Neoplatonic universals with verifiable empirical "particulars." While some traces of Neoplatonism's hieratic orientation still linger in Milton's early poems, the epistemology and cosmology of the mature epics reflect the full flowering of these empirical tendencies: through interactive material substances, "self-authoring" subjects (*PL*, 3.122) now ascend to God.

Nevertheless, these processes are already well under way in the early poems, as the "mixed" allegories of Milton's *Mask* and his "L'Allegro" and "Il Penseroso" attest. There we find personae who ambivalently balance the roles of active seekers and passive receptacles of divine truth, with the result that their quests themselves might be described as a search for a resolution of the authoritarian and individualistic models of personal discovery. Thus, in *A Mask Presented at Ludlow Castle,* the attendant Spirit is not the vehicle of universal charity or heavenly grace but merely a marker of the Lady's dialectical discovery of the larger meaning of her own particular chastity. Broadly understood, this virtue provides the principled self-governance underlying every form of human realization in the masque, including that of her brothers, who, like her, must struggle to "apprehend" (perceive, arrest, or seize) the meaning of Comus, the opposing principle of license. The equally mixed source of his defeat is thus imaged by Sabrina, the earthly principle of chastity that must supplement heavenly charity, the higher or more universal form of its completion now "disarmed" except through the interaction of particulars like the brothers, Sabrina, and the Lady herself.[5] The dialectic between universals and particulars is perhaps even more pronounced in "Il Penseroso," where the cosmic agency of "thrice great *Hermes*" is called on only to be replaced by the self-examination of a quester who can personally discover the fruits of passive contemplation only by descending ever deeper into a dark wood that refuses to yield transcendental answers. Hence, in the end, the young poet commits himself neither to the discipline of the "pensive Nun" of "Il Penseroso," nor to that of Euphrosyne or Mirth of "L'Allegro," but only to a personal search for his own "Prophetic strain" ("Il Penseroso," line 174).

Thus, by the time Milton writes *Paradise Lost* and *Paradise Regained,* even Satan recognizes that the enterprise of seeking universal meaning through natural correspondences is doomed. As he credibly affirms, nature's most seemingly "obvious" signs of ascent or descent amount to no more than "a sneeze / To man's less universe, and soon are gone" (*PR,* 4.458–59). While he establishes this credibility in the sly attempt to reconstrue such signs as the fateful "vehicles" of normative allegory, these are casually dismissed by a Son who is "not worse than wet" from his "ominous night" full of "terrors, voices, prodigies," and who therefore denounces these "foregoing sign[s]" "as false portents, not sent from God, but thee" (4.481–91). This episode effectively expresses the processes at work in both epics, which comprehensively condemn universal correspondences or "signatures" abstracted from their naturalistic contexts as false idols that become "fateful" only insofar as one accepts the reification at work in the (self-)worship of spirits malign. Yet, like alchemy, allegorical emblems are not therefore banished from the epics but given naturalistic employments misconstrued only by alchemy's fallen idolaters. Since like Descartes and Bacon before him Milton rejects "the ancient opinion that man was *microcosmus,* an abstract or model of the world that had been fantastically strained by Paracelsus and the alchemists,"[6] the only "true" alchemy at work in *Paradise Lost* is conducted by the solar processes of the "Arch-chemic Sun," although these remain hidden to an "Undazzl'd" (*PL*, 3.609–14) devil ignorant of what goes on beneath his very feet.

Insofar as Milton's great epic can attain the "prophetic strain," it must then be by struggling to realign the lost or fallen correspondences still existing between conjunct domains of the human and the divine. Much like the Lady of *A Mask* or the voice of the companion poems, the epic's narrator is confronted with the task of conducting an allegorical quest without succumbing to what Bacon referred to as the "preventing" of natural time through sacramental or alchemical magic.[7] To his empirical disapproval of these pseudosciences, Milton adds a Reformed disapproval not only of the idolatry of false essences but of all such Scholastic distinctions, as his prose works from *Eikonoklastes* and *Of Education* to the *Christian Doctrine* amply testify. As the "ancients" give way to the "moderns" and the nominalism and materialism of the seventeenth century produce the modern era, the realm of universal being loses its precedence over the ephemeral realm of becoming, which is now the privileged locus of "real" names and things and the domain of human inquiry into both. In the process, a passive language of knowing (via a speculative hermeneutics) gives way to an active language of doing (via an empirical epistemology). In the broader historical perspective, these epistemological changes evolve into the familiar paradigm shift of Western culture's "Classic Age." Its rational/empirical imperatives produce not only the secularization of theology and natural philosophy (both of which lose their "sacramental" orientations once modern science is born) but also a similar secularization of poetry as its theocentric orientation becomes anthropocentric. Collaterally merging with the rise of individualism and capitalism, these forces cumulatively produce what William Righter calls Reformation culture's "continually refined psychological exploration of man's inner life."[8]

As Foucault's *Les mots et les choses* more thoroughly details—the French title bearing the more telling trace of the triad of "words, things, and thought" at issue in the epistemic break it charts—by the middle of the seventeenth century the neodualist mechanics of Descartes had largely replaced the modified or ternary dualism of Platonic Realism.[9] As we have seen, this older system subdivided the cosmos into a lower order of material "things" or accidents and a higher or more "real" order of abstract essences, ideas, or forms.

Mediating between these phenomenal and intelligible orders was a third order that belonged exclusively to neither: the semipermeable "veils," traces, or material signatures that provided a semiconcrete channel or vehicle between the ephemeral and the eternal realms. These mystic shapes or characters were "written" on the phenomenal world but were indicative of the noumenal. In this capacity they translate the overlapping organization of microcosmos and macrocosmos, which Bishop Hall could imagine so layered "that as in an egg, the yolk lies in the midst encompassed round with the white, and that again by a film and a shell; so the sensible world is enclosed within the intelligible."[10] Through these cosmic correspondences, the higher realm of reality (the immovable, eternal shell) is made accessible to the lower realm (the malleable yolk) by the "veil" of the translucent white surrounding it, which is in turn encased or "informed" by the shell. Needless to say, this older epistemology was allegorical in essence: to ascend to things beyond mortal sight, one needed to decode the translucent sign that was in itself magically permeated with the ultimate level of divine reality. From an earthly perspective, these layers of correspondence could be extended almost infinitely; as the structure of the egg mirrored that of the cosmos, so the inner and outward aspects of the human form (soul, intellect, body) reflected both. The universe itself could be "read" as a divine allegory wherein the intellect reflects or translates soul to body much as the Son or Word reflects the divine essence in the earthly sun below and upward in the Father above, pure mind or light.

Yet, not much later, Milton's invocation to light acknowledges the problematic nature of the analogy between the corpuscular "expressions" of light, the "impressions" of divine energy, and the motions of the mind that they supposedly mirror. Is light in fact mere physical motion or some more fluent "etherial stream" informed by the divine presence? By alluding to light's "impressions," he concedes much to Galilean physics as well as Cartesian epistemology, although without eliminating the possibility that merely corpuscular impressions might still somehow "express" divine light. Because these ambivalent suggestions are never resolved into a new synthesis but displaced onto the characteristic baroque tension between the presence of light and the dark absences or enigmas in which traces of the old signatures or veils remain, the allegorical sense of correspondence between divine and human realms is retained without the details of its fantastically "strained" correspondences. At the same time, the quest for light is reframed as the "blind" seeker's journey down into the inner darkness of the self, not that of a progressively enlightened soul guided beyond itself by the sacramental symbols or steps up and out into divine light. Much the same processes are at work in Raphael's deliberately imprecise interrogative,

> . . . what surmounts the reach
> Of human sense, I shall delineate so,
> By lik'ning spiritual to corporal forms,
> As may express them best, though *what if Earth*
> *Be but the shadow of Heav'n, and things therein*
> *Each to other like, more than on Earth is thought?*
> (*PL,* 5.571–76; emphasis added)

Here, as in the second invocation's quandary over whether light can best be "expressed" as a "Coeternal beam" or a "bright effluence," stream, or fountain of that beam (*PL,* 3.1–8), the underlying epistemic problem is displaced onto the status of figures that are still ontologically interrelated, but only hypothetically, and no longer by means of the part/whole analogies by which the older correspondences were conveyed. Unlike Hall's synecdochic egg, Raphael's shadow analogy depends on the vaguer connections of contiguity and/or causality characteristic of metonymy. What, after all, *is* the relation between the "shadow of heaven" and its earthly substance? Is the latter merely the outline or image of the former, or is the reflection also more substantial as well as contiguous, as between parent and child? Finally, if there is a genetic or substantial relation (which seems most likely, given the non-Platonic context of Raphael's narration), is the causal relation alchemical or chemical in function? Raphael never directly answers such questions, rather displacing them onto a historical narrative darkly "shadowing" both the ruin and the re-creation of an evolving continuum of heaven and earth. From this perspective, heaven does seem substantially to "body forth" the things of earth through the molecular continuities within difference of Milton's "one first matter." Yet, at the same time, these material processes depend on an organic figure of evolution (from root and stalk to leaf and flower) that does not resolve the problematic correspondence between heaven and earth but further displaces them onto the enigmas of a monistic but also "mixed" continuum of dark root and bright flower (5.472–81).

As in the parallel passages clustering around it, this uncertainty

about causes and effects as well as signs stems from the metareferen-
tial process of equivocation itself. While Raphael's "shadow" at first
seems to allude to the old cosmic correspondences, where it would
signify no merely material or nominal resemblance but an actual
outline or impress of the divine order it signifies, the fluid associa-
tions of *ombra, vestigia,* and *nutus* (as well-established Scholastic
terms for God's presence or essential "identity" within representable
things) fail to rule out the alternate emphasis on God's infinitely
vitalistic dispersal throughout nature. As semiotic or signifying
"presences," shadow, trace, and sign are thereby freed from that ex-
cessive condensation of spatial expression so characteristic of both
Dantean and Spenserian allegory but so ambiguously deferred by
Milton's metonymic materialism. Far more than his use of paradox
or puns—both of which are conventional instruments of allegory—
this reliance on the causal rather than participatory character of
metonymy distances Milton's baroque allegorical practice from its
antecedents, whose mysterious layered cosmos of "plastic" substance
ultimately led to a synecdochic "experience" of ineffable divine es-
sence. In the form of the Neoplatonic and Stoic "channels" between
spirit and matter—the *logoi spermatikoi* or *rationes seminales*—this
occulted or plastic matter at once separates the entire universe from
God and conveys it toward his empyrean. But, for Milton, these
channels have at once been closed and opened by the material infu-
sions obscurely originating both in light's *ex deo* expressions and in
the formless darkness of its absence, in Night's prematerial realm.
This ambiguous "solution" to the lost correspondences and darkened
emyreal "ring of fire" lamented by Donne thus implicitly distin-
guishes the divine traces within nature from the participatory corre-
spondences of the old enclosed cosmos, all of whose overlapping
circles had by now been "put out" with the arrival of an infinite and
largely undifferentiated space.

In cosmic poetry particularly, this shift demands a new semiotics
as well as a new theology, for, if anything could be said to focus the
attack of Cartesian philosophy on the older occult resources force-
fully active in the doctrine of correspondences, it was not skepticism
per se but, as Foucault's work details, the notion of a monistic plastic
substance somehow unifying everything beneath the veil of a God-
given language. In overturning the mystical or ternary monism pre-
served in Neoplatonism and revived along with hermeticism, the
grand semiotic paradigm shift effected by Cartesian philosophy

would replace this subjective "somehow" (instantiated with a "Je ne sais quoi" or "I know not how" of mysterious resonances) with consensually agreed on, empirically verifiable rules of binary order. This quest for objective relations between names and things was preeminently expressed both in the mathematical search for unimpeachable laws of nature and in the search for universal principles of language— as in the Cartesian grammarians of Port Royal and in John Wilkin's principles of universal grammar (to both of which Noam Chomsky refers the foundation of his own linguistics).[11] Yet, before Newton crystallized the laws of the new physics into their definitive form, it was still possible for philosophers and poets like Milton to accept the Cartesian revolution without abandoning some form of material monism, which had not (contra Foucault) been thoroughly discredited and which has in fact latterly reemerged in post-Newtonian physics. Conceived as an alternative rationalism, this early modern version of monistic metaphysics could abandon the fuzzy logic of mystified correspondences for the rationalized "spaces" of Cartesian logic while conserving a semimystical role for the material vacuum as an invisible, infinitistically displaced, and hence implicitly divine dimension of space.

In other extensions of the new physical continuum, Platonist philosophers like Henry More attempt to project a logical category of newly "extended" spirit, which in more mathematical terms Blaise Pascal projects into the incommensurable disjunction between the finite and the infinite. Milton parallels but also diverges from both thinkers in returning to the pre- and post-Socratic atomist traditions summed up in Lucretius. Instead projecting a newly extended form of divine matter in God's infinitely "dark with excessive bright" (*PL*, 3.380) emanations, he replaces More's dualist reinterpretation of the traditional spirit/matter dichotomy with a monistic divinity hidden in the immanent, invisible, yet also ultimately material recesses of the universe. If this vanishing point of light is hardly as comprehensively "clear and distinct" as Cartesian ideas, such imaginings are grounded in precisely the same logical attempt at seeking empirical certainty by bracketing man's mystical quest for higher things. Yet, since in this case this quest is merely reformulated by the logical mathesis implicit in the laws of Galilean motion, it must proceed as Raphael teaches— not by adapting a strictly binary version of the "resolutive-compositive" method that opposes objective and subjective or discursive and intuitive reason, but by monistically fusing them (5.488–500).

Although Galilean science has completely restructured the param-
eters of a universe in which all objects are now naturally in motion,
not at rest (as they were in the static Aristotelian-Ptolemaic cosmos),
it has not yet eliminated the possibility of approaching God through
a comparable "science" of motion, a dialectic that differently re-
solves the pieces that its spatial logic decomposes.[12]

Yet, since emblematic essences and static correspondences are no
longer aesthetically available to conduct the quest for higher things,
the vital verbal "drive" or power previously associated with piercing
their iconic veils must be carried over into the vitality of the poem by
different means.[13] Milton reassimilates this power through two prin-
ciple devices: (1) the self-reflexive or meta-allegorical method of
"heroically" sifting the ancient syncretic system of pagan and Chris-
tian forms, which, by the late Reformation, had fallen into the "ruin
of our first parents" and, like them, had to be canceled or otherwise
"repaired" (*CPW*, 2:366–67); and (2) the self-reflexive, introspective
method that the poet models for his "fit audience" of readers as
virtually they read and "perform" its enacting assumptions—even
though to most of us the poem has by now been largely severed from
those originating assumptions. Yet, in the very act of expressing the
ruin of a transactional conception underwritten by conditions we no
longer share, the poem continues to project a subliminal "allegory" of
the very process of renewal and its mysterious vitalities. In that di-
mension, it differs from the norms of more conventional allegory,
which usually achieves its mysterious unification of cultural ideology,
not through explicit questioning of, but through an implicit com-
plicity with the dualist distinctions that must separate microcosm
from macrocosm or "letter" from "spirit" in order "anagogically" to
unite them. In contrast, Milton's monistic allegory of poetic force
creates the linguistic equivalent of perpetual dialectic, a self-reflexive
vehicle everywhere dissolving the borders of the literal and the figu-
rative dimensions that (re)organize it. Having "virtualized" the com-
positional experience of John Milton, the poet in *Paradise Lost*
himself becomes a figural antitype pointing the way (through and
beyond whatever simple literalisms his stance evokes) to an allegory
of individual poesis. He thereby projects a world only superficially
accessible to a binary dialectic of any kind—Platonic Realist, Carte-
sian, or Calvinist—for the self-determining freedom that his poem
ideologically defends is fully realized only in the poetic attempt to
pursue "with no middle flight . . . / Things unattempted yet in prose

or rhyme" (*PL*, 1.15–17), a pursuit that in dialectically transcending conventional allegory's segregation of literal and figurative registers also inevitably expands the parameters of selfhood.

2

As outlined above, the received theories of epic-allegory to which the opening invocation implicitly alludes typically presuppose a system of language consisting of a "false shell in front, within containing a hidden truth." In this system, poetry ideally imitates the "bilingual" style of Scripture, which Coluccio Salutati described as speaking "in *figura*, binding what it relates in verses" with the result that "all is full of hidden meaning, everything can be brought back to an allegorical meaning." As Mindele Treip's commentary explains, Salutati's intimate association of the *integumentum* or outer wrapping with the *involucrum* or inner essence illustrates the essential continuity between the Renaissance theory of allegory and the medieval concept of *symbolum*, the mysterious yet also semitransparent discourse of divine truth "concretized" in such examples as Bishop Hall's egg.[14] As the egg analogy suggests, by positing successively continuous layers of truth, these theories were able to reduce even such abstruse doctrines as the "hypostatical" union of the trinitarian godhead to such elementary visual "enigmas" as the union of the egg's shell, yoke, and white. Such visual *symbolum* thus precipitate the "unveiling" of essentially iconic, eternal, and communal forms of sacramental mystery linking the known with the unknowable. As the decline of the word *sacrament* from its original meaning of "mystery" into technical controversies over its actual efficacy suggests, these continuities were later shattered by the Reformation's skeptical approach to external signs, whose meaning was not only objectified but collaterally interiorized, temporalized, and individualized. To re-form the paradigmatic biblical myth of the human lapse, pardon, and return in what Jurij Lotman calls the "syntagmatic" terms of a more linear and/or "readerly" epic culture, the iconoclastic Protestant poet must then revise not merely the Pentateuch but also Plato, whose parallel myths of individual purification and trial (*Phaedrus* 247c) must be similarly demystified.[15] Yet, ironically, because Platonic method also forms the ultimate philosophical foundation of Cartesian certitude, this return also requires its more primitive dualism to be overcome with its own device, a method rooted in mythic binary oppositions ultimately resembling those of biblical myth.

Much later, the Classic Age will "mathesize" these oppositions into schematic tables of signs and things, subjects and objects, the elementary "correspondences" of empiricism and objectivism. Yet, as serviceable as these dichotomies might be to empirical modes of inquiry, they lack an adequate account of the agency of the mind's mediating "force"—which even in the twentieth century Heidegger could describe only as poetic "rapture," understood as the "form-engendering force" mediating between enactment (subjectivity) and representation (objectivity).[16] Earlier, Kant related this shaping power to the imagination's construction of the world through its transcendental intuitions of space and time, a "Copernican" revision of Descartes that Milton's "icastic" poetic imagination seems to anticipate—which suggests why the Romantics found Milton a better teacher than Descartes or Hobbes.[17] Milton provides an opposing model of the "Agent of the One Great Mind" (Wordsworth, the 1805 *Prelude*) by reconfiguring the traditional Platonic and Christian allegorical ascent from earth to heaven as a descent in which *each* material form will be seen to be more like heaven's than even an angelic sense might suspect, although even the intuitive sense of angels remains material in ways that pointedly exclude elaborately mystified correspondences or analogies. Without eliminating any of the traditional levels of spiritual ascent derived from Plato and still implicit in the monistic scale of a "one first matter" proceeding from and returning to God (*PL*, 5.469–72), he regrounds them in the soil of Chaos's mutable atoms, the anarchic abyss immanently corresponding to the indeterminate "voids" of human freedom and divine grace.

This cosmic reconfiguration can proceed only through a radical modification of traditional allegory's synecdochic symbols, formerly the *integumentum* or cosmic "exornations" of the divine world that had so intimately imparted the shell's essence to the yoke that "'mere' ornament no longer exists." According to Angus Fletcher, who labels these symbols *kosmoi* in order to stress the original Greek sense of their simultaneous reference both to the cosmos as a whole and to its ornament as a part of that whole, such emblems are no mere outer wrappings any more than they are arbitrary signs. Instead, they function as "daemonic" or magical fragments, subdivisions, or microcosms of the living, breathing macrocosmos descended through the *Celestial Hierarchy* of Pseudo-Dionysus from Philo Judeas, "the greatest allegorist of the ancient world." Because Milton iconoclastically cancels the ritual or sacramental "essence" of these symbols, his images lack the magical ability to act as parts vitally conveying the whole. Nevertheless, through a vitalistic form of metonymy, his allegorical emblems conserve some of the chief functions of the conventional emblazoned language described by Fletcher. As before, "the ornament of the world 'comes forth'; there is an *ex*ornation of matter which is primarily felt to be beautiful but which has hierarchic order for its basis"—but now by different means.[18] By focusing instead on temporal motions as the causal or dynamic aspect of cosmic forms, the metonymic language of Milton's epic conserves the effect of the old correspondences within Galileo's abstract system space. Through the fluidly transactional if still immanently sacramental medium of these baroquely extended images, he monistically reforms the traditional Phaedran hierarchy of inspirational levels. As a result, *Paradise Lost* retains the feeling of a divinely ordered allegorical "Idea" while rejecting its sacramental essence. As in no previous cosmic poem, the hierarchical order of the Ptolemaic/Dionysian universe is imploded into the disembedded secular power of unfallen language.

The result is a Benjaminian ruin in a "realm of thought," a baroque form of allegory compelled to record the deconstruction of the very tradition that it would at least partially reconstruct. For, as Benjamin demonstrates, the "ruined" allegory of the seventeenth century is the typical result of the exhaustion of the pagan mysteries that had sustained key elements of Christianity's transcendental logic in general and of its sacramental system in particular.[19] As noted above, these changes are reflected in the evolution of the word *sacrament* itself, which, in ceasing to translate the Latin sense of the Greek word for *mystery,* also ceases to embrace all seven "magical" vehicles for the ritual purification and release of the soul. By the later Reformation, only baptism and the eucharist were still generally considered as spiritually efficacious *symbolum,* although even these were no longer considered "channels in which the supernatural is imparted" so much as "paramount obligation[s] . . . expressly commanded by Christ Himself," although even these only *potentially* conferred "special spiritual benefits . . . from faithful use" (*OED*). Hence, among more radical English Puritans and Nonconformists of Milton's type,

the very word *sacrament* was eliminated as a term too easily associ-
ated with "opinions regarded as superstitious," the word *ordinance*
being preferred in reference to baptism and the Lord's Supper. In the
process, the ancient idea that these holy rites provide a kind of pu-
rified covering, garment, or ornament for the purified soul is gradu-
ally objectified into a mere ecclesiastical convention, until sacra-
ments will uncertainly be seen either as mere signs or tropes (as
Milton regarded them) or as external signs or appearances of radical
grace without any assured internal analog (as conventional Calvinists
regarded them).

Yet, as Bunyan's example suggests, conventional Calvinism's rig-
idly predestined separation of saints and sinners on the presumptive
basis of outward appearances or "works" (which in practice qualifies
its radical doctrine of grace) permits a far stricter and hence more
conventional allegorical segregation of good and evil signs than we
find in Milton's poem. In rejecting this revival of a quasi-legalistic
system of salvation in favor of an ambiguous Arminian or "free will"
theology, the poem thus registers that secular incertitude toward the
holy that Benjamin traces to Lutheranism's austere exclusion of ex-
ternal signs of grace from both communal and individual life. While
Milton seems never to have suffered from a melancholy, much less a
"Lutheran," uncertainty about his personal salvation, his tactic of
asserting the inscrutable indeterminacies of personal conscience as a
defense against the Puritan revolution's communal failure to exter-
nalize its mandates ironically produces much the same effect: an
austere celebration of sacramental/allegorical incertitude. In this
sense, this skepticism is at once anti-Calvinist and anti-Cartesian, at
least in the modified sense that would accept some tenets of both, as
well as anti-Spenserian in the sense that it can accept his "great
Original's" apocalyptic certitudes only in the context of a thoroughly
qualified prophetic mode. For Milton regarded the prophetic certi-
tudes of his faction as a chief contributing factor in the revolutionary
debacle to whose disappointments and sufferings his epic bears elo-
quent witness. Clearly, the "tragic" return of the Stuart court has
vastly reinforced his early hostility to the "wanton Mask, or Mid-
night Ball / Or Serenate" (*PL*, 4.768–69) as even a potential model of
the true kingdom of England, much less of God. If there is to be any
Protestant "mirror" of God's providential plan, it must then be found
in a kind of epic-allegory far different from Spenser's, which he
abandons along with the Arthurian-epic ambitions of his youth.

These revisionary impulses are already evident in Milton's early *Mask*, which as we have seen represents a fairly advanced experiment in the transitional mode of baroque allegory. But, like his antiprelatical treatises of roughly the same period, the masque also maintains a youthful confidence in the ability of God's "emergent revelations" to guide the revolutionary struggles of his nation, a confidence that naturally enough inhibits the melancholy or "ruined" sensibilities that Benjamin regards as the chief hallmark of the baroque. These attitudes are thus far more fully developed in the later poem's postlapsarian vision of paradise, where, along with any external signs of personal or public virtue, Adam and Eve lose any direct access to the divine presence.[20] This loss also historically "seals" the rupture between the secularized universe of Cartesian signs and the sacramental world system tentatively initiated in *Comus*. Here Milton plays on the ancient and uncorrupted sense of *virtue* as an actual power (from the Latin *virtus*, "strength or force") of individualizing agency, but one only indirectly and ironically sustained by a courtly community. In this central respect, the masque allegorically unmasks the idea that any external community can act as a vehicle of grace; like the sacrament itself, this "vehicle" is replaced by a more naturalistic (if still mythic) counterpart of the individual's internal "virtue," the river goddess Sabrina. Yet, because Sabrina is herself a pre-Christian water spirit, and because the Lady's own chastity reconfigures the more traditional virtue of charity to which it alludes, their joint victory over Comus "baroquely" renews, reorders, and reironizes the continuities of Christian with pagan ethics. Concluding with the Attendant Spirit's evocative allusion to Plato's Vision of Er (*Republic*, bk. 10), "Virtue" here becomes a simultaneously moral and physical force somehow pervading the universe but manifest only in individually generative song—the power allegorically imaged in the Lady's opening song to Echo. This spontaneous and unceremonial aria (arising from her inspired apprehension that she is attended by Faith, Hope, and Chastity, her instinctively self-referential version of the traditional theological virtues) thus returns "virtue" to a root meaning that symbolically reforms and restores its true significance. This linguistico-spiritual revision additionally reflects the uneasy late Protestant exaltation of grace over works and individual over communal meaning, thereby submerging virtue into what Benjamin calls "the depths which separate visual being from meaning."

In this intensified and refined Protestant culture, not only is the court no longer a condensed image of the larger harmonies of nature (as in Jonson's masques), but the old liturgical calendar and its harmonies no longer emblematically order the cyclic segregation/integration of the profane and the sacred. In contrast to Counter-Reformation Catholicism and its powerful penetration of secular life, advanced Protestantism at once divorces religious duty from public performance and paradoxically reunites the two through a "rigorous morality . . . [whose] teaching in respect of civic conduct stood in sharp contrast to its renunciation of 'good works.'" These attitudes contribute to a ruin of allegory that is in effect an implosion, not a complete effacement, of the form, both by denying works "any special miraculous spiritual effect" and by "making the soul dependent on grace through faith, and making the secular-political sphere a testing ground for a life which was only indirectly religious, being intended for the demonstration of civic virtues . . . , [which] did it is true, instill into the people a strict sense of obedience to duty, but in its great men it produced melancholy."[21] Milton's assimilation of this ethic is at once less mournful and more radical since it stems ultimately from a self-imposed, voluntaristic sense of Christian virtue that can alternately seem both bright and dark—as a source of strength and freedom derived from the oblique presence of a distant but relatively comprehensible God, but also as a burden imposed by the absence of a forever fragmented community.[22]

In a similarly ambiguous sense, the purely inward nature of Puritan ordinances and rites restores their "proper" and original form, even though they can now no longer securely "seal" God's covenant with his people. In place of such assurances, the individual gains the godlike freedom to "covenant" with God by means of purely personal but binding vows, although their meaning, enactment, and ratification remain almost wholly internal and inscrutable.[23] But, in characteristically Miltonic fashion, the more dubious aspects of this aporistic natural religion are overcome by personal, virtually "esemplastic" zeal, a sign or seal synthetically "evident" in his iconoclastic rejection of superstitious belief and his assertion of a quasi-divine rationality so powerful that it can be traced only to the re-creative motions of inner grace. Denying that the eucharistic "food of eternity" has any supernatural power or that baptism literally "seals" the righteous with anything more than a "grace already revealed," Milton's consideration of the sacrament thus characteristically begins by declaring the bread of "which *he who eats shall live for ever*" to be nothing more than a convenantal symbol; if it were otherwise, then "even the most wicked of the communicants, not to mention the mice and worms which often eat the eucharist, would attain eternal life by virtue of that heavenly bread" (*CPW,* 6:548, 553).[24] Yet, in indignantly pronouncing "consubstantiation and particularly transubstantiation and papal anthropophagia or cannibalism" utterly alien to reason, common sense, and normal human behavior, he avoids the melancholy of the unsealed saint by turning such declarations into quasi-"visible" acts of civic virtue capable of "convenantally" assuring that his ultranaturalistic theology still serves as a means of grace. Otherwise, how could he have regarded his *Christian Doctrine* as among the most precious of his possessions or "talents," had he not conceived its writing as somehow sacramentally rendering these talents back to the divine "taskmaster" of sonnet 7? Thus, Milton avoids the darker melancholy of the Germanic baroque primarily through a positive dedication to exposing the false enigmas or superstitions that he conceives as irreconcilable with sacred doctrine, with the actual nature and fruit of the sacrament, with the analogy of baptism, with the normal use of words, with the human nature of Christ, and, finally, with his as yet unfulfilled kingdom on earth. What other baroque allegorists would mourn he would doggedly regather, like his own redeemed Isis or Orpheus, reassembling the scattered limbs of Truth's truly numinous remnants with the help of the greater mother-muse Urania (*CPW,* 2:549; *PL,* 7.21–39). Only in this way can he begin to repay his talents a hundredfold, in the process blindly glimpsing God's bright face amid their mutual, if incommensurable, darkness (*PL,* 3.40–55).[25]

The sacramental critique of the *Christian Doctrine* is thus worth examining in fuller detail since its views inform Milton's view both of allegory and of all human/heavenly forms of accommodation, as he explains: "In the so-called sacrament, as in most matters where the question of analogy arises, it is to be noted that a certain trope or figure of speech was frequently employed. By this I mean that a thing which in any way illustrates or signifies another thing is mentioned not so much for what it really is as for what it illustrates or signifies. Failure to recognize this figure of speech in the sacraments, where the relationship between the symbol and the thing symbolized is very close, has been a widespread source of error and still is today" (*CPW,* 6:555). These formal errors derive from a theologically legalistic view of the sacrament as "absolutely necessary" for Christians

(*CPW*, 6:556), which produces the related literalism of locating transubstantiational mystery in mere signs or symbols. In harmony with the Cartesian preference for "clear and distinct" ideas, such criteria may admit verbal enigmas, but they hardly allow for any mystical identification of words and things: "what [a thing] really is" and "what it illustrates or signifies" are now at best tangentially related.

More tangentially still, these remarks illustrate Benjamin's conclusion that, in Reformation hermeneutics generally, the "imitation of nature [can no longer] mean . . . the imitation of nature as shaped by God," most especially not in anything resembling the easy "communion" of sign and signified presupposed by Renaissance thought. For, as we have seen, the most critical disjunction of this vast early modern paradigm shift lies, not in the recentering of the universe around the sun, but in the decentering of the sacral cosmos descending from heaven to earth through the "veil" of the supralunar sphere. In this disjunction lies the essential impulse behind baroque allegory's paradoxical resurrection/recancellation of the pagan nature deities, which in cultural-aesthetic terms means that, "with the revival of paganism in the Renaissance, and Christianity in the Counter-Reformation, allegory, the form of their conflict, also had to be renewed." Yet only a little earlier, before the Cartesian-Copernican revolution was complete, pagan wisdom could still be allied with sacramental truths since both were unproblematically derived from the *priscii theologiae*—Moses, Hermes Trismegistus, Orpheus, all providing part of a unitary chain in Spenser as in Ficino. Even Egyptian hieroglyphics thereby became "something corresponding to divine thought, since divinity surely possesses knowledge of all things, not as a changing idea, but as the simple and fixed form of the thing itself."[26]

In the late Reformation or early revolutionary period already reflected in *A Mask*, these hieroglyphic or hermetic symbols of courtly allegory had already become guilty both by association and by genetic lineage. Descending, as Frances Yates shows, from Ficino via the French academic allegorists who glorified courtly hierarchies as the visible extensions of eternal cosmic law, the English allegorical tradition had by this time been tainted by the incipient decay of an interdependent linguistic, cosmological, and political system of "natural" hierarchical authority—the system that Milton began his academic as well as his polemical careers by rejecting.[27] Nevertheless, as his masque also attests, Milton is hardly a Romantic enemy of all such authority—any more than he is of pagan or hermetic symbols. In discarding the symbolic signatures that point to a transubstantiation beyond language, he points instead to a sacramental power within language that has become newly capable of "realizing its potential to name everything," in William Kerrigan's phrase.[28] Yet, unlike the mystical language of correspondences, this power derives from the lingustic ambiguity at its root—tha natural "virtue" or force of its primally complex words. Thus, while Milton would agree with the rationalists that the presence of Christ's body and blood in the Eucharist is "merely" a trope, he also grants this trope the multivalent internal significance of the covenant itself. A similar approach to metaphor is evident in his understanding of ancient myth as literally neither false nor true but as a distant "shadow" of a reality that, like the "things" of heaven or of Eden, can at least partially be recaptured. This dialectical recovery of signs is partly sustained by the fact that, for Milton, repairing the ruins of our first parents means resuming a process of accommodation interrupted, not instituted, by the Fall. Given the partiality of Adam and Eve's *initial* "correspond[ence] with Heav'n" (*PL,* 7.511), among the many myths that his poem will demystify and renaturalize is that of an aboriginal purity. By situating the lapse of human language and virtue (in its multiple senses) in an Eden never excluded from the indeterminacy at the core of linguistic and ethical danger, the poem at once "ruins" pagan symbols and sacramental certitudes yet also recuperates what Milton regards as their original and fecund ambiguity.

In contrast, like Spenser's Garden of Adonis, Dante's paradise is conceived in terms of an Augustinian theology wherein God has indefinitely withdrawn from any primordial immediacy of real presence to human consciousness or language. Where once in unfallen Adam's apperceptiveness there was plenitude itself, now there are only signs of God's presence (*Paradiso* 26.106). In contrast, Milton's "magnanimous correspondence" with heaven places man on initially lower but ultimately higher ground. In his here and now, the regenerate mind is in far greater communion with God or with an illimitability that the mind conceives for itself, while, for Dante, the linguistic consequences of the Fall meant a forever impoverished ability to read the possibilities of the signs of God's presence, to think God absent when he is actually present in signs that either are not always readily decodable or are only marginally manifest in mysterious, quasi-transubstantiational signs, the very effect of whose mysteries was to signify a delimitability that could not even be theoretically breached.[29]

The "mysteries" of Milton's Eden are strikingly different in both form and content. Replacing the partially transcendent realm of trial of *A Mask* with a fully and immanently material arena of choice, his "fair field of *Enna* . . . which cost Ceres all that pain" (*PL*, 4.268–71) is summoned only as a clue to what it never was, a magically secluded and mystically decipherable paradise. Eden's experiential multi-valence, its problematic wantonness and wandering, thus forecloses the earlier episteme whose antique blazons, ciphers, and hiero-glyphics could turn "immediate resemblances [into the] . . . vast open book" of nature that sixteenth-century Neoplatonism saw as a mystical code linking it to its otherwise inscrutable God. Here, in-stead, like his Isis and Osiris, Milton's Ceres and Prosperine supply signatures of almost wholly canceled mysteries turned into baroque emblems that ambiguously herald the melancholy, irregular, incom-plete, yet immanently assured process of gathering up Truth's alle-gorical ruins.[30] Not only does the complex fragmentation/reunifica-tion of these certitudes inevitably blur the dichotomies behind any easy allegorical correspondence of place and person, vehicle and meaning, but it also forces Truth's incoherence to take on the natu-ralistically expanded vanishing points of infinite space and time in which God reemerges.

This expansion of the Ptolemaic macrocosmos and its microcos-mic correspondences thus completes the disintegration of traditional allegory's ritual magic, which is ruined along with its closed spa-tiotemporal coordinates. As Benjamin summarizes, "The mystical instant [Nu] becomes the 'now' [*Jetzt*] of contemporary actuality; the symbolic becomes distorted into the allegorical. The eternal is separated from the events of the story of salvation, and what is left is a living image open to all kinds of revision by the interpretative artist." These reorientations also account for the excessively realistic lineaments of Milton's God, whose "allegorical designations bear the seal of the all-too-earthly" impulses of the baroque:

Never does their transcendence come from within. Hence their illumina-tion by the artificial light of apotheosis. Hardly ever has there been a literature whose illusionistic virtuosity has more radically eliminated from its works that radiance which has a transcendent effect, and which was at one time, rightly, used in an attempt to define the essence of artistry. . . .

Any adequate masking of content is absent from the typical works of the baroque. The extent of their claims . . . is breathtaking. And they lack any feeling for the intimate, the mysterious. They attempt, extravagantly and vainly, to replace it with the enigmatic and the concealed.[31]

Yet this assessment of the mode also makes its application to *Paradise Lost* problematic insofar as it chiefly describes its least successful, least resonant moments, as when the Almighty gruffly reserves the role of prosecuting attorney, judge, and jury to himself in condemning "Man," his "ingrate" and "faithless Progeny" (3.93–98). This apparent defeat can be explained on two related grounds: first, that at his best Milton does indeed differ from the gloomier *trauerspiel* poets in the theological respects outlined above; second, that Benjamin's excessively gloomy view of these poets (who, as we will recall, include Shakespeare) seems to be darkened by his own preoccupation with the lost "aura" of religious faith in the harsher light of modernity.

As to the first point, we have seen that Milton understood divine Providence as functioning in two distinct modes, only one of which bears the seal of the all too earthly. As he suggests in *The Doctrine and Discipline of Divorce:* "The hidden wayes of his providence we adore & search not; but the law is his reveled wil, his complete, his evident, and certain will; herein he appears to us as it were in human shape, . . . binds himself like a just lawgiver to his own prescriptions, and . . . is commensurat to right reason" (*CPW*, 2:292). This formulation explicitly contrasts the deity's discursive mode, that of the legalistic lawgiver bound by his own precepts, with the simultaneously uncertain and self-evidently praiseworthy Providence hidden in his as yet incomplete design, the Providence outwardly represented by his austere pronouncements but more vitally enacted by the dances of angels or of the graces with the universal Pan. Since the dances of the latter are accompanied by the hours (*PL*, 4.266–67), like Raphael's "process of speech" their enactment of temporality figures forth the humanly "adorable" dimension of "time or motion," not the forbidding immediacy of an all too clear and distinct justice beyond human recall (7.176–79). Nevertheless, as both this gloss on divine accommodation and the frequent interjections of the narrative voice jointly reveal, the tension between representation and enactment or discursivity and delight at times threatens to "ruin" the contrapuntal harmony of temporally revealed and eternally rigorous law. This potential dichotomy thus at least indirectly corresponds to the baroque gulf between the mysterious (or unknowable) and the enigmatic (or merely unknown) pointed out by Benjamin—a gulf capable of producing "breathtaking effects," although perhaps in a more positive sense than he seems to have intended.

In lamenting this generative dichotomy, Benjamin thus seems to be operating in a more self-referential vein, which betrays the split within himself as Marxist critic of social aesthetics and one who more cabalistically yearns for a redemptive Providence that might somehow unriddle the mysterious intimations of the historical process. Certainly, his allusion to the baroque artist's melancholy rejection of "tightly woven, deliberately simplified schemes that unmistakably point to an external referent, usually transcendent for those members of a community who possess the key," suggests, first, that he mourns the loss of such schemas and, further, that he does not fully appreciate the reemergence of the numinous in the looser and more naturalistic motions of baroquely displaced time and space, where it appears, not in the absence of discursive reason (as in Dante), but actually in its midst. Yet, however he is interpreted, Benjamin's portrait of the " 'metaphysical homelessness' . . . of lonely creatures in despair about transcendence despite their conventional religiosity"[32] goes only so far in illuminating Adam and Eve's situation. While it clearly applies to many aspects of their expulsion, it hardly engages all the facets of their "paradise within." Even so, when, stripped of its elegiac and mystical flavor, Benjamin's model accurately isolates the "this-worldly" focus that Weber similarly glimpsed in Milton's epic: the celebration of a deritualized, uncertain continuum that supplies a marginal but by no means complete cause for lament.

If belated Romantics like Benjamin find cause for regret in what Eliot was at the same time lamenting as a "dissociation of sensibility," from another perspective the poem can be seen as a triumphantly iconoclastic celebration of revitalized yet still spiritualed "earthly" individualism.[33] Not only are its multiple frameworks responsible for the exhilaration produced by baroque art, but, in Benjamin's own terms, such distancing does not remove but merely "refracts" poetic apotheosis onto an indeterminate and deliberately illusionistic providential "screen." Reserving any other kind of transcendence for the individual's own "covenant" with the poem and its presiding Spirit, the epic's loss of concrete certitude is thus partially regained by a paradoxical inner paradise at once tragically limited and "happier far" (*PL*, 12.587). Yet, like Adam and Eve, the reader can earn this ironically mitigated joy only by accepting the unmitigated loss of an aboriginal Eden, although it might once have been, as Michael tells Adam,

> Perhaps thy Capital Seat, from whence had spread
> All generations, and had hither come
> From all the ends of th' Earth, to celebrate
> And reverence thee thir great Progenitor.
> But this preëminence thou has lost, brought down
> To dwell on even ground now with thy Sons.
>
> (11.343–48)

Nevertheless, this sad pronouncement reflects not so much a fallen as a necessary human condition, one not only possible but perhaps necessary from the first—at least insofar as every man and woman is an Adam or an Eve who must earn whatever "preeminence" is worth celebrating in the individualistic ethic of Protestantism. Of course, from the proleptic perspective of modernity, Benjamin is right; more than a mere revision, *Paradise Lost* also represents a rupture of myth, a world of lost perfection that has really been our world all along. This naturalized dreamscape is most likely what left Marvell "misdoubting" that his friend had gone too far in rationally ruining the "sacred truths": that in "perplex[ing] the things he would explain, / . . . what was easy he should render vain" ("On Paradise Lost," lines 6–8, 15–16). Yet only through such a drastic reorientation of epic-allegorical "truths" could the poet transcribe his culture's old songs into a new key since, as Friedrich Creuzer emphasizes in a text cited by Benjamin, it is only "allegory, and not the symbol, which embraces myth . . . , the essence of which is most adequately expressed in the progression of the epic poem."[34] Hence, only in an epic revival of biblical myth could the underlying framework of Christian/Greek culture be recast according to the central tenets of Reformation ideology. Here, a new form of heroic myth would express a new hierarchy of works and grace, which could reverse the old hierarchy previously celebrated in Christian poems organized around the grail of a contrary set of rituals and beliefs—"the daily celebration of the sacred liturgy, the sacramental system, the systemization of theology, the philosophical interest in being rather than becoming, the emphasis on the visual rather than the auditory, the elaborate system of static correspondences between the earthly and the heavenly, [which] all bespeak a primary (though of course not exclusive) interest in the timeless structure of eternity as physically manifested in the natural world and in the forms and symbols of daily life."[35]

3

William Madsen's by now familiar summary thus reminds us that the chief problem for a study attempting to analyze *Paradise Lost* from the perspective of Reformation allegory has less to do with the metaphysics than with the aesthetics of the mode. While its metaphysics have been extensively explored, its aesthetics have been notoriously confused by the contradictory polemics of the late Reformation and early Romantic periods, which are at once continuous and distinct. Although both superficially tend to reject mystical allegory, both also reinvent it in opposing ways—the Reformers by "translating" it into broad typological or historical schemas whose moral core remains allegorical, the Romantics by preferring a symbol whose temporal "unities" conceal the characteristic dichotomies of allegorical analogy, as Paul de Man's extensive work on this theme reveals.[36] Because modern critics have, like Benjamin, inherited both traditions, any discussion of Milton's allegorical poetics has remained essentially confused. Owing particularly to the onus placed on allegory by Coleridge's reductive opposition of the symbolic to the allegorical mode, whole generations of critical apologists have devoted themselves to discussing Milton's aesthetics as if they fell within the exclusive domain of the symbol. Thus, for C. S. Lewis, his was an art of "ritual symbols," while, for successive critics (who rightly suspected the high church overtones of this "praise"), Milton's epic art could be Platonic, metaphoric, mythic, typological—in short, anything *but* allegorical.[37] Yet, as Milton himself well understood, allegory by definition subsumes or includes all these forms or modes, of which it is merely a more extended or schematic elaboration (much as Scholes and Kellogg observe): "Typological significance precedes . . . moral (or 'tropological') significance" and inevitably shades into it.[38] Nevertheless, through a kind of inversionary logic, a resolutely anti-Platonic (and implicitly anti-Lewis) school of critics has ignored this continuity along with Milton's stated subordination of typology to allegory, thereby reading his poem as if his Protestant hermeneutics demanded a quasi-Hebraic insistence on the image's temporal completion in time, a fulfillment that would grant it the quasi-sacramental concreteness privileged by modern symbolist aesthetics and its Romantic forebears—both of which ironically conceal allegorical aspirations.

Thus, as Jon Whitman points out, what all these confusions have in common is the misapplication of "a distinction that is at once too broad and too narrow": "too broad in that the loose association between the 'sacramental' and 'symbolic' approaches tends to overlook the fact that these procedures may imply quite different values and operations for the figures of the natural world . . . [and] too narrow in that a strict separation between the 'sacramental' or 'symbolic' mode as a whole and the 'allegorical' mode in general seems to depend in general upon a problematic division between 'natural' and 'psychological' dramatization that overlooks the central principles shared by both strategies."[39] Benjamin himself similarly acknowledges the tendentious features of an aesthetic theory either directly or indirectly influenced by German Romanticism—itself ideologically inflected by Protestant thought of a later stamp. Nevertheless, his understanding of allegory as fundamentally the art of lost "aura" also reinforces late Protestantism's self-reflexive evaluation of a mode whose ideological underpinnings it nostalgically dismisses as either "beyond beauty" or actually complicit in Western art's process of "irresistible decay." That there remains ample truth in Benjamin's analogy between allegory as a ruin in "thought" comparable to that within the secularized "realm of things" is unquestionable; but it is also true that such generalizations fail clearly to discriminate between baroque allegory and its earlier, more vital and/or normative forms. Less prejudicially speaking, all allegories do in some sense "recollect" the ruined emblems of decaying cultural concepts, although only in baroque allegory will this recollection fully reflect the wholesale ruin of a formerly cohesive universe. But merely to rehearse the familiar Romantic conflict between "redemptive" symbol and "decadent" allegory—as Benjamin implies by suggesting that, "where man is drawn towards the symbol, allegory emerges from the depths of being to intercept the intention, and to triumph over it"[40]—is not to progress far enough beyond Coleridge's somewhat muddled reworking of German aesthetics. In dismissing allegory, he confines it to the Apollonian, didactic, or dualizing aspect of the symbol while mystifying the symbol as its Dionysian, dynamic, organic, and positive antithesis, where it remains implicitly submerged as its darker double or enemy twin.[41]

More recent and linguistically sophisticated approaches to the relation between symbol and allegory describe their conflict as a form of violence, the struggle of a lost world of timeless "being" with the petrified, historical space of allegory. Benjamin himself points toward this approach in acknowledging their underlying unity as follows: "The measure of time for the experience of the symbol is the mystical instant in which the symbol assumes the meaning into its hidden and, if one may say so, wooded interior. On the other hand, allegory is not free from a corresponding dialectic, and the contemplative calm with which it immerses itself into the depths which separate visual being from meaning, has none of the disinterested self-sufficiency which is present in the apparently related intention of the sign."[42] As Benjamin is no doubt aware, these related if antithetical rhetorical "intentions" are also inherent in the twin poles of all speech isolated by Nietzsche and later by Wittgenstein as the metaphoric pole of "self-effacing" seeing or *enactment* and the similitudinous pole of "self-sufficient" showing or *representation.* Since all discourse of any amplitude must alternate between both poles, there can be no such thing as a pure poetics of the symbol or of allegory. Thus, given the fundamentally metaphoric basis of language and the fact that nearly all narrative contains both the literal and the figural dimension of meaning employed by allegory (that of common reference and of "other" speaking or secondary meaning, as its etymology implies), Northrop Frye may have been closer to the truth in declaring all literature implicitly allegorical in scope.[43]

Yet such a definition does little to clarify either the specific rhetorical resources of allegory or Milton's relation to the mode. In part, these varying resources (as Gordon Teskey seems also to suggest) participate in Wittgenstein's familiar saying/showing or rabbit/duck dilemmas, dichotomies inherent in any self-reflexive or "meta" approach to language; in part, they remain embedded in obscurities that still surround our understanding of Milton's practice. Given the kind of compromise that Fletcher's useful "anatomy" of allegory strikes with this tradition, we should perhaps do best in following his refusal either to devalue the allegorical emblem or to oppose it to the symbol as the only true vehicle of "being" or "time." For, as a privileged language of metameaningfulness, any allegorical poetics will always particularly reflect the Western canon's internal conflict between being and time, representation and enactment, or synchrony and diachrony. At the level of language itself, this conflict is repeated in the disparate resources of synecdoche (part/whole tropes of synchrony) and metonymy (cause/effect tropes of diachrony), which again are not so exclusively disparate as the Reformers or Romantics assumed. Teskey presents a roughly similar assessment of the case in arguing that the "primal scene" of allegory is originally a place of "bold juxtaposition, unrestrained analogy, violence, struggle, and noise," which gradually succumbs to antiphrasis or irony in its triumph over polysemy or allegorical meaningfulness. Yet, despite his striking insights into the complexity of allegory's language games, his position does not ultimately account for the full creative potential of irony, diachrony, or metonymy to enact their own species of allegorical meaningfulness. At the same time it tends to recapitulate some of Benjamin's emphasis on the mode's lost numina as well as his assumptions about allegory's inability successfully to negotiate a world where eternity's "being" has been replaced by temporality's "becoming."[44]

What instead seems needed is a more Nietzschean evaluation of the Dionysian processes of remembering and recovery in which, not only Miltonic allegory, but the entire horizon of literary reception participates. From such a perspective—which at best can be explored here only initially—it would be possible to demonstrate the strength of Fletcher's insight that the baroque allegory of the seventeenth century dies only to come "alive again in a profoundly new notion of man's place in the cosmic order of things . . . not in awe of Nature, but in [a] direct confrontation and perception" that occasions "those same feelings that characterize man's attitude toward the holy."[45] Of course, from a more postmodern perspective Teskey's work seeks to establish a similarly comprehensive or "Nietzschean" analysis of allegory—one capable of isolating its underlying *structure,* while Fletcher's anatomical evaluation merely skims the surface; and from this perspective its divergence from the viewpoint presented here is almost exclusively historical, not methodological. Methodologically, Teskey's analysis of the generic parameters of allegorical structure that *Paradise Lost* directly engages is completely consistent with the terms of this study; historically, it remains too close to Benjamin's "tragically" ironic view of the baroque mode as a belated failure. Nevertheless, precisely this divergence makes Teskey's analysis of the mode's normative functions an extremely useful measure of the poem's engagement with the form that it has so often been seen as simply rejecting—particularly because his definition of *allegory* is much more restrictive than most. According to this definition, all the following functions must be present in a genuinely allegorical work: (1) "By concealing the underlying, originative work of instrumental meaning [or correspondence] allegory reinterprets the noise beneath the things we can see as the inner desire of those things to return to their origin in the One." (2) Allegory resolves the "otherness" implicit in such correspondences through "an ascending hierarchy of anagogic (upward-moving) meanings." (3) It also resolves that otherness by affirming the "identity of those opposites," that is, of the self and the transcendental Other that "we situate above the world in order to make that . . . macrocosm . . . coincide with the self," or microcosm. (4) A true allegorical poetics (as opposed to mere allegoresis) "contains instructions for its own interpretation."[46]

From the standpoint of even this rigorous definition, it should be apparent that, whether or not we would regard *Paradise Lost* as a failed allegory, it remains a profoundly allegorical text. Of course, the poem also ironizes the normative mode in ways we have already defined, with the result that at the same time (1) it reveals rather than conceals the original work of correspondence, thereby critiquing it; (2) it resolves the problem of otherness through a descending or historicizing rather than an ascending or "anagogical" movement; (3) it resolves the difference between the self and the transcendental Other by incorporating that other into a separate, inwardly inspired, or theomorphic man, a poet/Adam/reader who will still ultimately correspond to the macrocosm of the "All in All"; and (4) it ironically provides the most explicit instructions for its interpretation of any canonical allegory through its fourfold invocational structure and its intermediate narrative injunctions. These revisions suggest that some course between German Romantic optimism with regard to symbolic forms and the pessimistic reaction that belatedly succeeds it seems to us the best approach not only to the baroque mode generally but also to Milton's reinvention of allegory in *Paradise Lost*. At times Benjamin himself suggests a similar course, as when in commenting on Creuzer he astutely observes that, "if nature has always been subject to the power of death, it is also true that it has always been allegorical. Significance and death both come to fruition in historical development, just as they are closely linked as seeds in the creature's graceless state of sin. The perspective of allegory as a development of myth . . . [thus] ultimately appears from the same baroque [or pre-Romantic] standpoint, as a moderate and more modern perspective."[47] At least at this point in Benjamin's often contradictory "oscillation," baroque allegory is simply the maximal realization of the ephemerality in which all myth and symbol participate but that in more naive, premodern or prebaroque, perspectives is concealed by the homeopathic and ritual magic of diagrammatic "polysemy." Yet baroque works like *Paradise Lost* also resist the expected death of analogical polysemy by inverting allegory's "ritual" priorities and recuperating its noise as the resonance, not of a mystified or "absolute" truth, but as the resonance of the oscillational truth of language itself.

Of course, diagrammatically or analogically to "measure countries in the mind," as Francis Bacon understood the work of allegorical poetics, requires an overriding narrative schema, "Idea," argument, or "plan," a "figurative geometry" that would seem to inhibit the spontaneity, "suggestiveness and intensity of ambiguous metaphorical language" that this study associates with Milton's baroque poetics.[48] However, as Teskey's reference to "noise" and Frye's emphasis on the overlapping generic systems within allegorical "plots" differently suggest, this "geometry" does not necessarily inhibit genuinely dramatic or lyric moments. As Fletcher summarizes,

Allegory may also be taken as emotive utterance and in this light shows an internal structure of such force that we do not long remain cold analysts of the geometric paradigm. The popular appeal of many parabolic works, especially of those romances that are so modestly allegorical—the western, the detective story, the melodrama—lies in a countermovement; for the causal connections of scenes and characters—the reasons why they go together as they do, the way the characters influence and affect each other, and so on—these are not simply logical; they are not merely reasonable; they are to a high degree magical relationships which have only superficially the form of ordered arguments.[49]

Thus, as Fletcher also suggests, as meditations on the hidden mysteries of the human psyche's interaction with the "poem" of its culture, like magic, allegories are hyperlogical attempts to match form and content. In pointedly rejecting allegory's older, externalized magical correspondences in favor of a more naturalistic dialectic or "Ramist" logic of consequences, Milton's poem implicitly initiates these later protomodern, psychological explorations of "natural" human mystery. As its "diagram" of sin and salvation moves farther from plotting the primitive logic of contamination and closer to examining the psychic logic of self-deception, its correspondences thus also begin to resemble those of more contemporary psychodrama.

4

The task of detailing these complex reorientations is best approached by contrasting Milton's personified Sin and the verbal noise she disseminates throughout the poem with the primitive "symbolism of evil" discussed by Paul Ricoeur. In this ancient system, as in most normative allegory, purification is not conceived as ontologically separate from the "otherness" of evil, which it tries to capture or "annul . . . by a specific action" directly correlated to an external " 'impurity, a fluid, a mysterious and harmful something that acts dynamically—that is to say, magically.' "[50] Milton's doctrinal and poetic representations of the holy alike preclude the existence of these dualistic "essences," a Scholastic term he specifically rejects as an invalid explanation for the otherwise inexplicable hypostasis of the Trinity. His poetry remains consistent with this theology since there the only power capable of exorcising the "essence" of evil is through the fluid, subjective, and individual experience of grace. As a result, his poetry characteristically lacks that overwhelming sense of the merciful dissolution of the self into the transcendental Other, that *mysteriuum tremendum* so breathtakingly absent from his poem. Moreover, since there can be no transcendent mystery where there is no sequestering of the profane from the sacred, here instead "To the pure all things are pure, not only meats and drinks, but all kinde of knowledge whether of good or evill." Thus, "that which purifies us is triall, and triall is by what is contrary" (*CPW,* 2:512, 515). In dramatic contrast with Dante's earthly paradise, Milton's Eden admits not only evil itself, but Satan himself can say, "Et in Arcadia Ego." This dissolution of boundaries in turn depends on an evolving awareness of the self-conferred state of grace or sin without which this paradise would indeed prove at once hopelessly enigmatic and a truly tragic baroque failure.

Yet there is little enigma involved in the fact that in both prose and poetic form, Milton consistently denies that the good ever can or should be sequestered from evil. To ignore how this collapsed distinction creates a wholly different vehicle of regenerate action from the sacrament that it cannot in any ritualist sense imitate is thus willfully to misunderstand the poem on a fundamental transactional point.[51] Here, we confront some of the clearest of Milton's many "instructions" to his readers, which impose a morality of freedom and choice on the reading both of poetic and of historical meaningfulness. In *Paradise Lost* as clearly as in *Areopagitica*, when "God gave Adam reason, he gave him freedom to choose, for reason is but choosing," since, without the possibility of demonstrating merit or receiving reward, "he had bin else a meer artificiall *Adam,*" unable to turn his "rightly temper'd" pleasures and passions into "the very ingredients of vertu" (*CPW,* 2:527; cf. *PL,* 3.108). *Vertu* in this passage draws its force from the same redefinition that Milton's masque gives it: that of the primary source or wellspring of human agency, which only through self-purification can achieve its own proper power, the vital power that is collaterally that of choosing and imposing allegorical readings fully commensurate with the worthiest "trials" of self-authored subjects. Yet accepting these conditions also implies the acceptance of mortality, which Milton incorporates in his poem even to the point of placing his heretical mortalist doctrine in the mouth of the archangel Michael. Thus, not only in the poem's final books, but also in Eden, where the cormorant-like Satan darkly alights on the very tree of life, death takes no holiday but becomes, as in baroque art generally, the personified "figure presiding over this new sort of allegory."[52]

These twin conceptions of human freedom and self-purification functionally demystify Milton's verbal representation of the holy in all but the last instance, his paradoxical sense of God's humanly knowable yet also "boundlessly" incomprehensible grace. In the form of his dark brightness, this grace lends a baroque aura of enigma to the more or less conventional negations that frame God's boundlessness as that of the "Immutable, Immortal, Infinite, / Eternal . . . Author of all being, / Fountain of Light, thyself invisible" (*PL,* 3.373–75).[53] Imagistically, these imponderable mysteries are summed up in the angels' oblique glimpses of his hidden face as a form of chiaroscuro, in which

Dark with excessive bright thy skirts appear,
Yet dazzle Heav'n, that brightest Seraphim
Approach not, but with both wings veil their eyes.
(3.380–33)

Yet, apart from this ultimate transcendence, all God's accommodations to human understanding (even fate, which is now "what I will," or essentially a divine edict or rational law, not the mysterious *fatum* of Fortuna of normative allegory) have become riddles to be unraveled not *sub specie aeternitatis* but *sub specie temporalis.* Hence, sin itself is no fatal curse incurred before time began but merely a sign of the human liability to error inherited from Adam and Eve. This erasure of the ineradicable "spot" or "blot" that Ricoeur finds retained in the later notions of sin's contaminating power radically revises the human subject's relation both to the deity and to those sacrificial/sacramental "expiations weak" that Michael regards with some disdain.

Instead of a wrathful God who must be propitiated, the God of *Paradise Lost* has thus become a judge presiding over the highest tribunal of rational and natural law. This conception of the deity is unimaginable in ritual systems where a participatory form of sacrifice is needed to counter sin's mysterious "infection," where a magically fated ritual impurity or sin has nothing to do with technical or juridical notions of guilt. Such systems demand a purely symbolic compensation to a God for whom "no act of punitive justice is performed" on an altar that "can in no way be compared to a tribunal . . . [; for] expiation is not a punitive act, but a method of salvation."[54] This entire system is thus somewhat jarringly discredited once Milton's God insists on acting as his own defense council and disputing fine points of foreknowledge and free will before an angelic tribunal. So, too, with the charges that face the accused, which are simply those of deliberately transgressing their superior's "sole Command" (*PL,* 3.94), an accusation that makes their distance from sacrificial victims nearly as great as their prosecutor's remove from the traditionally wrathful deity of smoke, cloud, and fire. If more prosaic, this rationalization is also appropriate to Milton's Protestant reinterpretation of sin, which he no longer "superstitiously" conceives as a mythic violation, mysterious taboo, or primitive infection "caught" from a snake. Instead of being contaminated by the serpent's forbidden apple, Adam and Eve have committed a serious legal offense or "fault"—a word that in the mouth of Milton's God is so detached from the taboo placed on the literal Tree of Knowledge that the Hughes edition supplies a footnote to remind the reader of its reference (3.94–96).

The enormity of this revision can hardly be overstated, for the ironic gulf thereby inserted between the tribunal of Milton's heaven and the celestial sphere of high Renaissance allegory can lead to the mock-heroic response recorded by Pope, who sneered at Milton's God as a mere "school-divine." Yet, despite the inevitability of this reaction, its more positive and liberating aspect is manifest in a matter that Pope's Newton ("Essay on Man") had quite otherwise resolved: the matter of matter itself. In rationally moralizing evil, Milton situates its roots in the fallen mind and will, not in the material "spot" or infection that the Christian/Greek tradition had continued to associate with Original Sin. Previously, the multiple matter/mater associations of this primitive concept had embraced the whole complex linking the forbidden fruit to physical or maternal blemish, and thence to sexual and mortal contamination—the ancient Western love/sex/death complex that hardly needs to be rehearsed here. But, once sin is fully moralized, both physical matter and mater can be benignly revitalized. Sexuality itself can then be declared pure, despite those "hypocrites austere" who would disparage the rites not too "mysterious of connubial Love" or deny them to Eden (*PL*, 4.743–45). Here, as in *Areopagitica*, sin is not external in even the most intimate of senses, "For those actions which enter into a man, rather then issue out of him, and therefore defile not, God uses not to captivat under a perpetuall childhood of prescription, but trusts him with the gift of reason to be his own chooser" (*CPW*, 2:513–14). As the major poems and the *Christian Doctrine* alike reveal, this ethical position—scripturally based in Matthew 15:17–20 and Mark 7:15–23—remains central to Milton's entire corpus.

These views can be instructively contrasted with those of Milton's epic precursor, Spenser, who continues to regard sexuality as a harbinger of death, which intrinsically places it within the sacramental code of abstinence and/or purification. For Spenser, this aspect of procreation gravely saddens the Venus who presides helplessly over a garden where there is no "redresse for such despight: / For all that lives, is subject to that law: / All things decay in time, and to their end doe draw."[55] Gone with this Venus of fallen nature is also the temporal dualism that permeates *The Faerie Queene*'s Christian/Greek view of the "Great enimy": "wicked *Tyme*, who with his scyth addrest, / Does mow the flowring herbes and goodly things, / And all their glory to the ground downe flings" (*FQ*, 3.6.39). For, once Milton's Chaos becomes both "the Womb of nature and perhaps her grave" (*PL*, 2.911), matter can be linked to regeneration as well as to death, which innoculates it against the "hatefull darkenes and . . . deepe horrore" that Spenser associated not just with "eternal chaos" but with all the "substaunces of Natures fruitfull progenyes" that must die (*FQ*, 3.6.36). Where nature's "mutabilitie" (*FQ*, 3.6.47) need no longer be redeemed by the stasis of immortality, the mind/ body dualism that in Spenser's *Mutabilitie Cantos* assures final salvation also disappears. Once time becomes the benign universal measure of the ongoing creation in which man participates, organic life becomes the providential medium of "all things durable" (*PL*, 5.581), including regeneration itself. Before presenting us with an ultra-Levitical Milton, scholars would then do well to recall how he reverses the traditional dichotomy of body and soul, profane and sacred, by regarding "chaotic" or irregular time and space as the monistic medium of inward purification (sonnet 7)—that is, the medium of the free agent's self-conferred purity conjoined with grace.

For, from his earliest antiprelatical tracts and sonnets to *Paradise Regained*, Milton consistently rebukes Pharisaical legalism by asserting that God wants "mercy, and *not* sacrifice" (Matt. 9:13), words he takes to disparage sacramentalism in every guise. Not just the Laudian "wolves" condemned in "Lycidas" but all hypocritical "forcers of conscience" thus convict themselves of the charge that, beneath their sheep's clothing, "*New Presbyter* is but *Old Priest* writ Large" ("On the New Forcers of Conscience," line 20). These allegorical revelations also illuminate Milton's epic refusal to base either defilement or purity on any unambiguous "priestly" code conferred on Adam or the archangels and the care with which he develops a new symbolic language capable of expressing his thoroughly revised myth of sin and redemption. By definition, this language departs from the mystical terms of the traditional schema, which, as Paul Tillich explains, had nothing to do with a "theoretical knowledge about objects, but with cognitive participation in a new reality that has appeared in the Christ. Without this mysterious participation no truth is possible, and knowledge is [not only] abstract and meaningless" but lifeless, devoid of the means whereby the poison of mortality is overcome with the sacramental "drug of immortality."[56] Since the literary counterpart of this sacramental logic is the "contagious" or "imitative" magic performed by normative allegory's agents and personified abstractions, late Protestant allegory can realize its rationalizing impulses only through a symbolic metamorpho-

sis of its inherited terms. Mythically, *Paradise Lost* effects the meta-
morphosis implicit in its meta-allegory by converting the traditional
Platonic/Orphic idea of the exiled soul's return and ascent and the
corresponding Semitic cycle of pardon and return into a proto-
modern saga of self-inflicted disease, reform, and rehabilitation.[57]

Thus, wherever *Paradise Lost* contains remnants of the older view
of purification as the path to redemption, as to some extent any
biblically inspired Christian poem must, these appear either as
"ruined" fragments largely stripped of supernatural aura or, as in
Michael's Lazar House episode, as individualized exempla of the
physical suffering experienced by the victims of intemperance—the
willful disregard of the natural "science" of self-regulation. In dra-
matic contrast to the symbolic purification of Spenser's Redcrosse
Knight in the House of Holinesse, the scene from which this inci-
dent is loosely drawn, Milton's sinners receive no ritual purgation, or
even condemnation, but only bodily death, "thir chief good, and final
hope" (*PL*, 11.493). A similarly revisionist tactic underlies the alle-
gorical personification of Sin itself, whose malign energies continue
to run directly contrary to those of holiness or grace, but now in the
naturalistic terms of a wholly Reformed redemptive system. Just as
the sacramental "vow" has been recast as a "trope" sealing a sponta-
neous act rather than creating a magical channel or amulet of grace,
so Sin now acts as a verbally transitive and/or self-reflexive "mirror"
of moral error (2.764). Throughout the epic, these revised functions
surcharge the personified image with a new and more elemental
power, a form of causal efficacy derive from the subject's self-
authored, semidivine reflexivity. This reflexivity in turn sponta-
neously "creates" the shape, context, and, ultimately, the meaning
of such projected images, much as Satan spontaneously generates
Sin, and she Death. Thus, in place of the old magical, part/whole,
or synecdochal correspondences, Milton's meta-allegory employs a
metonymic reflexivity that allows them rightly (if also ironically) to
claim that "The mind is its own place, and in itself / Can make a
Heav'n of Hell, a Hell of Heav'n" (1.253–54).

Here, as with so much else related to the old ritual mode—zodiacal
signs, humoral psychology, astrology and its presiding "deity," the
goddess Fortuna or fate—the form of the allegorical emblem is con-
served while its operations are made to conform to a theology not
"alien to reason" (*CPW*, 6:554). A similar logic underlies Milton's
reconfiguration of the Orphic myth of the soul's return and ascent,

which he characteristically summons only to place under erasure. In the invocation at the epic's very center, Orpheus thus becomes a false double, a pagan prototype mothered by the wrong muse who cannot grant her son what only Urania confers since only a muse who has been restricted to the nondaemonic "meaning, not the name" (*PL*, 7.5), associated with the goddess of astronomy or spirit of heaven can

> . . . drive off the barbarous dissonance
> Of *Bacchus* and his Revellers, the Race
> Of that wild Rout that tore the *Thracian* Bard
> In *Rhodope*, where Woods and Rocks had Ears
> To rapture, till the savage clamor drown'd
> Both Harp and Voice; not could the Muse defend
> Her Son. So fail not thou, who thee implores;
> *For thou art heav'nly, shee an empty dream.*
> (7.32–39; emphasis added)

Although remnants of the "medieval allegory of vice and virtue" are retained both here and in Raphael's preceding narration of the "invisible exploits / Of warring Spirits," their sacramental logic has been subverted. Where only a radically individualized and interiorized experience of the quest can be either heroic or pure, the false heroism of Orpheus, of the fallen angels or an Eve too sadly and pridefully "bent" on seeking "temptation . . . , which to avoid / Were better" (9.364–65, 384), must be reframed as a false temptation sprung from the Realist allegories of hell.

Hence, Eve's unwitting pun on "bent" prior to her fall underscores at least three key epic revisions: (1) the superiority now accorded the more difficult trial of "standing and waiting," even when the soul is more "bent" on active seeking and service (sonnet 19); (2) the ambiguously transformative effect accorded the will, which can (as Eve's can and does) turn a potentially positive "bent" into the negative or crooked kind achieved by accepting Satan's magical-allegorical gloss on the apple; and (3) the ambiguous, transformative nature accorded language itself, whose puns can similarly generate either negatively reductive or positively expansive forms of polysemy. In this epic transformation of allegory, the very absence of normative heroic questers except in hell and their replacement by Reformed gardeners suggests both Milton's Puritan distaste for the contagious magic that underlies Satan's reification of heaven, hell, and Eden and his determination to reform his representation of sin and redemption along individualistic and antiauthoritarian lines. Thus, whatever "contagious" magic remains ritually embedded in "the Fruit / Of that Forbidden Tree, whose mortal taste / Brought Death into the World" (*PL*, 1.1–3), it is countered by the immortal tree of "one first matter all" that naturalistically erases its "taste" in time.[58] By temperately and patiently ingesting both the material and the intellectual "food" springing from that natural tree, men may attain such self-authorized "virtue" that their diet as well as their apprehension may, like Adam's, participate with that of angels (5.94–96).

For Milton, then, there is no ultimate distinction between eating the benign fruits of Eden and imbibing the divine Word, which is not merely their symbolic but also their moral and physical counterpart, especially in light of its multiple "fruits." Consequently, as in *Areopagitica,* the sacred remains essentially continuous with the putatively "profane" since the vehicle of both has become the free will and motivation of individual subjects who naturally "transubstantiate" its common elements. So long as these agents remain free, sacral "purity" inhabits "every lower faculty / Of sense," just as shadows of the celestial paradise inhabit an earth whose "varied . . . bounty . . . [of] new delights, / . . . may compare with Heaven" (*PL*, 5.410–11, 431–32). Both earthly purity and its ambiguous mutability are thus distant reflections of the bright/dark enigmas of the "one Almighty . . . from whom / All things proceed, and up to him return, / *If not deprav'd from good*" (5.469–71; emphasis added). Conforming to these mandates is far from enigmatic since it simply demands the freedom from depravity arising from a naturalistic rather than mystically "segregated" appreciation of his universal bounty. Thus, as Raphael explains to Adam:

> . . . Therefore what he gives
> (Whose praise be ever sung) to man in part
> Spiritual, may of purest Spirits be found
> No ingrateful food: and food alike those pure
> Intelligential substances require
> As doth your Rational; and both contain
> Within them every lower faculty
> Of sense, whereby they hear, see, smell, touch, taste
> Tasting concoct, digest, assimilate,

And corporeal to incorporeal turn.
For know, whatever was created, needs
To be sustain'd and fed. . . .
(5.404–15)

Although in this schema "The grosser feeds the purer, Earth the
Sea, / Earth and Sea feed Air, the Air those Fires / Ethereal" (5.416–
18), these distinctions of degree are ultimately relative in a monistic
continuum where "Great / Or Bright infers not Excellence" and
earth "so small / Nor glistering may of solid good contain / More
plenty than the Sun that barren shines" (8.90–94).

At the opposite end of this dialectic, Milton's ontology of evil,
defilement, and exile is by no means confined to hell but monistically
"erupts" in the holiest of holies, in heaven itself. From there, its
temptations (like its tempter) enters the holy mount of Eden by way
of Chaos, the nebulous void whose mutable ambiguities materially
anchor those of the entire divine continuum. Because the continuity
of spirit and will rests on a similar void, God's divine progeny need
only retain "unalterably firm his love entire" (*PL,* 5.502) in order
spontaneously to transform the passive imagination and even the fact
of temptation until "no spot or blame" is left behind (5.119). Hence,
no merely external contamination by "distemper'd, discontented
thoughts, / Vain hopes, vain aims, inordinate desires / Blown up with
high conceits ingendr'ing pride" can taint Eve (4.807–9), nor is any
"expiation" for her literal "infusion" with satanic desires needed be-
yond the simple dialogic understanding she shares with her husband,
especially since it is accompanied by her spontaneous emotions of
"sweet remorse / And pious awe that fear'd to have offended" (5.134–
35). Once again, the contrast with Spenser's parallel dream scene
proves instructive, for his Redcrosse Knight is immediately contami-
nated by precisely the kind of daemonic "infusions" that are here
demystified. Moreover, while it will take most of the first book of
The Faerie Queene to rescue and finally "purge" Redcrosse of Archi-
mago's spell, the effects of Eve's unconscious contamination are dis-
pelled within moments.

The rest of Milton's allegory of sin and redemption thus proceeds
along similarly naturalistic lines, largely guided by symbolically ex-
tended processes of digestion and elimination.[59] Since his conscious
sinners can be purged only by literally experiencing and/or "tasting"
the fruits of their acts, these processes begin and end in the "miser-

able pain" that results from willfully "conceiving" narcissistic desire (*PL*, 2.752–58), which brings forth the "noxious" fruits of its poisonous envy. The naturalistic effects of these "fruits" are also conveyed through Milton's characteristic strategy of underscoring the etymological origins of the processes themselves. In this case, his essentially Ramist strategy involves tracing the etymology of *taste* to its Latin roots in *temptation*—literally, "any attempt, trial, or test." The Latin verb for *taste, sāpere*, associated with Eve's fallacious "Sapience" (9.1019), further extends this psychology of temptation by appropriately signifying not only the interrelated stimuli of attraction through taste or smell, but also the act of becoming sensible of, discerning, or wise (an ironic half truth in relation to the fruits of the tree of knowledge), and that of *thinking, judging*, or *deciding*. Since Milton further links these rational and/or willed responses to the meaning of knowledge in both prominent biblical senses, to know the Tree of Knowledge is at once mentally to sense or discern good and evil but also more willfully to experience, taste, or enjoy its fruits (in the sense in which Adam "knows" his wife). By playing on these inevitably intertwined "senses," his text thus conveys the act of sin as consisting in a doubly erroneous if also natural "taste": a false evaluation of the value of knowing or tasting that "*fallacious* fruit" and a false enjoyment of its savor over the Creator's more "varied bounty," including, ultimately, his boundless love. Although the framework of this evaluation is allegorical, its imagistic processes are mimetic. Like the intemperate invalids in the Lazar House, or like Sin herself, Eve is literally eaten by what she ate, consumed by the false "fumes" (the alluring scent, aroma, and noxious aftertaste) of the apple's unsapient indigestion (9.1049). The couple's subsequent sexual and sensual intoxication produces an equally literal hangover (9.1008–15) that, along with other equally "natural" forms of indigestion (9.1047–51), punningly transfers the "noxious" distillation of this poisonous fruit into a "shame obnoxious" (9.1094). Thus, as with the intemperate sufferers in the Lazar House scene, the allegorical emblems surrounding the forbidden fruit result in a sense of sin closer to a psychological model of dysfunction than a ritual model of evil.

Sin's physical effects thus derive from the consequences of succumbing to a "fruit" that is partly a true illusion or deception and partly a real projection of Eve's self-deformed will. Much as Adam's falls by objectifying Eve, her own fall falsely but effectively "reifies" and/or "sacramentalizes" the substance of the fruit, which is further linked to the physical/psychical idolatry inherent in Satan's self-infatuation and the birth of Sin—ultimately, the conjunct moral and material "meaning" of her miscegenation. As in radical Puritan thought generally, Satan's incestuous self-worship constitutes real idolatry in the sense that his iconic and sacramental "realities" are empowered by his actual mode of consciousness. Hence, idolatrous "gods" can wield real authority and bear real fruits via the kind of psychic investment we understand as false consciousness, although not through any intrinsic "daemonic" or magical powers. By "sacrificing" and bowing to the Edenic tree "as to the power / That dwelt within, whose presence had infus'd / Into the plant sciential sap, deriv'd / From Nectar, drink of Gods" (*PL,* 9.835–38), Eve thus commits an act of narcissistic ego worship, which is generically, not genetically, akin to Satan's—who becomes the "father" of Sin and stepfather of Eve in a profoundly new psychological sense. He of course can and does literally "engender" this psychology in others, but only by imitation—which is why Sin is his image as much as his daughter. The psychic basis of this "contagion" is further underscored by the way in which it "spreads" to Adam, whose seminarcissistic or "effeminate" attachment to Eve almost immediately rebounds in its mirror or inverse image, his misogynistic inflation of her role in his fall. These lines thus complete a poetic naturalization of sin that, in synthesizing its moral and physical consequences, essentially reverses its primitive logic.

What then remains is a depiction of judgment whose ritual form is once again "emptied" by its mimetic content. Since they have already experienced the psychosomatic side effects of their hubris, Adam and Eve now must learn to abhor what they imagined they ate by experiencing the broader effects of its noxious reverberations. Eve is to sorrow in conceptions as painful as her first "conceiving" a selfish desire for a self-exalting fruit more desirable than any "never tasted" (*PL,* 9.786–90), while Adam is to taste the equally real labor pains that result from inflating an imaginary "Link of Nature" into an apparently self-exalting but actually self-imprisoning chain (9.914). The organic consequences of this false consciousness are further linked to those attendant on the fallen imagination of the demons in the following passage, where their joy soon turns to sorrow as they are forced to "taste" the bitter ashes of the forbidden fruit and the pains of its addictive desire. Similarly, after "savoring" and, with "true relish, tasting" this "delightful Fruit" that will so soon become obnoxious (9.1019–24), Adam and Eve had reclined on "Earth's freshest softest lap," only to discover "of thir mutual guilt the Seal." Here, Milton converts the literal experience of sin into its own sign or trope, which is also ironically the seal or covenant of their treason, "the Harlot-lap / Of *Philistean Dalilah*" (9.1041–43, 1060–61). This materially "binding" sense of our Grand Parent's self-defilement is then further "sealed" by means of a characteristic metonymy, as their common "mother" earth is caused "sympathetically" to groan with the pangs of this illegitimate birth (9.1000–1001).

A similar metonymy pervades the depiction of the demons' "contagious" lust, which operates through a parallel chain of cause and effect. Like the human couple (*PL,* 9.1036) submitting their lapsed moral bodies to physiological consequences "catcht by Contagion" (10.544), as in other "diseases" of intemperance, their faulty "taste" produces literal physical pains. Thus, the applause that "seals" the demon's approval of Satan's seduction of Eve (which inversely reflects their narcissistic seduction by Sin earlier [2.761–64]) also "seals" the sting "cast on themselves from thir own mouths" (10.547) into a self-pronounced hiss of shame, revulsion, and ultimate casting off. "Thir penance" then chiefly externalizes their internal condition: "parcht with scalding thirst and hunger fierce," they endlessly seek self-replicating trees laden with illusory fruit (10.550–56), fruit that, "not the touch, but taste / Deceiv'd" (10.563–64). While, as this line suggests, only the act or taste, not the mere "touch" or desire of tasting, eating, or knowing sin, produces its bitter aftertaste, as addictive indulgence in sin's self-contamination warps and finally deforms both perception and desire, which in seeming to make its worshipers "exact of taste / And . . . of Sapience" (9.1017–19) produces only ashy, empty self-"conceptions." Since for this kind of error there can be no sacramental remedy, Sin's hallucinatory experience will continue to attract and addict like a drug unless that taste is "repented." If not, then its victims must expect the dysfunctional fate of the demons, who

> Hunger and thirst constraining, drugg'd as oft,
> With hatefullest disrelish writh'd thir jaws
> With soot and cinders fill'd; so oft they fell
> Into the same illusion. . . .
> (10.568–71)

Finally, then, even the uppercase Sin is only a "Sign / Portentous," a potentially addictive allure in the moral and physical, not the ritual, sense. Hence she portends no external source or mark of divine wrath, only a turning in the path toward self-destruction that, until it addicts, remains subjectively reversible. Yet, unlike the ambiguous womb created by Eve's appetite, which after her fall continues to "conceive" both good and evil, that is, both Cain and Abel, the deformed womb of Sin bears only matricidal and fratricidal offspring to her mates, which include all those ensnared by the fruit of her "attractive graces" (*PL,* 2.760–62). Nevertheless, even this "fate" is baroquely ruined by the fact that Sin's curse largely consists in falsely conceived freedom, that *pharmakon* or poison/remedy that either cures or kills from within.[60] These ambiguities ultimately nullify the boundaries between abstract good and evil, much as Satan effortlessly violates the gates of Paradise—an entry that emphasizes the utter failure of such incursions in themselves to contaminate. As in Satan's "original" conception of Sin, every such lapse springs fully formed only from the heads of those who would be gods, from wills that when most free ironically *can* "deify" Satan's creatures, although in a far more ambiguous sense than his deformed imagination comprehends (2.755–60, 8.430–31).[61] Because only "reason [that] also is choice" decides the difference (3.108), salvation does not depend on either sacramental vehicles or the magical *kosmoi* that embody them, signs that would materially enact and/or represent the transubstantive processes now rooted only in the "miracle" of the freely chosen penance, absolution, and communion of every believer.

The affirmative aspect of this choice is modeled by no less a character than the Son himself, who, meditating on his own sacrificial role, effectively reduces the mystery of the atonement to a naturalistic process of debt and repayment. Thus, as his combined right reason and volition allow him to conclude, the payment of this wholly voluntary obligation "must" earn the victorious resurrection that the tribunal of divine justice accords to all other similarly "unspotted" souls (*PL,* 3.246–51). By this judicial logic, even pre-Christian figures like Enoch are freed from the literal "spot" of Original Sin—"Exempt from Death; to show thee what reward / Awaits the good, the rest what punishment" (11.709–10). Rather than rehearsing the drama of the Passion, a poem Milton could not complete, the final books of the poem therefore illustrate a "sacramental" victory of a quite different kind.[62] This logically consists in the choice of self-conquest through patience, moderation, and the healthful "rule of . . . temperance,"

In what thou eat'st and drink'st, seeking from thence
Due nourishment, not gluttonous delight,
Till many years over thy head return:
So may'st thou live, *till like ripe Fruit thou drop*
Into thy Mother's lap, or be with ease
Gather'd, not harshly pluckt, for death mature.
(11.531–37; emphasis added)

A less sacramental depiction of the last rites due to sin and death, or a more naturalistic absolution of Mother Eve's appetite for forbidden fruit, can scarcely be imagined.

5

Whatever its errors of fact or feeling from a modern or scientific perspective, there can be little doubt that *Paradise Lost* represents a vast generational shift away from Spenser's sympathetic magic or Sidney's astrology. As Yates notes, the Sidney circle remained indebted to hermetic traditions that still allowed them to follow "the sky with religious feeling, like Thamus, the Egyptian king," who typically conveys these sensibilities in Sidney's poetry.[63] But, a generation later, Milton's poem is preoccupied with debating the new cosmology even in Eden, while Thammuz and "smooth *Adonis*" are relegated either to hell or to the hell on earth of those "Idols foul" whose "wanton passions in the sacred Porch / . . . alienated *Judah*" (*PL*, 1.446–57). Moreover, whatever echoes of Spenser's "wanton Prime" (*FQ*, 3.6.42–45) remain in an Eden that wantons "as in her prime" (*PL*, 5.295), his mythical Garden of Adonis has metamorphosed into the almost wholly natural magic of an Eden where Pan as all-god has become a pantheistic nature spirit hymned by bird choirs who alone "attune / The trembling leaves" of his dance (4.265–68).[64]

This allegorical metamorphosis of epic convention ultimately goes far beyond an aesthetic transformation of the traditional sacramental "world picture" that underlies the entire system of magical pictorialism informing most normative allegory. Not only its sacramental symbolism but its implicit assumptions about human psychology, memory, and understanding are here comprehensively critiqued, along with the highly corporeal system of similitudes that had structured the inherited fabric of Christian thought from "mediaeval imagery in art and architecture as a whole . . . [to] great literary monuments such as Dante's *Divine Comedy.*" As Yates further details, in the seventeenth century these structures had lingered, not only in the hermetic memory systems of Dee and Fludd, but also in thinkers who are turning in new directions—Francis Bacon, Descartes, Leibniz. Yet, at the same time, the Ramist influence on radical Protestantism (and we must not forget that Milton wrote a Ramist *Art of Logic*) further erodes this earlier revival of the ancient attempt "to draw power from the cosmos into the memory . . . under the higher celestial images, the images of their 'causes.'" In place of the iconic system of visual similitudes that had once concretely linked the individual subject to the divine or transcendental world, the abstract "flow" charts of Ramist logic abolish the "emotionally exciting memory image" as at once superstitious and unnatural. The result, as Yates concludes, was "a kind of inner iconoclasm, corresponding to the outer iconoclasm" characteristic of Protestant thought.

Nevertheless, as a revisionary Platonist who thought of himself as restoring a tradition of Socratic dialectic "ruined" by the artificialities of Aristotle and his Scholastic heirs, Ramus (like Milton) retains something of the mystical Neoplatonic aspiration gradually to ascend to higher truths, which he liked to imagine as progressing as in "Homer's golden chain from earth to heaven, from heaven to earth."[65] Milton characteristically conserves yet radically recontextualizes this image by making Satan observe "this pendant world, in bigness as a Star," suspended from heaven "in a golden Chain" (*PL,* 2:1051–52). Without destroying either the image or its essential meaning, this reworking of inherited materials (which foreshadows our "satanic" introduction to Eden and, in fact, to the poet's revision of God's "mysteriously . . . meant" images as a whole) emphasizes the importance of perspective, method, and stance in the interpretation of its own epic-allegorical "machinery." For Satan fails to understand these enigmatic gates and ladders (3.515–18), not only because of his dialectical mishandling of these entry and exit points, but also because he misunderstands the common condition of all creatures in a universe where "So little knows / Any, but God alone, to value right / The good before him, but perverts best things / To worst abuse, or to thir meanest use" (4.201–4). His arena of trial is thus not inherently different from our own; rather, it occupies the same newly boundless and "viewless" (3.518) world.

Yet, just as Ramism itself preserves something of the characteristic baroque tension between a spatializing, naturalizing logic and a more transcendent yearning for a hermetic key to the secrets of nature, the playful or speculative hermeticism of Milton's early companion poems seems not to have wholly disappeared from the astronomical speculations of his mature epic. Here, we find the "Archchemic Sun" breathing forth *"Elixir* pure, and . . . / Potable Gold" by means of a natural alchemy that works on the dark matter of its "Terrestrial Humor." Producing amid the solar "dark so many precious things / Of color glorious and effect so rare" (*PL,* 3.607–12), these "realities" allow the narrative voice scornfully to condemn the "vain" medievalism of philosophers who would reproduce this alchemy on earth, which he suggests can "logically" be achieved only in extraterrestrial magnitudes, no doubt beneath the sunspots recently discovered by Galileo's "Optic Tube" (3.590). Although neither Milton nor any of his contemporaries could yet guess the atomic nature of the forces fueling the sun, here, as throughout the poem, he never ceases methodically and dialectically to sift the most "natural" from the more artificial, superstitious, or merely "antique" speculations on the substances and forces at work in the perceptible universe—even while borrowing their hermetic ruins, which would not be fully purged from science even in the age of Newton.

It is in these respects that Milton's poem most fully corresponds to the speculative "ruins" outlined in Benjamin's theory of baroque allegory since, in these excessively dark with bright auras, the epic seems to project a "ruined" sensibility reminiscent of what Gershom Scholem calls the "historical psychology" of the Jews in the aftermath of failed messianisms. As a matter not of influence but of an analogous historical experience, Milton's epic thus elevates the individual to the exemplary status of a quasisacramental vehicle of divine intention in ways also characteristic of the Lurianic cabala, a seventeenth-century exilic text that also seems to have influenced Benjamin's theory. As his friend Scholem tells us, this cabala focuses on three great symbols: *tsimtsum,* the self-limitation of God; *shevirah,* the breaking of or ruining of the vessels; and *tikkun,* the harmonious correction and mending of the floor that comes into being through the *shevirah.*[66] Together, these symbols map a simultaneously historical/secular process of recovery that curiously parallels Milton's "return" to the cosmogonic roots of allegory to which Luria (through Philo) is also bound. In addition to recovering this elemental form of Western speculation, Luria also conceives of the godhead as a quasi-Miltonic paradox. In submitting himself to mankind, this deity thus undergoes the same kind of self-limitation modeled by both the Father and the Son of *Paradise Lost:* an act of kenosis or "emptying" that also reciprocally limits yet empowers human beings since this divine withdrawal bestows on them the responsibility for completing a paradisal world left imperfect or incomplete, although it could and should have been otherwise, had Adam not fallen (*PL,* 11.339–46).

Additionally, for both Milton and Luria, the primordial space from which God withdraws is the pleroma, the "boundless deep" where the "I am" at once fills "infinitude" and "uncircumscrib'd" retires or retracts himself from it (*PL,* 7.168–70). In both cases, his withdrawal or kenosis thus at once permits the emanation of all things from God and the possibility of evil within Chaos, the root but not the essence of "one first matter." This cosmic equivocation between empty or *ex deo* and formed or first matter implicitly allows Milton's God to contain the potentiality, although not the actuality, of evil and thus to preserve an incomplete "goodness, . . . free / To act or not" (7.171–72). As an ambiguously passive and active divine potentiality, this goodness is figured by the twilight regions of heaven, themselves part of the "grateful vicissitude" (5.645, 6.8) whose alternations provide, not merely creaturely freedom, but also the free acts of love and grace darkly shadowed beneath their infinite light. This interplay between forms of light and darkness in God's "boundless" mystery virtually defines the baroque chiaroscuro of Milton's poem, which can also be linked to the intradivine view of exilic history characteristic of this period. Here, while the presence/absence of God maximizes the role of the individual virtually to the point of secularization, in its depths the divine becomes a metaphor for the immanent order self-organized out of a chaos "extracted" from God in shattered form. Thus, much like the Lurianic cabala, *Paradise Lost* provides an allegory of accommodation in a fallen world always about to be but never yet redeemed.

The main difference between these two "ruined" theologies thus lies in their ontologies. For Luria and his disciples, the light from the eyes of the demiurge (or Son) shatters the vessels in the very act of creation, with the result that from the very beginning the limitless becomes self-limiting. This moment provides the decisive crisis of all divine and created being, which according to the *Zohar* (the divine splendor) is caused by the dying of the primordial kings, which in turn produces ages of stern justice later tempered by love. Such concepts are very easily harmonized with Christianity in general and, in particular, with Milton's Protestant reworking of the myth of the Fall, where, in the very act of begetting and anointing his beloved Son, God creates the potential for evil immediately realized in Satan's envy against his "light" (*PL,* 6.658–65). Moreover, much as in Milton's Eden, the cabalistic *shevirah* or "ruining" of the forms can be traced to the lack of harmony between masculine and feminine elements of creation, which may explain not only Milton's elaborate reallegorizing of the relationship between Adam and Eve but, at deeper level, also the inherent conflict between Satan's masculine or "heroic" ethos and the Son's more "femininely" redemptive love. Mediating as well as potentially resolving these oppositions, like Luria's shattered vessels, Milton's repositioned Chaos thus acts as an ongoing and indeterminate vessel necessarily broken, rather than (as in Genesis) one necessarily quelled.[67] Operating under similar exilic tensions, this most fundamental revision recasts the Christian myth of Original Sin into something far closer to the Jewish myth of exile, thereby doubly "ruining" the sacramental tradition of Christian allegory by ploughing it back into its most native soil, in this case, that of Jewish/materialist mysticism.

Thus, Milton's baroque allegory of history also bears strange traces of a process resembling the *tikkum,* in which primordial man is reconstructed in phased stages where every renewed pattern of individual calling and failure symbolizes the simultaneously allegorical and literal "progress" of providence. Literally, the enactment of individual experience becomes the virtually transparent vehicle of providential truth, while, tropologically, its representations must remain incomplete "types and allegories" of a covenant finally "sealed" by a far more obscure conjunction of human will and divine grace. For Milton, then, as also for Luria, "the coming of the Messiah means no more than a signature under a document that we ourselves write; he merely confirms the inception of a condition that he himself has not brought about."[68] These mystical/rational paradoxes ground the baroque outlines of Milton's "dark with excessive bright" allegory, one structurally stripped of all ritual essences and signatures, all figures that we ourselves do not read or write and that can thus no longer be either mnemonically or sacramentally summoned as a means of grace. For the "real" seals of the covenant are found only in the book that we ourselves *do* read and write, in the transactions between the human and the divine beings of history: the vows, prayers, and poems, the living metaphors that Adam is assured will continue to conduct him to God.[69] In this highly rationalized sense, then, *Paradise Lost* is not antisacramental any more than it is antiallegorical; but, because both kinds of signs have been reinscribed within a newly immanent universe of words, things, and living beings, only its baroque tension between a historical rationalism and a quasi-mystical vitalism produces the poem's unique sense of a newly natural sublime.

Between the Visible and the Invisible

Agency, Being, and Time in the Relative

Universe

1

Allegorical writing tends to assume or project a structured cosmos against which to measure the actions of its cosmic agents, whose characteristics in turn dictate the scope, context, and ultimate significance of its symbolic narrative. The concentric circles and interlocking levels of the Ptolemaic universe thus in some sense provide an "ideal" framework for Christian allegory since they afford convenient "ladders" on which to measure the spiritual progress or regress enacted by its agents. Some of these allegorical hierarchies are more explicit than others, yet Milton's symbolic universe drastically departs from nearly all normative patterns in that its structure is explicitly presented as contradictory and/or ironic. This departure is immediately signaled by the strangely unconfining nature of his hell, whose "meaning" as a prison "reserv'd to more wrath" by the edicts of "Eternal Justice" is qualified both by its interactive construction and by its later evolution, which finally causes its "darkness visible" to burn with an almost wholly internal flame (*PL*, 1.54–71). Yet Milton even more fundamentally alters the moral ladders that Pico della Mirandola had taken from the story of Jacob and turned into an allegory of man's ascent in "a series of many steps, with the Lord seated at the top, and angels in contemplation ascending and descending over them alternately by turns" corresponding to the successive vegetative, sensitive, rational, and intellectual phases of creation. Here the regularly ascending chain "scal'd by steps of Gold to Heaven Gate" (3.541)[1] almost wholly ceases to convey Pico's order or meaning but, like Eden's Tree of Life itself, is turned into one of Satan's many ironic perches. Yet this radical inversion of the "heroic" quest does not constitute a simple reversal since now all forms of subjective perspective, not merely fallen ones, have been relativized in relation to intention, motive, and stance. Thus, while the reader allegorically notes that his "goodly prospect" is wholly lost on this "Spirit malign," a "Scout" seized with wonder but "more envy . . . / At sight of all this World beheld so fair" (3.548, 552–54), he or she also senses a shared meta-allegorical exclusion from the simpler stairs and passages once traversed by the angelic messengers to Israel's "happy Tribes" (3.532).

From its dual perspective on heaven and earth, this miniallegory provides an important key to the exemplary framework that charts both the expanded scope of subjective responsibility outlined in the following debate between Father and Son and the comparably expanded, ultimately involuted if not quite erased ladders of Milton's epic universe. A similar baroque hall of mirrors also frames Raphael's later accommodation of the apparently conflicting models of universal organization, for Milton's tactic of openly confronting the knotty cosmological problems of his period is logically of a piece with his unsettling decision to foreground the moral or "legal" conflict between divine justice and grace, foreknowledge and free will, in an open dialogue between Father and Son. Because these precarious tensions might just as easily have been settled by the poetic equivocations surrounding holy light in the opening invocation to book 3, their baroque elaboration may even seem "logically" absurd: why should the infinitely wise need to argue or the infinitely merciful need to plead for leniency to the God who is love? Both the normative and the neoclassical modes of allegory refuse to dwell on such enigmas, which they resolve either through mystical allusion or naturalistic simplification. Yet baroque aesthetics instead requires an elaboration of dilemmas that so centrally address the overriding problem of the period: the quest for a kind of selfhood that could cope with the subject's new situation in a spatially random and temporally evolving cosmos.

Both physically and morally, Milton's epic universe is thus correspondingly decentered in ways that radically undermine all previously "certain" senses of place, personhood, and transcendent virtue. Such stabilities were implicit not only in the hierarchies that Pico continued to take for granted but also in the static "ladders" of Aristotle's aggregate space and the fixation on eternity inherent in Christianity's metaphysical time. In replacing this stable spatio-temporal cosmos with the counterintuitive construction of Galileo's relative and empty space, where the location of objects is determined by force fields and mathematical measurements of motion in time, the scientific revolution of the seventeenth century introduced a profound questioning of all previously "given," perceptually "self-evident" propositions—including personal questions of natural place, virtue, and reward. This change was inevitable given that earlier conceptions of the state and progress of the human soul had reflected the stable structure of aggregate space decreed by Aristotelian physics, where "a certain element naturally strives upwards, and another naturally strives downwards, . . . [and] 'up' and 'down' possess their own fixed constitutions, their own specific *physis.*" As Ernst Cassirer further explains, in this "commonsense" system, there is thus always "a reciprocal determination of the fundamental elements: the places are defined by the bodies that belong to them, and the bodies by the places. . . . Just as objects are separated into eternal and mutable, into perfect and imperfect, so, too, an analogous division runs through the spatial world."[2]

In contrast, the new mathesis and its many interrelated methods— Ramist, Cartesian, Calvinist, and Arminian—produced a skepticism toward all outward appearances or predetermined physical directions and especially toward the symbolic concretion of sacramental and/or Neoplatonic scales of human ascent. This philosophical revolution links such seemingly diverse responses as Kepler's mathematical attempt to reallegorize the universe in *De harmonice mundi* (1619), Descartes's *Meditations on First Philosophy,* the Reformers' rejection of transubstantiation and deep suspicion of all outward ceremonies, the Counter-Reformers' ardent exploration of new forms of private meditation and casuistic logic, and the reactionary ambivalence surrounding the neomaterialist sciences of Galileo and Hobbes—a consequence Descartes was to avoid only with great care. This anxiety reflected a specter raised by the new science that proved more threatening than the idea that the earth no longer occupied the center of the universe: the attendant implication that the human mind had not correctly cognized the very ground on which it stood in either the literal or the figurative senses of the phrase. Thus, between the Copernican revolution and Newton's restabilization of an essentially Galilean mechanics, an interim world picture intervened in which the profound instability of matter provides a powerful source of both expanded speculation and expanded doubt. Yet in this period matter would also retain a residual element of occulted "force," a godlike fluidity or vitalism whose motions immanently preserve a trace, if not a static signature, of the divine. While this interim cosmology rejects the old concentric universe, the revival of a quasimystical atomism also allows it to regard the numerical calculations of Galilean physics as still somehow coordinate with the logic of God. Here, not only mystical numerologists like Kepler, but thinkers directly influenced by Cartesian logic (like the Cambridge Platonists, Pascal, Milton, and, later, Leibniz), remain relatively free to imagine new physical solutions to the question of how to reposition human and divine spirit within a material continuum that has lost its *primum mobile*. For Henry More, spirit will be paradoxically relocated in some hypothetical Cartesian "extension" ensuring its physical reality, while, for John Milton, it will be retained as the material essence of *ex deo* creation.

In opting for the fully materialist solution that More rejects, Milton must confront a different set of paradoxes that leads him to an inverse, if equally hybrid, form of universal order.[3] In their own right as exploratory as the flight in which Satan reconnoiters this newly emergent world, Milton's poetic flights are thus "spectacularly" situated (as a "spectacle," an allegorical "theater" like that of Revelation [*CPW,* 1:815]) in the volatile "ruin" of a transcendental and static order of things intuitively and immanently forecasting the emergence of a more dynamic order. As the preceding chapter details, the rubric of this ruin can be traced to Milton's radically Arminian, anticeremonial, and spiritually voluntaristic "free will" theology, which, together with his materialism, exalts the spontaneous natural order arising from the ashes of traditional Realist allegory.[4] The result is an allegorical cosmos whose only transcendence emerges from a "One first matter all" hierarchies immanently aspiring toward its God,

Indu'd with various forms, various degrees
Of substance, and in things that live, of life;
But more refin'd, more spiritous, and pure,
As nearer to him plac't or nearer tending
Each in thir several active Sphears assign'd,
Till body up to spirit work, in bounds
Proportion'd to each kind.
(*PL,* 5.473–79)

Yet, as this example suggests, the naturalistic and vitalistic elements of Milton's cosmos are not truly mimetic since they are designed to fulfill one of the most traditional demands of Christian allegory: the representation of the universe as primally spirit infused, providential, and meaningful according to the dispensation of its all-wise, powerful, and loving God. Insofar as the figurative indeterminacies attributable to the epic reflect a tension between theology and science, with theology (as in the case of the Cambridge Platonists) going on the defensive, these tensions are productive precisely because this rational theology can still be Cartesianly presumed to lead to new certitudes, although, as a poet, Milton was more concerned with the concealed, uncertain, and yet more intuitively "present" design of providential time than with its abstract outlines. Moreover, this design's hidden mysteries, the depths revealed within the depths of these tensions, seem to him most reflected in the organically evolving "mirror" of nature in which the Calvinist Reformers ultimately sought their God but that the Cartesians would reduce to the mechanical operations of mere automata. But the central philosophical contrast here is between two different species of induction. While one would in Cartesian fashion reduce all organic life beneath that of the human cogito to the status of robots (although Hobbesian determinism goes even further, ascribing this status to the human mind itself), the other would in Cambridge Platonist or Calvinist fashion extend divine spirit throughout the universe. Since even his animals "reason not contemptibly" (*PL,* 8.374), in most respects Milton is closer to the latter than the former, but, in a larger sense, he also characteristically synthesizes both forms of rationalism much as he reconciles the deity's revealed law with his concealed will (*CPW,* 2:292, 295). This synthesis makes his philosophical position even more hybrid and, hence, inherently more baroque than the more familiar interim cosmologies of the period. Although he rejects the philosophical dualism of the Cambridge Platonists, he also rejects the Cartesian neodualism that succeeds in collapsing divine into natural law—a course that secular Calvinism will later follow. In the process he also finds himself at odds, not only with the determinist tendencies of the Calvinists among his own party, but also with those of the Royalist proponent of natural law, Thomas Hobbes, the most thoroughgoing mechanist of the age.[5]

In the context of our postmechanist critique of empirical positivism, Milton's antideterminist agenda can thus begin to seem more prophetic than irrational or unscientific, as indeed even More's radical speculations on absolute space and time eventually proved to be once they were incorporated into Newtonian theory. Yet, as a far subtler apprehension of the implications of evolutionary time, Milton's distinction between God's revealed law and his providentially concealed will looks even farther ahead. At least in poetic form, these discriminations resemble the fundamental Darwinian distinction recently outlined by Daniel Dennett, who describes the evolutionary intelligential "game" of life as an interplay between an underlying order and an evolving design.[6] In Milton's case, viewing the natural order as fulfilled by a dynamic pattern or "design" immanently organized by God's inscrutable laws is both linguistically and doctrinally motivated by the most positive intellectual legacy of Calvinism—its reverence for the living Word and its underlying spirit of grace. Thematically, this inherently dynamic conception of providential design appears in the epic's predominant figures of the cosmic dance, which regularly performs the pairing of God's only partially determining "will" with the kinesthesia of cosmogonic matter. The imaginative virtue of Milton's baroque principle of freely emergent design then lies in its singular concordance with what Dennett might call the governing relation between evolutionary forms and the abstract, noncontingent order informing them. Adam and Eve are both morally and intellectually free to evolve within the teleological order intermittently guiding human progress, because this freedom is maintained by a correspondent loss of synchrony (or the immediate perception of order) and an ascendance of diachrony (or the "chaotic" aspect of evolutionary progress). The highly interactive form of self-determination thus produced demands a wholly internal balance of

> True patience, and to temper joy with fear
> And pious sorrow, equally inur'd
> By moderation either state to bear.
> (11.361–63)

Here the providential order's symbiotic relation to the mutable "guidance" of inner fortitude dramatically rechannels the normative allegorical ascent toward eternity into a "this-worldly" horizon dispersed into various states and proportions only irregularly and organically returning to God.

Thus, in place of the vertical hierarchies generally governing normative Christian allegory, the reader discovers a descending universal order in which a materially indeterminate, natural/alchemical chain aspiring toward God is "recycled" (although never fully subsumed) into the horizontal dimension of temporal existence. Because all salvation history, individual and communal, transpires in this dimension, such allegories leave behind the Realist ideal of ascent into a statically transcendent realm of truth, which retains only the lost aura conveyed in Michael's postlapsarian history. The resulting world image aptly mirrors the tensions of a universe as well as an epistemology in flux, where ultimately, as Michael Fixler remarks, once time is dissolved into space and both into a temporal perspective "oriented . . . on earth, between the heavens and the lowest depths," man is permanently thrust into the experiential continuum of secular existence. Yet, here, matter has become not the enemy but the plastic medium in which mankind at once discovers and shapes his relation to God, whose vitalism he shares. Moreover, because the *imago dei* in man is no longer conceived as an abstract "shadow" but as an *ex deo* continuity with the divine being, both man and God proportionately participate in an interactive cosmos whose "vast vacuity" (*PL*, 2.932) permits a parallel, if not equal, freedom.[7]

In this respect departing from the Protestant baroque's characteristically gloomy relation to the material "remnants" of the numinous, Milton's cosmic allegory traces a realm where words have lost an intrinsically magical relation to the universe (the correspondences facilitated by the old "inseminating power" of the *rationes seminales*), only to take on some portion of the power of the divine word of Genesis. This generative power is graphically displayed by Adam in paradise and maintained even after the fall of Babel since, as Milton argues, "languages, both the first one which Adam received in Eden, and those various ones, perhaps derived from the first, which the builders of the tower of Babel suddenly received, were without doubt divinely given" (*CPW*, 8:294). Thus, the demise of one set of natural correspondences gives birth to an epistemology based on the more radically contiguous powers of naming.[8] However, as Fletcher remarks, in this "nominalist" universe, "We have by no means destroyed authority. We have not destroyed the possibility of accidental . . . [or] marvelous events. We have not destroyed hierarchy. We have not made feelings of awe impossible. *All these ideal activities are preserved, but in a new framework.* The scientist (and now the poet becomes a sort of scientist) will be the conquistador of that new cosmos."[9] With Galileo as the prototypical hero of the new philosophy, the way is then opened for the bard to become the hero not only of his own poem but also of a new poetics of space, which entails the invention both of a new form of agency and of new instruments for navigating the difficult passage between the old hylomorphisms and the new science's abstract or system space, the newly trackless realm to be "navigated" by the dawning mathesis of abstractly related things.

Yet, if in one sense Milton's monistic continuum seems to solve the problems of Cartesian dualism in making Galileo and his discoveries the "hero" of a newly expanded and unified cosmos, it must also still struggle to resolve the problems of agency previously settled by the older or Realist mind/body dualism and now by the new scientific and religious rationalism. Just as Calvinism tends sharply to divide works from grace as body from soul, in the process placing both at an incommensurable remove from God, who has retreated into the inscrutable and virtually irrational space of absolute will or "irresistible" grace, so empiricist mechanics tends to isolate both man and God within a rational calculus that radically detaches the observer from the observed. Milton's "heretical" departure from both these rationalisms thus provides the key to his more affirmative synthesis of baroque despair and nominalist optimism. For, unlike these philosophical "isolationists," he regards imagination as a form of mediation, as the human apprehension of the indeterminate eruption of God's concealed will within his revealed law, not as a destructive phantasm. The poetic imagination's synthetic force thus potentially heals the ruptures instituted by God's absence from absolute space and time since it not only parallels but conjoins the subject's to the deity's capacity to "implant" his presence everywhere and nowhere in the "boundless deep" that defines their intersubjective creativity (*PL,* 7.168–73). When guided by right reason and grace, the "wild work" of "Fancy" can then imitate the benign randomness of the divine matter arising from Chaos's "vast immeasurable Abyss / Outrageous as a Sea, dark, wasteful, wild" (7.211–12), for, while it may "misjoin . . . shapes, / . . . and most in dreams," those "Aery shapes" are also the very "frame [of] . . . / All what we affirm or what deny." So long as it continues to distinguish the active or obedient intelligence from the passive distortions that intervene "when Nature rests" (5.105–12), the chaotic yet also dynamic imagination thus confers a vitally constructive and reconstructive capacity on the human agent. In blending the new mathesis with a new kind of occulted force, an atomic substance no longer structured by a half-hidden language of nature, like God himself the interchangeably "absent" and "present" rational imagination presides over the indeterminate generation of matter from Chaos. Symbolically mediating between the well-formed "light" of reason and the freedom of "mimic" or antic fancy, the dreamlike realm of Chaos's unformed matter provides the plastic "correlative" of the poet's esemplastic imagination, which like God's is inspirationally tuned to "the secrets of the hoary deep, a dark / Illimitable Ocean without bound" (2.891–92).

To reveal these secrets without returning to the imitative magic or idolatry of signs inherent in Neoplatonic philosophy's microcosmic correspondences and occulted substances, Milton improvises a characteristically Puritan and empirical solution.[10] On the one hand, he denies the literal sacramentality of matter's "embryon Atoms" (*PL,* 2.900) in their purest state (a form of *ex deo* matter mysteriously "retracted" from God's active will); but, on the other hand, he allows it to retain something like the immanent grace inherent in its source. Ultimately, this source is God himself, although more indirectly it corresponds to the dark lineaments of light, everywhere the blind poet's material correlative of Urania's bright but also darkly ineffable powers. This dark light's ambiguous powers thus monistically link hell, heaven, and earth since, even in the "continent of spacious Heav'n," it springs forth from the inchoate depths within its "etherous mould." There its dark roots are latently empowered to develop into the more ambient forms of "Plant, Fruit, Flow'r Ambrosial, Gems and Gold" (6.473–75), welling up from

> Deep under ground, materials dark and crude,
> Of spiritous and fiery spume, till toucht
> With Heav'n's ray, and temper'd they shoot forth
> So beauteous, op'ning to the ambient light.
> (6.478–81)

Thereafter, this "spume" begets more light from the dark fire of its root, apparently the same root that in Raphael's life tree culminates in God's "bright consummate flow'r," "more refin'd, more spiritous, and pure, / As nearer to him plac'd or nearer tending" (5.475–81)—although not less dark in origin.

One assumes that this evolutionary process is repeated wherever light is born, as when during earth's creation its eternal/temporal ray, "Ethereal, first of things, quintessence pure / Sprung from the Deep," begins her earthly "journey through the airy gloom" (*PL,* 7.244–46). The vital ambiguity of this substantial yet "increate" (3.6) light, here apparently feminine, but in the invocation to book 3

apparently masculine, thus mirrors the sexual and atomistic ambiva-
lence common to all three of Milton's cosmic realms, all of which
seem to be "grounded" in the fully indeterminate state ruled by
Chaos and his consort, Night. Here, as everywhere, light's indeter-
minate "effluence" can be used either imaginatively to create (or
enact) or rationally to illuminate (or represent), although, antitheti-
cally, it can also destroy in all three realms, as it most notably does
when Satan and his cohort convert the "dark Nativity" of heavenly
light "pregnant with infernal flame" (6.482–83) to malign ends.
These enigmatic continuities produce the chiaroscuro so characteris-
tic of baroque allegory and so foreign to the darker mysteries of
normative allegory. Of course, its mysterious aura remains within the
epic's infinitely receding "mirrors" of synchrony and diachrony, each
dimension of whose monistic order (space) and design (time) pro-
ceeds from the "dark unbottom'd infinite Abyss" of chaotic matter,
where "time and place are lost" in the commingled chaos of subjec-
tive and divine freedom (2.405, 893–94). Yet the theodical impulse of
the epic also conserves an assured vehicle of divine mediation, an
ineffable calculus of illumination or boundless grace hymned by the
poet as coordinating these emergent infinities:

> Hail holy Light, offspring of Heav'n first-born,
> Or of th' Eternal Coeternal beam
> May I express thee unblam'd? since God is Light,
> And never but in unapproached Light
> Dwelt from Eternity, dwelt then in thee,
> Bright effluence of bright essence increate.
> Or hear'st thou rather pure Ethereal stream
> Whose Fountain who shall tell? before the Sun,
> Before the Heavens thou wert, and at the voice
> Of God, as with a Mantle didst invest
> The rising world of waters dark and deep,
> Won from the void and formless infinite.
> (3.1–12)

Here, the language of struggle (which is continued in the narra-
tor's description of his escape "through utter and through middle
darkness" [3.16], although ironically blind himself) amplifies into
questions surrounding the problematic nature of light itself: is it
God's emanation, an inseminating "effluence" similar to the Aristo-
telian *logoi spermatakoi*, or a concatenation of the abstract physical

motions that "invest . . . the void and formless infinite?" According to Fixler, this uncertainty points toward a deliberate equivocation that usefully bridges the otherwise unbridgeable gulf between an abstract or a mechanistic God and an immanent creator capable of providing both the medium and the message of all existence. Rather than the pure "presence" that might be identified with the second person of the Trinity, Milton's "Co-eternal beam" is thus identified as both the creator of space (God's corporeal function) and the measure of time (his temporal/eternal function). By occupying this ambivalent status, his light coordinates the abstract mechanics of the new science with the older, transcendently active conception of the First Cause. Yet the primary "impetus for figural change in the matter of substantial light increasingly came from science itself" since, as Fixler observes,

The displacement of light from essentially the sign of an occulted quintessence, as in the light of astrological influence, to a type of corpuscular motion, had been relatively swift but gradual, the most dramatic changes coming in the period between the ending of the early period of Milton's poetic activity with his two elegies, *Lycidas* and the *Epitaphium Damonis*, and the ending of the late poetic period with the publication of his major works. By the time Newton came to write the *Principia Mathematica* he could point back, as in that work's opening paragraph, to the shift in understanding which had disqualified altogether any attribution of power to some hypothetical hylic substance of quintessential etheriality, a shift which sent him searching for a far more fundamental and verifiable form of universal force on the model of light itself, but for Newton by then, a force focused on the power of gravity. *Still, while Milton wrote, the world on its well balanced hinges still hung, albeit precariously, exactly between the old and the new science, which meant that in the light of the old science Milton could be either literal or figurative* when—relying on the identity of the hylic substance with the *logoi spermatikoi* of etherial stella power—he spoke of the cognate procreative inseminating power of the poet and the minister, making a creation like unto God's by infusing from that Sun of Righteousness God's Spirit into others. This was not merely a figurative notion, since *some* substantial power was involved in such motions of gracious spirit.[11]

Thus, while the light of Milton's God remains immanently concealed in the inner recesses or "cave" of the material world that emanates his "grateful vicissitude" in proportions accommodated to the varying "substances" that its inhabitants, like heaven's, can contain (*PL,* 6.4–8), he remains separate from any traditional scale of being that would utterly separate light from darkness, as in more normative epic-allegory. This equivocal empty/fullness ensures that the material freedom figuratively displaced onto such ambiguous figures as Eden's "mazy errour" (4.239) can be harmonized with the far more abstract vacuities in which matter now circulates, the empty or "system space" that replaces the old plenary continuum of aggregate space. If this "solution" was not entirely original with Milton— in fact, More also used the new scientific concept of the vacuum as a "place" in which the real "presence" of the spirit might be conserved—its materialist attempt to outline the grounds of a new and fundamentally divine linguistic creativity is most certainly novel. In conserving the divine status of this one talent that the poet must finally render to his great taskmaster's account, Milton's poem also conserves the by now ruptured but still vital form and content of Christian allegory, whose semi-effaced essence he would later pass on to the greater Romantic lyric and the quest romance of the novel, where it persists in similarly oblique and ambiguous terms.[12]

2

Yet, in terms of the seventeenth-century episteme, the breach caused by Milton's departure from the older system of aggregate space produces a more immediate and graver rupture than in literary works where spatial values are more subordinate. As noted above, like Platonic cosmogony and Ptolemaic astronomy, Aristotelian physics had provided an ideal groundwork for "framing" the moral hierarchies of Christian allegory. Unlike the spatial theorists of the new science, Aristotle "did not acknowledge the existence of space apart from substance and form, so where there was no substance and form there could be no space"—which essentially means that space is always associated with a specific place value. For that reason alone, the Aristotelian universe "abhors" both vacuity and indeterminacy, the latter of which is limited to the "inferior" realm of the sublunary sphere. In the Christianized version of this episteme, the ephemeral world will thus never fully reflect the stabilities of this ideal world before the *eschaton.* This spatial continuum is thus not a true continuum but a dualistic hierarchy sharply distinguishing between "up" and "down," fixed and mutable. In converting these dichotomies to continuities,

Milton can no longer conceive his deity in conventional terms. Where once he had been alternately "near" (in respect to the motions of natural man and his world) and "far" (in respect to the accommodated nature and character of his essential being), now, according to Georgia Christopher, "the metaphorical and metaphysical distance [of both dimensions] is so great that one can scarcely speak of a synthesis of traditions," for Milton conceives his God as neither near nor far but as both and neither.[13]

Illusionistically projected like light simultaneously behind and within each dimension, this deity (in a sort of anticipation of the Leibnizian Great Monad) can best be imagined as an absent point of triangulation between heaven and earth, between up and down, and, finally, even between being and time—directions that in themselves have become relative in becoming interactive. Hence, here, as in the earlier speculation on the boundless universe, God becomes "an infinite sphere whose center is everywhere and circumference nowhere." No longer the summit of a chain of being, nor properly speaking a "he" at all but what Andrew Milner describes as at once the "particular personage who stands by merit at the top of the cosmological hierarchy" but also as the "abstract principle which transcends that hierarchy altogether," this deity provides a paradoxically appropriate model for both a new form of agency and a new universal structure.[14] As "sighted" through the poet's intimation that the process of discovering this structure somehow parallel's Galileo's telescopic discovery of sunspots (*PL*, 3.588–612), God can now "concretely" be accommodated only by our observations of the mysterious operations of the "Arch-chemic Sun" (3.609). These operations allusively indicate the paradoxical divine presence that the poet figuratively brings in under Satan's very feet as he lands on the solar surface, where, as in the words of Psalm 19, "The Lord hath set his tabernacle in the Sun." Neither a sensuous object drawn from a hierarchical ladder nor any mystical sign of grace, Milton's God thus becomes an oblique chemical "projection" of the sun's natural philosopher's stone, the invisible force and principle behind light's "Magnetic beam" (3.583, 600–608)—as well as the Psalter's silent trace.[15]

In this sense he is also a "real" presence under symbolic erasure, the less than self-evident occasion for a hermeneutical exercise that not only permits but demands God's enigmatic realization as the invisible plastic force behind matter, as the baroque vanishing point of a world still slouching toward Newton to be born. Of course, as an image of primal power and authority, the godhead's revised epic representation is not merely theological or natural scientific but also social and political in scope. Inspired by the successful civil and ecclesiastical challenges to the monarch's authority, dissenters like Milton were also emboldened to challenge entrenched philosophical authority, as his mature epic's ambiguous recasting of divine truth reveals.[16] Insofar as God is spirit and truth, his revealed law remains unchallenged; but, insofar as this law is supplemented by his concealed will, it remains forever open to the interpretation of his emergent revelations and their self-authorizing grace. This unstable synthesis of abstract reevaluation and concrete ambiguation is principally responsible for the ambivalent aura of baroque or "ruined" allegory surrounding the godhead, which collaterally attests to the profound crisis of meaning produced by a world precariously balanced between a multitude of competing semiotic and philosophical rationalisms. In this context, Cartesian/Hobbesian empiricism is not merely a rival attempt at philosophical reformation but (among other things) also an opposing episteme directed at discrediting religious enthusiasm, which Milton's synthesis of rationalist with inspired or "icastic" imagination is just as clearly a means of countering. According to Edward Craig, these competing rationalisms comprise the period's main opposing branches, the "similarity thesis" and "agency theory" models of knowledge. While the similarity or Cartesian model presupposes an epistemology wherein the human mind reflects or "re-presents" the "mind of God," the proto-Kantian agency theory posits a mind capable of reenacting the innate and fundamentally divine intuitions of time and space.[17]

Whether invoking the inspirational qualities of light or announcing a voice "unchang'd / To hoarse or mute, though fall'n on evil days, . . . and evil tongues" (*PL,* 7.24–26), the poet's "agency theory" thus proclaims more than its cosmic sympathies. It also stakes out a fundamentally active role for the subjects of history, for, as Milton most certainly realized, in itself radical materialism need not be liberating. Differently applied, it can actually negate any potential for divine intervention or individual interpretation of natural principles according to the "inner light" of grace. Here, Milton's most obvious opponent is not Descartes but Hobbes, whose materialism virtually outlaws not only the light of "prevenient grace" but the unfettered imagination in all its forms. In insisting that "Whatsoever we imagine is *Finite* [and] Therefore there is no Idea, or conception of anything we call *Infinite,*" Hobbesian philosophy would limit the human mind and imagination to determinate, visible objects of empirical investigation, so that if our senses supply the source of all our knowledge, we can investigate nothing but God's "ordinary as opposed to his intermediate work" in time. Since this epistemology further dictates that our lack of any independent understanding of divine providence means that we have no reason to worship God other than as the civil authorities command,[18] it threatens to isolate both God and man from the operation of a universe abstractly set in motion by a First Cause and passively recorded by a secondary "effect." Thus, as Edwin Burtt memorably observes: "When the *how* of Galilean mechanics replaces the final *why*, both God and man are threatened with banishment from the system as either uncaused First Cause or as secondary and *in-efficient* cause: the former becomes a quasi-mechanical principle, and the former a mere 'bundle of secondary qualities.'" . . . [Hence,] Man begins to appear for the first time in the history of thought as an irrelevant spectator and insignificant effect of the great mathematical system which is the substance of reality."[19] This drastic reorientation poses an obvious problem for any project that would employ rational materialism to justify a deity whose primary role is to preserve the Christian liberty of "th' upright heart and pure" (*PL*, 1.18).

Milton's consistent commitment to the human realization of this liberty seems to have been a principle factor leading him away from both the transcendentalism of the Cambridge Platonists (desperately trying, through a doctrine of "plastic substance" that would replace the *vis rerum,* to harmonize Descartes and Plato) and the deterministic materialism of Hobbes. His intermediate position confines neither human nor divine self-determination by affirming a sphere of metaphysical indeterminacy wherein God would be absolved of all necessity, even that of creation itself. At once renouncing the Neoplatonic doctrine of the deity's automatic *egressus-regressus* still maintained by the Cambridge school and the Hobbesian doctrine of the automatic human obligation to contract an indissoluble social covenant, he also quite consistently rejects Calvinist predestination as yet another indissoluble covenant between man and God. Yet his Arminian or free will position is also ultimately less antinomian than either radical empiricism or Calvinism, at least in the sense that both of the latter tend to free the redeemed or "contracted" individual from prolonged metaphysical scrutiny. The Calvinist elect are freed to pursue their vocations in this world, much as the empirical "elect" are freed to pursue the laws of material necessity to their own best advantage. But, as an unrepentant revolutionary, Milton has an obvious investment in a theology that would maintain the individual's sense of personal connection with and responsibility to an ongoing rather than a closed revelation. By his objective acts alone, the irresistible and inscrutable God of Calvinism would join Hobbesian pragmatism in condemning the Good Old Cause—as a good many of its foes and friends believed he had. Combined with Milton's lifelong investment in progressive self-realization, his continuing commitment to Christian liberty thus seems the likeliest motive for his rejection of all immutable or legalistic notions of the deity—from Scholastic and Neoplatonic definitions of God as an "Actus Purus" to the Calvinist conception of a thoroughly voluntarist God.[20]

As Dennis Danielson similarly concludes, in purging terms like *nature* and *fate* of their deterministic connotations, "Milton establishes a metaphysical basis for conceiving of necessity and possibility as being real, even before creation . . . in a way that not only avoids dualism but also positively enhances the freedom and omnipotence of God." The same synthetic paradox that allows "all potentiality and necessity [to at once] inhere" in God then effectively cancels the traditional distinction between his temporal acts and eternal law:[21]

> (For Time, though in Eternity, appli'd
> To motion, measures all things durable
> By present, past, and future). . . .
> (5.580–82)

Because God implicitly contains everything now separately evolving in the universe, which in respect to him is no longer an inferior "material" or temporally subordinate creation, both time and motion now coexist with the deity before the creation of the world. In the process, since both God and his universe have become equally infinite, they are distinguished chiefly by the fact that "Nature or *natura* implies by its very name that it was *natam*, born" (*CPW*, 6:131). Yet, in every other sense, the eternal God coexists with a matter that reflects his infinite and spontaneous capacity of extension, retraction, and evolution (*PL*, 7.169–70), which can "in a moment . . . create / Another World" and "Of Spirits malign a better Race to bring / Into their vacant room, and thence diffuse / His good to Worlds and Ages infinite" (7.154–55, 189–91).

In order to maintain these benign infinitudes while rejecting the malign specter of an "aspiritual material universe" inherent in the empirical mechanics of the expanded cosmos, Milton then takes the even more radical step of denying *any* definitive disjunction either between the First Cause and his creation or between mortal body and immortal soul.[22] This step allows him to re-orient the new philosophy along spiritual lines that make his expanded God into another aspect of the project of Reformation—the recovery of those obscured ancient truths "Left only in those written Records pure" (*PL*, 12.513) of God's twin books of Scripture and nature (*CPW*, 6:318–25, 396–98). Like the new scientists of relative space, but unlike the Hobbesian mechanists who materialize all things but the intellect of the observing subject, Milton posits a fluid material agency or "first matter" that unites subjects and objects so that neither man nor God becomes an irrelevantly "transparent" spectator. Properly used, this synthesis allows the human agent's "twinned" abilities of right reason and spiritual liberty to approach God by imitating his active creative agency, itself the empty/full "vacuum" mediating the infinite reaches of the allegorical and real cosmos. Ultimately, then, the entire structure of this cosmos can be likened to its God, who can be seen as either empty or full (*PL*, 7.168–71), according to the stance of the spectator.[23]

In relation to the infinite temporal extension of the universe, this paradox corresponds to the "abyss / [of] Eternity, whose end no eye can reach" (*PL*, 12.555–56); in relation to its infinite spatial extension, it corresponds to that inscrutable vacuum into which God "uncircumscrib'd . . . retire[s]" (7.170). While such "spaces" are in one sense screened from secondary agents, in another sense they are reciprocally inserted in this boundless continuum both through the "godlike" spatial extensions of such inventions as Galileo's "Optic Tube" (3.590) and through the temporal extensions of God's infinite grace. Meta-allegorically, this dialectic between space and time, or deductive and inductive experience, corresponds to the act of reading itself, the material/spiritual synthesis whereby the individual in principle coordinates his inner experience of God's universe and its laws with his external *logos* or book, therein fashioning an *imago dei* that is not sacramentally or externally conferred but agonistically and creatively earned.[24] This model implicitly presumes that a poetry that exposes its own incertitudes must also be attuned to the speculative, self-reflexive poetics of historical process. By further assuming the inherent continuity of its "informational" processes with the actual information of the universe, Milton's poetry of virtue—of vital "inseminating" and ethical force—taps into the circulational energies of its universe by making the uncertainties of its freedom continuous with those of universal evolution. Although the laws of the "one Almighty . . . from whom / All things proceed" draw these things back "up to him [in] return," they do so primarily to rerelease them into the benign mutability of the process. Thus, while any of its elements or agents may choose to become "deprav'd from good" (5.469–71), when rightly used, a more "expansive" understanding of Providence is rightly rewarded with still greater freedom, as in the paradigmatic example of the Son. But, even when wrongly used, this understanding can be recuperative since the very depth of any self-chosen sphere of action is checked in the balance of nature, permitting (as in the case of Adam and Eve) a naturally corrective self-reflection. This kind of autopoetic "feedback" thus forms the groundwork of their baroque allegorical cosmos, where even the normative moral directions "up" and "down" remain self-reflexively, contextually, and, hence, meta-allegorically ambiguous and indeterminate.

Hence, God's repeated insistence on the words *free* and *freedom* (occurring three times in the five crucial lines defining human authority [*PL*, 3.124–28]) also implicitly foregrounds the monistic principles governing all levels of Milton's material universe, all of which are relatively unconstrained by hierarchical rank or external influence. Everywhere springing "lighter green" from a stalk that naturally blooms into more "sublim'd" "vital spirits," the various degrees of matter at work in its root, branch, and flower are harmonized by their common potential either to be "Improv'd by tract of time," to be "deprav'd" or degraded from good (5.470–97), or to be recuperatively recombined in the "pregnant causes mixt" (2.913) of Chaos. The same multidirectional potential is exhibited by more fully self-directed allegorical agents, who can paradoxically "rise" either by succeeding or by failing to fulfill their prescribed duties (as in quite different external circumstances Abdiel, Uriel, and Gabriel variously illustrate), so long as they retain God's "love entire" (5.502). Thus, despite the differences of degree or direction inherent in higher and lower "causes," the agent's outward course of rising and falling remains relative to its own subjective intention and self-understanding, which alone dictates its degree of personal growth in time. Of course, other agents may intermediately affect or even divert these internal directions, but neither to the extent nor with any of the lasting effects characteristic of normative Christian allegory, for here no "real" universals or "ideal" essences convey the abstract conditions of "accidents within substances," just as no external scale of value dictates the meaning of the agent's victory or defeat. As a result, Abdiel's spontaneous and solitary self-vindication against impossible odds actually merits far higher acclaim than Michael's more "momentous" defeat of Satan's forces on the second day of the War in Heaven since the archangel is not only under the direct command of the deity but backed by all the "Armory of God" (6.321). Even the great jubilation surrounding the Son's final victory is therefore framed as due to his perfected faith far more than to his perfected works since not only the Son's but all real force belongs ultimately to God. "Differing but in degree, of kind the same" (5.490), Abdiel and the Son are thus equally meritorious in exerting their freedom to make their faith and deeds answerable to their various degrees of knowledge, the course that Adam at last painfully learns to follow (12.582). In Milton's chain of being, any merit attached to extreme differences of kind is therefore confined either to demons or to the "painful Superstition and blind Zeal" (3.452) found in a Paradise of Fools "who in vain *things* / Build thir fond hopes of Glory or lasting fame, / Or happiness in this or th' other life" (3.448–50; emphasis added).

As it erases the "painful superstitions" of the older dualism, this Reformed epic continuum resolves many, if not all, of the conventional problems of divinity and agency posed by the neodualist mechanism of the new science. Since the contested world picture of the seventeenth century hardly permits any definitive solutions, Milton instead exploits its indeterminacies by forcibly juxtaposing the rational mechanics of nominalism's Classic Age against the closed structures of the Peripatetic/Ptolemaic universe. This technique results in the meta-allegorical practice that can again be compared to Shakespeare's strategy of juxtaposing the rigidly antiquated or "closed" drama of *The Mousetrap* against the baroque space of Hamlet's dilemma. Through this dramatic contrast, a new and more mimetic "space" is opened both to critique and to reinterpretation: a space of hermeneutical triangulation, a deductive fulcrum or baroque "vanishing point" capable of mediating the inductive differences and continuities between divine, human, and universal infinitude. This strategy is especially evident in the Paradise of Fools, where Satan ironically encounters

> . . . they who to be sure of Paradise
> Dying put on the weeds of *Dominic,*
> Or in *Franciscan* think to pass disguis'd;
> They pass the Planets seven, and pass the fixt,
> And that Crystalline Sphere whose balance weighs
> The Trepidation talkt, and that first mov'd;
> And now Saint *Peter* at Heav'n's Wicket seems
> To wait them with his Keys, and now at foot
> Of Heav'n's ascent they lift thir Feet, when lo
> A violent cross wind from either Coast
> Blows them transverse ten thousand Leagues awry
> Into the devious Air. . . .
> (*PL,* 3.478–89)

Here, Milton's parody both of the Dantean cosmos and of the Ptolemaic universe's "Trepidation talkt" (a means of accounting "for certain phenomena . . . really due to the rotation of the earth's axis" [*OED*]) coalesces with his Puritan disdain for these pilgrim's "disguises," which as a whole satirize the idea that any outer garment or ritual appropriation can possibly change the soul's internal condition. Thus, just as these pseudosaints seem to glimpse the keys of Saint Peter's kingdom, these ritually deluded and therefore vain or "light" souls lift their feet (with a buried pun on their condition's continuity with their lower *soles*) in a presumed ascent that only seals their final banishment—blown "ten thousand Leagues awry" into their own "devious Air."[25]

Milton's irony is lighter but equally apparent in his angelic "lecture" on astronomy, no doubt in part because the Ptolemaic system had not yet been definitively disproved. Nevertheless, his very inclusion of this system's "Crystalline Sphere" in the Paradise of Fools provides a strong clue that Raphael's "weighing" of the two rival cosmologies is no more impartial than the poet's sarcastic allusion to the light "weight" of those who pass through the "Trepidation talkt." Thus, without precisely denying the divine capacity to generate the immense "speed almost spiritual" (*PL,* 8.110) that the older theory requires, the archangel strongly hints at the inconveniences of a system that must "contrive / To save appearances" by girding

. . . the Sphere
With Centric and Eccentric scribbl'd o'er,
Cycle and Epicycle, Orb in Orb.
(8.81–84)

Contrasting this model's theoretical inelegance with the advantages of a "streamlined" Copernican system less conformable to Adam's physical sense, he then asks his pupil to perform the hermeneutical balance also required of his readers, asking himself why the sun may not

Be Centre to the World, and other Stars
By his attractive virtue and their own
Incited, dance about him various rounds?
Thir wandring course now high, now low, then hid,
Progressive, retrograde, or standing still,
In six thou seest, and what if sev'nth to these
The Planet Earth, so steadfast though she seem,
Insensibly three different Motions Move?
Which else to several Spheres thou must ascribe,
Mov'd contrary with thwart obliquities,
Or save the Sun his labor . . .
. . . .
. . . which needs not thy belief,
If Earth industrious of herself fetch Day. . . .
(8.123–33, 136–37)

In commenting on these scenes, like so many empiricists who considered Milton's science "retrograde," Arthur O. Lovejoy condemned Raphael for not dogmatically rejecting the "thwart obliquities" of the Ptolemaic system, even though it was still defended by many scientists in differing forms, including Tycho Brahe's "Copernican" compromise.[26] Hence, from a seventeenth-century perspective, such a rejection would not represent responsible science any more that it would accurately reflect the continuing debate over Bishop Wilkin's *Discourse that the Earth May be a Planet.* Yet, in the context of that debate, the poetic emphasis of Raphael's "simple, sensuous, and passionate" discourse (*CPW,* 2:403) quite clearly favors Wilkins's position, which echoes that of the Royal Society in general. Raphael's initial, if at first somewhat subtle, preference for the elegant rationality of the Copernican side of the argument is further hinted at by his remarks on the merits of an astronomical system in which an "industrious" rather than a "sedentary Earth" (*PL*, 8.32) participates in the motions of its surrounding universe. Distinctively Puritan as well as empirical, such a cosmology is clearly in harmony with Milton's characteristic preference for Kepler's "dancing stars" rather than Ptolemy's static spheres, for "eccentric" angelic orbs whose motions symbolically validate mankind's virtually unlimited spiritual and scientific capacity for progress in a newly mobile universe. As Raphael explains to his pupils in paradise, so long as "ye be found obedient" (5.501), these human capacities are virtually limitless.[27] Nor are they later nullified by our Grand Parent's subsequent exile; even after the human lapse, God continues to provide sufficient "prevenient grace" and angelic instruction to ensure that this prototypical pair can individually and/or socially (if also painfully) overcome most of the defects accruing to the Fall through objective, self-disciplined observation as well as faith. Far from the perversely backward-looking attitude of which Lovejoy accuses it, then, Milton's dialogue on astronomy reveals his deep regard for the role that both empirical and self-knowledge must play in exploring a materially expanding cosmos.[28]

Yet, largely because Milton rejects the idea that either human or scientific history affords a picture of inevitable ascent—but also because he persists in regarding this ascent in spiritual as well as material terms—intellectual historians like Lovejoy have dismissed his affirmations as mere window dressing even after most of the Enlightenment myths of progress have lost all credibility. However, since more recent historians of science now actually concur with Raphael in describing empirical progress as a pattern of shifting paradigms and outright errors, never as the result of an unbroken chain of assured empirical advance, Lovejoy's still influential view of scientific and theological "compromises" like Milton's as strange mutations or "missing links" deleted from his "great chain" needs to be discarded along with his dismissive approach to Milton's "superficial," "malicious," or "curious" theodicy.[29] For Raphael's probing of the conflicting systems of astronomy outlines a *skeptically* progressive allegory of the fundamental requirements of the scientific outlook, as even his conclusion reveals. In warning Adam to "Dream not of other Worlds, what Creatures there / Live, in what state, condition or degree" (*PL*, 8.175–76), he merely directs human inquiry toward more pressing empirical concerns—an epistemological position "ten thousand leagues" beyond the ritual universe of the older allegory, the world formerly enclosed by the mystic perfection of the "Crystalline Sphere" (3.482, 488). In refusing to "save the appearances" of this antiquated epic cosmos, *Paradise Lost* thus celebrates an infinitistic yet relatively unmechanistic universal continuum recentered in humankind's expanding perceptions.

Yet, in setting the old hierarchical system of aggregate space against the evolutionary ontology presupposed by his Chaos, the poet also probes beyond the empirical limits of human comprehension in search of its missing center, the divine source in which the whole coheres. In this most "baroque" aspect of its cosmic allegory, most of the poem's epic geography gradually evolves into the wholly internal spaces that his hell and heaven finally become (*PL*, 4.75–78, 10.598–99). Like the indeterminately "square or round" space of heaven (2.1047–48) and the "pendant world" suspended from it by "a golden Chain," these epic regions thus chart only contextually relative allegorical directions. Borrowing traditional emblems only to expand them to the point of rupture and/or ruin, Milton's ultra-Olympian and post-"*Pegasean*" angle of vision on creation (7.3–4) finally reconfigures even the conventional purity of heaven's mystically squared circle of perfection (2.1048). For, ultimately, its "Opal Tow'rs and Battlements adorn'd / Of living Sapphire" (2.1049–50) resolve into a kind of optical illusion, a semiopaque intensification of celestial perception as the viewer approaches the source of light. Moreover, to prevent less careful readers from missing the point that these figures are not literally but "mysteriously . . . meant" (3.516), Raphael empirically "corrects" earth's symbolic appearance as a link in a heavenly chain by describing it as actually "a cloudy spot" such as "*Galileo*, less assur'd, observes" (5.266, 262).

3

From these few examples alone, it seems evident that Milton's predilection for light imagery, no doubt stimulated by his blindness, also expresses his visionary faith that, within the "bright darkness" of the vastly enlarged cosmos, God remained a hidden but providential power materially manifesting itself. Thus, however accurately his celestial signposts of living sapphire testify to the yearnings of a sightless poet whose eyes "toll in vain / To find thy piercing ray, and find no dawn" (*PL*, 3.23–24), their intensification and expansion also attest to his awe before the majestic forces that bind such new and previously undreamt of universal distances. Because light has a power that can "tangibly" be communicated even to the blind who cannot see it (3.22), its paradoxes also suggest both the common human distance from divine light and its dark vanishing point in freely "inspired" interpretation. Light's primary force in the poem can then be traced to this interchangeably figurative and literal status, since the enormity of the distances that Raphael must traverse "worlds and worlds" to cover (5.268) can be adequately understood only in the context of its simultaneously transposible literal/figurative power, the measure of distance but also of perception, which here, as in Milton's invocation to book 3, presupposes a virtually boundless universe. In this context, the "golden Chain" connecting heaven and earth becomes a figurative allusion to the loose allegorical framework in which light's multiple interconnections now act as "concatenative" ciphers or symbols (*catena* signifying a "chain") for the "divine design penetrating the entire universe," as the Hughes edition notes.

Once this design has been detached from the certitudes of aggregate space, the very stairs of Jacob's ladder (*PL*, 3.510) cease to act as traditional steps to divine revelation. Instead modeling the abstract and intangible calculus accommodating creature to Creator, this ladder is ambiguously lowered either "to dare / The Fiend by easy ascent, or aggravate / His sad exclusion from the doors of Bliss" (3.523–25). Here, Milton's "either/or" suggests that, like the physical dimensions of his allegorical universe, moral choices have been reconceived as a kind of probabalistic, although not random, mental calculus replacing the pseudosciences of innate dispositions, creaturely humors, and ritual garments or ceremonies of purification. By focusing instead on the very real indeterminacies within which right reason must inform moral choice to negotiate the knowledge of external reality, the poet makes these same uncertainties the very foundation of all human freedom and its limitations, which is where alone (as Adam warns Eve)

> The danger lies, yet lies within his power:
> Against his will he can receive no harm.
> But God left free the Will, for what obeys
> Reason, is free, and Reason he made right,
> But bid her well beware, and still erect,

> Lest by some fair appearing good surpris'd
> She dictate false, and misinform the Will
> To do what God expressly hath forbid.
> (9.349–56)

Far from coincidentally, Adam issues this warning just as Eve is about to submit to the self-aggrandizing, superstitious aims of Satan's pseudoempiricism, here also a precursor of those later attempts to ascend to paradise by faulty methods, garments, or other "weeds." In this Baconian poem, such alchemical attempts to "prevent" natural time only reciprocally increase the randomness of human calculation by sending so far "oblique the Centric Globe" (10.671) that the true universal motions hinted at by Raphael will take centuries to rediscover.

From this belated, although also triumphant baroque perspective, Milton's "higher Argument" (*PL*, 9.42) replaces, not only the "long and tedious havoc [of] fabl'd Knights," but all the ceremonial places and dimensions of their "Battles feign'd" (9.30–31). Ploughed back into the soil of its Lucretian roots, Milton's epic space/time reallegorizes the older symbols of universal order much as it recasts the functions assigned to the pagan gods, which have become antiquated emblems or signposts of the advances achieved by a thoroughly Reformed mental and physical geometry. Within this geometry, ethical choices like Eve's can still be conceived as "morally" high or low, narrow or wide, but only in relation to their actual physical consequences. Yet the subtlety of this ethical calculus also requires Raphael's warning that, although Adam's relatively "late" creation from the ongoing "womb" of Chaos might cause him to dream of rapidly rising to "other Worlds" (7.92–93, 8.175), true "breadth" consists in focusing more narrowly and skeptically on the world now before him. In conformity with the powerfully inductive and empirical orientation of Puritanism, Adam is thus reminded that earthly wisdom consists in turning from abstract possibility to concrete probability. If grasped correctly, these probabilities reveal a more truly expansive finitude framed within the divine infinitude of grace: the immense power, bounty, and goodness of Eden and its wandering, wanton, yet also wise potentiality.

Because this potentiality exists not merely to limit but also to reward human apprehension, Adam's discursive understanding is designed to prosper to the extent that it combines his inductive understanding of Eden with Raphael's more abstract probing of the parameters of divine Providence, a synthetically intuitive and discursive (*PL*, 5.488) model designed to preclude both arid empiricism and reductive reasoning from limited premises (5.856–63, 9.716–26, 764–79)—the reasoning so conducive to the presumptuous sin of both Satan and Eve. Ironically, in following the humbler and more broadly inductive/intuitive course of Abdiel, the human pair would have attained to ever greater heights of understanding (5.497–99): the understanding of angels, but most certainly not of Descartes. Significantly, then, Eve falls into Satan's trap at the precise moment she agrees to accept the shortcuts of his deductive logic as the inductive demonstration that it is not: she reasons from the pseudo-evidence of a speaking serpent rather than from her own carefully weighed observations and assessments or what Abdiel calls the direct "experience" by which "we know how good, / And of our good, and of our dignity / How provident" the boundless godhead actually is (5.826–28).

The anti-Cartesian premises of this inductive method further suggest that, like his Jansenist contemporary Blaise Pascal, Milton was among the first of the moderns fully to grasp the problematic incertitudes accompanying the decentered spaces opened up by the new science and its mathematics. For both, accurately exploring these infinite vistas of extension and contraction also means recentering the observer within the creative void connecting him to God, an insight also implicit in baroque art's experimentation with multiple vanishing points.[30] Although this experimentation expresses the absence of origin implicit in the new algebra of the period's perspectival system space, as Brian Rotman has shown, this awareness does not simply "erupt" during the seventeenth century. Beginning much earlier, in fact with the very introduction of the number zero once the Hindu system of numeration replaces the Roman (which has no sign for nothing), it culminates as Euclidean geometry replaced by algebraic equations. In the process, the concept *zero* is gradually transformed from a merely negative to a positive absence, from a mere empty gap to a placeholder, the metasign grounding all variables in the system of differential equations. Thus, "the elaboration of the code of scientific discourse in the seventeenth century to accommodate the concepts and reality of 'vacuum' and 'empty space' was a question, not of historical causation to be traced through the supposed influence of Greek atomism, but the completion of an existing semiotic paradigm. Within this discourse the terms 'vacuum' or 'empty space' were obliged to signify the absence of what before them had been conceived as full, indivisible and all-pervasively present: the plenum of breathable air and the plenum of material (as opposed to divine) existence."[31]

As Paul de Man suggests, this new system of representation is then logically inclined to replace the idea of the divine existence as a *one,* a "total unfractured omnipresence" stabilizing the entire network of subjective presences, with the idea of this existence as an absence, a nothing, zed, or "zero" coordinating the multiple and/or triangulated vanishing points of the universe. De Man traces this new theodicy in Pascal, the Jansenist mathematician/theologian whose early experiments in resituating the "place" of God at the all-centering zero of the revised number line (formerly centered on the one) later form the basis of his "mathesized" "allegory of persuasion."[32] In this theodicy, the role of zero and of the void as determinative "agents" fundamentally inverts the strategy of Descartes's empirical reconfiguration of method in his *Meditations* since, in the latter, only the human observer is recentered as Rotman's "active constructing subject who, by taking part in a thought experiment, makes an abstraction [and] . . . is enabled to occupy a new semiotic space, one which relies essentially on a reference to the absence of signs that were previously . . . conceived in terms of a positive, always present, content."[33] In contrast, the Cartesian God remains a "one," which by now means an abstract "whole" or Prime Mover relegated to the role of hypothetical origin outside the new algebraic system entirely.

Pascal counters this tactic by conceiving both the human observer and the divine "center" of the universe as positive zeros, as null sets around which system space now revolves. Yet their divergences go even further than this insistence on conserving a universal space for his God since, as we have seen, the Cartesian system also ultimately makes the human observer a "zero" in the negative or subtractive sense that he merely reflects or transparently records the symmetrical "tables" of names and things that establish the fundamental binarism of the Classic Age. As Pascal was acutely aware, this nominalist system ultimately rules out all final causes, human or divine, in favor of a self-sufficient continuum of objectively defined "extensions," a grid, graph, or taxonomy of visible things and their mechanical relations to signs. Although this empirical model of reality has been challenged only recently, Pascal's objections have been confirmed as modern science begins to acknowledge the place of the observer in its calculations and the sciences of certitude are regrounded in those of probability and relativity. Prophetically, then, Pascal makes his zero not only the active agent centering the number line but also the infinitely transmutable factor multiplying all numbers into itself, the hypothetical juncture between all subjects and objects, ultimately including man and God.[34]

Although Milton hardly foresaw that the Cartesian model would lead to the mechanical or "clockwork universe" of the succeeding century, much less objected to it in such explicitly mathematical terms, as we have seen he also resisted its tendency to equate God with the mere necessity of a Prime Mover or with a logical postulate retroactively deduced from natural law. Moreover, like Pascal's, his theodicy is far more empirically innovative than merely mystical or nostalgic and, like it similarly allows his deity to announce that chance and fate "approach not mee," for "*what I will* is Fate" (*PL*, 7.172–73; emphasis added). This active rather than passive prime agent also suggests that he was among the first thinkers of the period fully to grasp the full theological/logical potential presented by the dissolution of aggregate space, although some of the Cambridge Platonists were working in similar directions—an association that most likely explains his keen awareness of the problem, if not his own contrary solutions, which bear some unexpected yet instructive resemblances to Pascal's. As elsewhere clearly accepting the dissolution of the Peripatetic universe, Pascal's *Pensées* combine his mathematical "proof" of God's necessary centrality with his inductive proof of the vacuum within nature by showing that in itself human logic leads to an inescapable "void" at the center of the new calculus.[35] In terms reminiscent of the probability theory he helped invent, he then demonstrates the probable "healing" of this gap in the newly boundless "circumference" inhabited by the deity. For the paradoxically unmeasurable yet certain vectors of the "double infinities" of microscopic and macroscopic space seem to require this "uncircumscribed" placeholder without which they would seem completely lacking in coherence. Although not positively calculable, the existence of this infinite placeholder becomes even more probable in that it also seems to correspond to the comparable void within man himself, the incalculable gap between his self-reflexive consciousness and his material condition.

These incomprehensible, although demonstrable, disjunctive infinities in external space thus illustrate the parallel incommensurabilities of God/matter and mind/body within mental time, which can be neither empirically nor mathematically conjoined. Further, any mathematical attempt to "measure" this inductive/deductive absence will merely magnify man's intuitive awareness of the even greater distance between a divine mind that could comprehend infinity and a human one that can merely postulate it. Like Milton using the inventions of the telescope and microscope as dramatic props to foreground the boundless immensity of this new metaphysical stage, Pascal then dwells on the disturbing fact that its receding dimensions remain both externally and internally disjunct. Yet because Zeno's paradoxes ultimately lack physical confirmation—that is, because the universe does indeed cohere—he postulates that we can and indeed must postulate the existence of a benign integrative agency uniting the mathematically deducible and inductively determinable vacuums of the universe: just as we can project infinity, we must/should also project its God. In a period that has not yet formulated the laws of gravity, this identification of an immanent or "hidden" God as the invisible force providing the probable coherence of an order no longer held in place by interlocking spheres must be regarded as far more ingenious than regressive, far more mathematical than medievalizing. This theodicy at once accepts the new discontinuities appearing at the heart of the spatial continuum and supplies a profoundly new solution to the problem of the physical and metaphysical "coherence gone" from a New Philosophy that calls "all in doubt," as Donne's *Anniversaries* famously lament.

De Man shows that Pascal's apologetic uses of this calculus can be traced to his *Refléxions,* which replace scholastic affirmation with a form of disjunction that "is not to be thought of as a negation" but as the reinscription of the heterogenous, "unnamable," yet also functionally ineradicable element of zero.[36] In ways that explicitly underscore the implicit aims of Milton's theodicy, Pascal here sets scholasticism against nominalism and defeats both with their own device. By showing that the obsolescence of the old Euclidean number line centered on one also invalidates the old theology of the divine "One," he demonstrates the logical necessity of the all-centering zero. For this heterogenous element, like his God, is at once the most necessary and ambiguous of ciphers, a nonnumber in its unique indivisibility and infinite multiplicability, but one also demonstrably "real" both in its role as a placeholder and as a cipher that can be added or subtracted. These "baroque" paradoxes allow Pascal to distinguish what according to Euclid is a nominally, although it is not really, an indivisible number, one, from the actually indivisible cipher, zero. In the process, zero becomes the new center not only of the number system but also of the universe, the metasign uniquely capable of signifying the absence/presence of a God who can no longer be conceived as a one. In the same way that infinity (of which the vacuum supplies a physical exemplum, an empirically verifiable, yet, in theory, also an "infinitely" empty void) has become the incommensurably absent "circumference" of nature, its hypothetical sine qua non, "nothing" has become its inner-worldly "presence"—which, by definition, is *there* only by human definition, by a paradoxically "certain" projection from the experienced to the nonexperiential.[37]

At this point, Pascal's divergence from what he calls the Cartesian "Romance of Nature" becomes absolute: for, as the latter grants reality only to extended things (thereby making spirit inexplicable), so Pascal's system grants reality primarily to emptiness, thereby ironically making matter itself (whose existence is here proleptically subjected to the later "doubts" of quantum physics) hypothetically inexplicable. Yet, even as Pascal's paradoxical subdivisions of atomistic "nothing" disappear into a vanishing point beyond the reach of the finite observer, they also approach him as an analogy of his center, the *arche* of his number line and of his absent self, whose otherwise "empty" conjunction of body and soul calls on him also to wager on the existence of God as the only comparable infinitude capable of filling it. Again ingeniously, the human being continues to be imagined in the image of his God, the zero, even while both existences are radically reinscribed in a metasign: in the infinitely multiplicable variable that alone among sublunar creation man can calculate. At once dividing and adding him on to the comparable nothing/everything of the deity, man thus becomes analogous to nothing but God, the absent center of both his external macrocosm and his internal microcosm. As the placeholder of being and number, motion and time, Pascal's zero thus inductively reunites the absences of relative space in the infinite absence of God, whose incommensurability paradoxically figures the lesser but equally incommensurable freedom of man.

4

As we have seen, the Miltonic form of a parallel rupture/suture unit-
ing the "double infinities" of man and God first appears in his repre-
sentation of God as a source of energy inevitably prior to light and of
light itself as an enigmatic, if also real, vanishing point, a "Bright
effluence of bright essence increate" (*PL,* 3.6). Thus, while God's
inapproachably *"dark* with excessive bright" (3.380) force cannot be
seen directly, it can be indirectly shadowed by the discursive "process
of speech" he shares with his rational creatures. This process of
accommodation then seems to follow much the same logical pattern
as Pascal's mathematical demonstrations since, as Raphael assures
his human audience, although God's Word exists in an indefinitely
remote infinity, the effect of his will can and must be understood as
analogous to its finite extensions in time and space: "Immediate are
the Acts of God, more swift / Than time or motion, but to human
ears / Cannot without process of speech be told, / So told as earthly
notion can receive" (7.176–79). In other words, the eternal and "in-
finite" gap between God's immediacy and his Word's enactment of
his will in time roughly corresponds to the role played by Pascal's
infinite but also additive and/or subtractable zero. The incommen-
surable disparity between the two functions is in this case coordi-
nated by the reciprocal "motions" of his Son, the visible "Word" who
gives temporal "effect" to his divine intentions (7.174–75), thus sup-
plying as the chiasmus between the dual infinities of human and
divine freedom. Through the positive gap thereby inserted in the
structure of the universe, although what God wills "is Fate" (7.173),
he can withdraw or retract his will in time to leave his creatures free
to act on their rational or pseudorational desires, "without least im-
pulse or shadow of Fate, / Or aught by me immutably foreseen"
(3.120–21). Either by negating or by neutralizing his foreknowledge,
the Son, his angels, and the race of mankind become "Authors to
themselves in all" (3.122) in their own relatively infinite dimensions,
dimensions where their accommodation of his functions to their
own creates a "process of speech" that does not limit but only ex-
pands the essential freedom absently yet also "concretely" linking
them as their common zero functions.

If not so fully hidden or absent as Pascal's *Deus absconditus,* Milton's epic God is also similarly revealed through a negative analogy of number. This analogy parallels Pascal's zero function in supplying a real, present, yet also abstractly "empty" basis of cosmic order. Because his decrees can be transacted and accurately "read" only in the abstract and relative dimensions of function or system space, God's presence remains only a relatively calculable, never a concrete or stable, projection of human signs. His universe must then be modeled on similar principles, since, if hell is as far from heaven "As from the center thrice to the utmost pole" (*PL*, 1.74), to imagine its space the reader must perform a kind of numerical wager in measuring a demonic descent itself calculated only through the triply binding direction of their downward motion. Far from the certain centers of Dante's concentric cosmos, this narratively and spatially decentered universe thus also precludes any assured allegorical means of measuring Satan's distance from God, for to measure this "space" before the creation of the earth would require a threefold equation here only inductively apparent in the relative distances between Satan's sensually "binding" allegory of persuasion and the divine act of withdrawal that defers God's judgment onto creaturely freedom. In pitting these two allegories against one another, Milton parallels Pascal's technique of discrediting the "absolute" realities of the Peripatetic and Cartesian universes (to which only Satan appeals) by allowing their internal contradictions to emerge in their juxtaposition. As the inverse of boundless grace, the satanic allegory of a completely chartable space—whether grounded in the old enclosed or the new scientific universe—can measure only the demons' distance from a heavenly perfection that is by definition absent and indeterminate. Hence, again like Pascal, the poet requires his readers to approximate their true "place" by probabilistically measuring heaven's vast remove from the narrow confines of the hellish council.

Thus, in contrast with Satan's unalterable "union" of "firm Faith, and firm accord" (*PL*, 2.36), the God of *Paradise Lost* offers an ongoing negotiation with his self-authorizing subjects, a constant realignment of covenantal accords that represent him, not as a static "one," but as an infinitely multiplicative zero, a variable vanishing point located everywhere and nowhere in the universe. This "absent" origin makes the deity at once a "boundless Deep," an "I am" who "fill[s] / Infinitude," and a self-emptying retraction into which he can "uncircumscrib'd . . . retire" (7.168–70). Completely "free / To act or not" (7.171–72), he becomes accessible to his creatures chiefly through a quasi-Pascalian system of analogies, for, as Adam's perfection allows him to grasp, if in one sense he is a mysterious unity "alone / From all Eternity, for none I know / Second to mee or like, equal much less" (8.405–7), in another sense he is also the mysterious placeholder of the creation to and from which he can add or subtract his presence. Wholly unlike this being except in their mutual sense of disparity, Adam acknowledges that their differences far exceed their similarities. While Adam needs a mate to expand his "singleness," for his creator there is

> . . . No need that thou
> Shouldst propagate, already infinite;
> And through all numbers absolute, though One;
>
> . . . .
>
> Thou in thy secrecy although alone,
> Best with thyself accompanied, seek'st not
> Social communion, yet so pleas'd,
> Canst raise thy Creature to what highth thou wilt
> Of Union or Communion, deifi'd.
> (8.419–21, 427–31)

Yet, if no true parity with God is possible even on the part of his "only begotten Son," God's very infinity permits him infinitely to "deify" his creatures so that they can "intuitively" participate in his discursive medium. Mathematically, this potential derives from God's dual nature as both infinite and nothing—"through all numbers absolute," but in his "secrecy . . . alone." As also a cohesive power that, like Pascal's zero, alternately expands and contracts his numerical reach everywhere and nowhere in the universe, Milton's God thus becomes the still point of the number line as well as of the turning world. Consequently, Adam can refer to him as a "One" when he contrasts God's self-sufficiency with his own, which is in "unity defective" (8.425); but, when he considers his propagation "through all numbers absolute," the godhead must be understood as both the beginning and the end of an infinite number line hypothetically, but not actually, contained in himself. In human terms, God's unbounded progression thus remains traditionally limitless in being and eternity, although his freedom has now been untraditionally dispersed to the finite subjects who can both discursively and intuitively intersect with his free agency in historical time. Because this time's "motion . . . measures all things durable / By present, past, and future" (5.580–82), its agents are functionally analogous to Rotman's "algebraic subject," who by ranging over all number signs "performs an operation of closure on the infinite proliferation of number signs that come into being with zero."[38]

This variable and illusionistic "proliferation of number signs" thus explains the parallel between the baroque perspective of Milton's epic universe and that common to the contemporary art of the period. Both use visual illusion to suggest invisible enigmas, and both are based on "schema and correction" paradigms. As E. H. Gombrich describes them, these paradigms incorporate the observer's subjective response as an element of its spatial schema, which is no longer conceived as a static structure but as an interactive process.[39] Of course, the elements of this interchange can be conceived in a wide variety of ways besides Gombrich's schema and correction: Dennett's (or Darwin's) order and design, the physiologist's systole and diastole, or the physicist's or information theorist's entropy and negentropy are but a few of the feedback processes that baroque forms seem proleptically to forecast. These variously interrelated "loops" also underscore the fact that no material monism can dispense with a dialectic of elements that interactively create new horizons of being, which in Milton's case are supplied by the dialectic between self-designed and providentially ordered subjects. Just as in the temporal order finitude must somehow intersect with divine eternity and infinity, so in the material order chaotic dissolution (entropy) must be integrated with reorganization (negentropy) to accommodate open-ended life forms. As in Raphael's life tree, the chaotic disordering of energy within any given level of the organism must "benignly" dissolve energies that are negentropically resolved into higher phases of order, which, in Milton's animist universe, continuously "feed" on one another, much as the sun "alimentally" "sups with the Ocean" (*PL*, 5.423–26).

Thus once Galileo's system space makes position relative to direction and mass becomes relative to velocity, "one first matter" itself must be conceived as relative to its alternative forms. In such a cosmos, ascent may lead either to descent or vice versa without generating any "cardinal" reorientation in allegorical space. Lucifer's high eminence provides the ground of Satan's decay, but the Son's descent is grounded in a "more tragic" yet "higher argument" (*PL*, 9.6, 42) in which ascent complexly interacts with descent. In theological terms, meta-allegory also recuperates the original "depth" of the paradoxes latent in John's Hellenistic gospel, where from the beginning the Word "was life; and the life was the light of men. And the light shineth in the darkness; and the darkness comprehended it not. . . . And this is the condemnation, that light is come into the world, and men loved darkness rather than light, because their deeds were evil. For every one that doeth evil hateth the light, neither cometh to the light, lest his deeds should be reproved. But he that doeth truth cometh to the light, that his deeds may be made manifest, that they are wrought in God" (John 1:4–5, 3:19–21). These circular orientations—that light is life and (implicitly) height but that many choose darkness, depth, and death because of the great "height" (or depth?) of expectation they place on their deeds—are then fused with the newly boundless and disoriented spatial configurations of a relative universe, where ultimately neither original direction nor position can determine the efficient causes and effects driving material processes to manifest their consequences in time. Yet matter still immanently marks moral or cosmic "direction" in this allegorical continuum, which remains algebraically and/or perspectivally variable except in the last instance—when all deeds are made manifest and when the All in All at last supplies the correction of all schemas.

Thus, the reader's final "vision," like that of Adam and Eve themselves, models the immanently divine process in which all participate, that of a self-referentially "ruined" allegory of agency circumscribed by a characteristically diffused baroque light. In its quasi-infinite extensions, time and space are not ultimately erased, as they are in mystical or Augustinian allegories, but remain rhetorically foregrounded from first to last, from the initial void of creation to the final abyss of eternity. If no eye can fully measure such spaces, the baroque imagination can and does, by means of its restlessly displaced vanishing points. In conformity with the characteristic hermeneutic of late Protestantism, this displacement finally initiates the resolution of the poem's interlocking hierarchies of vertical ascent with its horizontal or organic axis of temporality. Yet the primacy of this temporal horizon has also been implicit from the first, as the opening invocation reveals. Beginning with the primordial spatial image of "the Fruit / of that Forbidden Tree" and its mountain garden in Eden, the narrative voice next invokes an ascending series of typological mountains associated with spiritual fulfillment: the successive mountains of Eve's "chosen Seed," all of which historically surpass "th' *Aonian* Mount" (*PL*, 1.15) despite its apparent priority in the "space" of our cultural hierarchies. Surmounting this Apollonian peak, the poet ascends still higher, past Eden's telluric dimension and Zion's Dionysian or "purgative" phase into the initiatory height of divine love, a mount of inspiration ultimately dissociated from any stable geography, for this summit exists only in the indeterminate space and time that "Thou O Spirit . . . dost prefer / Before all Temples" (1.17–18).

Yet even these spatiotemporal progressions are uniformly relative rather than absolute in that the coming of the "one greater Man" (*PL*, 1.4) fulfills not only all successive peaks of the biblical mountains of God—Eden (1.4), Oreb or Sinai (1.7), and Zion (1.10), the sites of inspiration, creation, or re-creation—but also the pagan prototypes associated with the "th' Aonian Mount," which, according to the invocation's finale, they had ironically always transcended (9.40–47). As James Whaler has shown, the interlocking spirals of this proleptic, recuperative, or backward- and forward-looking temporal horizon are far more typical of Milton's epic perspective than the route traced by Raphael's vertical axis of descent and reascent, although, structurally, the evolution of this classical descent from heaven ultimately follows the same pattern.[40] In either meta-allegorical framework, graphic visual images are constantly subordinated to a regularly revised, reframed, and relativized geographic "place," which culminates in the Dionysian dimension of continuous temporal recreation, a horizon negentropically fulfilled only in time, much as the infinitely modified mountain of light surrounding the temple of "th' upright heart and pure" (1.18) is at last "horizontally" fulfilled only by the "paradise within" (12.587).

Yet the spirit of these places is never mystically disembodied or decentered but rather regrounded in allegory's lower, more Dionysian and tellurian levels. Just as the Holy Spirit at last appears in its "true" image of a dove "with mighty wings outspread," so Raphael at last emerges from his phoenix shape in the "true" biblical form announced by his six Seraph wings, "his lineaments Divine" (*PL*, 5.278). Greatly simplifying the allegorical shape and identity of these figures in comparison to the ornately iconic or "daemonic" shapes of the nine muses of Aonia or the full emblematic regalia of "*Maia's son*" (5.285), the literal and symbolic meaning of such figures remains clear in outline if not in detail, for such baroque enigmas as the meaning of Raphael's six wings or of his "Heav'nly fragrance" (5.286) remain to be fleshed out by the observer.[41] Such efforts are far removed from the more normative allegorical task of repiecing emblematic mosaic puzzles since they consistently call for a triangulated perspective spatially mediating between the heights of a Spirit/ Muse who "didst inspire / That shepherd, who first taught the chosen Seed" (1.8) and the depths of the Holy Ghost, who "Dove-like satst brooding on the vast Abyss" (1.21). Temporally as well, they mediate between the coming of the "one greater Man" and his complex fulfillment of spiritual, aesthetic, and cosmological history, the history of a spirit from whose "view" "Heav'n hides nothing" (1.27). This perspective is by definition self-referential, for, unlike the muses of all previous epic poets, the identity of this presiding spirit is never clarified but instead deflected onto the ever-changing, although enduring, role of that great agent who, from first to last, from its pregnancy on the "vast Abyss" to its pregnancy at Pentecost, much like the poet himself mediates between God and creation. As the Dionysian vehicle of the poem, the poet's prayer must therefore guide the reader's accurate understanding through rhetorical imperatives rather than through images or emblems: "Instruct me, for Thou know'st," "What in me is dark/Illumine" (1.19, 22–23).

The result is a meta-allegorical progression from the vertical axis of ascent and fall (Eden, its "Forbidden Tree," and all "blissful seats" of gain or loss in heaven and earth) into a horizontal vista of successive typological fulfillments at key historical "peaks": the beginning of the universe, the formation of the earth and of Eden, and the seizure of the fruit and the beginning of "all our woe," which in turn leads to the semirestoration brought by law given on Mount Zion, the law's greater fulfillment in Christ, and the new seat of the Reformed temple, "th' upright heart and pure." Although these directions are horizontally shaped by a swiftly superimposed, shifting, and partially blurred series of images, the vertical aspect of the various "mountains" is never fully obscured; all are clearly imaged as heights that flow from the original "Abyss," even though some (like the fruit) also represent depths that must be negentropically renewed through a seed that, as Corinthians describes, "is not quickened, except it die" (1 Cor. 15:36).

However dizzying this baroque dialectic may appear, the integrity of its central perspective or vanishing point is guaranteed not only by the poet and his God but by the spiritual medium his words "enact," the radically "empty" spirit of immanent grace, the invisible chain linking all creation from Spirit to poet to reader, which, since it must everywhere counter its satanic antithesis, is operative even in hell.

First seen as an enormous, semi-indefinable Leviathan-like shape "floating many a rood" (*PL,* 1.196), the satanic first cause of "all our woe" (1.3) thus also resembles the universe he helps "author" in being both expandable and contractible, if not ultimately incalculable in time. To illustrate this temporal calculus, the epic's first book concludes with his satanic legions shrinking to the size of tiny insects, then expanding to the "bigness" of dwarfs and elves:

> Behold a wonder! they but now who seem'd
> In bigness to surpass Earth's Giant Sons
> Now less than smallest Dwarfs, in narrow room
> Throng numberless, like that Pigmean Race
> Beyond the *Indian* Mount, or Faery Elves. . . .
> (1.777–781)

Yet, even in this gloom, if not caught unawares like "some belated Peasant," the alert reader can still calculate the true proportions of these half-mythical, half-historical enchanters who transfix their victims only insofar as they are committed to the iconic fixity of Satan's "darkness visible," the human idols, priests, magi, and pseudo-philosophers who deal in appearances, that is, in the outward things or appearances opposed to infinite spirit and truth.

Less confined than defined by their function in time, the inhabitants of Pandaemonium thus have a size and shape only accurately determined by the dual coordinates of motion and direction. In conformity with the new physics governing Milton's epic universe, these coordinates are fully comprehensible only after their trajectory is temporally charted. At that point, their common denominator can be used to approximate their true shape, which is also their accurate "number" in relation to their "darkness visible":

> Thus incorporeal Spirits to smallest forms
> Reduc'd thir shapes immense, and were at large,
> Though without number still amidst the Hall
> Of that infernal Court. But far within
> And in thir own dimensions like themselves
> The great Seraphic Lords and Cherubim
> In close recess and secret conclave sat
> A thousand Demi-Gods on golden seats,
> Frequent and full.
> (*PL,* 1.789–97)

Even though their magic allows them to appear innocuously small in earthly moonlight or in "close recess and secret conclave," like man, God, and his faithful angels, these spirits can be charted by a "calculus" that reveals their "own dimensions like themselves." For, although their legions are "without number," their Lords and Cherubim total a thousand, a figure that points toward the typological equation situating them within the endlessly multiplied historical repetition of error, yet also limiting it *sub specie aeternitatis.* While one thousand is a number that may be appropriated by demons, it belongs ultimately only to the multiplicative power of their God, the zero function and center of all number lines. Thus, while their shapes can expand and contract throughout history by "the will / And high permission of all-ruling Heaven" (1.211–12), Christ's thousand-year reign will finally limit them in space and time. This knowledge of God's revealed word, which for both Milton and Pascal is confirmed by his free grace, is needed to supplement the objective calculus of their approximate spatial dimension, in itself a mere "Romance of Nature." Not a depth in the absolute sense (since the dove too broods on the abyss), this "place" can then be identified as the utter antithesis of the expansive and uplifting regions wherein God "deifies" his creatures: the contracting and diminishing depth where "that infernal Court" convenes "secret" and "close."

Far from constructing the transhistorical memorialization of Adam's lapse from sacred space into fallen time (a traditional allegory still too often associated with the Miltonic cosmos), this space/time clearly constructs an evolutionary world of becoming in which a sacramental world of Being is always already canceled. Yet, like Pascal's universe, this cosmos still supplies a Christian allegory of persuasion, not despite, but because of its expanded architectonics. Moreover, as Gombrich and Rotman remind us, the baroque calculus underlying this architecture still demands some degree of closure on the part of its "algebraic" subjects, which in baroque allegory is situated at the vanishing point of divine transcendence. Yet even this point is achieved only at the price of excluding the traditional certitudes of the Realist universe, the concentric hierarchies and precise polarities that generate the symbolically meaningful places of the old sacramental/allegorical system. Here, instead of the endless correspondences generated by this mode, we find only a "one first matter" in which all differences are of degree, not of kind, and where teleological closure is immanent and oblique, not externally fixed by an assured prospect of transcendence. As the unknowable center of this creation and the immanent coordinator of the two planes of nature and history that take his place, the All in All is both fully responsible for and fully absent from his creation. Yet, through the free agency of his most knowable analogue and "image," the human will and intelligence, this hidden God remains both probabilistically "grounded" in and hence "present" to the discursive intuition of the reader/observer engaged in constructing this freedom in her own image.

In calculating the true distance between the journey of this meta-allegorical subject and the ascent of the soul in more traditional or Neoplatonic allegories, one inevitably arrives at a remove paralleling the great gulf between Milton's Puritan God and the God of Augustine or Dante. Similarly, the cosmological distance of Milton's "allegory of persuasion" from philosophical Realism can be measured only disjunctively, as a profound rupture, a gap in which God's eternal space as an analogue of his sacred linguistic and sacramental signatures has yielded to an imperfect language operating within an indefinitely perfectible time. This distance is thus at least as great as that between the enclosed cosmos and the expanding universe—but in some sense even greater since it also registers the immense rupture between older and newer notions of causality. Here the old final causes, sacred signatures or cosmic "ex-ornations" of the universe, have been replaced, not only by the epic's expanding picture plane, but also by the reader's reflexive perception of his or her own role in foregrounding its relative "places" against the dominant horizon of providential time.

From the Allegorical Kosmos
to Miltonic Space *Rhetoric, Image, Code*

Is all good structure in a winding stair?

GEORGE HERBERT, "Jordan I"

1

Typically, the Miltonic image is spatial, but its most comprehensive form, as in the modulation of the angelic dance into the movement of the heavens, tends to echo the expanded universe that in both poetic and actual time it delineates. In this respect, its allegorical extensions imitate the new science of motion heralded by Galileo, a science in which spatial location is no longer static position but temporal movement within an essentially empty space. Its rhetorical corollary is a form of imagery that characteristically exhibits a tension or a torsion between an absent but idealized regularity and the irregularity that signifies the implicit presence of divine freedom, the moving content of its absent form. Those who have seen the winding pillars and restless outlines of late baroque ecclesiastical architecture can thus assimilate its sense of space in motion to the trajectory of the Miltonic image, whose movement is "regular / Then most, when most irregular" it seems (*PL,* 5.623–24). Ironically, then, the effect of Milton's poetic architecture can also be likened to the unstable structure of the great hall of its own Infernal Pandaemonium. Analogically extended into an allegory of the fallen symmetries of the concentric universe, such spatial forms can no longer be providentially resolved in either heaven or hell except in time, the measure of all.

Yet the effect of such restless space also creates a sense of rupture that is neither wholly fallen nor "ruined" insofar as providential time remains Milton's ultimate reality, the basis of his underlying allegorical "Idea." The elements of this idea are already present in *Areo-pagitica*, which expresses his positive conviction that, short of their final separation, the progress of good and evil in this world must be left to unravel itself on the winding stair of history. The work of Christian rhetoric is therefore to arouse a commensurate motion in the mind individually prepared to disentangle evil by recognizing that good is everywhere intertwined with it, even in the most irregular revolutions of Chaos or, more remarkably, in hell's Vallombrosa itself. In the form of God's shadows, traces, or signs, its reminders extend everywhere that the human mind reaches, whether in the valley of the shadow of death (Vallombrosa's literal meaning) or in the Tabernacle of the Sun, where Satan contemplates a shadowless world ironically "shaded" by the darker and more "Terrestrial Humor" of sunspots. If many of these images contain vestiges of the transcendental investments of the old closed cosmos, like its "daemonic" deities—in this case, exemplified by Proteus and the "Arch-chemic Sun" (*PL*, 3.610–20)—they are remodeled by the intricate convolution or torsion of their temporalized context. This convoluted motion threads a labyrinth between the depths wherein the mind creates "its own place" (1.254)—in its supreme subjectivity risking a devolution into the splendid yet also stark isolation of satanic pride—and the counterbalancing revolution apparent in the anointed Son, where, "without cloud / Made visible, th' Almighty Father shines" in the "conspicuous count'nance" that diffuses his reflection of divine love to the rest of creation (3.385–86).

These complexly coordinated vanishing points suggest that, while Milton's poem distantly looks forward to the end of philosophical certainty reflected in Wittgenstein's remarks on epic prophecy, closer to home it anticipates the complexly coordinated subjectivities of Leibniz's monads. Like Milton's vanishing points, these monads are connected only to the extent that each from its own perspectival stance (or degree zero) reflects the light of its intelligential relation to God as the Great Monad. From this common focal point sharing an intersubjective intuition of the incommensurable distances between themselves, such coordinates in some sense recapitulate the role of Milton's epic agents and images, for in this epic universe, as in Leibniz's philosophy, agents are fashioned by the "image" of the Great Monad in which they interactively "choose" to reflect themselves. This choice includes such opposite extremes as Adam's dim groping for a way to relate his awakened subjectivity to the mind of

God and Satan's diametrically opposite assertion of his own self-begottenness, his refusal to recognize any mind or time prior to the current subjective moment (*PL,* 5.859–60). A similar competition of conflicting perspectives within a potential but never fully realized harmony can be found in baroque art, which generally shares Milton's and Leibniz's concern with the problems of establishing the extensions and coordinates of subjective freedom within a newly relative or system space.

In Milton's poem, the hypothetical conjunction between the doubly absent presences of human freedom and divine grace is reflected in the verbal and imagistic interplay between the concepts *author, authority,* and *authentic.* Everywhere, Adam learns to realize, God as author is in the details surrounding his authentic observers; but nowhere, we come to realize, can Satan see the authoritative presences of God allusively adumbrated in the perspectives canceled by his self-imposed blindness. Thus, from Satan's self-chosen or "begotten" standpoint (*PL,* 5.860), the vast spaces of the universe become only more empty, whereas, for Adam's apperceptive or regenerate progeny, God is implicitly everywhere. As befits a cosmos bound together by forces Newton had not yet rationalized as gravitational, the "monads" of Milton's poetic universe remain free to determine their own center of gravity, which, like the signs relatively coordinating the cosmos, are neither static nor random but variably determinate.

As Milton's etymologizing rhetoric also implies, a balanced focal point of discursive and intuitive understanding allows subjects to become "authentically" authorial to the extent that they approach the Son's/sun's shadowless expression. Yet such expression is neither transparent nor static, for, just as authentic signs must strain to capture a cosmos fundamentally in motion, so authentic understanding must strain to reflect the essential ambiguity and metaphoricity of the ultimate Author. Thus, emblems that in a more normative allegory would restrain their ambivalent "meaningfulness" by deflecting their significance onto the higher mysteries incipient in their source are here expanded into more vitalistic or fully virtualized forms of verisimilitude. The difference is simple but profound: where traditional allegory presents a speculum or "dark glass" that is ultimately to be discarded so that we may see the divine or Real world "face to face" (1 Cor. 13:12), Milton's baroque allegory presents a monistic continuum where God's images remain forever "transfus'd," diffused, or darkened by his disappearance into the "Begotten Son, Divine Similitude," in whom "th' Almighty Father shines" but "Whom else no Creature can behold" (*PL*, 3.389, 384–87). Thus, where the emblematic abstractions of normative allegory strain toward an ornate "clarity" that signals their synthesis of the successive levels or veils of a reality that is to be unveiled in the penultimate instant, Milton's allegorical figures strain toward a vitalistic obscurity, a transmutation of spatial figures into the play of a final paranomasia whose formal blurring of semantic distinctions mimetically tends toward the ambiguity of the real.

If this virtually mimetic use of metaphor has often caused Milton's epic rhetoric to be superficially confused with the form of naturalization prescribed by neoclassicism, its ultimate difference from the concretized abstractions or "sensuous analogisms" of the later mode is actually profound—as Johnson's *Life* shows he was well aware. For Milton's figures are never merely decorative in the rationalistic manner recommended in Johnson's famous critique of Milton's Sin and Death episode. Here, as in allegory generally, he suggests, if "Fame tells a tale and Victory hovers over a general or perches on a standard[,] Fame and Victory may do no more."[1] Yet, because not only Sin and Death but all the poem's images represent vital interactions with the "track divine" (*PL*, 11.349), much like Milton's God, the Miltonic metaphor never conducts merely an abstract law, fate, or symbolic effect but the potentially active or immanent agency at work within the "Divine Similitude." Its indeterminate figuration therefore resists any more than hypothetical resolution in either time or eternity precisely because its variability signals an oblique resonance with divine grace. This free grace also informs the "adventitious" play that Johnson perceptively recognized in the poem: the free play between the Word as inspired or "true sign" and the word as independent monad derived but also detached from its divine source. These tensions too are characteristic of baroque allegory, which, as we have seen, bridges the gulf between the extremes of philosophical Realism, where the lost language of Adam is deemed obscurely if actually present in signs, and nominalism, where signs are relegated to the role of arbitrary human creations with no intrinsic relation to things. The intermediate mode of the baroque spans this enormous gap by regarding language as retaining the remnants of an original or divinely imparted "code," although not through the magical or "hieroglyphic" correspondences that translate Spenser's syncretically layered "forests" of symbolic meaning.

Thus, as in the central incident discussed in chapter 1, where Milton surrounds Sin with the polysemous connotations of a sinister "sign portentous" (*PL*, 2.760–61), he does not exclude the verbal mazes implicit in this pun but rationally underscores them through mimetic rather than hermetic means.[2] Rather than leading us through ever deeper labyrinths resolved by a numinously transcendent icon, the poet supplies the key to what this ominous portent portends through her literal "fruits." No longer an emblem mystically figured by her name or her insignia, unlike Spenser's Errour Milton's Sin does not require even a "semiveiled" etymology as an extraneous key to her unriddling. Yet, also unlike Johnson's Fame or Victory, neither she nor his lowercase *error* can be reduced to a univocal sign. With quasi-Spenserian inscrutability, Milton continues to pun on error as a form of "wandering" even in the very midst of Eden, although its "mazy error under pendant shades" also pointedly refuses the segregations that his great "original's" "nice Art" (4.239–41) would demand. The effect is not merely to cancel Spenser's ritual boundaries but also to cancel one form of visual depth in favor of another.[3] Now, gone with the confinement of Errour to her cave is that hidden key, that "ungraspable third term," that "mysterious geometric depth" in the heart of a natural space that normative allegory conceives as a divine labyrinth threaded by mysterious signatures of Being.

In Milton's epic, we find instead the fully naturalized baroque space of becoming that Alberto Pérez-Gómez traces to the influence of the new science and its "thinning and objectification of space . . . assumed to be transparent to mathematical reason." Yet, much as in Milton's Eden, the numinous itself has not disappeared but is instead "theatrically" transformed by the human world's new self-referentiality. As in meta-allegory generally, a residue of the older mysteries remains as a thin patina of "metaphysical light" created by resolving various "points of epiphany . . . [or] perspective vanishing points . . . [where] the sacred or profane representation attained its supreme coherence and meaning." Thus, "much less ambiguously than in the Renaissance, man now contemplated the space of God, represented exclusively as a geometrical entity. . . . To experience this epiphany, human beings literally had to leave aside their bodies and binocular vision, to assimilate themselves with the geometric vanishing point—now truly a 'point at infinity.'"[4] These remarks aptly summarize the fundamental intellectual-historical processes at work as the expanded cosmos passes into the expanded images of Milton's epic: a naturalization of space that in its initial phases tends to replace one form of ambiguity or depth with another. As Renaissance mysteries of concentric space generally give way to baroque mysteries of perspectival extension and displacement in time, so Spenser's tightly encoded mysteries are replaced by Milton's Ramist expansion of vestigially enigmatic etymologies.

The "archetypally" paradoxical passage in question here thoroughly exemplifies this metamorphosis,[5] as Eden's "nether Flood" emerges from "his darksome passage" to divide into "four main Streams," all of which merge in a single

> Sapphire Fount [whose] . . . crisped Brooks,
> Rolling on Orient Pearl and sands of Gold,
> With mazy error under pendant shades
> Ran Nectar, visiting each plant, and fed
> Flow'rs worthy of Paradise which not nice Art
> In Beds and curious Knots, but Nature boon
> Pour'd forth profuse on Hill and Dale and Plain,
> Both where the morning Sun first warmly smote
> The open field, and where the unpierc't shade
> Imbrown'd the noontide Bow'rs. . . .
> (*PL*, 4.231–33, 237–46)

In this unfolding space receding into "unpierc't" and ineffable distances, a benignly "boon" nature communicates its vital ambiguity to a language in which "mazy error" announces only a positive sense of rupture with the older, enclosed sense of space; fountains liberally spill on sands that their subliming waters turn to pearl and gold, while the infinite bounty of Edenic vegetation spontaneously receives the nectar that it in turn distills. Although this baroque circulation is far less constrained than the "nice Art" and "curious Knots" of Renaissance emblematism, it is not entirely less enigmatic. In place of the overcoded, self-contained, and/or "daemonically" segregated puzzles of the emblem book or impresa, the Miltonic metaphor generates puns framed by the reader's self-referential awareness that these innocent mazes of vegetative delight will ultimately yield erroneous mazes not unlike those of the demons (2.561), overly confining or self-contained labyrinths that lead to greatly diminished forms of wandering in a number of interrelated senses.

To guide the reader through these alternate mazes, the winding branches of Ramist dialectic chart the variable courses of wandering by linking root cause to consequence through a complex chain of "efficient" or intermediate causes. The allegorical relation to *etymon* or *truth* established by this metonymic chain is not only more literally etymological and less fancifully figurative but also more logically (rather than mythopoetically) expansive. In place of the often bizarre polyglot etymologies that the earlier Renaissance employed in the "hieroglyphic" associationalism of its correspondences, as in the above example, the "flow charts" implicit in Milton's Ramistic form of punning foreground the root English sense of words *alongside* their Latin derivations. Thus, the Latinate "error" or wandering of Edenic nature simultaneously indicates a classical labyrinth or maze, a straying that might go astray, and also an uncontained or open exploration utterly unlike the caves of Errour or of Minotaur: a simply "amazing" or wondrous display of nature's endlessly fecund playfulness.

Another example of this unhermetic etymologizing occurs in the self-referential range of play on the words *safe* and *safety* in the late poems generally, but particularly in the "risky" middle passages of his invocational descents from light: "thee I revisit safe" (*PL*, 3.21); "with like safety guided down" (7.15); "More safe I Sing, with mortal voice unchang'd" (7.24). Here, *safety* carries the evident or plain sense of a protection from danger alongside the Puritan significance attached to its Latin or salvific sense. As used by one of the Miltonic Smectymnuans, Stephen Marshall, the latter sense provides a key pun in his sermon before the House of Commons, where he turns the common political dictum of *salus populi suprema lex* into a new supreme law of *salus*, where the principle sense of *safety* now concerns the people's *salvation*.[6] This double sense of safety also invokes as its binary opposition the double sense of *ruin*, which in Milton's usage retains within the English noun of destruction the Latin verb *to fall*, the poet checking his own potentially "erroneous . . . wander[ing]" and downward "fall" by virtue of the "safety" offered by the ultimate inspirational "cause" of his poem in divine grace (7.20). These opposing vanishing points of "ruin" and "safety" are mediated by the indeterminacy of irregularity and error, whose variable place values in the relative spaces of heaven, earth, and hell are caused or "propelled" by the differing "weight," "force," or (in its own multiple sense) "virtue" of its agents' choices.

We have no difficulty, and Milton even less, with the resonance of such doubled or amplified language, but in both post-Restoration prose and neoclassical epic, the Cartesian preference for the plain sense of clear and distinct language tended to prevail over a metaphysical or baroque style that was waning even as he composed his poem. In the dogma of the Royal Society as well as that of many contemporary theologians, this preference commonly dominated even the meaning of Eden, with the result that recovering its language was often "scientifically" equated with overturning the "ruins" of Babel. Yet Milton counters these canons in a way that also parallels many of his epic's aims. By exalting a rationalized form of metaphoric ambiguity, he too seeks a form of mimesis that would at least partially regather the scattered limbs of Osiran truth. Yet, as he warns in *Areopagitica,* in these remnants lie "so many cunning resemblances hardly to be discern'd, that those confused seeds which were imposed on *Psyche* as an incessant labour to cull out, and sort asunder, were not more intermixt" (*CPW,* 2:549, 514). Thus, as opposed to the Cartesian rationalists, Milton attempts to rejoin the literal and the figural poles inherent in all verbal art, not by reducing, but by amplifying the connections between these falsely sundered poles.

Here, of course, as earlier in *Of Reformation,* he seems to have imagined the potential for more complete correspondences, a "concurrence of signs" apparent first to the most "holy and devout men," furthered by others "trying all things, assenting to the force of reasons and convincement," and concluding in "some new and great period in his Church, ev'n to the reforming of Reformation itself" (*CPW,* 2:553–54). While the revolutionary fervor coloring this view of divine signs did not last, there is no doubt that he later clung to a similar if still more oblique conception of God's ongoing, emergent revelations. Of course, after the Restoration, it was also obviously more safe to sing of God's providence in the equivocal language of baroque epic-allegory; but it is equally clear that this language remains relatively consistent with the principles earlier advocated by the dissenting ministers with whom Milton was associated, the brethren of the Westminster Assembly. As they put the case for the proper human response to the uncertainties of the light shed by the "candle of the Lord" on history, in

all such cases wherein we saw not a cleare resolution from Scripture, example or direction, we still professedly suspended, untill God should give us further light, . . . we having this promise of grace for our encouragement in this, . . . that in *thus* doing the will of God we should *know* more.

A second Principle we carried along with us in all our resolutions, was, Not to make our present judgement and practice a binding law unto our selves for the future . . . to alter and retract (though not lightly) whatever should be discovered to be taken up out of a misunderstanding.[7]

This emergent or "suspended" view of human accountability to divine providence as conducted by the aroused spiritual/linguistic sense should be contrasted with the Hobbesian version of Cartesian epistemology, where all such exercises of "subjective imagination" constitute error pure and simple.[8] Nor is this view of the imagination wholly original to Hobbes since many of its biases can be traced to the Augustinian tradition that Sidney's *Defence of Poetry* counters and Calvinism reinvigorates. In the latter, as in Spenser's idiosyncratic synthesis of Neoplatonic and Calvinist conceptions of the sign, *wandering* is archaically linked to error and error to evil, which, like the unrestrained imagination, is in the eyes of God ultimately nothing—simply an absurdity, a nonexistent illusion.[9] Here, Milton's epistemological position is once again more linguistically and historically "mixt": because his divine signs point to no wholly preordained sacramental or empirical reality, the imagination may be "irregularly" inspired as well as misled. As a result, this position virtually defines the baroque attitude toward the word as an ambiguous vehicle of becoming in which the realm of Being has been infinitely displaced. The same twisting stair of winding and wandering language that leads to the fall of the "infernal Serpent" in "ruin and combustion down" (*PL*, 1.34, 46) also leads upward, away from Eve's collateral ruin into a new maze or wilderness that in time regenerates her seed as from "a second stock" (12.7), although, like all successive forms of regeneration, this process remains virtually endless and hence intrinsically "mazy."

A suggestion of how such a "sinuously" intertwined language manages to retain at least the outlines of allegory's geometrizing effects is found in the pedagogical aims of Milton's *Of Education*, which purports to outline a program capable of repairing "the ruins of our first parents." Because the results of these ruins are originally interwoven with the combustive "ruin" of Satan, they can be overcome, not by erasing his language or its imaginings, but only by reversing his course: "by regaining to know God aright, and out of that knowledge to love him, to imitate him, to be like him, as we may the neerest by possessing our souls of true vertue, which being united to the heavenly grace of faith makes up the highest perfection" (*CPW,* 2:366–67). The movement here from a literal description to an implicit personification of "vertue" and "faith" also suggests their conjunct capacity to unite letter and spirit in a newly synthetic "soul." This implicit personification of the cardinal virtues is of course almost unavoidable within Christian discourse, yet when he so chooses Milton will dramatically expand the power and limits of its analogies to the extent that his Ramist logic and rhetoric will bear. In defending his views on divorce to Parliament, he warns: "Advise yee well, supreme Senat, if charity be thus excluded and expulst, how yee will defend the untainted honour of your own actions and proceedings: He who marries, intends as little to conspire his own ruine, as he that swears Allegiance; and as a whole people is in proportion to an ill Government, so is one man to an ill marriage" (*CPW,* 2:229). If strained, this analogy does not burst its limits, causing his audience to conclude that "charity" demands that the laws of national allegiance should be as revocable as those of the marital bond, but rather the reverse: here, the domestic sphere becomes the microcosmic image of the national macrocosm in a new and dramatically vital sense, extending from the bottom (or common household) level upward, rather from the top (or royal household) downward. Because good marriages create good citizens, the elastic social contract governing both should be designed to ensure Milton's vastly expanded valorization of interpersonal virtue or good intention as both the literal and figurative root of public "safety."

This upwardly propulsive sense of repairing "ruins" at once contrasts with the predominantly downward and hierarchic focus of the older macrocosm of eternal truth and creates the new context of the poet's dynamic, Dionysian struggle to regenerate linguistic truth. Rather than merely being "in-formed" by his heavenly muse, he must also struggle to inform his readers by discrediting the mystifications of false muses and false Orpheuses, lest he fall onto "th' *Aleian* Field . . . / Erroneous there to wander and forlorn" (*PL,* 7.19–20). His success in escaping a fate that would also leave him fatuously "rapt above the pole" (7.23) depends on avoiding both the superstitious logic of Calliope—the mother of the old Orpheus or Apollo of Neoplatonic tradition, whose "Muse" now fails to "defend / her Son" (7.37–38)—and the absurdly anti-imaginative logic of the nominalists and Calvinists, from whom he parts company by calling on his muse's higher "meaning, not the Name" (7.5). In short, allegory is not a Pegasean horse that will throw the poet, for his language is possessed of a libertarian sense of invention that goes far beyond the abbreviated poetic license or "fancy" authorized by either the main-line Christian or the neoclassical tradition. In this respect, he has become even more a poetic "maker" than Sidney's *Defense of Poetry* would authorize since Sidney's theory merely grants poets the priv-ilege of reflecting or recapitulating the role of the greater maker with whose spirit the narrative voice now actively participates. By Diony-sianly pitting himself against both the old enclosed space of hermetic correspondences and the literalistic tables of nominalist empiricism, the poet thus ultimately propels himself beyond their limits into the new imagistic trajectory whose "adven'trous Song, / . . . with no middle flight intends to soar / Above th' *Aonian* Mount, while it pursues / Things unattempted yet in Prose or Rhyme" (1.13–16).[10]

2

Yet fully to explore Milton's double deviation from the older and newer rhetorical modes operative in his period will require a far more specific discussion of how his metaphorized and metonymized alle-gorical figures come to constitute the kind of tertium quid I am sug-gesting. Here, we turn first to the normative function of the allegori-cal "kosmos," which, as outlined by Angus Fletcher, functions as both a microcosmic fragment and an ornament of the macrocosm: as indicating both the "*large-scale order* (macrocosmos) and the small-scale *sign of that order* (macrocosmos)." These interlocking functions provide the source both of the normative emblem's power and its limitations: its lack of "mimetic naturalness" combined with its abil-ity "to force . . . [the] reader into an analytic frame of mind." A similar logic governs its normative visual effects, which (as typically in Spenser) if surreally intensified to the point of artificiality, also in turn signal their emblematic authority. Measuring Milton's allegori-cal figures against this standard produces paradoxical results: while the multiple frames of his etymological elaborations certainly gener-ate something like Fletcher's "analytic frame of mind," the organic functions of his images make them closer to the tropes he identifies with "true metaphor." In contrast, the normative kosmos characteristically "produces something at the same time deader than the lively effects of metaphor and clearer than those effects. When allegory is called 'pure,' the adjective implies that it lacks ambiguity in the same way that a diagram essentially lacks it. For the suggestiveness and intensity of ambiguous metaphorical language allegory substitutes a sort of figurative geometry." Although by no means the univocal mental shorthand that Coleridge's mistaken understanding of allegory disparages, such signs do chart something like a geometric "map" of the oppositions and correspondences coordinating their figurative universes.[11]

Thus, while the dichotomy necessary to such figuration may be suggestively polysemous in a surreal sense, its diagrammatic context deprives it of the indefinite expansion and resonance inherent in metaphor per se. For, as Paul de Man's definition further specifies, the true metaphoric figure does not set "up an adequation between two experiences" but

deploys the initial experience into an infinity of associated experiences that spring from it. In the manner of a vibration spreading in infinitude from its center, metaphor is [thereby] endowed with the capacity to situate the experience at the heart of a universe that it generates. It provides the ground rather than the frame, a limitless anteriority that permits the limiting of a specific entity. . . . Far from referring back to an object that would be its cause, the poetic sign sets in motion an imaging activity that refers to no object in particular. The meaning of the metaphor is that it does not "mean" in any definite manner.[12]

Yet of course Milton's epic metaphors do "mean," even though the expanded medium of their message vastly dilates the relational "pull" between tenor and vehicle. As in the case of the teleology semantically "ruined" by baroque allegory, generally, any transcendental adequation of tenor and vehicle has become wholly problematic, if not erased. As in Milton's miniature allegory of Isis and Osiris, the set of fragments that should be reassembled only further fragments, as if permanently to confound the identification that both normative allegory and the Cartesian system of signs seek by means of their opposing linguistic logics.

As observed above, both these logics exhibit the Judeo-Christian tradition's dominant bias against metaphor as ultimately superfluous. Ideally, the "figurative use of words does not add or produce anything new, but cancels itself out. Figures of speech are thus merely ornaments and not generators of meaning."[13] Milton's poetics are often erroneously placed in this general framework, not only because of his dominant place in the English metaphysical and religious traditions, but also because his work verges on the period in which its classical ideals were about to be restated in the privileged terms of modern philosophy and science—the Lockean/Newtonian ideals of noiseless communication, which collaterally established the standards of professional literary criticism. As an heir of both traditions, Douglas Bush logically analogized Milton's Tree of Life to Yeats's "artifice of eternity" as an image of self-effacing, transcendental stasis, in the process creating a paradigm of his poetics still maintained long after the waning of his Christian humanist school of interpretation. To appreciate precisely how the force of the Miltonic metaphor does *not* lie in its ability to project bodily forms "out of nature" and far from "any natural thing" ("Sailing to Byzantium," line 25), as Bush assumed, a concrete reinvestigation of the general process by which Milton's paradisal symbols bloom their "vegetable gold" should also usefully dispel the equally persistent idea that Milton's rhetoric creates a landscape under erasure or, in Stanley Fish's terms, a "self-consuming artifact." For, insofar as its motions can be isolated at all, the "winding stair" of Milton's baroque allegory actually moves in precisely the reverse direction: not toward the refinement and eventual effacement of a Neoplatonic ladder of truth, but toward ever more naturalistically expansive, metaphorically ambiguous, yet also concrete definition.[14]

Rather than ascending, the poem's readers must therefore retrace the trajectory of invocational descent explored above: a direction that in imagistic terms provides an unusually vitalistic experience of meta-allegory's virtual reality, the self-reflexive baroque mode outlined by Pérez-Gómez. In contrast, most critics still adhere to the influential model outlined by Fish and Anne Davidson Ferry, which is essentially in conformity with Bush's assessment. Here the Miltonic image continues to conform to the standard laws of Christianity and Neoplatonism, whose suspicion of metaphor is then expanded to include Milton's "antiallegorical" practice.[15] Like most post-Romantic critics, Ferry thus draws an especially sharp line between the "fallen" allegorical images and the highly refined "sacred metaphors" of *Paradise Lost*. Yet, as in the case of Coleridge, her drastic separation of these "impure" and hence ultimately illusory and empty emblems of sin (allegory) from Milton's truly "living" metaphors or sacred symbols confuses the very terms she would define. If, as she argues, the symbol's dynamic mingling of "essence and quality, thing and meaning," is ultimately "frozen" into an abstract identification with "the world made by God," then she is actually assigning the symbol the transcendental stasis belonging to the allegorical emblem. As in Bush's "artifice of eternity," the presumed vitalism of Milton's "symbolic" poetics is thus falsely identified with Christianity's characteristic attempt to transcend the literal in the metaphysical Word; and so, in place of the kinesthetic dynamism of the baroque image, the reader of *Paradise Lost* supposedly discovers an archetypal world of mystified metaphors that doubly bond abstract with concrete qualities. Here Ferry argues that the essentially allegorical correspondences of what she insists are Milton's "sacred symbols" exclude secondary qualities in order to emphasize essential conditions: locations and duration rather than colors, shapes, or surfaces. The result is a language so stripped of extensive or conflicting connotations that the terms of the metaphor become fully reversible: "By joining a concrete and an abstract noun . . . , Milton equates them; each borrows the properties of the other, like the terms in a metaphor. . . . [Thus,] the place is not an invention to depict the feeling, nor the feeling simply an explanation of the place."[16]

Here, Ferry's practical observations are far more discriminating than her theory, which goes a long way toward explaining their influence. Nevertheless, at the theoretical level, two characteristic problems besetting this general view of Milton's poetics quickly emerge. The first has already been noted; although she hardly realizes it, Ferry's rhetorical theory actually describes the allegorical poetics far more accurately associated with Dante or Spenser than with Milton. As Fletcher's anatomy details, once concrete and abstract terms of a metaphor merge, the result is a "fixed" image conducting the personifying functions of allegory, a key element in its construction of transcendent symbols. The second problem is also clarified by Fletcher's analysis. Although the synthesis of part/whole relations (synecdoche) with cause/effect relations (metonymy) is common to all "teleologically ordered speech," for an image actually to be stabilized into an abstract personifying function it must be systematically isolated from naturalistic contexts and included in a network of "large-scale double meaning." The real question that must then be confronted by a novel rhetorical approach to the Miltonic image is how it avoids the normatively iconic, isolated, and static ritual landscape characteristic of the mode, which (as Fletcher would also agree) has already been "ruined" in Milton's early masque.[17] Further, if elements of this practice continue in *Paradise Lost,* then how do the poetic personae and their motives, feelings, convictions, and concepts generally fail to be personified as "things," even while natural things continue to act as allegorical vehicles interchangeably translating the moral conditions of subjects into the physical status of objects? For Ferry seems clearly right in observing that, instead of conveying an order that resides elsewhere, the Miltonic image reverses the process so that "the place is not an invention to depict the feeling, nor the feeling simply an explanation of the place."

One solution to these questions is suggested by returning to my initial thesis that the paradoxes of Milton's "allegorical" images parallel those of his God; although they are not, like him, eternal, they are, like the *imago dei* imparted to his agents, "Sufficient to have stood though free to fall" (*PL,* 3.99). Only in this "monadic" sense are Milton's allegorical metaphors "isolated," although they are never fixed, "ritual," or "mosaic" in the manner Fletcher finds characteristic of normative allegory.[18] Unlike the mosaic's flat, iconic surface or the geometric design coordinating allegory's self-contained images according to a preconceived, authoritarian pattern, the only mosaic created by his baroque poesis consists of mutably "dark with excessive bright" (3.380) images. Relayed by a receding series of oxymorons, this anti-iconic chiaroscuro institutes patterns of shifting light and motion that characteristically create the illusion of perspectival depth. By refusing to resolve themselves into any stable hierarchy, Milton's tropes further disperse into panoramic distances where they acquire the ambiguous aura of semiconcrete indices of the divine circulation between concrete and abstract properties. These effects stand in clear contrast to those of normative allegory, which, as Maureen Quilligan remarks, usually creates a mosaic "maze" of allusive paths supplemented by external signposts or keys to guide its readers back to some unifying center, some central "mount of contemplation."[19] Instead, in *Paradise Lost* the immanent source and meaning of its teleology emerge gradually, naturalistically, and utterly apart from any even hypothetical stasis in eternity, the "abyss, / . . . whose end no eye can reach" (12.555–56). Before that end lies the entirety of the epic's development, its linear, historical impetus constructing visual and verbal fields whose relation is relentlessly subject to reinterpretation and change.

Nevertheless, the fluidity resulting from this vital and highly nuanced freedom does not fully attain the degree of concrete definition or frameless anteriority that for de Man defines the "true" metaphor, although it does borrow a considerable degree of its visual self-realization. For, like God's other emanations, the Miltonic metaphor attests to its divine source through its indeterminacy, the only visible imprint of the "track divine" on creation. Thus, much as Milton uses the hierarchies of the Peripatetic universe as symbolic signpoints to point away from their traditional unification, so he employs the language of "hermetic correspondences and signatures" of the earlier hexameral tradition as semierased images on which to superimpose a largely naturalized continuum.[20] As in so much else, this practice is continuous with the antinomian tendencies of radical Protestantism, which Keith Stavely argues produces "an appreciation of natural process that verged upon pantheism." But, because this affirmation of a universe in which "every creature hath a beam of God's glory in it" is at once pre-Romantic and postutopian, in *Paradise Lost* it produces an even more exaggerated opacity of signs than the overt pantheism of Romantic neoallegory. Moreover, because Milton's Calvinist understanding of divine Providence and election is ambiguated by his Arminian or "free will" theology, his emphasis on the free responsibility of subjects is transferred into the unusual freedom of images whose teleology is not mystically "present" but indefinitely displaced onto an "emergent" course of history.[21] Thus, in his epic, as in the Protestant view of signs that Milton both inherits and advances, God is discerned only through the language or the agency of a synecdochic "word" converted into metonymic process or efficient *effect*.

With this theory in mind, we then revisit the scene that has either directly or indirectly provided the standard exemplum of Milton's reputedly static landscape. For, if we are to ascertain whether his poetic images participate in the functions of the normative allegorical emblem, where "language foregoes its autonomous creative value and assumes a symbolic significance," or whether his images form a vitalistic "correction" to such schemas, then surely Eden's tree of immortal life should supply the archetypal test case.[22] Here, in God's holy garden of symbols,

> Out of the fertile ground he caus'd to grow
> All Trees of noblest kind for sight, smell, taste;
> And all amid them stood the Tree of Life,

High eminent, blooming Ambrosial Fruit
Of vegetable Gold. . . .
(*PL*, 4.216–20)

The first clue that the tree's "vegetable gold" does not actually exemplify Bush's frozen poetic time is the unusual use of *blooming*, a
verbal usage that avoids intransitives by converting a present participle into an active verb.[23] By later linking its active fruits to the
"bright consummate flow'r" (5.481) of Raphael's universal life tree,
the reader can further glimpse an eternity entirely subsumed in its
own bloom-, fruit-, and seed-producing cycle. As Raphael will soon
explain, the way to both divinity and eternity is as metonymically
material as the simultaneously mental and physical "fruits" of obedience. This Edenic tree prepares for that lesson by depicting the
immortality "blooming" on the Tree of Life as a life chain of concretely divine processes to be felt and tasted, not a static edifice or
ladder to be climbed. Existing both for themselves and for the whole,
the parts of this chain are isolated neither from each other nor from
the whole; rather, they develop in and through time, the vehicle
of the endless processes of evolution and devolution (5.469–70), but
never of an atemporal eternity. Semantically, this process remains
allegorical in essence; but, imagistically, it has become largely naturalistic in function.

With this in mind, it becomes easy to see that the capacity of
Eden's "high eminent" Tree of Life simultaneously to "bloom" and
bear fruit is not halted or canceled by its paradoxical "vegetable
gold." Despite its oxymoronic form, this fruit is mystical only in its
adventitious expansion into pantheistic directions, for *vegetable* refuses to function as a fixed adjective or even as a "clarifying" substitution of a noun for an adjective, but, like *gold* (ambiguously either a
color or a precious metal), it seems to be both and neither. Yet, even
if on the basis of word order we assumed that *vegetable* must in some
sense modify *gold*, because it also acts as an appositive for the ambrosial *Fruit*, no stable identification is actually possible. As Ferry
would suggest, each term fluidly modifies the other, nouns "diffusing" into their signifying kinds or colors and returning to their adjectival "stems," but without establishing a stable hierarchy of cause and
effect. Does the vegetableness of the gold define its transcendent
value, or does the enigmatic gold hidden in the vegetable (eternal
life) magically create this immortal "Fruit"? Either possibility, or

both, is plausible. Thus, while J. B. Broadbent has pejoratively compared Milton's Tree of Life to the paradisal tree of Marvell's "Bermudas," in many ways Milton's "vegetable gold" image is actually far more animate and indeterminate than the transposed biblical emblematism of Marvell's "golden lamps in a green night."[24]

In further contrast to the more conventional neo-Edenic symbolism of the Marvellian orange tree, as a fruit, the ambiguous golden color, shape, and kind of Milton's "vegetable gold" is also more "fertilely" expansive. Leaving the qualities of apple, pear, peach, or more exotic fruit to be filled in by the reader, the poet is able to suggest all and none. Similarly, while its golden essence or texture must somehow act as the vehicle of its golden value or luster, the ambiguous fluidity of these properties suggests their generically but also concretely organic functions. Instead of an "artifact" of Eden's unfolding age of gold, the fruit thus represents the ripening "food" of a vitally blooming life process inherently linked to every "natural thing." Because here the organic cycles of temporality, not their eternal stasis, transmit the divine aura of its golden fruition, Eden's ephemerality has become the very medium of its holy or "golden" purity, itself merely the outward expression of a vital immortality that can be transacted only in the immanent sanctities of earthly space and time. Hence, as Michael Fixler remarks of another aspect of Eden, here even the sharing of food between men and angels is "deliberately calculated to inhibit any symbolic—and therefore [traditionally] sacramental—resonance to the action." As a result, the poem's sacramental character is "generally symbolic and diffused, as if communication had for Milton replaced communion. A sacrament for Milton was a visible seal of great significance, but any man might offer it, and in any form representing God's mercies to the elect."[25] Through a suggestive opacity that cancels extensive allegorical correspondences by deferring them onto the circulation of things, their colors, their textures, their temporality, and their freedom, the teleological design of the poetic image is also comparably diffused.

Nevertheless, it should also be conceded that Bush's association of Milton's Edenic vegetation with the imagery of Yeats's magical tree and its golden bird, one "such . . . as Grecian goldsmiths make / Of hammered gold and gold enamelling" ("Sailing to Byzantium," lines 27–28), was not entirely fanciful. Most probably it was suggested by the reader's introductory glimpse of the garden, where, nestled within ranks of "Shade above shade," we find that, within the "verdurous wall of Paradise" (*PL*, 4.141–43)

> And higher than that Wall a circling row
> Of goodliest Trees loaden with fairest Fruit,
> Blossoms and Fruit at once of golden hue
> Appear'd, with gay enamell'd colours mixt:
> On which the Sun more glad impress'd his beams
> Then in fair Evening Cloud, or humid Bow,
> When God hath show'r'd the earth; so lovely seem'd
> That Lantskip. . . .
> (4.146–53)

Commenting on this scene, even Stavely concludes that "here is a vision of static perfection if there ever was one, the yearly cycle transcended in a perpetual synthesis of spring, summer, and autumn." Despite the pantheistic currents he finds elsewhere, for him the garden's "gay enamelled colours mixt" here suggest essentially the same sort of artifice that occurred to Bush, Ferry, and Fish: "Paradise . . . [as] a work of art, a mythic construct, that . . . belongs to the venerable tradition of our imagined forms of escape from vicissitude and struggle." To recuperate the "divine vitality and purpose" he finds in both the poem's medium and message, Stavely therefore argues that the surrounding similes (4.159–71) serve to disrupt and frame this stasis as a satanic temptation—a "self-canceling" strategy he evidently learned from Fish.[26]

The problem with this reading is threefold: it fails to convince first because we see nearly all of Eden over Satan's shoulder, so to speak; second because Stavely ignores the subsequent allegorical figure of the dance of Pan as a synthetic space/time figure; and third because he (like Bush) ignores a powerful alchemical tradition that, going back to Plato's *Timaeus,* takes "gold" as a quintessentially "protean" element exemplifying the very essence of natural transformability. In the character of the scene as dance, we again note that *Pan* is a name for God in nature, the "all"-creating Word inspiring the play of the Graces and the Hours, the latter being the Horae or the seasonal as well as the daily cycle. As Milton employs them, these figures, like those of the Graces, serve as consummate images of the natural harmonization of space and time, the Graces also personifying motions of God's descending and ascending grace such as the seraphim downwardly and cherubim upwardly mediate. The implication, albeit allusively hidden, is that paradisal perfection, which Milton elsewhere represents as the blissful dance of the blessed "quaternion'd" in heaven, remains essentially kinetic rather than static: not "cloy'd with repetition of that which is prescrib'd," but "orb[ing] it selfe into a thousand vagancies of glory and delight, and with a kinde of eccentricall equation be as it were an invariable Planet of joy and felicity" (*The Reason of Church-Government, CPW,* 1:752). Thus, in both poetry and prose, Milton characteristically lacks any sense of the homology of significant forms of divine revelation except within a dynamic nature, a pattern reaffirmed as the angels celebrate the Son's anointing

> In song and dance about the sacred Hill,
> Mystical dance, which yonder starry Sphere
> Of Planets and of fixt in all her Wheels
> Resembles nearest, mazes intricate,
> Eccentric, intervolv'd, yet regular
> Then most, when most irregular they seem:
> And in thir motions harmony Divine
> So smooths her charming tones, that God's own ear
> Listens delighted.
> (*PL,* 5.619–27)

The transformative principles poetically summarized here (which remain both philosophically and imagistically or theoretically and practically constant throughout these works) may be summarized as follows: (1) Images of "eccentric" or "mixt" dances or (what is much the same thing) of wandering mazes or planets (for a planet is a wanderer) are invariably, if "irregularly," affirmed, for Milton echoes Heraclitus in maintaining that "elementall and mixt things . . . cannot suffer any change of one kind, or quality into another without the struggl of contrarieties" (*CPW,* 1:795). (2) The statically conventional, overly "adorned," or "gaudy" ceremonial image is invariably rejected in favor of naturalistic excrescences of the "track divine" since, for Milton, all other "corporeal resemblances of inward holinesse & beauty are now past" (*CPW,* 1:828). Of course, what these principles mean in regard to the "clothing" of ecclesiastical ceremony in *The Reason of Church-Government* is evidently not quite the same as what they mean in regard to the related but hardly identical "clothing" of paradise. In the latter, gilded or "enamelled" verbal images may be appropriate insofar as they are understood as emanating from the protean context of the living Word. Hence my third and final objection to Stavely's commentary, which overlooks Plato's equally equivocal treatment of the "undecidable" matter of Timean gold called to our attention by Derrida's analysis of the role of the *khora* in his *Timaeus*. This reminds us that whether Milton's Sun alchemically concocts "potable gold" or old Proteus is alchemically called up from the sea and "drain'd through a Limbec to his Native form" (*PL,* 3.605), he is subtly bombarding us with the generative or kinetic properties concealed within apparently static created forms.[27]

While, like "vegetable gold," the "golden-hued" fruits and flowers of these Edenic passages initially suggest an identity of substance (jewel tones mingled with metallic images) with static, eternal value (the lost wonders of the Golden Age), these identities thus rapidly dissolve into the limbec of creative plasticity that Milton's similes thereafter expand, not create. In the passage under discussion, this natural alchemy commences as soon as the apparently atemporal coexistence of fruit and flower is ruptured by the unexpected personification of a Sun "more glad" to impress his beams on these "goodly" trees than on evening clouds or rainbows, for even this hyperemblematic Sun seems to understand that his role is far from ornamental; like the sun's presiding angel, Uriel, he chooses how and where to shine. Reflected through the Pan-theistic fertility god "ripening" its rainbows, sunsets, and "enamelled" fruits, Eden's hidden god baroquely reveals his immanent presence chiefly through ongoing gifts and the intensification of their "theatrically" variable light. Through this semiopaque medium, Eden's life-giving, light-enhancing vapors concentrate and dispel his reflected presence in ways more consistent with the cloudy, shifting vistas of the postlapsarian universe than with any surreal form of stasis. For, in this Eden, as in our world (if in the latter chiefly at sunrise or sunset), such vistas belong to the eye of the beholder as much or more than to the eye of a transcendent father-deity. Since for "our general Sire" (*PL,* 4.144), as for ourselves, the garden's "perfect" synthesis of outer beauty and inner worth must remain unstable in order to fulfill the divine purposes of freedom in delight and delight in freedom, the jewel-like hardness of its fruits (one neither possible nor desirable in organic fruits and flowers) is dissolved through an alchemical "undecidability" soon deferred onto the revolving space of Edenic time. Its being constituted by its becoming, its essence by transformation, the garden's only ultimate difference from our landscape is that its balance of mist and light is always benign.

The continuity of this beauty with the muted splendors of what Benjamin would call the "all too earthly" can here be traced directly to a historical horizon from which danger can never be exiled. The "Evening Cloud" and "humid bow" that appear "when God hath shower'd the earth" remind the cautious reader that an intrinsically mutable divinity directs both the Sun and its variable temporality— from its daily rising and setting to the larger rising and falling cycles of pre- and postlapsarian history. Not only the baroque ephemerality of ambiguously shaded and softened vistas illuminated by sun's eye-altering light but everything about Eden reminds us of evolutionary time and its latent dangers long before Eve eats the "fallacious fruit" growing "fast by" the tree of life. This ill-chosen "wandering" is already implicit not only in the overarching "frame" of Satan's presence but even in Eden's rainbow and its oblique allusion to the Noatic Flood (11.865–66). This essentially meta-allegorical allusiveness also registers the difficulties of interpreting a newly temporalized and active nature in accordance with the hidden designs of its God. Although not an absence *toute court*, this divine immanence in natural signs and things then completes the poem's imagistic "ruin" of standard allegorical teleology by generating a sense of an ending no longer hierarchically imposed on the microcosm by the macrocosm but instead intrasubjectively coordinated through the multiple vanishing points of nature and naturalized history.

Of course, chief among the symbolic subjects dis- and reintegrating this history is Satan, himself, whose presence in Eden thoroughly disrupts whatever liminal sense of stasis it may have had. A typical instance of this disjunction occurs as the "purer air" of Paradise not only fails to cast him off but

> Meets his approach, and to the heart inspires
> Vernal delight and joy, able to drive
> All sadness but despair. . . .
> (*PL*, 4.154–56)

Obviously this "despair" primarily alludes to a Satan who has just acknowledged that "all Good to me is lost" (4.109). Yet it also subtly includes the reader, who has so far seen our doomed "general Sire" largely through his eyes, for, if then as now "vernal delights" are able to drive away "all sadness but despair"—and if even more then than now—their potential to produce loss and despair has become virtually integral with those delights, as the successive frames of Edenic experience consistently emphasize. Thus, for Adam as for us, there is no escape from transience, from the potential despair and joy inherent in a purity inseparable from danger. Because Eden can no longer be imagined apart from its internal potential for deception, illusion, and loss, we all live under the same sun, more or less deceived, and more or less "glad."

Not only is this baroque evaluation of the image structure of *Paradise Lost* much closer to the Protestant epistemology that both Weber and more recent historians have traced in the poem than to the classically Augustinian or mystically "self-canceling" models that still dominate considerations of its rhetoric, but it also seems more accurately attuned to Milton's characteristic insistence on the continuities between the sign systems of fallen and unfallen creation. As in his prose treatises, this insistence is linked to the twin concerns of Christian liberty and self-reformation, the "allegory of inwardness" to which he dedicated his life. Yet to continue these projects in the post-Restoration climate meant even more emphatically rejecting any externally determined or objectively "clear and distinct" theory of signs, theories that by then had become instruments of the Stuart court and the Royal Society. Such consensualist conceptions were used not only to cast the entire revolutionary enterprise in doubt but collaterally to promote precisely the type of political/empirical pragmatism that *Paradise Regained* later dismissively interrogates. If after Adam's fall " 'the Book of Knowledge fair' (III.47) is further obscured both objectively, with reference to the perceived sign, and subjectively, with reference to the perceiver," so that, as Robert Entzminger points out, "nature . . . cannot communicate directly God's 'goodness beyond thought' (V.159)," this goodness still provides a benignly opaque mirror of the "track divine" within the natural continuum. Effectively constituting an alternate scriptural text, the providential design now evolving within nature thereby replaces a more deterministic with an "open" teleology in which God remains active even though the immediate "corporeal resemblances" of his transcendent order have ceased. In its place, we gain an allegory of inwardness, of the ever-ambiguous *freedom* of individuals to "choose / Thir place of rest" with only "Providence thir guide (12.646–47).[28]

Thus, even more than *Samson Agonistes, Paradise Lost* is a poem about coming to terms with harsh realities and deferred expectations. Although its final objective may well be "to escape from history as a circular treadmill," as Christopher Hill remarks, the poem acknowledges that this "escape" can be accomplished only by accepting the fact that "there will be no miraculous intervention by an external Saviour merely because we impatiently expect it. It is Satan who offers short cuts."[29] As a result, its eternity is posed, not as a secure emblematic stopping place, the top of a Platonic ladder, but only as the vanishing point whose end "no eye can reach" (*PL*, 12.556)—nor should reach. In rejecting transcendence in favor of immanence as the concrete sign and path to human salvation, the secure filiations of all allegorical emblems of truth are simultaneously encountered and ruptured. Yet, in affirming the new potential emerging from this rupture, the poem is also far from exhibiting either a Calvinist or a rationalist distrust in the authenticity of signs. Instead—cosmically, imagistically, and experientially—the poem traces a winding stair between the antithetical rationalisms of the Renaissance and the seventeenth century, in the process also providing an alternative both to Realist allegory and to an allegory of erasure. Through this compromise, the Miltonic image becomes a recuperative rather than a mystically escapist, self-consuming artifact—the concrete forerunner of a new poetics constructed somewhere between the ruins of Renaissance allegory and the Romantic reconstruction of metaphor.

3

Yet, while the metonymic or "metaphorized" emblem provides the tropological foundation of Milton's baroque allegory, as Stavely suggests, it does not carry the full thrust of its dispersive, temporal/ horizontal drive, a function that has long been associated with his epic simile. In further extending the already expanded function of the kosmos, Milton's epic simile creates a fully multidimensional perspective, featuring baroque vanishing points that now end only in (as Pérez-Gómez remarks) a "point at infinity." The panoramic effects thereby achieved thus stand in striking contrast to the iconic or mosaic effects created by traditional allegory, which Michael Murrin traces to its tendency to view "past and future . . . [as] different parts of a common human pattern . . . judged implicitly or explicitly in relation to a mythic past, which itself possesses a transcendent per-

fection and can apply to any stage of human history."[30] This univer-
salizing or "flattening" vision of human space and time results in a
ritual vision of history as merely the shadow of an eternity filtered
through tropes that exhibit the "extreme degree of 'condensation,'
'displacement,' 'negation,' 'timelessness,' and . . . 'wish fulfillment'"
that in Fletcher's view also lends them the fictive atemporality of
myth. In this waking dream each figure then becomes a "gemlike
talisman, bounded by very strict lines, . . . because each detail is
integrated into a highly systematic order of [ritual] acts."[31]

In setting this static universe in motion, baroque allegory not only
vivifies its space but also concretizes its time. In *Paradise Lost,* this
final metamorphosis is conducted by similes that perform far more
naturalistic relational functions than those of the traditional mode.
Rather than the relatively detachable and abstract emblems em-
ployed in varying degrees by Homer and his successors, Milton's epic
similes "reciprocally influence and expand each other, often so or-
ganically that a detailed relationship is interpretable only in terms of
prolepsis," the forward-driving vehicle of its concrete and linear
time. Homologization, a comparative technique, carries the usual
freight of Christian typology; but, as James Whaler's seminal anal-
ysis concludes, in Milton's case it is temporally extended through
the forward- rather than backward-looking vehicle of prolepsis.[32]
Hence, the conventional moral exempla of the traditional epic give
way to a dynamic recontextualization of myth, legend, and biblical
narrative within the framework of secular patterns of events that
recall the past chiefly to reinvest it with present and future mean-
ing. Rejecting "classical amplitude" for "Hebraic intensity," Milton's
"images cluster around central nodes of Biblical significance, rather
than 'splay out' in all directions after the Homeric or Spenserian
manner," so that, as Harold Fisch concludes, "precise geographical
and physical notation takes the place of mythological transcen-
dence." Instead of the simile's more normatively digressive, atem-
poral "intrusions," the Miltonic trope thus creates tightly focused
homologies that expand into the concrete historical time of the
reader, who in coordinating its self-reflexive allusions must set aside
mere "binocular vision" to entertain the "geometric vanishing point"
tending toward infinity—the formal structure we have come to un-
derstand as baroque.[33]

Departing as well from the conventional mythic and/or sacramen-
tal homologization of history, these similes model an experience of

time that must be concretely and personally rather than communally or ceremonially apprehended. Although its meaning is still moralized, the historical process is now no longer mosaic or "aggregate" but largely mimetic in perspective, even in its most surreal reaches. Yet this elemental naturalization of space/time also allusively reprises Homer's "naive" epic mode, particularly in its rejection of the highly stylized or "sentimental" allegorical symbolism of Neoplatonic and Virgilian epic.[34] Thus, Satan's fall is no mere metaphor of the vice that must be overcome by virtue, no more than his obdurate "fate" is a judgment to be overcome by *pietas,* but a quasi-naturalistic account of the rise and fall of civilizations as the systolic forces of self-destructive wrath encounter the diastolic forces of self-abnegating love. As a result, evil itself is no mere abstraction, no mere passive Augustinian absence of good, but an active contraction of the self into the self-consuming cancer of evil. Like a literal tumor, this "growth" thus may be traced to nonexistence only in the philosophical sense that *all* motives now originate in the "nothingness" of free will. Since all motivation is thus rooted in the indeterminacy that Augustine's *horror vacui* attributes only to sin, Satan's fall cannot any longer be Neoplatonically understood as the passive failure of a properly active will or even as a lapse from proper devotion. Like the similes that frame the baroque experience of hell, the contractions of evil expand into ever deeper, more inward, and yet also more concrete historical existence.[35]

In rupturing the iconic tradition of Christian history stemming from the Augustinian opposition between an ephemeral city of man and an eternal city of God, the poem is forced to revert both to its Homeric and to its biblical roots. As in Auerbach's seminal analysis of biblical art, it then returns to a narrative sweep synthetically "rang[ing] through all three domains [of] . . . legend, historical reporting, and interpretative historical theology," at last creating a vision where "the sublime influence of God . . . reaches so deeply into the everyday that the two realms of the sublime and everyday are not only actually unseparated but basically inseparable."[36] Auerbach also contrasts the Hebrew text's deep structural centering around narrative gaps to be filled by the "space" of interpretation with the Homeric text's cohesive textual surface, a contrast that further suggests the depth of Milton's innovative synthesis. As the Miltonic simile's newly tightened connections between tenor and vehicle produce "clusters" around Homeric epic questions, they also open Hebrew "gaps" at the heart of this mimesis. Further, because the simile's tightened focus blocks the mosaic "splaying out" of motifs into merely superficial or formal answers, despite its brilliant surface, ultimately it self-reflexively implodes into the internal questioning and (meta)historical expansion that Auerbach associates with the Hebrew Scriptures. Only in this meta-allegorical or baroque manner, and not by altogether "refus[ing] allegory," as Gordon Teskey argues, is it possible for Milton's revival of Homer to claim that its "events are incorporate in the truth."[37]

The foundational questions of *Paradise Lost* thus pose Homer's questions concerning Achillean wrath in even more systematic and naturalistic terms: Who and why is this envious "original Serpent," and how does he explain the ruin of so many "heroes"? The baroque elusiveness/allusiveness of the narrator's answers are transmitted through ironic similitudes that convey the "aweful" ambiguity of Satan's verbal and physical transformations, as

> . . . Him the Almighty Power
> Hurl'd headlong flaming from th' Ethereal Sky
> With hideous ruin and combustion down
> To bottomless perdition, there to dwell
> In Adamantine Chains and penal Fire,
> Who durst defy th' Omnipotent to Arms.
> Nine times the Space that measures Day and Night
> To mortal men, hee with his horrid crew
> Lay vanquisht, rolling in the fiery Gulf
> Confounded though immortal: But his doom
> Reserv'd him to more wrath; for now the thought
> Both of lost happiness and lasting pain
> Torments him; round he throws his baleful eyes
> That witness'd huge affliction and dismay
> Mixt with obdurate pride and hate. . . .
>
> (*PL*, 1.44–58)

Here, the repeated aspirants of "hurl'd headlong" and "hideous," combined with the resonant plosives (chiefly *d*'s and *p*'s), form an attack of hissing consonants that verbally mirror Satan's fall, while the echoing "rue" of his "ruin" assonantly repeats itself in his "doom" before dying away in the "affliction" of his "bottomless perdition." These echoes suggest that hell is a round and empty place, real and perhaps measurable, although chiefly through the coordinates of mortal pain. The effect is achieved as a typically Miltonic oxymoron, "bottomless perdition," fuses an abstract noun with what is, especially in hell, only apparently a concrete adjective, *bottomless,* and then ambiguously "measures" it with the equally obscure duration of the demons' fall. For how can "Nine times the space which measures Day and Night / To Mortal men" have any computational meaning when there is as yet no earthly day or night, much less any known speed by which such a descent might be measured? By thus using a riddle to "measure" an oxymoron, the narrator expands and paradoxically implodes the conventional space/time of Homer and Hesiod.

Unlike that of Zeus, the space of this Omnipotent's creation can then be measured only by similitudes whose temporality is far from unidimensional, formulaic, or "flat." Yet such misleadingly "concrete" contradictions not only introduce us to hell's dimension, but they also darkly explore its essential experience. Hell contains "no light, but rather darkness visible" (*PL,* 1.63); hope never comes here, although it "comes to all" (1.66–67). Its landscape is composed of "ever-burning Sulphur unconsum'd" by "a fiery Deluge" (1.68–69) in which it temporally began—and will end—although it has ironically *not* been eternally prepared by an Eternal Justice who acts in time (1.70). The numerous similes analogizing this deluge to that of Noah and Pharaoh further deepen the historical meaning and enigma of these relentless oxymorons, which, like hell itself, condense the causes that they organically and historically disperse. What becomes most concretely manifest is not its geographic but its causal dimension, a relativized space/time metonymically shaped by Satan's verbal, ethical, and physical hubris. For, while Satan's claims to deity are as inherently contradictory as the images of his fall, in poetic time they are as "really" related to and independent from their temporal source as Sin herself. Since their meaning at once springs from and stands beside their author, the metonymic images surrounding Satan only initially portray him as a self-authored "part" condensing the whole of the Fall. Because they soon become as alienated from him as his Sin-ful progeny themselves, both his psychic projections and the geography of hell are even less synecdochic than those of Eden, although both are best perceived through the gaps and inconsistencies that meta-allegorically "measure" the self-initiated aspects of their growth and/or decay in time.

Yet Satan's self-exoneration at first sounds convincingly consistent, for, at least indirectly, the Almighty can be said to have "tempted his attempt" (*PL,* 1.642) by intentionally concealing his power; and "till then who knew / The force of those dire Arms?" (1.93–94). However, as in all his arguments there is here an implicit disjunction between cause and effect, between the tempting and the attempting, which progressively makes the source of Satan's "republican" aspirations, like his followers' "rightful" temptation to "dislike his reign, . . . mee preferring" (1.102), as rhetorically dubious as his dubious battle itself:

> . . . What though the field be lost?
> All is not lost; the unconquerable Will,
> And study of revenge, immortal hate,
> And courage never to submit or yield:
> And what is else not to be overcome?
> That Glory never shall his wrath or might
> Extort from me. To bow and sue for grace
> With suppliant knee, and deify his power
> Who from the terror of this Arm so late
> Doubted his Empire, that were low indeed
>
> . . . .
>
> Since through experience of this great event
> In Arms not worse, in foresight much advanc't,
> We may with more successful hope resolve
> To wage by force or guile eternal War
> Irreconcilable to our grand Foe,
> Who now triumphs, and in th' excess of joy
> Sole reigning holds the Tyranny of Heav'n.
> (1.105–14, 118–24)

Beneath the bombast of this speech lie propositions that clearly contradict nearly everything that either the narrative voice or Satan himself has revealed about hell, heaven, and its God. The Almighty is depicted on the one hand as "Potent . . . in his rage" (1.94) and on the other as having impotently "Doubted his Empire." Then again, Satan claims never to be vanquished or changed almost immediately after remarking "how chang'd" and dimmed Beelzebub's mirroring "luster" (1.84–87, 97) appears. These inconsistencies consistently undercut his rousing challenge to continue his mission "In Arms not worse, in foresight much advanc't," and with much "more successful hope." While this "lustrous" rhetoric convincingly illustrates his ability to motivate this host, the il-lustrious absurdity of his refusal to

"deify" God's power—a darkly punning euphemism for actually de-
fying him—makes this verbal assault as clearly self-defeating as the
temptation or "at-tempt" that drove him from heaven. By making
himself the false icon of "the mightiest" with whom he raised him-
self to contend (1.99) when he scarcely has the power to raise himself
from the floor of hell, Satan embodies the historical hubris under-
lying all the successive falls traced in the poem's epic similes.

By thus foregrounding the psychological basis of evil in the adver-
sary's own rhetoric, the poet prepares the reader for the later transla-
tion of narrative and personification allegory in the first two books
(respectively, the Pandaemonium and Sin/Death episodes) into the
self-reflexive mode of meta-allegory. Yet, before this synthesis is
complete, the process is proleptically historicized by two related
strategies: the displacement of abstract nouns onto transformative
verbs, and the ceaseless expansion of the simile through tightly
linked forms of nominal and conceptual homologization. In con-
densed form, both processes are initiated as the former Lucifer or
"light-bearer" renames himself not merely in word but in deed: "To
do aught good never will be our task, / But ever to do ill our sole
delight, / As being the contrary to his high will / Whom we resist"
(*PL*, 1.159–62). Redefining himself with the active verb *resist*, he
thus becomes Satan (or Satanas), the Hebrew (or Greek) name for
he who resists. At once opposing himself to the epic "I am" (cf.
7.168, 8.316) who primarily *is* and linking himself to other similarly
self-begotten historical/typological resisters, Nimrod and Pharaoh,
this formula equates their chosen form of existence with sin, the
disposition that in making "ever to do ill our sole delight" denies the
priority of the life principle itself.[38] For, as a verbal noun, *delight*
in/as self-seeking desire concretely images the process by which sin
attracts, conceives, and bears the fruit of death, which also homolo-
gically reflects the source of Satan's temptation. As this oblique bib-
lical allusion reminds us, no man may "say when he is tempted, I
am tempted of God: for God cannot be tempted with evil, neither
tempteth he any man" (James 1:13). Moreover, as Milton would have
known, the Greek *epithumia* or delight that the Authorized Version
of James 1:14–15 mistranslates as simply "lust" at once implies plea-
sure, enjoyment, and indulgence of a potentially sinful longing or
desire that "is put to the test" (*peirazetai*)—at which point it can be
either indulged or rejected. But, if allowed to "act as a bait" (*de-*

leazomenos), it becomes fertile and gives birth to sin (*tiktei hamartia*) after the bait is seized, enjoyed, or delighted in (*sullabousa*).

As in Milton's later personification of Sin, here the self at once psychically and physically "conceives" an illegitimate "delight" that, when violently seized, gives birth to a still more illegitimate off-spring: a fallen, self-perverted "conception" that, in philosophical terms, still represents an actual *res* or accident in a substance. The deformed psychosomatic mutations "conceived" by Satan's sin thus stand in ironic contrast to his mystical claim to remain unchanged, to possess the daemonic immutability of a classical allegorical kosmos, when his very description of heaven's "retreat" rests on a simile that invokes the broader historical horizon of his own transformation:

> But see the angry Victor hath recall'd
> His Ministers of vengeance and pursuit
> Back to the Gates of Heav'n: the Sulphurous Hail
> Shot after us in storm, o'erblown hath laid
> The fiery Surge, that from the Precipice
> Of Heav'n receiv'd us falling. . . .
> (*PL*, 1.169–74)

Not only does this corrosive, externally propelled hail deconstruct Satan's utopian attempt to "reclaim" hell in his "Hail horrors, hail / Infernal world" speech (1.250–51); it also suggests the absurdity of supposing that the "angry Victor" (whom he, as the resister, charac-teristically avoids naming) will forever condone the activities of its "new Possessor" (1.252). Like Homer's Agamemnon as well as his Achilles, this resister is thus overthrown by his *own* inability to recognize any source of authority higher than, much less equal to, himself. For, like his own cannon, Satan's rebellion has already back-fired in a cloud of hail that, "o'erblown," precedes him into the hell that "receiv'd us falling" in a dubious blaze of glory: one propelled by the self-consuming fires of Envy, Rage, and Pride, which as much as the Son's ascendancy "cast him out from Heav'n" (1.35–37).

Hence, even when Satan "successfully" perverts divine laws, his own accusations recall that they merely reconfirm the ironic internal "consistency" of this biblical "accuser," along with his ultimate (if not immediate) inconsistency with the life principle. His mosaic depic-tion of the "Tyranny of Heaven" and the cruel envy of a "Potent Victor" who has unjustly thwarted his "Glorious Enterprise" (*PL*,

1.89) is so tightly homologized with the more mimetic scenario he would conceal that it is nonetheless revealed as the more dialectical and authentic allegory of the fall. From this perspective, hell is ultimately merely the most objective of all the reified conditions in which Satan participates through his delight in Sin, the allegorical "essence" of which he misprizes and misidentifies in ways that further illustrate the causes of her fatal birth.[39] On this false schema, the narrator is thus warranted in superimposing the baroque correction inadvertently and spontaneously revealed by Satan himself, for not even the resister can thoroughly disguise the fact that God's universe is neither as static nor as univocal as he claims. From this vantage point, the reader can already predict that he who lives by false allegory must also perish by it, as Satan ultimately does in book 10, chewing the delusive ashes of his own diminished flame and false fruit (10.566)—which, typologically or historically speaking, are also those of the historical Sodom and Gomorrah.

As in Eden, this more evolutionary allegory requires the emergence of a more ambiguously mimetic physical geography, a hellish landscape that reflects Satan's "own place," the effects of "A mind" tragically "not to be chang'd by Place or Time" (*PL,* 1.253). *Because* Satan was free to create a "Hell of Heav'n," his self-determined changelessness now dooms him to as vainly striving to make a "Heav'n of Hell" by creating it in his own image. The hell of his mind will first be projected onto the false magic of Pandaemonium (1.727), which, through an ironically natural "magic," will later pervert the real splendors of Eden once Adam and Eve fall into a similar illusion. Yet, like that of this hellish "place," the splendors thereby created are real illusions: temporal actualizations of a "horrid Vale" or space of recurring error and alienation in both psychic and physical senses. Although the external expansion of this state is historically gradual, its internal condition is immediately homologized with the "unusual weight" Satan feels, "till on the dry Land / He lights, if it were Land that ever burn'd / With solid, as the Lake with liquid fire" (1.227–29). Sealed with the stamp of his darkened mind and its lost light-bearing capacity, the permutations of this oxymoronic landscape finally reflect only the circularly downward spiral of increasing alienation and infertility. Utterly lacking in heaven's "grateful vicissitude" (6.8), this dark perversion of a truly free or fertile causality can no more really reproduce heaven than Satan can reassume his role as Lucifer. For, although sardonically half right in claiming that, "To reign is worth ambition though in Hell," his alienated ideal of fame, not here even that "last infirmity of noble mind," creates only a self-subjection that is outwardly projected into hell's tyrannous hierarchies. Unable to effect authentic change or reciprocity, which in Milton's epic universe is virtually synonymous with authentic freedom, Satan's anticreative wish "not to be chang'd by Place or Time" then condemns him to his own version of eternal allegorical recurrence. At the intratextual level of meta-allegory, the distance of hell from paradise can thus finally be measured as the distance of the "Mineral fury" (1.235) forging Pandaemonium's "ascending pile" of inlaid gold from Eden's living "vegetable gold."

Nevertheless, these reifications lend hell its own organic shape as well as its own baroque historical vistas. Guided by the horizontal and self-reflexive work of the epic simile, the poet's "Optic Glass" (*PL*, 1.288) first "sights" the ruins of satanic allegory as his angel legions lay on the lake of fire like the autumnal leaves of Vallombrosa. Although this much-discussed simile has multiple sources and contexts, its typological level points toward the "*Etrurian* shades" (1.303) of Rome's ancestors.[40] Therein also recalling Aeneas's descent into the underworld in just such a "high overarch't" wood (1.304), it ironically details a far different lineage than the one Aeneas gains from Anchises—a typological progression of fallenness extending back from the defeat of Pharaoh's army in the "flood" of the Nile to the Flood of Noah, and thence to the primordial "deluge" of fallen angels. The Vallombrosa image thus proleptically depicts the fallen angels as the debris of all these floods, the ruins of time emerging as so much "scatter'd sedge," "floating Carcasses / And broken Chariot Wheels; so thick bestrown / Abject and lost lay these, covering the Flood, / Under amazement of thir hideous change" (1.304, 310–13). As the first stray leaves cut off from the Tree of Life, their "amazement" at once foreshadows and exceeds the "confounding" of all their descendants. Yet, just as the drowning of the Egyptians and of the "giants in the earth" in Noah's day destroyed one world and delivered another, so here we are reminded that "the safe shore" awaits the "Sojourners of *Goshen*" (1.309–10). Because there will always be those who walk through the shadowy waters of this Vallombrosa to another baptism in another Promised Land, the simile then anagogically points forward to the deluge of the Last Day, when those washed in the blood of the Lamb will once more triumph over their adversaries who have been "hurl'd headlong" into the final "flood" of the Lake of Fire.

In fusing these biblical typologies with Homeric accounts of fallenness, the pattern of epic similes in book 1 also recalls one man's present perspective on the autumn(s) of his life and times, which, like that of Satan and Achilles, is ambiguously intertwined with a long history of revolution, part just, part unjust. For when he considers the overriding patterns in the histories of Israelite, Greek, Egyptian, or English kings, their common denominator in the uneven history of injustice, tyranny, and final release of their captives seems to reside here, in Pandaemonium. Once again, this vast moralization of historical process is conducted by the simile's homologization of a vast range of mimetic causes and effects. Expanding outward from the central simile in which the demons "yet to thir General's Voice . . . soon obey'd / Innumerable," this baroque epic process of condensation and displacement is set in motion

> . . . As when the potent Rod
> Of *Amram's* Son in *Egypt's* evil day
> Wav'd round the Coast, up call'd a pitchy cloud
> Of *Locusts*, warping on the Eastern Wind,
> That o'er the Realm of impious *Pharaoh* hung
> Light Night, and darken'd all the Land of *Nile:*
> So numberless were those bad Angels seen
> Hovering on wing under the Cope of Hell
> 'Twixt upper, nether, and surrounding Fires;
> Till, as a signal giv'n, th' uplifted Spear
> Of thir great Sultan waving to direct
> Thir course, in even balance down they light
> On the firm brimstone, and fill all the Plain;
> A multitude, like which the populous North
> Pour'd never from her frozen loins, to pass
> *Rhene* or the *Danaw*, when her barbarous Sons
> Came like a Deluge on the South, and spread
> Beneath *Gibraltar* to the *Lybian* sands.
> (*PL*, 1.337–55)

Both stylistically and structurally, this simile builds on the preceding one by intensifying the interplay between its terms and by expanding its historical patterning. As in the journey begun at Vallombrosa, it traces the winding historical path from hell to the plagues associated with the exodus, in the process comparing its leader, Satan, both directly to Moses, "Amram's Son," and more obliquely to the first cause of Egypt's curse, Pharaoh himself. For, in an ironic sense, Satan is like Moses in that both are dividers of the waters, leaders who homeopathically "cure" the plagues visited on Pharaoh by allowing their poison full play. Moreover, by aligning Pharaoh's land with the same "plagues" Satan has visited on Pandaemonium—the fires of magic, illusion, and self-consuming changelessness—these infections metonymically "spread" to his fellow rebels, the "pitchy cloud / Of *Locusts*," food of prophets, but now the curse of the false priests whose magic consumes their own land. In this regressive "progress," "Sultanic" tyranny—whether hellish, Egyptian, "Rhenish," or Visigothic—is consistently linked to the insidious allure of an illusory "delight" that self-enslaves first its pseudoprophets, then their historical communities, and, finally, their literal land. In this sense, like his moral condition, Satan's empire begins and ends in the deluge of "barbarous Sons" descending from the North, the site of his original throne (5.688–89).

4

The critique both of tyranny and of its hierarchical allegories implied in this simile as in Satan's subsequent speeches thus prepares the reader for the final tour de force with which the book concludes, the catalog of demons and the construction of Pandaemonium itself. Yet in this progression there is no standard allegorical schematization of vice, no emblematic parade of the seven deadly sins, only a depressingly redundant history of the mental, moral, and social reifications of sinful psyches. Although each demon in Milton's epic catalog is given personal attributes, like Pharaoh and his barbaric hordes, each participates in the "gay Religions full of Pomp and Gold" (1.372) that "with thir darkness durst affront . . . [God's] light" (1.391). Because this critique of idolatrous worship is at once spiritual and aesthetic, its external forms can be synthesized with its internal motivations: lust or false desire/delight and pride or false aspiration/ inspiration. Since these dual "fruits" of Satan's sin causally "infect" his misled cohort, the catalog of demons is designed to represent variations on the same relatively mimetic theme, not an iconic or ritual examination of vice. Thus, in every case, misplaced desire for preeminence, becoming fertile, gives birth to lust for power, whence it demands luxurious "pomp" and its metonymic "double," licentious self-indulgence and pride.

Yet, at the meta-allegorical level, these apparent metonymies, lust, pride, and idolatry, are also synecdoches, the part of one representing the whole of the others. These final condensations replace a sacramental catalog of sin with a psychological unraveling of the processes through which self-enslavement monotonously expands into social enslavement. Reciprocally, the condensing/mirroring process conducted by part-whole relations is again shifted onto the horizon of history, where sexual/social license is seen as a "natural" by-product of the false heroism of barbarous war-mongers like Moloch, of the sybaritic sloth of Belial, and of the idolatrous greed of Mammon. Subsuming cause to effect as it subsumes the part to the whole, the book's progression of epic similes incorporates all these energies in the linear typology of Satan/Pharaoh/Sultan, which is ironically "fulfilled" in Christian kings like Charlemagne. Also looking forward to the final allegory of miniature enchanters that concludes book 1, such passages ask the reader to estimate the causes and consequences of an entire history of classical, pagan, and Christian chivalry, whose leaders' hearts, like Satan's,

> Distends with pride, and hard'ning in his strength
> Glories: For never since created man,
> Met with such imbodied force, as nam'd with these
> Could merit more than that small infantry
> Warr'd on by Cranes: though all the Giant brood
> Of *Phlegra* with th'Heroic Race were join'd
> That fought at *Thebes* and *Ilium*, on each side
> Mixt with auxiliar Gods; and what resounds
> In Fable or *Romance* of *Uther's* Son
> Begirt with *British* and *Armoric* Knights;
> And all who since, Baptiz'd or Infidel
> Jousted in *Aspramont* or *Montalban*,
> *Damasco*, or *Marocco*, or *Trebisond*,
> Or whom *Biserta* sent from *Afric* shore
> When *Charlemain* with all his Peerage fell
> By *Fontarabbia.*
> (*PL*, 1.572–87)

As the original standard-bearers of pride, Satan's army is immensely larger and more "heroic" than those fielded by his bellicose human descendants. This expanded homology allows the poet to interweave fact, fable, and romance in these military encounters much as in the earlier catalog he had mixed fictive demonic prototypes with their actual progeny, the pagan gods. Since the causal principle remains in either case the same, fiction and fact blend into a baroque architectonic spectacle demonstrating the sin-uous consequences of Satan's fall. Beginning with "the Giant brood / Of *Plegra*," the narrator first names the heroes of the Trojan War, then the exploits of the Arthurian and Ariostan knights, all of which "giants in the earth" typologically spring from the miscegenation of the fallen "sons of God" and men (Gen. 6:4). This demonic ancestry thus supplies the fictive yet real etiology of human militarism and its architectural "pomp," for, in retracing the "effects" of palaces and temples to their "causes" in the idolatry of trophies and armorial devices, the simile recasts Satan, not merely as the metaphoric foundation of this complex edifice, but as its actual embodiment: "he above the rest / In shape and gesture proudly eminent / Stood like a Tow'r" (*PL*, 1.589–91). Taking on the dimensions of hell, his noble face, form, and aspect are clouded with a sinister attraction, the only "tangible" sign of the moral distance between his heavenly and his current "light." Signaling not the transcendence but the ambivalence of even hellish signs, his obscure size and shape recast the hard mosaic outlines of the allegorical kosmos in baroque perspective:

> . . . his form had yet not lost
> All her Original brightness, nor appear'd
> Less than Arch-Angel ruin'd, and th' excess
> Of Glory obscur'd: As when the Sun new ris'n
> Looks through the Horizontal misty Air
> Shorn of his Beams, or from behind the Moon
> In dim Eclipse disastrous twilight sheds
> On half the Nations, and with fear of change
> Perplexes Monarchs.
> (1.591–99)

Through this alluring chiaroscuro, the penumbra of the etymological play on the "Arch-Angel *ruin'd*" conserves the traces of his continuing "fall," an ongoing enactment within the terms of its epic representation through simile. Moreover, because *ruin'd* bears more

of an elegiac, tragic sense than the more moralistic *fallen,* the face of
the ruined angel also traces the homological attraction that human
conquerors will share with him:

> Deep scars of Thunder had intrencht, and care
> Sat on his faded check, but under Brows
> Of dauntless courage, and considerate Pride
> Waiting revenge: cruel his eye, but cast
> Signs of remorse and passion to behold
> The fellows of his crime. . . .
> (*PL,* 1.601–06)

Through a naturalistically reciprocal rather than magically ritual
process of homology, Satan's followers are then similarly shaded by a
"sublime" half light:

> . . . from Eternal Splendors flung
> For his revolt, yet faithful how they stood,
> Thir Glory wither'd. As when Heaven's Fire
> Hath scath'd the Forest Oaks, or Mountain Pines,
> With singed top thir stately growth though bare
> Stands on the blasted Heath.
> (1.610–15)

In these examples, the allegorical sign is metonymically distanced
from its signified in a way foreign to Spenser, who, to image the
attractiveness of evil, divides the emblematic synecdoche into two
symmetrical halves. In his allegorical cosmos, there are thus neither
noble demons nor a sublime Pandaemonium, only an Errour hu-
manly beautiful to the waist but serpentine below or a Castle of
Lucifera splendid before and rotten behind. In contrast, Milton's Sin
begins in time as a wholly lovely creature who is later fully disfigured
by narcissism, incest, and rape—the psychosomatic manifestations of
her father's objectification of himself and others, a form of desire that
similarly "erupts" in Pandaemonium's brittle splendors. Yet, since its
"towers" exceed all subsequent imitations of its fallen glory to the
same extent that its inhabitants make later heroes look like pygmies,
the narrator looks ahead to its most ironic historical realization—the
glory that was Greek heroism ironically seduced by the same hubris
it had thought to overthrow in oriental form. By simultaneously
alluding to the myth of Amphion, builder of Thebes, the poet thus
suggests that the barbarous splendor of Pandaemonium is like a

Greek temple tragically complicit with his enchanting "oriental" music and therefore also like the golden net fashioned by his apparently Olympian but actually hellish prototype, Mulciber/Hephaestus, to reveal the base carnality of the gods of love and war. Like all such work, this idolatrous artifice thus prophetically ensnares both conqueror and conquered in its iconic "work"

> Of Dulcet Symphonies and voices sweet,
> Built like a Temple, where *Pilasters* round
> Were set, and Doric pillars overlaid
> With Golden Architrave; nor did there want
> Cornice or Frieze, with bossy Sculptures grav'n;
> The Roof was fretted Gold. Not *Babylon*,
> Nor great *Alcairo* such magnificence
> Equall'd in all thir glories, to inshrine
> *Belus* or *Serapis* thir Gods, or seat
> Thir Kings, when *Egypt* with *Assyria* strove
> In wealth and luxury.
>
> (1.712–22)

Of course, in true Miltonic style, only by contextualizing this architectural icon of narcissistic splendor with the epic catalogs and similes tracing it to the energies of Mammon and Moloch, the "horrid King besmear'd with blood / Of human sacrifice, and parents' tears" (1.392–93), can its full meaning become apparent. For, just as Moloch perverts the human life principle, so Mammon "orientally" "sacrifices" the gold fit only for the floor of heaven (1.678–82) by recasting it as the roof and capstone of this self-constructed, gilded prison. Thus, in every case, Babylonian, Egyptian, Greek, or Christian, living gold idolatrously contained or "trodd'n" treads and contains its containers, (con)sealing them like the murky asphaltic lights of its ceiling, "pendant by subtle Magic" (1.727). As in other similes tracing the descent of demons who at last appear in "their own dimensions like themselves," Mulciber's "ruinous" fall from morning to noon, from noon to evening, all on "a Summer's day," at last suggests a true meta-allegorical calculus of demonic history. As always, this calculus is also variable and self-reflexive—more variable even than the varying length of a day and night attuned to shifting equinoxes. Yet, while a cosmic "day" must be infinitely more indefinable than an earthly one, God's time, like the present tense of the reader, ultimately has a fixed beginning and end. By once more measuring this space in terms of that time, the reader can then escape the golden net of Pandaemonium along with the idolatry of its signs.

Of course, it is precisely this temporal dimension that, like the peasant viewing the demonic fairy revels, the reader is liable to forget, sharing as he does the condition of Adam, who falls because he forgets the temporal dimension of God's providence—their mutual freedom to intervene in time. By opposing an iconic image of God to his own idolatrous image of Eve, Adam forgets that all motives and images are best intuitively calculated through their temporally relative motions, which are "fixed" only in the eternal recurrence of Satan's hell. Such idolatrously static "spaces" are thus here discredited as the first offspring of transfixing desire, the desire to be like an imagined God who "prevents" or controls time. In this desire, all pseudoallegory originates, as the demonic saga of book 1 reveals. Here, the allegorical overestimation of places and signs consistently leads to an underestimation of time and change, which in turn results in a "ritual" enslavement to idols. Later, Michael must forcefully remind the partially regenerate Adam of this lesson since he cannot begin to comprehend the dialectic of Christian history until his own most compelling icon—that of Eden itself—is shattered,

> To teach thee that God attributes to place
> No sanctity, if none be thither brought
> By Men who there frequent, or therein dwell.
> (11.836–38)

Yet this lesson merely reinforces the fundamental epic design that Adam has partially forgotten since all the poem's imagistic spaces, not only hell's but Raphael's, are created by a fluid circulation between location, duration, and meaning. While in hell the fluidity of this circulation is reduced in proportionate degree to its inhabitants' self-enslavement, even that degree is rhetorically negotiated with its present-tense audience, whose perspective supplies the final shadings implicit in its eery "darkness visible."

At a maximum remove from Dante's "cathedral" or Spenser's "courtly" architectonics, the panoramic rhetorical structure of *Paradise Lost* thus proleptically and homologically expands Christian allegory far beyond its normative picture plane. In rejecting the stylized correspondences of the high Renaissance mode, Milton's epic also embraces the more "naive" or naturalistic fusion of myth, legend, and interpretative history common to biblical and Homeric narrative. This expansion of myth into history seems also to have motivated Arnold Stein's comparison of the poem to the "moving likeness of eternity" that emerges in Plato's *Timaeus,* a comparison that implicitly records its own epic "fall" from the Christian height of eternal correspondences—and thus from a static "artifice of eternity" into a Benjaminian "ruin in the realm of thought."[41] For representing a forever-absent structure, the ongoing present tense of *Paradise Lost* thus not only prophetically cancels the eternal moment of Augustine, Dante, and Spenser but also proleptically undermines the belated mysticism of Yeats. Hence here Death itself is no metempsychosis but merely a brief temporal disruption, a blank space of interpretation followed by "a gentle wafting" to an ongoing, endlessly variable "immortal life" (*PL,* 12.435), not a Spenserian reversion to immutability. This mortalist depiction of human redemption makes history, not bodily extinction and the resurrection of the immortal soul, the vehicle of all salvation. Thus, when at last "time stands fix't" (12.655) in the final judgment of eternal Providence, the individual's subjective, experiential understanding of signs may be changed but not fundamentally halted or reversed. For, in rupturing the finite spatial dimensions of the concentric universe, the poetic, intersubjective perspective of the human observer must comparably expand its static temporal configurations. If time can still be used to measure space to achieve some form of accommodation between them, such attempts are now successful only from a proper human vantage point—not one mystically "rapt above the pole" (7.23). From this perspective, the poem's simultaneously naturalized and expanded epic panorama at once approaches and recedes from the enclosed satanic spaces now consigned to the "ruins" of an antiquated allegorical place by definition unfit to encompass the temporal reparations of the poem's complex organic rhythms. In this meta-allegorical design, time is thus now of this world, while eternity is of the universe reserved only for God.

4

Some Versions of Allegory

The Personified Physics and Metaphysics of "One First Matter"

1

If both neoclassical and post-Romantic criticism have unnecessarily obscured the aesthetics of Milton's allegory, some essentially philosophical preconceptions have also impeded our appreciation of his allegorical personifications. Chief among these is the assumption that the relentless dichotomizing of symbol and substance required by personification allegory would seem to contradict Milton's material monism, an apparent inconsistency that encourages the standard view of his abstract allegorical personae as insubstantial, self-canceling, or otherwise "expendable" agents of no enduring import.[1] Since the previous chapter explores the aesthetic and formal foundations of this critical misunderstanding (which is generally compounded by a misunderstanding either of allegory, of the baroque mode, or of both), the current chapter will examine the broader philosophical sources of this illusory "contradiction." As it attempts to show, Milton's personifications actually support rather than contradict the workings of his material monism, which in fact largely explains their very real deviations (in every sense) from the far more limited personae of normative allegory. This demonstration thus requires an examination both of their divergence from more normative "daemons" and of their conformity to the requirements of material monism. In the process, we will discover that, in accord with the ascending scale of Milton's "one first matter all" (*PL,* 5.472), these personified material agencies operate within a fundamental binarism of interchangeable physical processes not unlike the monist oscillations posited by modern theoretical science.

In *Paradise Lost,* as throughout Milton's work, the evidence for his characteristic dichotomizing of monistic wholes is overwhelming.

The epic's multiple forms of alternating "male and female" light recall the poet's much earlier distinction between the "harmonious Sisters, Voice and Verse," in "At a Solemn Music" or the masculine "twins" of "L'Allegro" and "Il Penseroso." Yet, as the continuity of first matter's dark root and bright flower also suggests, these are not absolute or Platonically Real dichotomies but harmonic phases of a unitary dialectic conducted through the mutable mediums of light and sound, leaf and branch. Nevertheless, in almost all instances, within any given duality this dialectic involves an imparity—as, for example, where light is privileged over dark, verse over voice, sense over sound, masculine over feminine. Yet Milton's personifying "moralization" of these terms also equilibrates such imparities by elevating them into substantive self-referentiality as incipient alternations in the "currents" of the opposing type. Thus, instead of radically objectifying the moral dimensions of their universe, these personifications participate in the same fluid processes demanded of writing and reading subjects, who alternately "ventriloquize" different genders or modes of being. Of course, like those subjects, these personifications usually participate in the creation of qualities that are ultimately positive or negative in character, although, also like them, this character is revealed in their functioning, not in any mystified essences.

The same fundamental monism describes Milton's Chaos, which, since it serves as the macrocosmic foundation of his entire epic schema, represents this schema's most ambivalently mutable degree. For the monist materialism underlying his poetic theodicy demands, not only that Chaos supply the profoundly fluid conditions conducive to both good and evil, but also that it supply a life principle incipiently opposed to an evil here redefined as the negation of difference—and hence of life itself. Thus, in contrast to satanically disintegrative forms of organization, Chaos represents the far more benign harmonic divergence of mutable but potentially integrative life energies. The difficult task of discriminating these subtly but essentially different forms of disorder has fortunately been made simpler by recent refinements in scientific terminology brought about by chaos or complexity theory itself. Like the previous advances made by information theory's study of noise, these recent attempts to formulate a "disorderly" theory of order provide highly refined dialectical models for understanding the creative interchange between competing dissonances. As opposed to the largely mechanistic models supplied by the tradition of Newtonian physics, this nonlinear dynamics suggests a physical model of universal order where disorder is no longer mere "noise" to be eliminated but an integral part of the feedback system of life. As opposed even to the relatively advanced thermodynamic theories of nineteenth-century chemistry, in these models physical interference, inertia, disorder, or energy loss—technically, *entropy*—no longer leads to meaninglessness, or (much the same thing) to the prospective "heat death" of the universe, but to disorder's "negentropic" reintegration into new forms of order.

The necessary alternation of phases of entropy and negentropy in such systems thus suggests some important new solutions to the recurring problem of Satan's obvious influence over Chaos, which had earlier caused many critics to assume that, at least in this episode, Milton had succumbed to the old "daemonic" or dualistic "habit" of personification allegory and to its still more ancient association of chaotic matter with evil.[2] Yet, ironically, these assumptions themselves seem to have been influenced by the habits of thought fostered by the Newtonian paradigm, predispositions that are still very much among us—especially since similar biases exist in traditional philosophy and theology. However, in contrast to their familiar subject/object, content/form, or energy/matter dichotomies, nonlinear systems—whose prototypes are already present in seventeenth-century atomism—regard disorder or entropy as the very medium of reintegration or order itself. If they use a more advanced and less theistic vocabulary than Milton's contemporary John Ray, more recent theorists would then generally concur in regarding chaotic matter as a neutral state whose elements are "variously confused and confusedly commixed, as though they had been carelessly shaken and shuffled together; yet not so but that there was order observed by the most 'Wise Creator' in the disposition of them."[3] Of course, from the short-term perspective of an organism caught in the decline of a confused, "carelessly shaken," or entropic cycle, disorder may seem *and be* evil. Milton's theodicy avoids this dilemma by ascribing the long-term persistence in such cycles solely to the satanic cohort, whose self-referentially rigid adherence to this mode constitutes both the definition and the personification of evil.

Nevertheless, it must also be admitted that the difference between an allegorical personification and a physical description of chaos is that personification brings into bolder relief the implicit properties of agency that remain far less disturbing as organic manifestations of "one first matter all." Hence, in what follows, I will be proposing that Milton uses this paradoxical personification both to dramatize the gaps in a nature that could not otherwise be harmonized with the existence of evil and to suggest the immanent links between the void's randomly creative capacity and the more highly ordered mutability of Raphael's benign first matter. In the process, Chaos also provides an imaginative bridge between the realms of physical and metaphysical causality, which were already threatened with disruption by the new philosophy. Galilean mechanics had established the conditions of this rupture by demonstrating the empirical advantages of focusing exclusively on material and efficient causes, thereafter effectively relegating final causes to the hypothetical or intangible domain of metaphysics. Chaos at least potentially spans this gap by synthesizing the "elements" of material, formal, efficient, and final causality in an *ex deo* realm of primordial particles, which ultimately impart their root energies to the refining stalk, leaf, and flower of first matter as it ascends back to God. At the same time, the primitive and indeterminate nature of chaotic energy permits it negentropically to consume the self-consuming "draff and filth" of Satan, Sin, and Death" (*PL*, 10.630). This in turn requires a subtle distinction between two otherwise similar forms of entropy stems from Milton's crucial discrimination between mere disorderly or chaotic "commixtures" and more rigidly determinate or satanic disorders. This discrimination is also implicit in the word *entropy* itself, which alternately indicates "the amount of energy unavailable for useful work in a system undergoing change" and "the degree of disorder in a substance or a system [where] entropy always increases and available energy diminishes" (*Webster's New World Dictionary*). Here, the first or neutral sense describes chaotic entropy, the second or negative sense the "heat death" fostered by satanic entropy—which then reciprocally triggers the negentropic response of Chaos's merely inertial matter.

As this feedback loop suggests, Milton's philosophical rehabilitation of Chaos also supplies the key to understand his paradoxical personification allegory—and, ultimately, of his baroque allegorical poetics as a whole. By providing a materially real, atomic substitute for the old daemonic of "occulted substances" (*chora, logoi spermatakoi, rationes seminales*) that previously mediated allegory's macrocosmic and microcosmic correspondences, his personified material agencies also supply an innovative model of how the "one first matter" of earthly existence might still plastically and irregularly reascend to God. Hence, the function of the old cosmic correspondences is restored, but in entirely remodeled form: where once ideal essences or supralunar forms had mystically in-formed sublunar "accidents in substances," here the divinely descending hegemony and even the notion of ideal forms as final causes is replaced with an irregularly ascending "stair" of material, formal, and efficient causes centered in a chaotic substrate ambiguously created by but also withdrawn from God.

As the most paradoxically passive/active agent of the poem's revitalized personifications, Chaos also models the ambivalent potential for cosmic ascent or descent more substantially (and fatefully) enacted by the poem's fully formed personae. Thus, like Chaos, none of these personae are merely abstract "conductors" of final causes in the sense that the "daemonic agents" of normative epic-allegory typically are; rather than acting as the "division of some larger power" bearing "hieratic emblems . . . so there will be no mistake that a specific Idea possesses him and governs all he does," even Milton's most surreal personified abstractions demonstrate their allegorical significance through their organic and "efficient" effect on the material continuum.[4] In this, they even more strikingly deviate from the shadowy emblematic devices or "machinery" of the neoclassical mode, whose proponents have regularly objected that Milton's Chaos, Sin, and Death refuse to do the right thing by doing everything. For, as Samuel Johnson notably (and correctly) complained, to give Sin and Death "any real employment, or ascribe to them any material agency, is to make them allegorical no longer, but to shock the mind by ascribing effects to non-entity."[5] What Johnson evidently had in mind (the meaning, not the name) was that Milton's personified abstractions not only exercise the efficient agency normally reserved for epic protagonists and antagonists but even possess more of that agency than allegory's traditional agents—the knights and distressed damsels, sorcerers and saints, conventionally governed by their reigning vice or virtue. Yet, in Milton's baroque epic, we find what we assume to be abstract emblems like Sin and Death incongruously deliberating, confiding, reciting personal histories, developing their characters, and even resisting higher authorities like God (as Sin does) and Satan (as Death does). Unlike the older personifications associated with good (Eden and heaven), evil (hell), or some intermediate domain like limbo, purgatory, or chaos, the personae of Milton's epic thus follow the same laws of organic cause and effect that are usually limited to the highest reaches of the allegorical universe. Not nonentities at all, these "accidents within substances" must then be substantially and naturalistically, not ritually or homeopathically, erased from the benign network of "one first matter."

A different but inherently similar neoclassical reaction to Milton's personification allegory (although one more often associated with the Paradise of Fools or the War in Heaven episodes) takes a comic or mock-heroic perspective on these devices, who, like Pope's cosmetic sylphs in "The Rape of the Lock," are then understood as performing a merely parodic emblematization of vice and virtue. Yet, unlike these interludes of mock-heroic parody, the cosmogonic activities of Milton's Sin, Death, and Chaos effectively structure the entire epic journey beginning in book 2 and ending in book 10.[6] Nor can this journey be dismissed as merely satanic since it involves a vast number of equally abstract or symbolic agents that the Christian poet evidently regarded as both holy and real—not only Uriel who presides over the "Arch-Chemic Sun," but a whole crew of angelic guards posted about the universe much as they are in Milton's fully "mimetic" sonnet on his blindness. Yet, even when viewed outside the lens of neoclassicism, the partially fabulous nature of these figures tends to confuse the reader since their literal functions are devoid of any systematic framework for translating these actions into a metaphysical hierarchy of meaning. At times, this lack makes their psychological and physical realism genuinely disturbing, for, as Johnson notes, while it is one thing to stage a symbolic encounter between Satan, Sin, and Death in hell, it is quite another actively to employ them in building a bridge to earth. Here, as throughout Milton's personification allegory, the reader has no guidelines but Raphael's vaguely personified "one first matter" to determine whether this bridge is symbolic or literal, metaphysically or physically real.

The most contextual solution to these problems is thus to take the functions of this universal life tree as an unusually organic clue to this missing metaphysical hierarchy since it after all exemplifies every level of matter's cosmic "exornations," whether healthy or "deprav'd from good" (*PL*, 5.472). As Raphael himself consistently implies, unlike the either/or dichotomies of most allegorical narratives, these binaries must be understood as both abstract and real, as physical and metaphysical bridges in the dialectically synthetic or nonlinear sense outlined above. The impetus toward breaking down and resynthesizing these binary oppositions into entropic and negentropic phases can once again be traced to the metaphysical rupture created by the rise of new scientific and Cartesian forms of thought. Whereas earlier Christian theology, natural philosophy, and literary allegory had assigned final causes to the highest and most privileged level of the Aristotelian hierarchy of material, formal, and efficient causality, the new empiricism would effectively invert this older hierarchy. In the following century, it would be further truncated as final causes were relegated to purely metaphysical forms of speculation, until, from the perspective of empirical science, God himself becomes a kind of afterthought. Yet, in his own period, Milton is far from atypical in shunning the extreme "atheistic" implications of the new philosophy, for, like the atomist John Ray, many of his contemporaries similarly embraced its findings while striving to conserve the divine prerogative and priority of the First Cause.[7] As particularly befits the author of a Ramist *Art of Logic,* Milton seems to have had an especially heightened sense of the importance of reformulating the logic of causal relations in ways that could recenter God in a newly decentered universe. As we have seen, his macrocosmic solution to this problem is to associate God with infinity, which means that, at the microcosmic level, he corollarily associates him with the material, formal, and efficient causes now determinately active but also infinitely random in the formerly inert or fully subjugated matter of Chaos.[8] As a result, the chaotic deep or "Tehom" of Genesis is no longer silenced but ambiguously paired (although never identified) with Milton's infinitely free God.

In this reorientation, as in so much that has seemed aberrant about *Paradise Lost,* Milton empirically reformulates the traditional fourfold hierarchy of Being without fully replacing it with the Newtonian mechanics that superseded it. In the traditional paradigm of descending causes, the final cause or Prime Mover creates the universe by instructing his efficient cause, the demiurge or Word, to "impress" his abstract formal design on inert matter. In the mechanistic universe, the "prime" movers are the efficient causes or motions that propel inert matter, thus bracketing both the final movers and the formal causes that had previously served as the tenor of their vehicle. While some final cause is still hypothetically needed to set the universe in motion, its operation is assigned either to an abstract clock-maker deity or, as in more recent physics, to a mysterious empirical "event" like the Big Bang. But, in the transitional period explored here, early modern science tends to mediate between these extremes by seeking the designer through his design, now primarily conceived as his efficient laws of motion. Milton's cosmos incorporates this characteristic tendency by tracing the deity's concealed will through his revealed laws of nature, which are traditionally regarded as accessible through the same exegetical practices as his revealed word. Yet, because Miltonic exegesis follows a highly skeptical and advanced hermeneutic logic, here "revelation" proceeds according to the self-referential dialectic characteristic of Raphael's "process of speech." In his intuitive angelic discourse, we therefore find a highly subordinated, reflexive, and continuously recycled "feedback loop" of causal connections, a complex network in which material motions exhibit the synthetically efficient and formal agencies similarly deployed by his personified abstractions. Although these agencies are inherently linked to final causes, they organically enact rather than abstractly represent those ultimate causes, which themselves terminate only in the higher spiritual void of free choice and its "chaotic" agency, the indeterminate freedom of rational subjects "demiurgically" to invest matter with their choices.

This synthesis of old and new models of causality becomes even more ambiguously "commixed" once we realize that, in leaving behind the inert stabilities of Aristotelian matter for a form of chaotic vitalism, the "embryon atoms" of Milton's Chaos become volatilely active in ways that make them partners rather than mere formal vehicles of creation's higher causes. Yet the system itself is not fully chaotic, first because higher forms at least in the long run, if also interactively, prevail over lower ones, and second because this interactive system makes all levels of the revised causal hierarchy into quasi-efficient agents determined primarily by their own viability and by the will of the First Cause only in the last instance. This last instance is illustrated by the tendency of Raphael's life tree naturally to incline toward its maker in time, although paradoxically without canceling its own independent impetus toward self-realization, which may temporarily lead in the reverse direction. Like the other binary "twins" that populate Milton's poetic imagination, the life tree thus incorporates the contrary directions personified in Chaos and Night in more stable form. Yet these stabilities themselves continue to disperse in contrary directions, personified on the one hand by the reifying "constructs" of Sin and Death and on the other by the harmonic dances in which Pan leads the Graces and the Hours. Since none of these more or less "free" improvisations on the divine schema would be possible without chaotic mutability, it provides not only an extended "gloss" on first matter but also an incipient correction of less viable emanations that, like satanic entropy, prove ultimately inefficient. Here, as the "green stalk" of the life tree formally channels the dynamism of its chaotic roots into the more fully efficient causes emanating in its "aery" leaves and rational/spiritual "flower" (of which God remains the most sovereign and immanent final cause [*PL*, 5.479–82]), Aristotelian teleology is at once reversed and recycled. Where once he sat securely at the top, God has now become the baroquely ambiguous top and bottom of a life chain everywhere informed by his vitalizing force, which is free because it is good and good because it is indeterminate even to the point of self-denial.

The "thermodynamic" paradoxes inherent in these energy transfers are thus framed by matter's ambivalently entropic impulse at once to return to God to decline from his life and light, which in itself may be meta-allegorically benign or malign. For, within each level as well as between them, root, stalk, leaf, and flower retain their own relative degrees of independent force, which, as the free will and first law of God's sovereign universe, roughly resembles the laws of the conservation of matter and energy: matter must undergo change even as its energy system is preserved. Without wholly eliminating the psychomachia of virtue and vice, the "daemonic" conductors of normative allegory are then ultimately replaced with the one enigmatic "final cause" reigning in the Miltonic universe alongside its God: the incomprehensibly blank or vacuous space inhabited by free self-determination, the benign mystery "Beyond [which] we cannot go." In discussing this enigma, John Tanner traces the ultimate indecidability of the poem's most significant events to the "etiological tautologies" produced by ethical freedom, its most "unnatural" form of determination.[9] Yet this tautological "degree zero" in no way invalidates the otherwise mimetic behavior of the poem's allegorical agents or personified abstractions, even though this new mixture of mimesis amd allegory may confuse the reader more accustomed to a relatively rigorous separation of the two. In this sense, too, Johnson was right: although all literature requires some Coleridgean "suspension of disbelief," the process is facilitated when fictions consistently employ mimetic, fabulous, or ironic modes, not an unstable mixture of each. Nevertheless, he was also wrong in misunderstanding how mixed modes of the baroque or meta-allegorical type purposefully jar readerly sensibilities in the interest of provoking the kind of engaged or "metatheatrical" self-reflexivity required by Milton's readers.

Rather than a detached censuring of Milton's decorum, the poem thus seems to demand an active reevaluation of personifications who, like ourselves, can no longer be taken as mere allegorical embodiments of good or evil. For conversely, to regard their epic confrontation as melodramatically theatrical is to risk rehearsing the largely discredited either/or response in which our sympathies are univocally identified with Satan or God. The narrative voice itself discredits this response by reminding his readers that not only Satan but even unheroically "depraved" spirits like Belial neither "lose all thir virtue" (*PL*, 2.483) nor all their freedom. Measured by the standard the Aristotle's *Nichomachean Ethics* sets for authentic self-determination, each such agent mimetically retains the ability to decide "the originating cause of his actions; deliberation has for the sphere of its operation acts which are within his own power of doing them; all that we do is done with an eye to something else. It follows that when we deliberate it is about means and not ends."[10] Nevertheless, this standard also suggests the equally important ways in which the poem's symbolic agents exercise a more liminal degree of freedom than Aristotle's ethical subjects, who act within a cosmos ordered by human logic, not divine decree. As a result, the more or less mimetically "free" choices of Miltonic agents are inscribed within an ascending scale of metaphysical freedom that relegates them to relatively higher or lower places in the global scheme of things even while they are most directly concerned with the naturalistic deliberation over means, not ends. Yet, in enacting judgments meditated within a relatively uncircumscribed sphere of action, the choices of these agents are determined chiefly by their own previous decisions and by the material laws of a universe that they just as freely perceive and interpret. Hence, in this relatively chaotic universe, as William Madsen observes, "Neither places nor things have any inherent moral or spiritual meaning or value . . . , or if they do, their meaning is ambiguous."[11]

Here, even though God remains the ultimate determinant of the fate of this universe and of its material agents, his will operates only as a truly first and final cause—not as a preordained law of absolute reason and virtue. As a result, the Prime Mover has become precisely that: the initiator and ultimate conserver of its material, formal, and material laws, but not their univocal judge and executor, as the Son's intercession and his own "permissive will" remind us (*PL*, 3.685).

For, if as his angels beatifically attest, God knows how to bring forth good from evil, so do "the Spirits damn'd / [who] Lose all thir virtue" (2.482–83). Characteristically spiritual liberty is not for Milton a fixed commodity but a variable merely minimized by those who "*still* revolt when truth would set them free."[12] Since it is alternately maximized by those who understand that the exercise of liberty demands the divinely creative restraint of the "wise and good" (sonnet 12, 10–12; emphasis added), freedom is naturalistically circumscribed only by faulty perception and illicit choice, which limit without nullifying additional and/or future deliberations.

As the emblematic good angels (Abdiel, Michael, Ithuriel, and Gabriel) illustrate, the range of rational action that "also is choice" (*PL*, 3.108) thus increases along with the individual accountability to divine law, just as that available to Beelzebub, Moloch, Belial, and Mammon is reduced in accordance with their particular abuses of its principles. Yet, even subjectively, this ethical system of accountability is vastly more mimetic than a ritual distribution of abstract vice and virtue. To much the same extent as Aristotle's ethical individual, the pragmatic choices of agents are framed by the inevitable necessities contingent on freedom itself: the exercise of a personal logic, interpretation, value system, and/or psychology. As a case in point, Moloch favors a militaristic ethos because both his innate disposition and his self-chosen "gifts" lead him to this "vocation," which in itself might be used either for good or for ill, as the other martial angels illustrate. Similarly, Mammon's innate predilection for splendor leads him to seek the false wealth and glory of his largely self-constructed Pandaemonium, although the "heroic" aspect of his enterprising efforts is not innately evil (1.678–92). Further, because each of these psychologies and their aspirations are open to either benign or malign transformations, the poem's only fully fated actions are limited to those who "still" persist in a willful misprision of their own best means and ends. For those hopelessly self-imprisoned by persisting in this self-alienation, God's decrees provide only a final "revelation" of their freely chosen access to ends that organically cause their poetically and ethically just fate.

Beyond these diffuse allegorical parameters, no form of choice, malign or benign, leads magically, independently, or "fatally" to a salvation or a damnation that Milton's meta-allegory leaves to the agent's own self-construction, which fundamentally involves his or her interpretation of the divine life principle. Unquestionably, the epic also moralizes the operation of this life principle in Puritan terms by affirming temperance as freedom and condemning unrestrained sensuality as idolatry and/or enslavement. Yet, because this moral system also includes the Puritan and/or Arminian principle of individual self-determination, it notably excludes any Bunyanesque anatomy of the emblematic acts, attributes, or ritual passages of the elect enrolled in the Book of Life. While the names of the elect are available to divine foreknowledge, at no point in time before the apocalypse does this knowledge influence decisions that "without least impulse of shadow of Fate, / Or aught by me immutably foreseen," require all God's creatures to become "Authors to themselves" (*PL,* 3.121–23). Even though his edicts are prophetically foreknown, their material and temporal "providence" remains obscure to all but the Son, who at least in the human space/time of *Paradise Regained* is only somewhat more assured of their meaning than Satan himself. Hence, if the teleological design of divine Providence has hardly disappeared from Milton's epic, it has also been reduced to a gravitational pull like "the curvature of the earth, indisputable but also invisible." As G. K. Hunter's incisive remark then implies, the causal and ethical consequences of the poem's meta-allegorical design extend the cosmic reaches of its material paradoxes far beyond the normal metaphysical limits of abstract personification into a realm of virtually, if never wholly, mimetic agency.[13]

2

With this framework in mind, we can now narrowly focus on Raphael's seminal personification of Milton's monism, the fourfold dialectical "tree" through which he would have his pupils imagine Being continually being converted into becoming:

> O *Adam,* one Almighty is, from whom
> All things proceed, and up to him return,
> If not deprav'd from good, created all
> Such to perfection, one first matter all,
> Indu'd with various forms, various degrees
> Of substance, and in things that live, of life;
> But more refin'd, more spiritous, and pure,
> As nearer to him plac't or nearer tending

Each in thir several active Spheres assign'd,
Till body up to spirit work, in bounds
Proportion'd to each kind.
(*PL*, 5.469–79)

The immediate question here is how, within this scheme, the funda-
mental but mutable integrity of these universal molecules tends to-
ward order if not through the Neoplatonic ladder or "chain of being"
whereby matter autotelically ascends to spirit. Despite its superficial
resemblance to this conventional chain, William Kerrigan convinc-
ingly argues that Raphael's tree so thoroughly reworks the schema
that "All being is unchained." Although matter becomes more "spir-
itous" by degrees as it approaches the "one Almighty," its relative
"degree" is not solely determined by whether it is "nearer to him
plac't or nearer tending," for, "if all things 'up to him return,' they
must be 'plac't *and* 'tending.'" Much like the quasi-indeterminate
causality of the Miltonic metaphor itself, this causal system thus
replaces a hierarchy of innate orders with a mutable system of in-
teractive "degrees," for, as Kerrigan further points out, not only is
Milton's chain of being more random than Pico's, but its immutable
essences have been dissolved by an atomistic continuum of multi-
valent causation. Where Pico had regarded man's place in the uni-
verse—but not the universe itself—as mutable and relative, Milton's
"profoundly heterodox view" resembles Giordano Bruno's equally
radical reformulation of universal order. For Bruno, two species of
the same order are no longer differentiated by distinct material sub-
stances that have been infused into the same formal essence, but
"that which is common has the function of matter; [while] that
which is individual and brings about the distinction, has the function
of form."[14] In other words, formal causes have now become an aspect
of efficient causality operating within a relatively uniform (if also
randomly "plastic") matter.

Thus, Bruno and Milton similarly anticipate the profound re-
orientation of thought in the Classic Age, which, by replacing for-
mal with material and efficient causality, fundamentally destroys the
principle of analogy that Foucault regards as the fundamental feature
of traditional Renaissance hermeneutics. Where a series of abstract
correspondences had previously connected each level of the old chain
of being, now only physical and/or organic interactions conduct the
workings of the universal laws of matter. Instead of conceiving each

order or level of being as an interlocking link in a hierarchy of parallel forms—so that, for instance, in the vegetable, animal, mineral, and human kingdoms, oak is to lion as gold is to king—now organic continuities of the root-stalk-leaf-flower variety structure material forms of evolution and causation. Where formerly the rational soul had been understood as the microcosmic "king" of the commonwealth of the body, now both are regarded as corpuscularly continuous. In this transitional phase of seventeenth-century natural (and, by extension, political) philosophy, spirit, like God and king, begins to lose its absolute ontological primacy as first and final cause—a consequence that in Milton's case is registered by his semi-mystified, seminaturalistic substitution of these authorities with the abstract ideals of free will and spiritual liberty. Yet, partly as a result of this substitution, his reformulated final causality gains a complementary, if also equivocally real, relevance in the causal hierarchy as the most open-ended and therefore viable level of this destabilized scale of value. Viewed now as a naturalistic series of gradations on an infinite scale of "dense to rare," this new material continuum of interlocking cause and effect also informs the logical hierarchy of Ramistic causes personified in Milton's various degrees of densely material, efficiently interactive, but also ultimately rare substances ascending toward God. Yet, in the process, this hierarchy has been so thoroughly destabilized that (as the Son affirmatively, and Satan negatively, shows) even falling may lead to rising.[15]

This mutability prevails within every level, not merely between its unorthodoxly interactive top and bottom, since, in accord with Galileo's abstract science of motion, even "natural" directions like *up* and *down* are subjected to iconoclastic critique. While the material root of creation tends upward, this tendency does not in itself create a new framework of absolutely meaningful directions or places, a new ritual scale of value. Although Raphael's power and rank greatly exceed Adam's, Raphael encounters no physical obstacle nor incurs any metaphysical loss in converting Adam's hospitable offerings "to proper substance." At the same time, while Raphael assures him that, if he continues to improve, "by tract of time" he will be able to enjoy heavenly food as "No inconvenient Diet, nor too light Fare," the choice is entirely his as to whether "Here or in Heav'nly Paradises [to] dwell" (*PL,* 5.492–501). Thus, in place of a Platonic ascent from body to soul or an Aristotelian hierarchy of spatial levels, Milton's cosmos reflects the contemporary atomist revival of the *potentia materiae* that late classical (Stoic as well as Epicurean) philosophy derived from Aristotle's revision of Plato. Here "there is no true difference . . . between matter and form; they are only abstractions and are in reality two aspects of the same entity."[16]

Metaphysically, this form/matter continues to act as an ontological "chiasmas" within creation, although it no longer mystically conjoins "cosmic place and abstract space" as it had in the *Timaeus;* physically, however, this *potentia materiae* has become a protoscientific postulate, even while continuing to perform the essentially metaphysical or moral harmonization of material freedom with the freedom of "right reason," whose perfect fusion is personified as the divine first cause of the universal design.[17] This synthesis seems even less mystified in a period in which physics had not yet been divorced from metaphysics and still less when considered as a prophetic vision outlining the vitalistic feedback processes of modern complexity theory. Of course, Milton's terms are obviously quite different, for, in his system, matter becomes spirit and spirit matter in ways that make the evolution of men and angels not fundamentally different from that of fruits and flowers. Yet both spectrums are now uniformly organized by constant physical laws that, as in modern materialism, govern the rational soul or mind much as they govern the flowers of earth or of heaven, the latter of which include the sun's alchemical fruits, "bright"

> Compar'd with aught on Earth, Metal or Stone;
> Not all parts like, but all alike inform'd
> With radiant light, as glowing Iron with fire.
> (*PL*, 3.591–94)

All such fruits thus mature by synthesizing lower substances (such as the sun's "Terrestrial Humor" [3.610]) into their natural flowers, whose seeds are in turn recycled to feed other links in this hyperorganic chain. In its broadest spectrum, even the vicissitudes of life and death, light and darkness, have been reconceived as binary phases of a monist continuum that contains the equivocal potential for expansion as well as contraction, rising as well as falling. While more rarefied, spiritous, and pure forms like Uriel or Raphael are freer and hence can access a fuller and more varied range of experience and understanding, matter's spontaneously self-transforming mutability remains a more essential aspect of its continuing freedom than its relative rarity or density. Except for love, at once the essence of creaturely obedience and its only fully free or adequate sign, only the comparable, if also incommensurable, freedom of divine grace externally determines "Whose progeny you are" (5.501–3).

These paradoxically "twinned" internal and external determinants of creaturely "place" within an essentially fluid hierarchy of being metaphysically mirror the determination of place in both Galilean physics and Lucretian natural philosophy. While Galilean mechanics seems to have influenced Milton's uniformly and "efficiently" ordered conception of the spatial continuum, the more overtly metaphysical implications of Lucretian atomism seem to have influenced his conception of the randomness of subatomic, chaotic structures as both the complement and the medium of divine necessity, not as its opponent. As Michel Serres similarly notes, the pre-Newtonian context of Lucretian science thus ironically anticipates the post-Newtonian models of modern chaos or complexity theory, which once again regard randomly entropic molecules as irregularly but also predictably regenerative in systems far from equilibrium. In these evolutionary systems, chance (irregularity, unpredictability, or noise) is opposed, not to orderly necessity, but to the nonconservation of energy itself.[18] In far more primitive form, this vitalist affirmation of material randomness is available not only in Lucretius's *De rerum natura* and Plato's *Timaeus* but also in the pre-Socratics' commentary on Hesiod, an allegorical tradition of natural philosophy with which both Milton's *Of Education* and his allusion to Heraclitus in *The Reason of Church Government* (*CPW*, 1:795) show he was familiar. In resynthesizing this vitalist philosophy from its mythopoetic roots in Hesiod's Chaos and its classical commentators, Milton thus "prophetically" recuperates randomness as the natural medium of the interchangeable processes of cause and effect, the fluid diads operating at every material level of his cosmos, including that of his personification allegory.

To demonstrate convincingly how such diads support rather than undermine Milton's monism, two governing assumptions must be reemphasized: first, that this mythopoetic or protoscientific form of monism generically conforms to the principles of modern scientific materialism; and, second, that, strictly speaking, neither Milton's nor ours is a pure monism but a postulated unity always expressible as the function of two phases. As we have seen, in physical theory, this elemental binarism is denoted by the dual phases of thermodynamic entropy: the "chaotic" disordering of energy within any given closed system and the reordering, by way of negentropic recovery, of energy entropically degraded in one closed system and reassimilated into another that is open-ended with respect to the first. Humanly speaking, this means that each of us is a self-organizing system negentropically feeding off the entropic degradation of another system's ordered substance, turning the matter originally constituting it as a closed system into our open-ended accommodation to the exigencies of life within this binary-phased universe, where everything is simultaneously breaking down and building up.

In the largely animistic terms of *Paradise Lost*, the fundamental binarism of something like the material forces of entropy and negentropy is most apparent in Chaos and Night. Chaos disperses the "embryon Atoms" (*PL*, 2.900) over which he presides as a pseudo-"Umpire" whose "decision more imbroils the fray / By which he Reigns" (2.907–9), while Night seems negentropically to conglobe the dark materials later used to "create more Worlds." Their realm is thus simultaneously the "Womb of nature and perhaps her Grave," a random continuum of "pregnant causes mixt / Confus'dly" (2.911–14), but fertilely, since its fluid indeterminacy supplies the source both of the death principle (the "black tartareous cold Infernal dregs" purged from the newborn earth) and of the life principle (the "vital warmth" that engenders its evolving forms). Thus, as the chaotic Abyss is summoned to participate in earth's creation, its differently valenced matters "dispart" some elements and conglobe others, until, as "Like things to like" adhere, a pregnant residue congeals at earth's "self-balanct" center. Yet these double valences continue to inform the fertile dichotomies of "Male and Femal Light, / Which two great Sexes animate the World" (8.150–51), which less "confusedly" conserve traces in the "Matter unform'd and void" (7.233) of Chaos and Night. As a result, its more mutable Anarch can without out logical contradiction obey both the creative voice of "Paternal Glory" (7.219–21) and the entropic voice of his adversary, who promises only "Havoc and spoil and ruin [as his] . . . gain" (2.1009), for, in the broader or more "negentropic" perspective, this very ambivalence provides the material/molecular basis of the life chain's regenerative capacity. Far more vitally and materially than its "higher" relatives— the "grateful vicissitude" of heavenly twilight or of Eden's benignly revolving seasons—this double-valenced personification supplies the plastic roots of creation that may be either malignly or benignly "engrafted" by the poem's more efficient agents—and thus the basis of their material freedom.[19]

Within the parameters outlined above, this freedom is necessarily shared by agents who have been "deprav'd from good," with the result that the efficient agency of Sin and Death becomes a logical corollary of rather than an "aberration" within the naturalized (if still teleo- logical) causal system of baroque allegory. Far from behaving like fictions that "have no real effect on paradise," as Maureen Quilligan claims, these allegorical agents demonstrate a range of deliberative and material freedom as temporally real and as limited as Satan's own.[20] Acting no longer as "hieratic" but as efficient "daemons," Sin and Death perform acts of destruction calling for real exclamations of divine wrath and satanic exultation. Unilaterally "deciding" to ravage earth, they thus exhibit both the "natural sympathies" imparted by their "original" and some of the genuine creativity in which, for Milton, freedom consists. Moreover, if they did not, Milton's the- odicy would fall into the trap that normative allegory avoids only through its transcendentalizing impetus: that of implicitly placing the blame for the Fall on the Prime Mover, who designed its pre- determined hierarchies and their agents. In contrast, God is here exonerated at the paradoxical price of his own supremacy, which could but will not violate his own natural laws by interfering with the free will of agents who by definition are far more than mere fictive "nothings." Because their organic self-alteration makes the malig- nant effects of Satan, Sin, and Death on our Grand Parents the result of a cruel disease rather than of a cruel test, once again the physical effects of entropy and the psychic effects of dysfunction replace the ritual purification of sin on which both the traditional sacramental system and its allegorical manifestations are based.[21]

Like that accompanying his prophecy of Adam's disobedience, these alterations explain the wrath that God expresses in watching the ravages of these "Dogs of Hell" (*PL*, 10.616), further emphasiz- ing his self-imposed inability temporally to interfere with what ei- ther his sons or his daughters—or even Satan's—choose. For, unlike the Calvinist God who failed, Milton's deity is less a voluntarist God or a personal savior than the personalized guardian of his primary natural laws of free self-determination. An additional, if somewhat startling, corollary of this position is that he must experience real anguish when these laws are transgressed by others. Not divinely aloof, Milton's God therefore reacts more on the model of a human parent who is at once grieved and offended by the inevitable consequences of a transgression that his children were warned to avoid but that he is personally powerless to ward off. Although his powers of retribution naturally exceed those of a mortal father, like him he can best display his justice and mercy by relying on the redemptive example of the faithful Son, who understands not only the value and the limits of his gifts but how best to balance his law with love:

> . . . well thou know'st how dear
> To me are all my works, nor Man the least
> Though last created, that for him I spare
> Thee from my bosom and right hand, to save,
> And by losing thee a while, the whole race lost.
> (3.276–80)

This answering and unqualified approval of his Son's willingness to ransom back the "whole race lost" at once changes the entire meaning of "Die hee or Justice must" (3.210) and demonstrates the vital role accorded efficient causes throughout the epic.[22]

Here, as elsewhere, God's decrees are not proactive but retroactive, negotiating and then renegotiating decisions that are worked out in accordance with the course his creation has first chosen for itself. Thus, without fail, what initially looks like divine intervention turns out to be the clarifying function of divine Truth, the cornerstone of both God's justice and his mercy or love. The conjunction of these three traditional "final causes" within his newly interactive agency also suggests some additional reasons for the paradoxical expansion and contraction of the deity's role. As the redefined "last instance" or cause of the epic action, he determines the outcome but not the intermediate shape of a dynamic universe in which his self-willed restraint makes him peculiarly vulnerable to the injury of misinterpretation. In this instance, the general outlines of Milton's revision of the relation between natural understanding and natural law seem particularly Baconian. Final causes (both the divine First Mover and his laws of nature) are meant to guide the perception as well as the activity of the human agent, who is at once "free" to interpret yet "bound" to respect their principles. Hence, if "the road itself has been mistaken, and men's labour spent on unfit objects, it follows that the difficulty has its rise not in things themselves, which are not in our power, but in the human understanding, and the use and application thereof, which admits of remedy and medicine."[23] As the signpost but not the gatekeeper of this path, God must "stand and wait" while his subjects recuperatively remedy their understanding by realigning it with the actual nature of things, pursuing the "road mistaken" until they turn around—or terminate in a cul-de-sac.

Milton's personified Sin herself illustrates this logic when she "decides" to unlock hell's gates for her father, a decision-making process that illustrates not a failure of true choice but a perversion of its more medicinal uses. Nevertheless, if her obedience to Satan constitutes disobedience to God and to her own ultimate health, she is at least accurately assessing where her immediate interests lie, which may constitute a road permanently mistaken but a real road nonetheless. Further, where a traditional allegory would make it unquestionably clear that Sin must simply repeat Satan's error, her deliberations ironically reveal a daughter who is even more sinisterly self-interested than her own half-repentant father, as the eery logic with which she justifies her course reveals: since God did not directly create her, she hardly owes him the "natural" affection that she feels for Satan and with which he is sinisterly repaid in kind.[24] Rather like the "good" daughter of an abusive father, she thus betrays an obsessive concern with her family line, a trait we might expect in a mimetic character but not in an abstract vice lacking a metaphysical future. In Sin's behavior, then, there is the same potent mixture of allegorical schema and correction that characterizes the new *potentia materiae* of chaotic matter. If in some ways she is appropriately and traditionally daemonic in copying her demonic source, her imitation of Satan's behavior also caricatures and expands it to reveal its self-determining entropy, for his firstborn exhibits both a congenital resemblance to her depraved original and an instinctive taste for his reductive remedies that actually increase the efficient poison of the "medicine."

Born along with and probably from a sin-uous deformation of Satan's higher substance, Sin's very limitations (like those of more conventional personified abstractions) nevertheless allow her to identify her original's error with a clarity that his greater rhetorical freedom willfully obscures. Maligning God in his own image, the supreme liar and tempter had argued that his fall was caused by God: he "his strength conceal'd, / Which tempted our attempt, and wrought our fall" (*PL*, 641–42). But, as we have seen, this response also obliquely testifies to his ironic "faithfulness" to his divine original since it unwittingly demonstrates both the Father's refusal of coercive force and Satan's own insistence on misconstruing its meaning—which, in the broader allegorical context, effectively "defines" his own self-begotten temptation. In this context, his daughter Sin represents something like a full-scale return of the repressed, although chiefly in the sense where myth and psychology meet, for her allegiance to her disloyal father is not only natural but sensible, remaining as he does the only realistic hope for either her or her son Death. Yet, even if she can neither genetically nor logically avoid the "secret harmony" (10.358) drawing her to Satan, her inversion of heavenly restraint and affection is portrayed as mimetically "efficient" rather than predestined or immaterial. If her conception and development doom her to be less free than the children of innocence, she still receives some portion of Satan's divine inheritance, which, like a "natural" daughter, she interprets according to her own quite personal lights—or darknesses. Because even the fallen Satan remains free to change and, at least momentarily, almost decisively to repent (9.465), he is also able to relay these naturalistic energies to his children to a degree far exceeding those accorded the daemons of Realist allegory.[25] Moreover, because the genetic links between him and his children are organic rather than magical, their perversion of "one first matter" is substantial and psychological rather than merely symbolic, as soon becomes apparent as they invade Eden.

In this invasion, the full range of material and efficient causes "ruining" paradise is conveyed by the simultaneously verbal and nominal sense of the word *outrage*. Nominally, *outrage* signifies the "lateral noise" of divine disapproval as winds and storms burst "thir brazen Dungeon" somewhere to the "North" of Chaos (*PL*, 10.697); verbally, it conveys the psychosomatic consequences of the human lapse. These twinned part-whole (synecdochic) and causal (metonymic) effects are doubly appropriate here since, like Satan and Sin, Adam and Eve have holistically diverted benign natural causes to fully discordant or inefficient ends. By committing this simultaneously ethical and physical outrage, the two human "Lords of the World" literally turn neutral matter into a destructive force in which Chaos has come again. Yet, at this juncture, it comes with a particularly entropic or satanic vengeance, as a new grandchild enters Satan's personified but scarcely abstract family:

. . . Thus began
Outrage from lifeless things; but Discord first
Daughter of Sin, among th' irrational,
Death introduc'd through fierce antipathy:
Beast now with Beast gan war, and Fowl with Fowl,
And Fish with Fish; to graze the Herb all leaving,
Devour'd each other; nor stood much in awe
Of Man, but fled him, or with count'nance grim
Glar'd on him passing. . . .
(10.706–14)

As a meta-allegory within an allegory, the story of Death's sister
Discord completes the epic definition of the causal agency possessed
by personified abstractions of all valences, entropic or negentropic.
By inducing his sister to disrupt the lower relations "among th' irra-
tional" creatures after Satan's "efficient" ambitions have spread dis-
cord to the rational ones, Death assists Sin in relaying the final causes
of free choice into the psychically efficient emotional causes soon
materially to alter earth's life chain:

. . . nor only Tears
Rain'd at thir Eyes, but high Winds worse within
Began to rise, high Passions, Anger, Hate,
Mistrust, Suspicion, Discord, shook sore
Thir inward State of Mind, calm Region once
And full of Peace, now toss't and turbulent:
For Understanding rul'd not, and the Will
Heard not her lore, both in subjection now
To sensual Appetite, who from beneath
Usurping over Sovran Reason claim'd
Superior sway. . . .
(*PL*, 9.1121–31)

In this downturn of the entropic cycle, the fruit of "sensual appetite"
is linked to its material root, the temptation that gives birth to Sin,
Death, and Discord—whose psychic role in hell is allegorically sup-
plied by the hounds gnawing at their mother's entrails. These paral-
lel effects suggest that the same selfish causes that produce Satan's
"Anger, Hate, Mistrust, Suspicion," and, ultimately, this infernal
triad of his offspring, have similarly "infected" Adam and Eve. By
disrupting the truly efficient causality inherent in the proper order of

"one first matter," they have tyrannically overthrown reason and reaped the illusory, self-aggrandizing fruit that degeneratively seizes and entropically disorders each level of their internal and external chain of being.

Through these relentlessly twinned material/efficient agencies, these personified causes conduct the physical and metaphysical met-amorphosis induced by succumbing to their addictive allure, the double vision and the double bind that cause their victims to sacrifice themselves to an illusion. Yet, once this magical illusion is accepted as real, its appearances become a new reality, although hardly in the way their victims imagined. Through a chain so tight that the reveal-ing golden net in which Vulcan ensnares Mars and Venus seems reborn in the terms of a protomodern ego psychology, Discord and her incestuous siblings produce mirroring images of themselves throughout the Oedipally fallen world. She appears first in Adam's "discordant" "at/tempt" to lay all blame, not merely on Eve, but even on her formal shape: the golden hair and feminine curvature he now misidentifies as serpentine (*PL,* 10.869–71). Self-deceptively ignor-ing the Fall's "higher" and more ultimately efficient causes in his own free desire (which will soon be pointed out to him by the Son), like Satan's children Adam attempts to exculpate himself by means of a naive allegorical "fate" magically "caught" from a "daemonic" shape, "Crooked by nature, bent, as now appears, / More to the part sinister from me drawn" (10.885–86). Like the satanic family "twisting" Eve's vital elements by sin-isterly reifying the form he had not long before praised as "manlike, but . . . so lovely fair," made to his deepest "heart's desire" (8.471, 451), he now reduces her body to a ritual allegory of contaminating "places." For this misprision, like the oth-ers, Adam will have to pay by experiencing the entropic causes and effects of his self-serving reductions of a far more benignly random material reality. While some of these consequences, like Death itself, are external and physical, in this allegory the most disabling ones are internal, like the deformations besetting Sin herself. Disfigured by incest, her stubbornly narcissistic energies later take the expanded shape of the interpersonal discord that will return to haunt her new sons, who, as Adam predicts, will reprise his own lapse as they find themselves "Wedlock-bound" to "hate or shame," which "infinite calamity shall cause / To Human life, and household peace con-found" (10.905–8).

As a negative formal potential activated by the efficient power of these perversely reifying (although at first also potentially liberating) aspirations, illusion and deception are here imaged as the twinned forces operative within fallen perception and desire, which are in turn traced to a unitary perversion of the will and its higher potential. Thus, like mother, Sin, and brother Death, sister Discord's psychosomatic "work" is "sin-uous" chiefly in the baroque sense of producing a tortuously winding, convoluted, and entangling displacement of physical and metaphysical desire that disappears into the ultimate vanishing point of free will. Originating in the same "unruly" or unruled desires that cause Adam and Eve to ignore God's commands, Discord's sway is extended by the further corruption of natural reason, whose "true" exercise demands the same obedience to the free law of benevolent love and desire as other natural reflections of the divine will. Once this corollary of right reason has been divested from them, the animals' "rational" regard for and obedience to Adam and Eve is overturned, along with their mutual regard for one another, and the earthly war between the species and genders begins. But meta-allegorically, this misrule corresponds to the disruptive entropy Satan and his offspring introduce into Chaos's merely mutable matter: the formal disparity between perception and substance exhibited by all his tribe. This "disease" acts like a cancer or corruption within the harmonious relay system uniting root, stalk, leaf, and flower, which, in response to their intervention, reverses its normal ascent and produces a more "dense" or restrictive earthly hierarchy. By corrupting the final or intellectual cause of freedom (the life chain's universal "flower"), fallen motives bear diseased perceptual "leaves" that thereafter poison the stalk, which then physically perverts the roots, leading to new but abortive growth. Yet, these organic interactions remain fundamentally allegorical, as these highly symmetrical correspondences between perception, emotion, physiology, and sociology suggest. Through natural causes whose symmetries are far too strict to be fully naturalistic, Discord reproduces the narcissistic psychology at work in the satanic family romance as well as its ethical and social effects—pride, incest, and household destruction. Thus, as Sin herself observes of this allegorical "romance," as in light and life, so in "Shade," "Death from Sin no power can separate" (*PL*, 10.249, 251).

3

Nevertheless, because God's active will can be harmonized only with an ultimately benign universal design, which causes the profoundly mutable diads of Chaos also "evolve" into an important third term, a negentropic antithesis to the double valences of ascent and descent. As in all the dimensions of Milton's baroque cosmos, this vertical schema is then "corrected" by the horizontal vector of temporal evolution. In narrative terms, this means that threefold Chaos first occupies an initial and relatively inertial state as nature's "eldest birth," then undergoes an ambiguous phase where it alternately interacts with the opposing formal/efficient causes represented by Satan and the Son, and finally enters its own fully efficient phase where, in conformity with its *ex deo* origins, it absorbs the necessary recoil of Satan's dissipative entropy into itself. In this final phase, it spontaneously returns to the providential design by "swallowing" the dregs of evil and death, much as it had spontaneously "recycled" the "tartareous" waste produced by earth's creation. Although there seems to be some concealed prophecy of later science fiction in these personified chaos wars, their main features are most likely borrowed from the classical commentaries on Hesiod's *Theogony* alluded to above, which generally exhibit a similar three-phase development.[26]

As also suggested above, these phases can also be understood in thermodynamic terms, which when fused with those of theodicy would mean that only when a determined alienation from *ex deo* or neutral entropy replaces an indeterminate one—or only when evil enters Chaos—does the second physical sense of the word *entropy* replace the first: instead of existing simply as a "measure of the amount of energy unavailable for useful work in a system undergoing change," evil makes entropy "a measure of the degree of disorder in a substance or a system [where] entropy always increases and available energy diminishes." Yet, if like energy Chaos remains "open" to both the benign and the evil strife of creation, it also remains essentially true to its divine origin in providing an arena for disorder that not only initiates but at last conserves its benignly random design. Although in the short run it may serve the purposes of evil, in the long run it serves the divine purpose of supplying the negentropic or "final remedie" for the "filth" of Sin and Death (*PL,* 10.630)—the ultimate "grave" (2.911) that perverted matter unconsciously craves.

Here, as in Heraclitan atomism (which, like most of pre-Socratic philosophy, serves as an extended gloss on Hesiod), "change from one to another brings about a total change of name, which is misleading, because only a superficial component has altered and the most important constituent remains."[27] Applied to Chaos, the dictum suggests that, even apart from its personification of a paradoxical indeterminacy or freedom, its principles are no more logically contradictory than the thermodynamic laws stating the principle of entropy: for here, as in the first law of thermodynamics, however converted, matter/energy is always conserved.

While these principles had not yet been formulated by seventeenth-century science, their basic assumptions are patently present in the poem's natural philosophical foundation, as Harinder Marjara's commentary suggests: "The process of change from one element to another and from one substance to another is not, in Milton, a mechanical process of rarefaction or condensation, though the images of 'dense' and 'rare' occur frequently in *Paradise Lost*. A qualitative change is taken for granted, but at the same time, Milton assumes that the essential matter which they are made of remains the same. There is no real duality between corporeal and incorporeal substances, and the vertical rise is merely a change from a lower to a higher degree, and not a transformation into a different kind."[28] Thus, matter is conserved even as it is alternately transformed into more dense or rare, more entropically stable and "heavy," or more regeneratively mutable and "light,"

> For hot, cold, moist, and dry, four Champions fierce
> Strive here for Maistry, and to Battle bring
> Thir embryon Atoms; they around the flag
> Of each his Faction, in thir several Clans,
> Light-arm'd or heavy, sharp, smooth swift or slow,
> Swarm populous, unnumber'd as the Sands. . . .
> (*PL*, 2.898–903)

As throughout Milton's work, here destruction is inherent in creation, but in a strikingly contemporary sense: because every action has an equal and opposite reaction, both satanic destruction and human recuperation "chaotically" emerge from the same indeterminate source.

In *Paradise Lost*, the processes begun in Chaos end allegorically with the final transmogrification of the demons into serpents, which then anagogically forecasts the final end of Sin, Death, and Discord even as they begin their destructive work. Although this fate is at the same time "sealed" by God (*PL,* 10.616–40), the "organic" roots of their demise can be traced to the little-noted simile in which Satan begins to slog through Chaos's liminal realm, which is "neither Sea, / Nor good dry Land" (2.939–40). Here he is described

> As when a Gryfon through the Wilderness
> With winged course o'er Hill or moory Dale,
> Pursues the *Arimaspian,* who by stealth
> Had from this wakeful custody purloin'd
> The guarded Gold: So eagerly the fiend
> O'er bog or steep, through strait, rough, dense, or rare,
> With head, hands, wings or feet pursues his way,
> And swims or sinks, or wades, or creeps, or flies.
> (2.943–50)

Physically, this description of Satan's material interaction with the ambiguous "bog" foreshadows both his prelapsarian transformation into the "subtle serpent" and his offspring's postlapsarian transformations of earth's benignly "creeping" and "flying" animals into beasts of prey. Metaphysically, it emphasizes his connection with the griffin, a traditional allegorical emblem of moral alienation from the warmth of the Holy Spirit. But, at an even deeper level, the analogy underscores the monistic thesis, synthesis, and antithesis of chaotic matter by means of a typically trifold energy or light symbol. Not only does Satan's griffin-like attempt to recapture his "guarded gold" emphasize the "precious bane's" common yet disparate uses in heaven, earth, and hell, but it also suggests how heavenly gold excels chiefly in being most variable, liquid, and free. Whereas in heaven it is merely the gleaming foil for the living roses and amarant of angelic crowns cast down on heaven's floor, the essence and flower of spontaneous joy (3.350–54, 362–64), in hell it is hardened into the deadly capstone of Pandaemonium, the native seat of the griffin.[29]

Here, as throughout the Miltonic universe, higher or more "efficient" causes remain free to flow or to enclose, limit, and/or objectify originally mobile matter, yet they must also suffer what they create. Matter may be "purloined" at every level of the monistic universe, whether from heavenly rivers rolling "o'er *Elysian* Flow'rs her Amber stream" (*PL,* 3.358–59) or from the less peaceful, if more "pregnant," tumult of "hot, cold, moist, and dry" in Chaos. The influx of satanic entropy at both levels occurs as it interferes with this more potent flux in corrosively subduing volatile elements that would otherwise remain pregnantly "mixt." The essentially unnatural or energy-depleting aspect of this "heat-death" is proleptically contextualized in the similes surrounding Satan's preliminary "reunion" with Sin and Death. When challenged by a son and king who uses his reign only "to enrage thee more" (2.698), Satan will confront his still more entropic alter ego, a shape "tenfold / More dreadful and deform,"

> Unterrifi'd, and like a Comet burn'd,
> That fires the length of *Ophiucus* huge
> In th' Artick Sky, and from his horrid hair
> Shakes Pestilence and Warr.
>
> (2.705–11)

This confrontation thus confirms Satan's material collusion with the fiery "instruments of cold, pestilence, and war," which, like *Ophiucus*, the "serpent-bearer" comet, he "disparts" from the naturally mixed flux of Chaos as if to reappropriate the "tartareous" elements rejected at the Son's creation of the earth.[30] The result of this mortifying collision of satanic or positive negation with the utter negation of Death is thus likened to

> . . . when two black Clouds
> With Heav'n's Artillery fraught, come rattling on
> Over the *Caspian*, then stand front to front
> Hovr'ing a space, till Winds the signal blow
> To joyn thir dark Encounter in mid air:
> So frownd the mighty Combatants, that Hell
> Grew darker at thir frown, so matcht they stood;
> For never but once more was either like
> To meet so great a foe. . . .
>
> (2.714–22)

As this simile implies, the logical opponent of the father is found in his still "icier" son, whose midair encounter threatens Satan with a premature head wound (cf. *PR,* 4.568). Death's similarly "self-begotten" misappropriation of the Son's role is then signaled both by the substitution of the latter's righteous sword for the former's mortal dart and by the halting or "freezing" effect that this encounter has on hell, whose fires thereupon grow darker, not brighter, as they might in a more naive epic cosmos. These deviations also underscore how Sin's "merciful" preservation of Satan from Death's "mortal dint" (*PL,* 2.813) or thunderclap (*OED* 1b) ironically promotes an even deadlier collusion of cold energies diverted from their proper source, the benignly balanced mediation of divinely random energy contained in the fertile entropy of Chaos. The psychic parallel of this material diversion then appears in Satan's attempt to distance himself from his own offspring, to whom he declares, "I know thee not, nor ever saw till now / Sight more detestable than him and thee" (2.744–45). This ironic echo of the final judgment on those who fail either to give or to receive God's mercy—"depart from me, I never knew ye"—also indicates Satan's simultaneously metaphysical and physical alienation from the benign source of divine creation. Precisely because he has carnally known Sin, he now knows her not (this incestuous experience and its fruits having physically deformed her beyond recognition), with the result that, like a gothic self-portrait, his "perfect image" more closely resembles him the more he denies her, who is indeed remains the "perfect image" of his own perversion. Through the same "attractive graces" that produced her self-consuming conceptions, Death and his pack of "yelling Monsters" (2.762–66, 795), Sin then reflects back the deadly kind of "love" her father and son have for her, which narcissistically inverts and "hardens" the divine, life-giving love that all three deflect from each other.

Nevertheless, once he has sufficiently recovered from his initial shock and learned "his lore" (*PL,* 2.815) from his daughter, Satan gladly "claims" this dreadful duo—for a price. Bartering his recognition of them for their own acceptance of the effects of sin, this exchange will only increase their mutual hardening and psychic disintegration—as Satan's answer "smooth" implies:

> Dear Daughter, since thou claim'st me for thy Sire,
> And my fair Son here shows't me, the dear pledge
> Of dalliance had with thee in Heav'n, and joys
> Then sweet, now sad to mention, through dire change
> Befall'n us unforeseen, unthought of, know
> I come no enemy, but to set free
> From out this dark and dismal house of pain,
> Both him and thee, and all the heav'nly Host
> . . . .
> And bring ye to the place where Thou and Death

Shall dwell at ease, . . .

. . . .

. . . there ye shall be fed and fill'd
Immeasurably, all things shall be your prey.

(2.817–24, 840–41, 843–44)

Trusting in these false promises to free them from a perpetual state of famine that can be filled neither in hell nor on earth, Sin and Death thus await a new world of light and bliss even as their father effectively consigns them to the forces of a far more abortive entropy than any congealed in Night's "original darkness" (2.984). Yet, if for all three the prospect of an ascent to light is clearly a hallucinatory inversion of their entropic decay, once again the material effects of this delusion are not in themselves unreal. Since, both in word and in deed, Satan's misprisions at last imprison them all, behind the "bars" of his final allegorical transformation he will at last see the reality of his own "perfect image," as

His Visage drawn he felt to sharp and spare,
His Arms clung to his Ribs, his Legs entwining
Each other, till supplanted down he fell
A monstrous Serpent on his Belly prone,
Reluctant, but in vain. . . .

(10.511–15)

Seeing at last the death's head behind the beautiful "mask" of Sin and himself, Satan must at least recognize that, like the self-image that urged his "vain at/tempt" to usurp God's throne, his creations must retroactively recoil into the shape of his own self-conquest. Punished by assuming his own sinuous, self-chosen shape, he and his cohort are then finally damned by their own "sentences":

. . . Thus was th'applause they meant,
Turn'd to exploding hiss, triumph to shame
Cast on themselves from thir own mouths.

(*PL,* 10.545–47)

At this point, the hermeneutical circle is closed, and Satan and his cohort are appropriately allegorized to death, extinguished as immediate agents of any epic action, for by now Realist allegory and its magical illusions have been parodically exhausted as a fallen mode of reading that "reifies signification," even as Milton's naturalistically "ruined" mode meta-allegorically rises from its ashes.[31] In this ironic sense, the entire satanic cohort has all along been less real than the "pregnant causes" forever "imbroiled" by Chaos and Night, whose continuous and hence quasi-divine evolution permits no such "tartareous" self-extinctions. Unlike the elements ceaselessly circulating in a realm bordered by light (2.1035–39), satanic darkness contains a positive form of negation whose degrees of fire and ice increase in geometrical proportions inconceivable in a "Nethermost Abyss" (2.956) materially incapable of geometry or proportion.

The real yet also mixed darkness presided over by Chaos and Night thus exhibits a quite different state of entropy, an "Eternal *Anarchie*" where dimension, time, and place are lost but where negentropic "confusion stand[s]" (*PL*, 2.893–97) so as not to fall. In this sense, Sin and Night represent the consorts of two utterly different kings. While the darkness of Sin constructs a progressively deepening abyss where, as her sire later discovers, "in the lowest deep a lower deep / Still threat'ning . . . opens wide" (4.76–77), the darkness of Night is visited by ceaselessly alternating forces adhering or "ruling" for only "a moment" (2.906–7) and differing from heaven's "grateful vicissitude" (6.8) chiefly in their greater volatility. Thus, in contrast with Moloch's hellish determination that God shall yet "hear / Infernal Thunder, and for Lightning see / Black fire and horror shot with equal rage" (2.65–67), the Anarchs' state of "ruinous" noise (2.920) merely resembles a war that they can never wage. In this realm of all sound and no fury, thunder brings no lightning, much less any "efficiently" destructive fire or ice. Only with richly appropriate irony, then, does Chaos sympathize with Satan, confusing his own unarrayed confusion with the determined disarray of the forces he sees falling "With ruin upon ruin, rout on rout, / Confusion worse confounded" (*PL*, 2.995–96). Whatever his "natural" sympathies with this melee, no concerted effort on his part can actually affiliate him with Satan, for his entropic drives are limited by the very "illimitab[ility]" (2.892) of the mutable material energies (potentially both positive and negative) that inhabit his state. Consequently, he can neither accurately recognize nor aid a fiend whose banishment from light consists in the pseudoliberation that is limitation itself. Rather than real assistance, his pathetic offer of "all I can . . . [to] serve, / That little which is left so to defend" (2.999–1000) then merely marks Chaos's inevitable confusion in the face of a ruin whose direction and "speed" (2.1008) is far better organized than he can possibly imagine. His utter ineffectuality in the face of active evil (or good) is further underscored by the fact that the faithful angel Uriel, as his name indicates, the angel of the Sun, unwittingly renders far more aid and comfort to the enemy than Chaos can provide his mistaken "friends" (3.722–35).

If like Satan he thinks himself "impair'd" (*PL,* 5.665) by the recent encroachments on his realm, unlike him what Chaos actually opposes is more, not less, order. While Satan champions the static "Orders and Degrees" (5.792) that the new heavenly order has "entropically" leveled, Chaos prefers the "hubbub wild" (2.951) of the endless dissonance that he correctly associates with demonic ruin but that he incorrectly assumes is identical with his own. Again, his very "illimitability" makes it impossible for him to conceptualize the process whereby satanic misrecognition inevitably decays into psychic dissonance, the regular and predictable process whose metaphysical causes are intimately and nonrandomly bound to their physical effects. This misunderstanding is further compounded by the fact that these discordant effects are the dialectical by-products of a form of decay inherently alien to Chaos: a decline in which the extremes of objectification and projection, diseases of too much consonance, precipitate their own inversion, diseases of too much dissonance.[32] As a result, Chaos is ultimately as inept as he is confused: a true "anarch" and no monarch, he completely miscalculates the fact that the Infernal Triad will encroach on his territory far more than the heavenly forces now at rest. As parts of a mimetically extended personification allegory, the contrasting "dissonances" of ancient Chaos and his new guest, Satan, have of course been signaled by their initial appearances—the Anarch's "falt'ring speech and visage incompos'd" (2.989) inefficiently reflecting the tyrant's darkly "obscur'd" but still fiery brightness and glory (1.591–94).

Finally, then, although Chaos's erratic entropy does and must contrast with heavenly irregularity (*PL,* 5.622–24) and its counterpart, an earthly fertility "wild above Rule or Art" (5.297), its differences from the hyperorganized depredations of Satan's overly efficient causality go far deeper. As appropriate to an unformed, random state of matter, some formal parallels with the negative entropy of the Infernal Triad remain in Chaos's "dreadful halls of gloomy night" (*Theogony,* 744), for, even if the noisy combustions of Chaos are less

pernicious than those of hell, neither can induce the peaceful genera-
tion that results from an ordered alternation of dark with light. Yet,
despite its lack of the benign dichotomies procreatively informing
heaven and earth, Chaos's "hollow dark assaults [on the] . . . ear"
(2.953) are equally remote from the hell where Sin's birth pangs lead
to the fatal dissonance of her outcry "Death" (2.787–89). Taking the
hollow no shape of a form filled only with "lust and rage" to repeat
himself (and consequently his father) by raping his mother, Death's
repetition of Sin punishes her repetition of their father through the
"ceasless cry" (2.795) of his devouring sons, the hounds of hell. This
dissonance is reflected both in their "hollow" affections and in their
complete lack of the potential for kindly rupture (7.419) latent in
Night's "womb." For the cruel ruptures of a Sin-ful body can give
birth only to sterile Death, the cancerous scourge rather than the
vital remedy of misbegotten life that Chaos provides (7.90–93, 220–
21). While these cancerous mutants are increasingly alienated from
the path of light, chaotic entropy remains negentropically receptive
to reorganization long after Death's "Mace petrific, cold and dry"
(10.294) uses its fertile "waste" to pave a passageway to hell. Ex-
tracted from but essentially unlike the inertial entropy of Chaos and
Night, this anticreative causality can produce only a form of entropic
degeneration that, if as physically and temporally real as that of other
efficient causes, eventually triggers its own feedback into Chaos.

4

As the material analogue of the problem of metaphysical freedom
that his epic straddles, Milton's Chaos thus supplies the most fun-
damentally indeterminate and physical aspect of its open-minded
causal chain. In actively evolving, this realm at once "grounds" the
functions of his other epic personifications and synthetically accom-
modates the physical and ethical implications of a noisy universe to
the purposes of theodicy. Far from a merely destructive or disorderly
principle, his void should then be understood as the material, formal,
and efficient source of creaturely intervention and thus as the *ulti-
mately* immutable substrate of the divine law of self-determination.
From this perspective, to regard Chaos as inherently hostile or sim-
ply benign is substantially to miss the point of Milton's insistent
material monism and its fundamental bearing on his epic design.[33]

Alternatively, to grasp that chaos is the wasteful, noisy, but also providentially plastic source of productive order is in part to return the poem to the context of the atomist revival that lends so much support to Milton's reconciliation of physics with metaphysics. Since, in this context, order and disorder are necessary components of both heaven and hell, only by persisting in his univocal obsession with fixed "Orders and Degrees" (*PL,* 5.792) does Satan gradually corrupt his own efficient energies into a parody of their original form. Yet, since he is not "authorized" to contain the natural energies of other agents indefinitely, Chaos can at last naturally purge off what his cohort has artificially and reductively forced to "conglobe" within it—the physical/metaphysical bridge of Sin and Death. For on some things Chaos does express a firm and consistent commitment, as when he reacts "indignantly" to his betrayal by Satan's hyperorganized forces, which in the form of his offspring "scorn" and "scourge" his libertarian domain (10.311, 418). As the prior and inherently divine entropic principle, his mutability then becomes his ultimate weapon against their divisions and desolations. In this final phase of alternating entropy and negentropy, Chaos not only recoils from permanently harboring evil but also deflects evil back onto its own origin in higher, if also ironically "lower," causes: the spiritual degeneration of self-willed subjects.

Ultimately, then, as a poet for whom differentiation and ambiguation of the scale of "one first matter" was literary *materia prima,* Milton seems to have made an imaginative Lucretian leap in personifying the Grand Anarch "Chaos" as, *au fond,* a neutral and plausible mediator of its extremes and thus as also an incipient condition of good. Here, the same libertarian logic that allows even degenerate forms like Sin and Death "efficiently" to work their will on matter also permits Chaos to remain guiltless of any active complicity with them, even though his more elemental causality may be passively contaminated by their more "efficient" evils. An additional advantage of this dialectical schema is that now even Death is no longer simply the mortal enemy of mankind (as in Donne's famous sonnet) but also an efficient ingredient in its "final remedy," a form of negentropy that, as Michael teaches,

. . . after Life
Tri'd in sharp tribulation, and refin'd
By Faith and faithful works, to second Life,

Wak't in the renovation of the just,
Resigns him up with Heav'n and Earth Renew'd.
(*PL*, 11.62–66)

From this penultimate perspective, all matter (even the self-wasting substances of Sin and Death) affirms the ambiguously positive potential of indeterminacy personified in the womb/tomb capacity of Chaos. Utterly unlike the purely destructive "womb" of Sin, the twinned capacities of entropy make its matter no longer evil or needful of external redemption in an eternal stasis such as Spenser's *Mutabilitie Cantos* project. Here, the tables have so far turned that uncreated matter and natural flux, not immutability, are now linked to spiritual good, a condition attainable only through freedom, mobility, self-determination, refinement, and change—the central values one would expect to find allegorically valorized by this most radically Protestant poem.

Although Milton's cosmos still ultimately reflects a transcendent order, his universe remains both physically and metaphysically consonant with this order through the immanent or "Baconian" compliance of its agents, who must choose the route of freedom over the dead-end of satanic tyranny, which can in itself ironically supply its own "remedy and medicine." Further, because the negentropic regeneration of prime matter is primarily achieved through the free cooperation of the will, not only material causality but every level of God's interdependently "free" causal chain has been "unchained." In place of static or hierarchic order, there are only prophetic glimpses of the baroque vanishing point of a final, providential reintegration, as when the negentropic return of Chaos's original innocence or benign entropy is forecast by the Anarch's final epic appearance. At its opposite remove are the rigidly self-destructive currents of hell, which approach Chaos

As when two Polar Winds blowing adverse
Upon the *Cronian* sea, together drive
Mountains of Ice, that stop th' imagin'd way
Beyond *Petsora* Eastward, to the rich
Cathaian coast.
(*PL*, 10.289–93)

Besides imposing their icy fixity on the fecund abyss (which also means, as Alastair Fowler notes, blocking the entrance to the earthly paradise), Sin and Death "fix" (10.295) its "rich[es]" (10.292) with "*Gorgonian* rigor . . . And with *Asphaltic* slime" (10.297–98)—a punning use of the adversary's northerly "adversity" to depict the depths of its "reign" of rigor mortis (10.289). At this point, the enormous contrast between the satanic offspring's icy fire and the benign anarchy of chaotic fluidity (*PL*, 10.283) finely discriminates the overriding physical, ethical, and political values personified throughout the rest of the allegory. Swooping down into Chaos's fertile "damp and dark," and "hovering upon the Waters" (10.283, 285) like an insane parody of the Holy Spirit's "brooding" on the abyss (7.234–35), Sin and Death immediately begin to parch and freeze its mutable seas into an "aggregated Soil" (10.293) pointedly compared to the bridge with which Xerxes tried "the Liberty of *Greece* to yoke" (10.307). With tongue not much in cheek, the poet calls this imperial "scourge" a work "of wondrous Art / Pontifical" (10.311–13), a sign of the ultimate spiritual tyranny: a specious "liberation" (10.368) effected by "reducers" (10.438) who would in every sense pontifically bridge, subject, enchain, mystify, and diminish the metaphoric Greek "home" of liberty itself.[34]

The injustice of this enslavement of the once-libertarian Chaos is reemphasized in the following simile, which again describes the efficient causes of Satan's legions as conducting the moral equivalent of an imperial assault in linking the Persian prince to the barbaric Tartar who "leaves all waste beyond / . . . in his retreat" (10.431–35). Here, punning on the double meaning of their "wasting" or ruining of Chaos's once fertile "waste" (10.282) or undeveloped expanse, the passage then concludes by prophesying the reciprocal "wasting" of those who "waste and havoc yonder World" (10.617)—which includes the benign indeterminacies of both Chaos and the earthly paradise. Thereafter punished in the fashion of their crime, the satanic cohort is reduced to the "sharp and spare" (10.511) shapes reminiscent of the bars that Sin and Death had used to restrain its chaotic energy (10.417), with the result that, in the form of grovelling serpents, they are appropriately drawn to chew the "bitter Ashes" (10.566) of their own hellish fruit, the proleptic equivalent of the "tartareous dregs" they are later destined to become. This fate has been sealed by their desire to "taste" the fire that Chaos's damp "Anarchie" would have put out (10.283) had they not "mortified" it since, in this allegory of naturalistic action and reaction, God merely announces what their self-destructive interference with his most turbulent of steady states achieves. Yet not even "the folly of Man" that "Let in these wastful Furies" (*PL*, 10.619–20) can forever alter the quenching capacities of its pregnant deep, which, if not unalterable, is more resiliently reactive than the fateful forces of Sin-ful rigidity. Thus, once the Sin-ful family's energies have at once allegorically and actually exhausted themselves, the bitter morsels of their wasteful rigor mortis will "naturally" be digested and excreted by the very chaotic organs they had attempted to enslave. In the end, these great reducers, King Death and Queen Sin, will themselves be reduced to stoppers of that cosmic "bung hole," the giant mouth of hell, the pit whose "ravenous Jaws" they will "for ever . . . seal" (10.636–37).

This final framing of Satan, Sin, and Death as the self-destructive oppressors of both Chaos and the creation it conceives plainly indicates that all such forces, even Satan's, monistically participate in material principles that, as Anna K. Nardo remarks, now transact a "voluntary covenant between human will and divine commandment."[35] Rather than the mere impression, reflection, or cloudy shadow of an eternal macrocosm of Ideas, matter has been correspondingly converted into the literal material or "stuff" in which creaturely choice can either passively cooperate, actively alter, or malignly impede—although it can never utterly destroy the divine essence embedded in the active *energia* of its embryon atoms, for "fixed" perversions are far more degeneratively entropic than chaotic negentropy itself. At this point, the metaphysics of Milton's reciprocal causality recapitulates its physics, and these perverse agents become spiritually and physically bound to a frozen lake of fire, the effect of their own ice (Rev. 20:14). Ancient but not subject to old age, in itself chaotic entropy is thus no more intrinsically inimical to God than the heavenly subsoil that permits a similarly real yet temporary perversion of matter. This epic state is thus more than merely consistent with the hypothesis of the *Christian Doctrine* that "original matter was not an evil thing, nor . . . worthless: it was good, and it contained the seeds of all subsequent good[:] . . . a confused and disordered state at first . . . [that] afterwards God made . . . ordered and beautiful" (*CPW*, 6:308); it is also inherently opposed to the reductive "heat" of Sin and the "cold" of Death. The universe in general and Chaos in particular are thus empirically imagined as being renewed through the wisest of Providence's provisions: the primeval imbalance of uncreated matter, the divine check on the balances of the rest of God's creation. Because even the most "eccentric" of angelic dances (*PL*, 5.623) cannot in themselves nullify the overorganization of satanic energies, only through the *ex deo* force of chaotic matter can the divine law of freedom be fulfilled, at which point the Son can retroactively "sling" earth's "Hell-hounds" (10.633, 630) back through nature's womb and grave (2.911). Then, freed at last from Satan's "Universe of death . . . / Where all life dies, death lives, and nature breeds, / Perverse" (2.622, 624–25), the fundamental alterability of primal entropy provides the cosmic agency whereby "Heav'n and Earth renew'd shall be made pure" (10.638) from its source—in Chaos.

According to current physics, chaos abounds within attenuations of difference into the vast samenesses of interstellar and even interior spaces, which suggests that, like hell, Chaos is an everywhere. However, because Milton's universe conserves the priority of final causes, unlike the physics of hell or of modern science, *in potentia* its physical properties remain essentially on the side of the life rather than the death principle, as Adam and Eve discover during their own regeneration. By affiliating its vacuities with those of divine freedom, Milton's baroque Chaos is thus equivocally affirmed as an ambivalent medium of regeneration and choice, a vanishing point of causality that further meta-allegorizes cosmic directionality. For, while the space of *Paradise Lost* allows "up" and "down" to preserve some of their old dichotomizing power, the poem's multiple causal and temporal schemes mandate that both space and time now have merely local and relative meanings: Satan falls by "rising" to the challenge of conquering earth by invading Chaos; the Son rises by "falling" to serve a sinful race after he has temporarily pacified its Deep; while Raphael both falls and rises in the process of faithfully informing mankind of its "efficient" ability to manipulate the formal causes of physical and moral "space," the province of "one first matter." This allegorical movement, too, is ethical, even as in myth, although the normative processes of myth have been reversed: moral meaning is not projected onto the symbolic screen of the physical universe, but the laws of natural action and reaction have become the paradigm for the "physics" of moral law.

In the expanded and partially anamorphic picture plane of baroque allegory, even the vectors of matter thus create two conjunctive yet antithetical perspectives. Its original "steady state" in the subatomic forces of chaos (or dark matter) may either explode into the superatomic evolution of the galaxies (or angels) or implode under the adverse gravitational pull of negative entropy (or demons). Yet, since in principle matter is always conserved, these dichotomies are again subject to reconfiguration after the death of stars like Lucifer/Satan. Thus, like the dialectical name *Satan/Lucifer* itself, the negentropic principle only equivocally presupposes a closed system—by no means a stable model of the universe. From this final perspective, then, Milton's poetic version of chaos theory suggests why the canonical is always in some sense contemporary. Open-ended in its freedom and irregularity, the ordered integration of the angels' celebratory dance with the irregular/regular dancing stars of the heavens seems elliptically to reconcile the poem's oppositions and antitheses; yet it does so only in terms of the decentered "loopiness" of irreconcilable and ultimately interminable "vagancies," the optimally mutable matter outside of which Milton's androgynously gendered angels can scarcely be imagined at all.

5

Milton's Meta-Allegory of Action

Psychomachia, Battle, and Cosmogony

1

I have been referring all along to Milton's meta-allegory on the basis both of his evident practice and of his specific allusion to Revelation as a self-referential allegory of historical typology, which is in fact fully developed in the poem's central episodes—the War in Heaven and creation "epics" of books 5–7. Since the epic as a whole is a figurative fable reframing salvational and historical "truths" that are themselves figuratively represented in Scripture, what is then intrinsically problematic about its main meta-allegorical actions is not that their sense comes "after" or in "addition to" scriptural meaning (as Aristotle thought of metaphysics as "after" physics) but that in the more recent linguistic sense such self-referentialities create undecidable gaps or *aporias*. The application of these terms will then need more extensive justification, if only for the quite obvious reason that Milton had not read Wittgenstein. Here, one would need to show, not only that the inductive "truths" of modern linguistics might at least intuitively have been grasped by a master poet and logician, but also that an extended application of such truths would have been conducive to his poetic purposes. Yet nowhere in the poem is a demonstration of these linguistic and aesthetic possibilities more evident than at its epic core, beginning with the perplexingly inconclusive war between faithful and rebel angels that Murray Roston describes as "a baroque clash of forces such as Rubens would have delighted to paint." Since G. K. Hunter agrees that Milton here adopts a self-consciously inflated or baroque method that increasingly involves the reader in Satan's "grotesque mismatching" of perceptions, there is at least some precedent for regarding this episode as meta-allegorical in the sense that I have outlined.[1]

Moreover, like the Chaos, Sin, and Death episodes discussed in the previous chapter, the War in Heaven has long been considered deviant in relation to the normative psychomachia, itself the oldest form of Christian allegory. Yet, while no one would suppose that Milton sets out to imitate Prudentius, disagreements about his actual intent have been profound. Generally speaking, these disagreements are more similar to those associated with his allegorical Chaos than to those associated with his Sin and Death since most critics agree that Milton would have regarded his fictive War in Heaven as a typological instance of an actual historical conflict that had occurred once before and would recur once again *after* human time as we know it. There is also general agreement that this contest outlines a figurative type of the Christian warfare occupying all human time in between, in the indefinite present tense that the poet shares with his readers. To emphasize this complex interleaving of historical typology and future-oriented anagogy with present-centered allegorical or "moral" meaning, Raphael opens his account by representing the war's events as both more and less literal than the occasion would otherwise seem to demand. At first underscoring its accommodated moral meaning for his as yet innocent primary audience, Raphael's multileveled allegory ends by focusing on the Son's triumph as the prophetic vehicle of Adam's anticipated, although still literally unnecessary, epic redemption. In this most "meta" dimension of allegory, the past of the warring angels becomes the quasi-literal template both for the future of Adam's moral progress away from Sin and Death and for humanity's progress toward the redemption forecast in Revelation. Yet, intermediately, the war and the subsequent parable of creation also chart a self-reflexive course of moral interpretation aimed at all the inquiring servants of God here symbolized by Abdiel, a "readerly" contest that exists everywhere on earth as in heaven, in past as in present, and future metamorphoses.

Yet, after a lengthy digression carefully outlining how "what surmounts the reach / Of human sense, I shall delineate" (*PL*, 5.571–72), Raphael somewhat incongruously concludes the first half of his story by suggesting that there is after all a "simple" moral to be drawn from these complexly framed investigations: to have learned "By terrible Example the reward / Of disobedience" (6.909–11). But in reducing his complex medium to this simple message, this warning also refocuses his listeners' attention on the problematic nature of true obedience, a "meta" problem that in fact underlies his narrative's unstable synthesis of biblical history with parable and fact with fiction. This problem is all the more inescapable in that the good angels fail to defeat the bad, and the respective rewards "earned" by either are hardly as self-evident as in the morality play that Raphael ironically reminds us has failed to materialize here. Yet, because the rebels are expelled from heaven, we are prepared to accept the substance of his remark, even while at every level we have been prevented from accepting its literal outlines—which, as Johnson wryly remarked, only children might be expected to do. As in metatheater, the proscenium has already been crossed too many times for us to forget that the writer/director seems to be underscoring a philosophical point about the intractably obscure crossovers between representation and enactment, vice and virtue, merit and reward. The actual ambiguities involved in these "neat" polar oppositions are additionally underscored by the inconsistency between the grand operatic scale on which the angelic warfare is conducted and the mock-heroic scale of its actual results, which produce the enigmatic finale of the Son's single-handed victory.

Nevertheless, previous attempts at a thoroughgoing mock-heroic or parodic interpretation of these scenes tend not only to overlook their more meaningful *aporias* but Raphael's evidently serious pedagogical purpose as well.[2] For, in educating both his primary and his secondary audiences about the failures of conventional heroism, he is also clearly supplying the basis for a Reformed heroic ethic of a more naturalistic and/or individualistic type. The need for such an ethic becomes all the more evident after the failure of the heroic/apocalyptic "certitudes" of the Puritan revolution, which seems to have influenced Milton's epic refusal to portray any self-evident triumph of good over evil in the immediate context of the angelic battle. Yet this reluctance can also be traced to his lifelong preoccupation with the more internal and enduring rewards conferred by the "unsung" heroics of the solitary individual's ethical and interpretive struggle (*PL*, 9.32–33). As Mary Ann Radzinowicz's useful synopsis indicates, Milton's rejection of Calvinistic certitudes requires that "the ethics of purity through election is modulated into an ethics of purification through trial in free choice."[3]

Milton's use of Raphael's asides largely to problematize the relation between narrative voice and readerly reception thus becomes far less problematic if we assume that the War in Heaven is waged primarily over these fundamental libertarian principles, which help explain why he repeatedly emphasizes that the War in Heaven is the interpretation of an interpretation. From this remove it is far easier to see that his multileveled "veils" can conceal no secure moral or political truths, only a multiplicity of competing interpretations that will again be reactivated by Raphael's failure to safeguard his pupils from Satan's simpler, more "accessible" and appealing hermeneutics. Yet this failure also implicitly foregrounds incertitude and indeterminacy as the safeguards of liberty, a stance consistent with a well-established nonconformist tradition of biblical exegesis. This sectarian rather than church-based tradition emphasizes the self-referential ironies behind the biblical motif that regularly shows winners becoming losers and losers winners.[4] In more sophisticated form, this theme involves not only the deceptiveness of appearances but also the vagaries of choice, both strands of which are clearly involved in the parable of Abdiel as the atypical prodigal son and servant of the Father. To foreground the corrective difference between this version of the theme and the more naive schemas of the conventional psychomachia, Raphael begins by asking his hearers to "calculate" both the disparities and the continuities between the literal and the figurative dimensions of his truths. Turning the "higher" certitudes of accommodation into a form of equivocation, he begins by posing the centrally self-referential question of meta-allegory: "what if Earth / Be but the shadow of Heav'n, and things therein / Each to other like, more than on Earth is thought?" (*PL,* 5.574–75).

At this juncture, Raphael at once represents and enacts the decentering of the macrocosmic correspondences and moral homologies central to normative allegory, for, as Lee Jacobus points out, his analogy suggests an inherently unstable combination of comparison and contrast, a method more or less like measuring "a large hypotenuse with a small hypotenuse. They are both hypotenuses but they differ in size and fact."[5] Thus, while the war seems clearly to have occurred once at the beginning of history as it will recur again at the end of time, its uncertain correspondence with the ongoing, earthly psychomachia foregrounds a fundamentally meta-allegorical form of accommodation, one that must be continually transacted with its internal and external readers. For, in an allegory where losers are most often winners, crooked is most often straight, dark most often bright, and irregular most regular—although these asymmetries are themselves most "regularly" upset—the ethical meanings of action must be constantly viewed and reviewed in relation to an ever-shifting, easily reversible context that can situate but not stabilize the meaning of ethical action. Moreover, because Satan and his host most excel in imitating the dark brightness of the divine, the ascending stair of the normative mode cannot simply be reversed: while the more morally difficult choice is generally associated with true obedience, the truly worthy action may or may not entail the more obscure, solitary, or doubtful "strife of Glory," as Satan so tragically discovers (*PL*, 6.290).

The resulting disruption of the psychomachia's normative symmetry also subverts its normative complement, a "ritual progress" only roughly recapitulated in Milton's creation episode. As Fletcher remarks, in the ordinary course of such allegorical actions, "the reader is expected to follow . . . [as] in a sort of procession" a triumphal march or pantomime mirroring the ritual ceremonies of the liturgy. As a result, the literary conventions of the allegorical battle and progress normatively feature the same "steady propulsiveness and exact symmetry," an alternating centripetal and centrifugal progression rigidly structured by a syntactic alternation of parataxsis with hypotaxis. This highly formal "hierarchic system" also tends to "list . . . rather than more freely display . . . the cosmic order therein."[6] The epic exfoliations of the War in Heaven immediately invert this process by questioning a cosmic order that is never fully "listed" but instead freely displayed in a creation episode that vitalistically transacts a highly detailed revelation of God's organic continuum. Thus, while the war metatheatrically subverts the normative psychomachia by thwarting our suspension of disbelief in its highly formal conventions, the creation subverts the normative ritual progress by liberating the general into the particular rather than "the particular into the general"—as in the "normal" allegorical paradigm outlined by Gay Clifford.[7] The human history emerging from these episodes then requires a self-referential interrogation rather than a passive ritual or homiletic assimilation of the meaningfulness of its scriptural truths. Rather than a mere typology of God's providential design, the reader is confronted with a far more problematic and advanced hermeneutics of schema and correction.

At the most elementary or literal level of his narrative, Raphael's account seems to supply a psychological motive for Satan's rebellion missing from the biblical account: his envy over the exaltation of the Son and his resulting refusal to serve him. Yet, more than merely psychologizing Satan's sin (an objective already largely achieved by the peculiarly "mimetic" allegory of Sin and Death), this crucial addition already self-referentially links the history of biblical naming to the meaning of both true and false obedience and resistance and thus to the whole history of human strife. For Satan's acquisition of the new name *Satanas* (resister and accuser of God) occurs in ironic conjunction with the Son's acceptance of his new title of mediator and assistor to both men and angels. In order to determine what it means to have gained either title "by Merit more than Birthright" (*PL*, 3.309), books 5 and 6 then gradually explore competing models of heroism. Because a true understanding of their contrasts requires further renaming, this exploration centers, not merely on the Son and Satan, but also on the neological angel, Abdiel, the emblematic "servant of God" who stands for all who ever have or will resist the resister in the face of overwhelming odds. In echoing Jesus' reply to Satan (Matt. 4:7), Yahweh's reply to Job (Job 40:2), and Milton's own historical reply to tyranny, Abdiel thus comes to stand for a form of liberty that is at once divinely ordained and mimetically represented yet also meta-allegorically enacted by the comparable "covenant" between poet and reader.

In refuting Satan, Abdiel also models the ways in which those who inductively apprehend the fundamental premises of Christian liberty are able to give laws to themselves, a process that forms the basis of a far more rational and authentically emancipating covenant than the satanic attempt deductively to give them to God. Thus, in openly confronting his hierarchical superior (as Satan never does), Abdiel begins his liberation by demanding to know why it is

> . . . unjust thou say'st
> Flatly unjust, to bind with Laws the free,
> And equal over equals to let Reign,
> One over all with unsucceeded power.
> Shalt thou give Law to God, shalt thou dispute
> With him the points of liberty, who made
> Thee what thou art, and form'd the Pow'rs of Heav'n
> Such as he pleas'd, and circumscrib'd thir being?
> (*PL*, 5.818–25)

Satan's subsequent refutation of Abdiel's defense of a divine sovereignty that in fact secures the very conditions both of angelic liberty and of subjective existence then implicitly exposes his own delusory investment in a role that only the Almighty can rightfully claim or fully maintain. For behind Abdiel's response lies the substance of God's cross-examination of Job on the ontology and meaning of his own and all previous existence: "Knowest thou *it*, because thou wast then born? or *because* the number of thy days *is* great?" (Job 38:21). In appropriating the Almighty's rhetoric of divine knowledge, sovereignty, justice, and freedom to himself, Satan's contrary position implicitly outlines the issues actually at stake in the War in Heaven. Instead of a conventional illustration of the superiority of virtue to vice, the conflict between the faithful and the rebel angels will thereafter be concerned to demonstrate the nature, extent, and justice of God's "divine right" since after all

> . . . who saw
> When this creation was? remember'st thou
> Thy making, while the Maker gave thee being?
> We know no time when we were not as now;
> Know none before us, self-begot, self-rais'd
> By our own quick'ning power, when fatal course
> Had circl'd his full Orb, the birth mature
> Of this our native Heav'n, Ethereal sons.
> (5.856–63)

In the context of the contemporary natural law debates—and particularly Milton's dissent from the absolutist natural law theory of Hobbes—these questions raise issues far broader than the self-justifying rationale of a prideful, blasphemous, or rebellious angel. In this context, Satan becomes a figurative proponent of "clear and distinct" logical principles applied to ends opposite to those of Milton/Abdiel, who place their faith not in his absolutely deterministic but in a more negotiable and individually responsible rationale of creaturely freedom.[8] Thus, in the very interest of defending this conception of liberty, the reader is asked to give the devil his due as he questions the freedom of heavenly harmony, which he defines as an exercise of sloth and servility rather than of true "natural" freedom:

> At first I thought that Liberty and Heav'n
> To heav'nly Souls had been all one; but now
> I see that most through sloth had rather serve,
> Minist'ring Spirits, train'd up in Feast and Song;
> Such hast thou arm'd, the Minstrelsy of Heav'n,
> Servility with freedom to contend,
> As both thir deeds compar'd this day shall prove.
> (*PL*, 6.164–70)

In comparison to these charges, Satan's blasphemous assumption of deity is frivolous, for here, as in *Samson Agonistes*, atheism is not really at issue. Abdiel is certain that "by his Word the mighty Father made / All things, ev'n, thee, and all the Spirits of Heav'n" (5.836–37), just as he is confident that Satan's "perfidious fraud" (5.880) stems from his resentment at losing the full privileges of his rank. Yet, as the Romantic reading of the poem illustrates, the issue of who plays the tyrant in heaven is considerably less clear, as is the closely related issue of whether Satan's empirical instruments are superior to a more ambiguously "open" interpretation of God's heavenly hierarchy of grace.

2

Even the less Romantically or more meta-allegorically inclined reader might therefore question the true worth of heaven's unmerited and equivocal liberty as opposed to the innate "equality" that Satan offers his followers: "if not equal all, yet free, / Equally free; for Orders and Degrees / Jar not with liberty, but well consist" (*PL*, 5.791–93). For not only had something like this principle seemed to define the heavenly hierarchy of the previous books, but, of all Satan's legions, only Abdiel suspects that Satan's defense of liberty is more disingenuous than it appears. Abdiel's emblematic role is thus at once to challenge and to reveal the false, vainglorious, inauthentic, and ultimately enslaving libertarian rhetoric of this rebellion and its "heroism"—a tall order for any psychomachia, conventional or not. Given the broad natural law territory on which this contest is waged, this epic defense cannot rest on any merely prophetic vision of God's benign plan but must also include a narrative illustration of the far more authoritarian and hence ultimately reactionary political assumptions of the rebels. Thus, Abdiel's initial function is well chosen: he counters Satan with the hypothesis (nowhere clearly listed or announced) that the Son's exaltation is not intended to destroy but to enhance equality, replacing "Orders and Degrees" with a freer commonality "under one Head more near / United" (5.830–31). Most relevant here, however, is the fact that this inference is not that of a great or powerful cherub but that of a free agent emancipated by his lack of envy even more than by his faith or mental agility. In contrast to the cleverly convoluted rhetoric of a Belial or a Mammon, Abdiel exhibits the saving grace of true disinterestedness, which in this poem ranks higher than abject humility, for, in Abdiel, the individualistic standards of inductive and ethical clarity triumph over the seductive rewards conferred by satanic wit, status, or fraternal consensus. These values will ultimately confer on him the truly higher gifts reserved for the prodigal or "lost" sheep returned to the fold not through innate merit but through a personally reacquired birthright. Ultimately, because unlike Satan he does not think "himself impair'd" (5.665) by the disapprobation of his official superiors, he is received with great rejoicing and honor "before the seat supreme" (6.27).

Yet Satan's stance also fails to afford a simple contrast to Abdiel's for a number of cogent reasons. In accepting Lucifer's subtle objectification of value, his cohort confuses their loyalty with what appears to them as an Abdiel-like obedience to "natural" principle. The unmeritorious aspect of this confusion accordingly reflects the deceptive nature of communal appearances and consensual status, since their adherence to the fallen light bearer can more accurately be traced to their overreliance on his lofty preeminence and authority:

> . . . for great indeed
> His name, and high was his degree in Heav'n;
> His count'nance, as the Morning Star that guides
> The starry flock, allur'd them, and with lies
> Drew after him the third part of Heav'n's Host. . . .
> (*PL*, 5.706–10)

Yet, the function of this error is far more complex than Raphael's exhortation to obedience had conveyed, for, in unanimously awarding Satan the victory in his debate with Abdiel, his obedient troops have actually committed themselves to a spurious idolatry of place and name—the very kind of idolatry the reader must "meta-allegorically" learn to associate with the false allure of the conventional fable's abstract moral tags. By relying only on the "obvious" evidence of appearances, like Job's "wise" companions (but unlike the prodigal son's father) the fallen angels have become secret sharers in Satan's fraud, a collusion obliquely reflected in their "Hoarse murmur echo'd to his words applause" (5.873). Yet, if unlike him they unwittingly barter away their divine birthright, their situation even more ironically parodies that of Job himself, whose losses of place and name ultimately serve to exalt the true source of creation (5.894–95). Thus, even at the outset, in "forgetting" this source they as much as the faithful angels testify to the life-giving powers of God's "boundless deep," which is here echoed in their "answering," although also "hoarser," hollowness, the "sound of waters deep" (5.872).

Abdiel, too, inverts the usual symmetries of parable or psychomachia in the act of straying from his fallen flock. In this, the atypical lost sheep thereby becomes his own good shepherd, the "one / Returned not lost" through his own decision to wander (*PL*, 6.24–25). Fusing the images of sheep, shepherd, and victorious scapegoat, he completes the inversion of biblical paradigm as he is greeted with great rejoicing despite the loss of the other "ninety-nine." This individualistic revision of a scriptural tradition that (despite its emphasis on the supreme worth of each human soul) more conventionally emphasized the transcendent importance of the communal flock is conveyed through Milton's use of the word *number*. The faithful angels are able to rejoice even though ninety-nine perish and only one is saved since, in their understanding, numbers themselves cease to figure as either strict typological symbols or straightforward accommodations. In meta-allegorical terms, singleness is thus not a number but the opposite of multitude, which conversely signifies the satanic confusion of quantity with quality:

> His Loyalty he kept, his Love, his Zeal;
> Nor number, nor example with him wrought
> To swerve from truth, or change his constant mind
> Though single.
> (5.900–3)

Here, not merely truth, but loyalty, love, and zeal are all such single nonnumbers, which reside solely in the province of consistent individual interpretation and action, the exercise of "constant mind" unaffected by multitude.

In contrast, the "fuller" number of the "ninety-nine" signifies not merely multiplication but repetition, a redundant loss of individuality through faith in the false symmetry of mass conformity, a sacrifice of quality to quantity. Framed in this way, the main "moral" of Milton's revised psychomachia pits the false polarities and symmetries of Satan's enslaving hierarchies against Abdiel's asymmetrical, Job-like "singleness" of mind. This aspect of their contest is emphasized by Abdiel's echo of both the Almighty's reply to Job and Jesus' reply to the Pharisees, which in turn reechoes the poem's thematic indictment of the "infernal Serpent" "who durst defy th' Omnipotent to Arms" (*PL*, 1.34, 49): "how vain / Against th'Omnipotent to rise in Arms; / Who out of smallest things could without end / Have rais'd incessant Armies to defeat / Thy folly" (6.135–39). The true creator's ability to elicit witnesses from the "smallest things," including the very stones of creation (Luke 19:40), also reveals why the Son finds Satan's resistance more risible than truly derisive or divisive (5.735–37), which further suggests that the ensuing battle will in some nonnormative sense further test the true meaning of *number*. For, if Satan's defeat is the foregone conclusion that everyone knows it to be—not merely poet and reader, but also Abdiel and the Son—then the battle must supply some appropriately pedagogical contest rather than a mere test of force. However, this residual element of the traditional psychomachia—where the issue is always not if but how virtue will triumph over vice—is itself baroquely reframed by the battle's self-referential exploration of the very tools of the allegorical trade: not only its symbolic numbers, but all of its emblematic instruments, places, and actions. Thus, as Raphael's prelude warns, here everything, all symbolic actions and correspondences, must be reassessed in the context of the semicalculable relations between heaven and earth, divine obedience and individual responsibility.

The requirements of reassessment will ultimately upset the neat division of the contesting forces into equally balanced armies (which had seemed arranged to demonstrate something about number through number) with a victory won not through Abdiel's or the Son's singleness of mind but through an overwhelming "infusion" of divine power. Yet, in overturning the standard structure of the psychomachia, this puzzling finale also peculiarly reinvigorates the issues of individual accountability around which the contest centers. Although the battle's intermediate actions do answer Satan's damaging charge that the loyal angels serve God only for the sake of "Feast and Song" (the same charge he will later level at Job), the distinguishing traits of the faithful are undercut in a way that tends to ironize the entire passage. While marginally illustrating the advantages of liberty over license or of integrity over overreaching, the first two days of battle also ironically deny a Job-like victory to either party. In essence, then, the external physical attributes of beauty, strength, and reason, which are at first aligned with the spiritual qualities of faith, integrity, and constancy (or, as Abdiel terms it, spiritual "realty"), are ultimately canceled in favor of an almost wholly "placeless" and internal form of virtue, which not only allows but requires the faithful to stand in the faith of the Messiah alone.

This startling condensation of the traditional virtues is subtly signaled throughout the battle, beginning with Abdiel's opening challenge of Satan to single combat. Here, he is immediately astounded at how this false "Idol of Majestie Divine" (*PL*, 6.101) remains essentially undiminished by his treason:

> O Heav'n! that such resemblance of the Highest
> Should yet remain, where faith and realty
> Remain not; wherefore should not strength and might
> There fail where Virtue fails, or weakest prove
> Where boldest; though to sight unconquerable?
> (6.114–18)

Disturbingly, no answer is provided for this all too "human" question. Foreshadowing the later stalemate between faithful and fallen angels, the failure of Abdiel's faith and reason physically to triumph over Satan's fraudulent virtue suggests that the bold sinner does not always the "weakest prove"—especially since, in its root sense, *virtu* also signifies physical strength. While Abdiel's rational integrity is sufficient security against satanic wiles, it can no more increase his native physical force than Satan's infidelity can destroy his "resemblance of the Highest." Thus, virtue is here only equivocally tied to "puissance"; although not divorced from all forms of physical power, it is not necessarily able to overcome social and political, much less military, forms of evil. If in one sense Abdiel has conquered Satan by holding fast to reason and truth, in another sense his standard allegorical attempt to test or "try" Satan's objective worth is therefore mistaken:

> His puissance, trusting in th' Almighty's aid,
> I mean to try, whose Reason I have tri'd
> Unsound and false; nor is it aught but just
> That he who in debate of Truth hath won,
> Should win in Arms, in both disputes alike
> Victor; though brutish that contest and foul,
> When Reason hath to deal with force, yet so
> Most reason is that Reason overcome.
> (6.119–26)

Yet the ability to see through a false idol is one thing, while to cast it down and put another (personal victory) in its place is merely another false symmetry to be avoided. While Abdiel's intentions are good (he desires to vindicate God as much as or more than himself), the expected aid from the Almighty therefore never comes; his blow fails to conquer or even to halt Satan, merely setting him back ten paces. Of course, this "stumbling" constitutes a kind of vindication, especially since in traditional numerology the number ten signals earthly or worldly victory. Yet it also suggests that his forcing Satan momentarily to recoil on "bended knee" (6.194) is a more temporary than temporal or eternal victory, for the personal vindication through "trial" that Abdiel seeks, and to some extent deserves, never materializes in anything but Messiah himself.

Implicitly, then, because all such tests properly concern the individual's relation to God alone (although they may be indirectly exemplary to other wayfaring Christian soldiers), the same pattern of partial success and defeat recurs in Michael's meeting with Satan. Although the mighty archangel proves a more formidable foe than the righteous Abdiel, even his sword of Truth cannot eradicate the undeniable power of satanic evil. Sneering at Michael's ineffectuality, Satan thus taunts him with the partiality of his own "fables":

> . . . Hast thou turn'd the least of these
> To flight, or if to fall, but that they rise
> Unvanquisht, easier to transact with mee
> That thou shouldst hope, imperious, and with threats
> To chase me hence? err not that so shall end
> The strife which thou call'st evil, but wee style
> The strife of Glory: which we mean to win,
> Or turn this Heav'n itself into the Hell
> Thou fabl'st, here however to dwell free,
> If not to reign. . . .
> (*PL,* 6.284–93)

This speech affords an especially significant glimpse into Milton's meta-allegorical technique since its tangled web of conscious and unconscious ironies again reveals that Satan's "virtue" or strength consists in telling lies that are never simply delusions. Thus, he is eerily right in asserting that his ethereal substance is as imperishable as his pursuit of Glory, for it is imperishable to precisely this extent.

As Raphael explains, ill/ustrious glory is finally blotted out when the Book of Life (6.379) is opened at the Day of Judgment: "For strength from Truth divided and from Just, / Illaudable, and naught merits but dispraise / And ignominy" (6.381–83). Yet, until then, its external and/or interpersonal "brightness" remains as ambivalently present/ absent as Satan's indeterminately fading substance.

Hence, in the short term—which from our perspective is ironically the long term of recorded history—neither Abdiel's reason nor Michael's strength can utterly disarm the attraction of Satan's romantically "obscur'd" glory (*PL,* 1.594) or prevent its power to ruin heavenly peace with hellish violence, here achieved as both factions are buried in "dismal shade . . . / [and] infernal noise" (6.666–67). Whether or not the poet consciously planned it, the line numbers of this description (book 6, line 666) clearly sign the temporary victory of the Beast of Revelation. Yet, despite this anagogical reference to the apocalypse, the war to end all wars, the temporal aspect of the psychomachia's moral allegory (which is also the historical perspective of its primary and secondary audiences) is not typologically but meta-allegorically concerned with these "last things." For, in a merely typological sense, Satan is essentially right to boast of winning this battle, at least in the same sense that he is right to claim an ability to "dwell free, / If not to reign" in *some* heavenly hell of his own choosing. In a similar sense, he *is* free to purchase a spurious victory that costs him all real life, hope, and glory—none of which exist apart from God's benign natural laws—just as he is free to reign over a multitude of well-earned followers. Yet the internal disparities of such victories and their ironically hollow virtue cannot be confined to the conventional oppositions or typology of the traditional psychomachia any more than Satan's internal hell can be consigned to a conventional Hades. In short, if the War in Heaven at all resembles a traditional contest between truth and error, this proceeds only by displacing its real conflicts onto the largely invisible and internal principles of natural law, the baroque vanishing point of the War in Heaven and its "virtuous" readers.

In order to escape the almost inescapable "romance" of naive theodicy and its idols, the plot of the narrative is therefore "collapsed" in the manner of an antiphrastic romance, whose happy ending is ironically foreshortened by the Son's effortless victory. Nevertheless, because meta-allegory, like metatheater, remains parasitic on the normative mode, it continues to hover asymmetrically between conventional psychomachia and the mock-heroic mode. Although matching the loyalists in strength and courage, the rebel angels do receive a substantial setback from the force of Michael's sword in the manner of normative allegory. Like the ultimate weapon of Revelation, this two-edged sword of Truth (Rev. 19:15) tempered in the Armory of God (*PL,* 6.320–23) typologically reveals the demons' falsehood, which, when "felt" appropriately, makes Satan "taste" the truth of his pain (6.327). At its own apparently symmetrical remove, God's army is impervious to pain, "Such high advantages thir innocence / Gave them above thir foes" (6.401–2). In the sense that it is ultimately authorized by the Almighty, good is thus traditionally and magically empowered to outgun evil. Yet, just as these symbolic interventions seem about to upset the more naturalistic/ironic collapse of symmetry already under way, strictly proportional justice is once again subverted. Although the armor and military strategy of the two camps have so far mirrored their cosmic affiliations, now Abdiel and the reader learn that God and nature do not always bid the same, or at least not as immediately as Abdiel supposes. While remaining as sinless as the merely mistaken Uriel, Abdiel's well-meaning chastisement of Satan thus reveals a logic as partial as the adversary's fallen truths, which as he says deprave

> . . . with the name
> Of *Servitude* to serve whom God ordains,
> Or Nature; God and Nature bid the same,
> When he who rules is worthiest, and excels
> Them whom he governs.
> (6.174–78)

Yet what Abdiel has not fully discovered is that, if God and nature bid the same to those who dwell in unfallen harmony, Satan's rebellion will considerably reroute this natural course, not only initiating history as we know it, but inaugurating an interpretation of a history that is anything but rationally objective or "naturally" fair to its truly heroic champions—who in other narratives may well (and do) seem either the true martyrs or the false idols of truth (2.546–55).

Hence, Abdiel's disappointment ultimately "proves" only the familiar truism that the swift do not always have the race or the mighty man his spoil, which in moral allegorical terms means that the godly cannot always ascertain what nature and God bid, except that it is ultimately the same. This postulated unanimity exists only in a state of nature partially if not irrevocably lost once Sin has been conceived and brought to birth by Satan. From that point on, all signs and all interpretations become more radically polysemous than formerly, so that antiphrasis or irony becomes one of the first fruits of the War in Heaven—as the Son's wry remarks and God's reply immediately reveal. While the psychomachia continues to maintain the ultimate reliability of divine law, this now exists in a problematically canceled/upheld relation to traditional heroic emblems and their instrumentality, for, in both insignia and action, the innocent and fallen angels can be distinguished only by largely invisible mental states like pain, which have little or no effect on the success of their military endeavors. At this point (i.e., after the pyrrhic victory of the fallen angels on the second day), the abstract upheavals and secure certitudes of the psychomachia are fully abandoned, leaving in their wake only the even more amorphous truism that "war is hell." In human terms, the Son's utterly transcendent victory on the third day does nothing to reverse this truism since it reveals only the tautological truth of the Almighty's infinite power.

The inconclusiveness of this finale from a mundane moral perspective is proleptically foreshadowed by the collapsed symbolism surrounding the war's heroes and villains. Instead of the standard psychomachia's characteristically "willless" or featureless figures armed with emblems of good and evil, here no emblematic insignia (not even Michael's sword, although it comes the closest) displays the warrior's affiliation with vice or virtue, which is instead conveyed by a far more complex relation between his motives, perceptions, and rational choices. Abdiel remains the primary exemplum of this indeterminacy since his divine Nature not only seems to lack the iconography that he expects but is even bewilderingly neutral to the moral states of the combatants, as the not-so-subtle resemblances between the parties suggest. Not only does their angelic substance remain essentially the same despite the relatively minor transformations in sensation and appearance traced above, but both faithful and apostate angels pervert heavenly nature in ways only marginally related to their guilt or innocence. When Satan invents a suitably diabolical counterpart to Michael's sword, even this new superweapon fails to emblematize any abstract polar opposition between the two since the faithful resist it with the barbaric boulders of Hesiod's titans. Moreover, since, as Kester Svendsen remarks, gunpowder and gold now equally originate in a heaven where they become self-induced temptations only to the fallen, these episodes may be taken as an essential "proclamation of the neutrality of matter."[9]

In Milton's meta-allegory of action, the meaning of "things" thus resides not in their material form but in the efficient uses to which they are put, and even these uses only imply, without fully signaling, the psychological attributes of the opposing parties. Although God will someday restore some of the natural symmetry of his universe, temporally speaking, not only may virtue not be victorious, but at times it is not even its own reward. As a result, Satan himself derives a relatively naturalistic proportion of punishment and reward from his diabolical scientific experiments with hidden causes. Where the reader would expect to find a sinisterly self-destructive magician or alchemist at work, his brilliant inventions and shrewd calculations instead suggest that the "unhurt mind" (*PL*, 6.444) of the twisted genius remains the most hurtful thing in creation, a newly "natural" means of successfully derouting nature through a synthesis of sound reason with unsound motives and desires. Here again wavering between mimesis and allegory, the war falls into neither category, for, in deconstructing every remnant of symmetrical difference between good and evil, Milton finally turns both into exercises in meta-allegorical interpretation by imploding allegory's external devices— or exploding them, if the devils' invention of gunpowder is given its appropriate due.

This allegorical irony seems the more inescapable in that, although Milton was by no means the first poet to consider gunpowder a diabolical invention, he was indeed the first to give it strategic rather than merely emblematic significance. In comparing Milton's account with that of Valvasone's *Angeleida* (often considered the episode's primary source), Stella Revard's remarks suggest some sources of the vast gulf between Milton's meta-allegorical account and that of normative epic allegory:

Both demonstrate the hellishness of Satan's conduct of heavenly war. Valvasone makes no use of the cannon beyond this set description, however. We do not see it employed by the rebels in their warfare, nor does it function to surprise or overthrow the loyalists. He describes the cannon merely to show what monstrous weapons the rebels, themselves metamorphosed into monsters, have at their disposal. Milton, on the other hand, not only has given us a set description in which the monstrousness of the cannon is illustrated, but has also created an episode in which the cannon serves as the centerpiece for Satanic strategy.[10]

Yet, as Revard neglects to mention, even when Satan's strategy is most "monstrous," it most closely parallels the deity's deployment of his "dreaded bolt" (*PL,* 6.491). Thus, while the difference between satanic expropriation and genuine creation is indeed allegorically reflected in the differences between hell, heaven, and earth—the latter of which dynamically arises from the dismal ashes of the former, a process foreshadowed by the heavenly soil's rebirth as the Son/sun approaches to expel the demons (6.780–84)—these differences are always organically displayed rather than emblematically listed.

The same mimetic impulse makes Satan's military logic "meaningful" only insofar as its motives and ends prove organically and gradually rather than emblematically and immediately self-destructive. This impulse is clearly apparent in the continuities between his personal and his tactical hubris, which at least in the short term grants him the kind of success that we might mimetically expect from such a leader. His bombastic rhetoric and egregious punning thus seems to stem naturally from his abrasively creative genius, making his blind disdain for convention far less the external emblem of a vice figure than the logical result of the narcissist's implicitly self-parodic delusions. Satan's verbal assaults then miss their mark precisely to the extent that they exceed the Father's mildly understated irony, a self-possessed "process of speech" also reflected in Raphael's gentle puns. Both the continuities and the differences between the vicious and virtuous uses of punning are thus framed as variations on a common theme whose core ambiguities stem from the benign equivocality of the divine universe. For Milton does not regard punning as essentially "fallen," as many critics assume, but only as a potentially corruptible form of language like any other."[11] Thus the self-deceptive purposes behind Satan's boast that he and his cannons will "discharge / Freely our part," like his "cannonical" orders to "Do as you have in charge, and briefly touch / What we propound" (*PL,* 6.564–67), chiefly reveal his cruelly excessive and also ultimately self-defeating exaggerations of a form of wordplay not at all foreign to heaven. Hence, when Raphael wryly observes that Satan's cannon "with hideous orifice" was but pre- or "portending hollow truce" (6.577–78), the "sociable spirit" is merely following the example of "Jehoviality" set by the Almighty—most notably, in his ironic aside to his Son, "Nearly it now concerns us to be sure / Of our Omnipotence" (5.721–22) "lest unawares we lose / This our high place" (5.731–

31).[12] This remark puns on the word *nearly* in at least three senses: "closely," "approximately," and "somewhat or almost resembling." In applying the last sense to the Omnipotent, "somewhat to be concerned" about his power more *nearly* and ironically means "not at all."

However, in Satan and Belial's hands, this "gamesome mood" (*PL*, 6.620) loses the pleasantness of pleasantry, beginning to distort and obscure rather than to play on the truth in order to dramatize its ambiguities. Satan, like the bullying outlaw of the epic Western, rejoices to see his enemies "dance" (6.615) in the face of his guns, while Belial exults that, since they have "stumbl'd many" (6.624), "our foes walk not upright" (6.627). Yet these punning distortions of their opponents' standing also obliquely reflect the multiple senses of the strangely "literal" truth that they have not *understood.* Just as we expect the epic outlaw later to become the butt of his own nasty joke, we find that Satan's boastful flyting "celebrates" a quite different victory than he had expected, eventually winning him only the much-deserved rewards of his verbal and military hubris:

> So they among themselves in pleasant vein
> Stood scoffing, highth'n'd in thir thoughts beyond
> All doubt of Victory, eternal might
> To match with thir inventions they presum'd
> So easy, and of his Thunder made a scorn,
> And all his Host derided, while they stood
> A while in trouble; but they stood not long,
> Rage prompted them at length, and found them arms
> Against such hellish mischief fit to oppose.
> (6.628–36)

Combining strategic with perceptual error, Satan's fallen "understanding" finally proves as illusory as its object, the diversion and perversion of a divine subsoil or "design" that can only temporarily undermine his adversary but must permanently "stumble" the self who stands "not long" on such shallow and self-vitiated soil. Beginning with his confusion of his place with the Son's, and continuing in his myth of self-creation (as usual, an ironic half truth), Satan's self-inflicted defeat becomes complete when he confuses his creative/destructive powers with those of God and nature.

Not truly a new creation but a miscegenation of elements withdrawn from God's "ambient light" (*PL*, 6.481–82) into a "dark Nativity," Satan's authentically but also deceptively powerful invention thus proves more fatal to himself than to the patient enemies securely standing and waiting on "the bright surface / Of this Ethereous mould . . . adorn'd / With Plant, Fruit, Flow'r Ambrosial, Gems and Gold" (6.472–75). By converting heaven's subterranean elements to his own destructive designs, he, not they, will remain permanently impaired by its "materials dark and crude, / Of spiritous and fiery spume, . . . pregnant with infernal flame" (6.478–79, 483). In bringing this pregnancy to birth, Lucifer, the light bearer, realizes his dreams of power, but only by perverting both, for a self-lost light bearer can only distemper, darken, and corrupt the power of light. Because the undiverted rays of this "fiery spume" provide the chaotic elements of truly creative freedom, in corrupting it, Satan ironically begins to fulfill the self-enslaving course on which Abdiel had already announced him engaged, "Thyself not free, but to thyself enthrall'd" (6.181). In this respect, Abdiel, the self-found sheep, completes his own rational triumph over Satan, even though he had been physically unable to defeat him. At this point the moral of the tale begins to resolve itself into a neat allegorical equation: while the perverted tactics of perverted minds are able to defraud the righteous of their spoils, they cannot deprive them of their own understanding, which alone determines their true standing in the sight of God. Yet even this obvious message is destabilized by the separate, if not quite equal, truth that, in a very real sense, the mind is "its own place, and in itself / Can make a Heav'n of Hell, a Hell of Heav'n" (1.254–55).

Chiefly in this imaginative sense, then, the counteraction of the loyal host creates its only "place," although not in any sense that can be symmetrically contrasted with that of the demons. Although their place ultimately reflects their zealous standing before God, like Abdiel's own logic, the strategies of the faithful angels are not wholly free from misinterpretation and error. To be vindicated in what is at once a literal contest and the symbolic warfare of Christian soldiers, they must not only resist Satan's tactics without adopting them for themselves but also avoid the temptation merely to stand under God by displaying their passive understanding of his principles, for freely to combat Satan means sharing his creativity while rejecting his hubristic motivation. Yet, as the conclusion of the war suggests, always maintaining this perfect balance is impossible even for angels. The strategies of the contestants thus more accurately define the meaning of their individual efforts than the final outcome of the war, although even this individual meaning is ultimately ambiguous, particularly in the final stages that produce their stalemate. Here, the righteous heavenly warriors ironically achieve some external vindication merely in rejecting the external armor to which the devils stubbornly cling, the traditional insignia of classical and/or Christian heroism (Eph. 6:11–17) that now only "help'd thir harm" and "wrought them pain / Implacable" (*PL*, 6.656–58). But, again, even this partial success is soon partially subverted. For, while the fallen and faithful angels' differing attitudes toward outward signs obviously contrast authentic freedom with the ethically enslaving standards of military heroism or other conventional "idolatries," the loyalists are also trapped by their decision to use the hills of heaven as a form of artillery. Since this tactical and ecological lapse points to the partial understanding of even the free, we are once again reminded that

> . . . So little know
> Any, but God alone, to value right
> The good before him, but perverts best things
> To worst abuse, or to thir meanest use.
> (4.201–4)

At this point, the advantages of a meta-allegorical reading become most pronounced: without it, the reader would assume, along with Revard, that the reciprocity between both parties makes the war "Satanic in essence" since "rebel and loyal angel alike—even though the loyal are upheld by truth and justice—subscribe to the classical ethic of war making wherein skill and strength determine victory."[13] The problem with this assessment is that it too thoroughly subverts the program of moral allegory, thereby making the entire episode either a comically misguided or a pointless exercise with no relation to its heroic pre-texts—even though Milton's final invocation proclaims his intent to sing "the *better* fortitude / Of Patience and Heroic Martyrdom" (*PL*, 9.31–32; emphasis added). Here it helps to recall that, in the Hesiodic war to which these actions allude, the giants assist Zeus, not merely because of his strength, but because his "exceeding" "wisdom and understanding" authorizes him to act as the "defender of the deathless ones."[14] As a result, when the more reasonable giants crush the lawless titans beneath a shower of boulders and send them down to Tartarus, their punishment fits their crime: those who oppose a higher rational order deserve to be confined to subterranean disorder. This same high/low distinction between the opposing parties remains operative in Milton's psychomachia, although with all the meta-allegorical refinements of secondary or tertiary epic.[15] Thus, while it remains emblematically significant that the good angels instinctively look to the "high hills" of God's wisdom, power, and justice for victory, it is even more significant that they do not attain it. If their reliance on these symbolic places is sufficient to distinguish their actions from Satan's abortive appropriation of subterranean principles ("Th' originals of Nature in thir crude/ Conception" [6.511–12]), without the complete understanding of divine principles vouchsafed the Son, their excessive zeal would confound its object.

Moreover, the contrast between the literal resources of the faithful and apostate angels cannot be as meaningless as Revard's remarks imply since the "height" of the holy hills where the Son's exaltation was celebrated obviously provides one kind of symbolic ammunition, while the unrefined bowels of heaven supply another. These hills and their "mazes intricate" (*PL,* 5.622) also implicitly represent the "height" of God's mysteriously spontaneous but not secret harmony, which irregularly and asymmetrically (5.622–65) counters the unrighteous depths of satanic secrecy. In contrast, like his cannon's, Satan's energies are ironically most fraudulent and darkly irregular when most roundly regular and brilliant they seem: "approaching gross and huge; in hollow Cube/ . . . impal'd / On every side with shadowing Squadrons Deep / To hide the fraud" (6.552–55). Yet, once again, even the irregular symmetry of these oppositions is undercut when no clear-cut victory for the proponents of "high" and "open" versus "low" and "closed" tactics emerges, with the result that once more the immediate rewards accorded the champions of God's holy mountain as opposed to those bestowed on the despoilers of his sacred subsoil remain roughly the same. Just when we think we can clearly trace motive to modus operandi, the Father is forced to recall his own troops lest "all Heav'n / Had gone to wrack" (6.669–70). Of course, if the good angels' symbolic reversal of demonic strategy is on most accounts a failure, it does maintain their standing before God, although this standing does not bestow the single-handed power to exterminate evil. The very inwardness of their "Heroic Martyrdom" thus implodes the numerous biblical allusions implicit in the battle besides the most obvious one, wherein the faithful now put off rather than put on the "whole armor of God" (Eph. 6:13). Thus, if God is a "strong tower" (Ps. 61:3; Prov. 18:10) who dwells in certain holy mountains and gives his faithful the strength to move others (1 Cor. 13:2), why are they so powerless over demons "now gross by sinning grown" (6.661)? This is a question for which the traditional psychomachia holds no answers, a fact signaled both by the poet's relentless ambiguation of its conventional signs, places, and actions, and by his sudden shift of its resolution onto the overwhelmingly asymmetrical image of the Son mounted on the Chariot of Paternal Deity.

3

A careful analysis of this battle's grand "anagogic" finale thus reveals some possible solutions to the particular questions posed above as well as to the problem of defining meta-allegory in general. As we have seen (and as Benjamin's theory of baroque allegory would predict), one of its crucially defining inversions derives from the Protestant redefinition of the meaning of place. Yet a comprehensively iconoclastic redefinition of status can only partly be achieved by replacing traditional hierarchies and symmetries with a more individualistic representation of the psychic, strategic, and motivational factors involved in "true" merit, for substituting other absolute criteria of even this kind would implicitly reinstate a new idolatry of form. The iconoclastic conclusion of Milton's War in Heaven thus seems designed to complete the critique of this idolatry only erratically achieved in its earlier episodes, thereby completely overturning the psychomachia's abstract and external order in favor of a wholly internal and relative one. While Raphael's narration of the war continues to inculcate some basic moral precepts—as, indeed, a didactic novel might—its inconclusive finale finally subverts the moral naïveté of the inherited form, where, generally, "the allegorist assumes that, when virtue imitates vice at the moment of attack, it can, by that very isomorphic imitation, destroy its opposite."[16] In avoiding these strict isomorphisms and polarities, Milton's psychomachia also avoids the implicitly arbitrary and authoritarian imposition of reward and blame on relatively empty or abstract ethical oppositions between otherwise "willless" agents. Along with the arbitrary symmetries conventionally attached to opposing places, emblems, numbers, and instruments, he not only blurs but finally undermines the innate meaningfulness of military heroics, thereby critiquing all the external criteria associated with heroism itself. Because both tactical differentiation and even the self-won signs of victory have been rendered suspect, true worth is now posed as an essentially ambivalent and ultimately inscrutable form of virtue. What then remains are the real ambiguities and choices of human struggle, processural choices that not only will vary according to place, time, and subjective insight but will also succeed or fail as such varying contexts decree—until the certain but transcendentally deferred victory of Messiah.

Until then, the merit of the Christian warrior remains fundamentally internal and ambiguous, finally manifest only in a complex and intensely personal relation to the Word of God. By allowing the loyal faction to establish their voluntary perseverance and zeal (and perhaps overzealousness) in the fray, not only God but each individual angel has *already* resolved the true issues of the conflict before it is over. After refuting Satan's potentially damaging accusations against the slothful and servile motivations of the faithful, they need only invalidate his assertion of the complete relativity of natural law. Prominently excluded from these issues is the preservation of the saints from any liability to error since their creaturely weaknesses have been all too painfully demonstrated by their misjudgments and ultimate failure. In the terms established by this struggle, the external signs of victory or defeat are thus only tangentially related to "true" rewards except in the last instance, when, as in this finale, their meaning will be revealed by the unrelativistic recoil of natural justice. Nevertheless, the earlier loss of the saints' expected victory also requires a naturalistic reappraisal of the mystified values of Christian warfare and its revolutionary ideals, for, while both must continue, the eschatological promise signified by the typology of the *Merkabah* or chariot throne in which the Son rides to victory may not come on the expected day—or even in the day of need. As a result, the superhuman, supratemporal "designs" of providential intervention inscribed on the chariot itself are so overwhelming that they seem to de-sign themselves, collapsing under the ponderously self-referential elaboration of this vehicle of unimaginable power.

With its "four Cherubic shapes," each with four faces and wings set with eyes (*PL,* 6.753–55), the chariot's symbolic excess of jewel-encrusted, biblically emblazoned signs—including a rider garbed not only with Hebraic emblems but with those of the Greek gods of justice, light, and victory (6.760–64)—is thus not simply a "type" taken from Ezekial's vision.[17] The excessive emblematization of this iconoclastically overdetermined icon is here in some sense blindingly invisible as well as unimaginable, becoming humanly perceptible chiefly in its baroque aura of enigmatic vindication. Like the deity's own "dark with excessive bright" aura, it is shaded by peripherally perceptible emanations—emblems of historical vindication drawn from the entire span of the prophets, beginning with Moses at Sinai (as "about him fierce Effusion roll'd / Of smoke and bickering flame, and sparkles dire" [6.765–66]) and ending with Revelation. As the counterpart of the sword-bearing rider of the apocalypse but also of the enduring Spirit of the opening invocation who "didst inspire" that first Mosaic shepherd (1.7–8), the figure of the Son collapses all the Bible's historical "peaks" into the historical "now" of the spirit-inspired reader, its true "temple" (1.17–18). Like so much of the War in Heaven, this movement away from Ezekiel's visions and toward the prophetic tradition stemming from Moses is as significant for what it does not as for what it does suggest. Conventionally, Moses symbolized the concealment of higher truths from the grosser sensibilities of the multitude since, as Michael Murrin explains, "what the initiate knew as paradox could only exist as contradiction for the multitude, if they had everything told to them at once . . . the many simply could not bear a direct presentation of truth. The Hebrews gather around Mount Sinai recoiled in fear from the thunder and lightning of Yahweh's voice and asked for a mediator . . . reserving the terrors of the 'unheard of' for the few who could bear it."[18]

For Milton, however, "the few who could bear" the unimaginable power and majesty of divinity have been reduced to one, the Son himself. Poet and reader, like angel army, thus stand outside this colossal "tower" of overdetermined symbols, as in a comparable moment in *Samson Agonistes* they only indirectly apprehend the cathartic collapse of the temple destroyed by its iconoclastic hero and his God. This collapse of the satanic forces is of course more directly witnessed by the loyal angels, but, in repeatedly alluding to Revelation, the poet suggests that their experience ultimately stands outside time or place altogether. Raphael sees the "ten thousand thousand Saints" and their twenty thousand chariots of God (*PL,* 6.767–69), but the full experience of the scene is actually beyond even him; as he acknowledges, "I thir number heard." Thus, while his expression of divine power through these magical numbers undoubtedly points to some kind of transcendental truth, it also illustrates the impossibility of making any literal calculation or producing any tangible correspondence to it on earth, as either an actual or an imaginary "hypotenuse." Yet, paradoxically, God's unutterably and innumerably terrible power is also the most literal aspect of the deity or his prophets, as the Son reminds us:

> Vengeance is his, or whose he sole appoints;
> Number to this day's work is not ordain'd
> Nor multitude, stand only and behold
> God's indignation on these Godless pour'd
> By mee. . . .
> (6.808–12)

Vengeance is mine, saith the Lord, and so is number, adds his poet. Although it will come, it arrives in a "day's work" beyond number and multitude, although also as an eruption of eternity into history. This inversion of the usual ritual beatification of the One thus tacitly announces the end of all mystically meaningful numeration and, along with it, the ruins of its allegory, for, as earth is no longer merely the shadow of heaven, its saints are no longer merely the daemonic agents of that correspondence.

Nevertheless, as earlier, the poet can dispense with neither signs nor allegory in depicting the cosmogonic implications of these events. The fact that the Son's expulsion of the demons is reserved for a literary "place" that falls close to the exact center of the epic also suggests that not all sense of the meaningfulness of places or shapes has been superseded since, at some level, such principles remain indispensable to order itself. However, the Messiah makes it unreservedly clear that the imputation of absolute meaning to number, strength, and place are forms of satanic idolatry incompatible with his divine calculus, as he does in announcing to his faithful that they need "stand only and behold" a contest whose "numbers" Satan has attempted to calculate only to earn wrath beyond measure. As a result, he reappropriates his rhetoric, ironically announcing that

> . . . they may have thir wish, to try with mee
> In Battle which the stronger proves, they all,
> Or I alone against them, since by strength
> They measure all, of other excellence
> Not emulous, nor care who them excels;
> Nor other strife with them do I voutsafe.
> (*PL*, 6.818–23)

Like the terms of allegory, the demonic terms of this contest are here accepted only in order to prove how incapable they are of measuring true strength or merit, for the Son's single combat against the entire demonic host makes a mockery of their rebellion by demonstrating their infinite miscalculation. Having earlier proclaimed themselves "beyond / All doubt of Victory," they are here forced to understand how much useful doubt they have thrown away. Finally, then, only the rod of the Son's severity and wrath (6.825–26) can truly serve to measure their fate or complete the utter exorcism of their interference with heavenly bliss.[19]

Yet, while this, like the other miraculous signs that the Son performs, clearly justifies Abdiel's initial contention that "by his Word the mighty Father made / All things, ev'n thee, and all the Spirits of Heav'n" (*PL,* 5.836–37), it fails to support any ontological hierarchy that might otherwise be attached to heaven's natural laws. As we have seen, it is Satan, not the Son, who favors primogeniture over meritocracy, a point underscored by nearly every biblical allusion that Milton attaches to the Messiah. His paradigm for the Son's authority predictably stems from the Old Testament tradition favored by the Reformers, one in which God's adopted sons and true heirs receive their spiritual birthright by merit before place or birth order. Thus he bases his biblical epic not only on Job and Revelation but on the two books of Samuel, which trace the heroic saga whereby the youngest, least-favored son, also of obscure family, attains the kingship over an Israelite chieftain of greater stature and charisma. Although the Messiah's closer proximity to the Father would appear to invalidate any analogy making him a David to Satan's Saul, other details of the episode strongly reinforce the comparison. Like the flocks of the good shepherd, David's heir and redeemed "type," the hills of heaven "heard his voice"; like him, the Son is first made King "by Sacred Unction" (*PL,* 6.709) before coming into power; like him, he has been held back from the war against the Philistines by his father; and, like David, the Son achieves an effortless conquest of his enemy by faith, while a Goliath- or Saul-like Satan vanquishes himself through idolatry. Girding on his Davidic "superweapon," the Son singly confronts the entire army of his enemies by expressing his loyal love of his Father in his descendent's words: "whom thou hat'st, I hate" (*PL,* 6.734; Ps. 139:21).

These allusions complete our understanding of the paradoxical baroque dialectic of both power and standing. In this late or "meta" form of allegory, perfect faith conceived as empathic emulation is its own place and rests assured of its own power, even if this is, properly speaking, derivative from God. While Satan and his crew display a symmetrically similar understanding of authority and place, their distortions and misapprehensions gradually become more parodic and mock heroic, as Satan's inevitable devolution from the rigid symmetries of the "own place" of his mind reveals. This paradoxical expansion/implosion of allegory is further revealed in the poem's definition of *reflection,* which is somehow neither a shadow nor an imitation but an act of full interpretation informed by grace and love. In its most highly perfected, fully transparent form, it becomes the flawless translation that makes the Son the living, literal *Word* of God: "hee all his Father full exprest / Ineffably into his face receiv'd" (*PL,* 6.720–21). The joy that accompanies this pure poesis of apprehension renders the sense of imparity fueling overreaching ambition unimaginable, for its oblique reciprocities resemble the irregular harmonies and the placeless elevation of heavenly song. In putting on his Father's power, the Son thus already looks forward to resigning it "when in the end / Thou shalt be All in All" (6.731–32) and he shall be free to join the other angels as simply the chief among those who sing "unfeigned *Halleluiahs* to thee" (6.744–45). In this highly transactional model of his role as Word or Truth, the Son also steps down from his traditionally hypostatized place in the Trinity and also from any eternal order apart from that voluntarily imparted by God and accepted by him.[20] Here, as in his final encounters with Sin and Death, this corrected schema "reframes" Satan as a spirit who has fallen victim to his own hoax: for there actually is no Anointed King (as he conceives it) to oppose, only the grace imparted by communication with the Father that he has rejected for the "fairer" image of Sin, his second and more rigid self.

Thus, while the Son does retain certain prerogatives stemming from his birthright, he continues to merit them through his unfailing acknowledgment of these gifts as not properly his own but as those of the Father who freely grants them:

> . . . Into thee such Virtue and Grace
> Immense I have transfus'd, that all may know
> In Heav'n and Hell thy Power above compare,
> And this perverse Commotion govern'd thus,
> To manifest thee worthiest to be Heir

Of all things, to be Heir and to be King
By Sacred Unction, thy deserved right.
(*PL,* 6.703–9)

This "graceful" transfusion of power not only explains some of the mystical excesses surrounding the Son's progress astride the "Chariot of Paternal Deity" but also serves to demystify this vision in advance. Since the chariot belongs neither to the Son nor to any intermediate force in the universe, its transcendent meaning is confined to the source of the unimaginable primal power whose vehicle this is. Overwrought with this symbolic charge, its devices finally signal only the failure of signs and even, except by faith, of seeing. The hypermystical intrusion of this chariot at the climax of what had appeared to be a relatively mimetic psychomachia thus mark it as a baroque vanishing point, after which the traditional heroics of epic-allegory can only become a diminished thing.

In its place, we receive the "readerly" or interpretive heroic model supplied by the Son, whose "transfus'd" and hence irresistible power in this ultimate warfare suggests that his true victory consists in his perfected rejection of the false icons, instruments, and heroic myths of Satan's invention. Somewhere ambiguously below him in natural merit stand the other loyal saints, who, overbalanced by the twin imperfections of excessive zeal and hermeneutic literalism, win no more (and no less) than a faithful standing before God. Yet, without the divine grace issuing from his Word, their mediator, their firm "stand" on God's holy mountains would collapse entirely, for, as the passage ironically suggests, if faith without perfect love and understanding is sufficient to move mountains, it cannot restore them. As Paul similarly cautions, "Though I have the gift of prophecy, and understand all mysteries, and all knowledge; and though I have all faith, so that I could remove mountains, and have not charity, I am nothing" (1 Cor. 13:2). The Son, preeminent in faith, knowledge, prophecy, and charity, thus becomes the only model for God's elect, the divinely "fit audience" of his exemplary freedom from place or name:[21]

By merit more than Birthright Son of God
Found worthiest to be so by being Good,
Far more than Great or High; because in thee
Love hath abounded more than glory abounds. . . .
(*PL,* 3.309–12)

Because the charity or love that the Son shares with the Father not only guides the interpretation of his will but also interprets it for the rest of creation, the essential task of the saints is to recognize its signs through a necessarily asymmetrical process of exchange. Again resorting to paradox in order to represent the dual but not dualistic reciprocity of cause and effect, the poet represents this mutual reflection as synthetically, if also obliquely, revealing what in the Son's "face invisible is beheld / Visibly, what by Deity I am" (*PL*, 6.681–82). Fusing sound and sense, this verbal, rather than nominal reflection also echoes Jehovah's name, "I am that I am"—a name consisting of a pair of reversible verbs that "define" both the divine essence and the self-referential basis of Milton's meta-allegorical technique. Although the Son possesses the unique capacity to coexist on the same plane with God's transcendent verbs of Being, as a creature he can only indirectly or "invisibly" reflect the invisible deity in the visible realm of becoming. In this ambiguous sense, the Son is also the amorphous or interactive shadow of the Father's shadowless presence, just as earth is the shadow of heaven or the echo the shadow of the utterance. As both metonymy and synecdoche, this double linguistic conjunction replaces the paratactic displacements of normative allegory with the dialectical or hypotactic reflexivity that is the rhetorical essence of the meta-allegorical mode. In place of a digressive propulsion of symmetrical correspondences leading beyond time and space, this rhetoric leads to a readerly reengagement with the resoluable if also enigmatic ambiguities of the linguistic signs guiding human interpretation and action.

Just as for the reformed reader an interpreter's Bible replaces the eternal sacramental Word, so the Son here finally replaces the static homologies of allegory with a perfected principle of spontaneous signs as the transposible vehicles of absent and/or invisible causes. This revision is signaled in his final entry into battle, which generates a series of emblems dynamically erasing their own heraldic designs:

> When the great Ensign of *Messiah* blaz'd
> Aloft by Angels borne, his Sign in Heav'n:
> . . . .
> Before him Power Divine his way prepar'd;
> At his command the uprooted Hills retir'd

Each to his place, they heard his voice and went
Obsequious, Heav'n his wonted face renew'd,
And with fresh Flow'rets Hill and Valley smil'd.
(*PL*, 6.775–84)

As the signal for the final confrontation of the cosmogonic battle, Messiah's "ensign" first appears as an assurance of the peace that his conquest will restore. Although not the source or purpose of his victory, this symbol is metonymically linked to the "Power Divine" that has been granted him, itself a synecdoche for order. Miraculously, then, it instantly reunites heaven's "Crystalline Sky" (6.772) with its hills and valleys, the mutual reflection of landscape and sky natural to the Kingdom of God.

Yet, characteristically, Milton also partially cancels this hyper-allegorical device of converting a metonymic or causal sign to synecdochic effect by leaving it open to misinterpretation and, later, misappropriation:

This saw his hapless Foes, but stood obdur'd,
And to rebellious fight rallied thir Powers
Insensate, hope conceiving from despair.
In heav'nly Spirits could such perverseness dwell?
But to convince the proud what Signs avail,
Or Wonders move th'obdurate to relent?
(*PL*, 6.785–90)

The "insensate" devils remain doubly hardened, "obdur'd" and "obdurate," in their self-enthrallment becoming ever more confirmed misreaders of signs. Yet, since not even the heavenly saints can consistently interpret God's ways correctly, the demonic condition cannot be represented with proper allegorical symmetry. The careful reader perceives that neither internal nor external truth is fully contained in these signs, but only in her own perception of them as double-edged inscriptions expressing their senders only insofar as they are not narcissistically "redesigned" by their receivers.

Of course, the direction in which they are sent, like the one from which they are received, does indicate something about both authors and audiences, but only as their mutual "weight" is measured against their temporal field of gravitation: "For Time, though in Eternity, appli'd / To motion, measures all things durable / By present, past, and future" (*PL*, 5.580–82). At this level, Raphael's warning to Adam and Eve becomes primarily an admonition to avoid an idolatry of signs by contextualizing their "realty" with their temporal experience. Fulfilling his role by "Thus measuring things in Heav'n by things on Earth / . . . that thou mayst beware / By what is past" (6.893–95), Raphael cannot then be held responsible when Adam and Eve forget to measure themselves by these well-established natural laws or his "past" angelic warning. Once they reject the rigors of interpretation for the allure of idolatrous "ensigns," the fallen pair cannot at first even "see" the image of the Son except as their "Judge" (10.126). In forgetting their meta-allegorical role model, their Fall thus parallels Satan's "Realist" tendency to lend too much credence to apparently concrete but actually fluid and unstable natural signs.

4

For the unfallen human pair, however, the full import of Raphael's lessons cannot be considered complete with the victorious finale of the War in Heaven since they must also attain the fuller understanding of the link between destruction and creation that (ironically) their lapse will require. That human beings know life only from death, perfection or redemption only from sin and error, is a commonplace, yet Raphael's narration of the hexameron meta-allegorically reworks this theme by paralleling and inverting the example of Satan's rebellion and fall in ways that again exceed all the usual analogies, even Milton's own. Although the newborn earth is suspended from heaven "to that side" whence Satan's legions fell (*PL*, 2.1006), the progress of book 7 does not merely repair that desolation but more intensely resumes the themes of reflection and interpretation surrounding the war's conclusion. This exploration appropriately begins with the poet's invocation to Urania:

> Descend from Heav'n *Urania*, by that name
> If rightly thou art call'd, whose Voice divine
> Following, above th'*Olympian* Hill I soar,
> Above the flight of *Pegasean* wing.
> The meaning, not the Name I call: for thou
> Nor of the Muses nine, nor on the top
> Of old *Olympus* dwell'st, but, Heav'nly born,

Before the Hills appear'd, or Fountain flow'd,
Thou with Eternal Wisdom didst converse. . . .
(7.1–9)

More than another invocation to the heavenly spirit, these lines should be understood as invoking the muse of meta-allegory, who resists names, numbers, and places: "The meaning not the Name I call." As both the enigmatic sister of Wisdom (*PL,* 7.10) and a muse defined chiefly by her lack of analogy to Athena, Minerva, or Calliope, Urania subverts the usual allegorical tendency merely to rework its characteristic blend of classical and Christian myth. The sibling and perhaps even the "muse" of the unidentified voice of Proverbs 8:30, she is defined as *not* one of the traditional "muses nine" to whom her name alludes, the eighth and penultimate muse before Calliope, the last. "Heav'nly born," she remains as insubstantial and problematic as her sister Wisdom, who has often been identified with that model reader, the Son himself. All that then seems clear about this nonfigural figure is that, because she can be associated neither with number nor with name, she somehow aids the narrator in producing an accommodated interpretation of these cosmogonic events. As a Christian poet with a Christian muse, this narrator then uses her to express his higher hope of escaping the fate of Orpheus or Bellerophon—the mythic fall from divine favor that parallels Satan's actual defeat. Here, as in the War in Heaven, asymmetrical parallels are reflected by puns, in this case concerning in the poet's ironic "fear" of falling into Bellerophon's "lower" decline, for, just as Greece is situated in a lower geographic climate than England, so Bellerophon's fall from his winged horse occurs in a lower moral sphere than the narrator's descent from the heights of cosmic Christian warfare. Nevertheless, both are proportionately threatened by satanic hubris and iconic allegory, which he must avoid

Lest from this flying Steed unrein'd, (as once
Bellerophon, though from a lower Clime)
Dismounted, on th'*Aleian* Field I fall
Erroneous there to wander and forlorn.
(7.17–20)

Without heavenly inspiration, without the visionary Wisdom of Proverbs or Urania, the poet could never regain his "Native Element" (*PL,* 7.16)—generally, earth, but particularly, Christian England, where he hopes to find "fit audience . . . though few," if he can escape the "barbarous dissonance / Of *Bacchus* and his Revellers" (7.31–33), the monarchists and/or idolists of the Restoration. The poet's hopes for a Son-like victory thus depend on his ability to sing truth, not idolatrous myth, thereby avoiding the fate of Orpheus, who did not escape "that wild Rout" (7.34). Since the latter's mother-muse, Calliope, could not save him even in her lower sphere, the Christian poet regards his own danger as both more and less grave. With no knowledge of the Messiah's victory, myth was Orpheus's "Native Element"; if his divine gifts finally failed to save him, at least he never risked his eternal salvation in the process. At worst, his defeat would only accelerate the condition in which he already found himself: half blind and dying, the pagan poet could become fully blind like Bellerophon, or crazed like Tasso, or dishonored and dis-membered like Orpheus himself. In contrast, the Christian poet is blind but can still "see" the truth, unless he has mistakenly "pre-sum'd, / An Earthly Guest, and drawn Empyreal Air" (7.13–14). This misstep might hurl him down to the Aleian Field—like Satan, fall-ing the maximum distance of the spiritual universe, not merely from the "Plain of Heav'n" (1.104) to the "dreary Plain" (1.180) of hell, but from the highest plain of truth to the lowest stair of mythology.

This complex interleaving of similes expresses no mere virtuosity on the poet's part; rather, it serves to remind him and his reader of the ever-present dangers of the idolatry of form. By associating Satan with all of the many forms of this idolatry—mythological, psychological, and allegorical—these dangers are condensed into a psychologized, semierased personification, the antithesis of the Spirit of the invocation. Should the Christian poet prove "errone-ous," this Satan effect may overtake both him and/or reader, an association that implicitly translates satanic error back into a cause rather than a literal person, place, or thing. Yet this awareness further concretizes the poet's fears, since in psychologizing and thus effec-tively canceling the ritual or Spenserian effects of contamination, they also become more strongly "re-presented" than ever. In this sense they become part of the present-tense psychomachia pitting Satan against the poet as well as his readers. Thus while Satan be-comes a "vice" under erasure much as Urania is reduced to a highly ambiguous and transformative kind of "virtue," the very process of canceling their energies also upholds them in important new ways. In Urania's case, the result is that after initially acting as an interpretive guide on the order of Dante's Virgil or Milton's Spirit, she gradually becomes more than a symbolic warning without a place, a reminder of the dangers of all symbolic forms and places—in short, the Protestant muse of meta-allegory.

As a result, time, not place, weighs all creative images by tracing their development through a "process of speech" that here further recontextualizes the epic invocation to Urania, who in this sense is also the new muse of the new astronomy. From the "higher" and broader perspective of its expanded universe, the poet must then calculate his own epic "place" as a moralized function of shifting time rather than of concrete space:

> Half yet remains unsung, but narrower bound
> Within the visible Diurnal Sphere;
> Standing on Earth, not rapt above the Pole,
> More safe I Sing with mortal voice, unchang'd
> To hoarse or mute, though fall'n on evil days. . . .
> (*PL*, 7.21–25)

If at the poem's temporal midpoint the speaker must return to his spatial midpoint, earth, here the "cause" is no longer ritual or eternal but pragmatic and present tense: in the spiritual climate described by the poet, earth is clearly the proper element for a "mortal voice," not some absurdly mystical standpoint "rapt above the Pole." From here he can more suitably reflect on the latter course of England's "evil days," on which his expectations of an even smaller audience than he had anticipated in *Eikonoklastes* hinge. In the latter, he had also anticipated finding out worthy "readers; few perhaps" (*CPW*, 3:339–40), but even now while "In darkness, and with dangers compast round" (*PL*, 7.27), his situation may not yet be hopeless if he can find the proper "stance" dictated by a proper under*standing* of his times. This stance, along with his refusal to be silenced, may then earn him the invisible and interactive gifts of Urania: "yet not alone, while thou / Visit'st my slumbers Nightly, or when Morn / Purples the East" (7.28–30). Like his poem, the earth on which the poet concretely places himself is thus actually a frame or experiential medium more than a fixed place—a time/space halfway between Night and Morn, between Satan's fall and Adam's redemption, and between original Creation and the final Apocalypse.

This emphasis on the middle of things as a temporal medium demanding knowledge of fit seasons and processes also frames the treatment of creation that follows. Cosmically, the new earth represents a recuperation from the spiritual death that Satan has introduced into the world, a dialectical recoil of life against death that in turn frames all the processes of material history. To emphasize the interdependency of these rising and falling cycles, the earth's founding begins, not only precisely where Satan's expulsion left off, but also in reverse order from the events of book 6. This reversal is inaugurated as God informs the Son that his divine design will prevail (*PL,* 7.150–56) despite Satan's incursions and, in response, receives the hallelujahs his Son had promised him on confronting Satan (6.742–44) and defeating him (6.882–89). The angels' glory hymn (7.182–91) thus fuses the celebration of vengeance and re-creation in ways significant both for book 7 and for the remainder of the epic. Since evil is here not an Augustinian "nothing" but a cancer on the good that must inevitably atrophy into its own waste, the relation between good and evil has all along been naturalistically grounded in this birth/death distinction. Yet here its entire historical cycle panoramically emerges as the angels celebrate the expunged or "vacant room" of the "Spirits malign" in the same breath and in the same words that they will use to hymn Christ's nativity: as promising "good will / To future men, and in their dwellings peace," finally extending his "good to Worlds and Ages infinite" (7.182–91).

Not only the large-scale motions of this cycle but its minutest details follow a similar pattern. Thus, when the Son appears in glory, "Girt with Omnipotence, with Radiance crown'd / Of Majesty Divine, Sapience and Love / Immense" (*PL,* 7.194–96), his entrance at once repeats and reverses his preparation for battle. Again, God infuses the Son with his Omnipotence, as "all his Father in him shone" (7.196), but now in order to propel new existence into being rather than to expel decadent spirits out of their former home. Displaying the same symbolic emblems of power, the Son again accepts his role as Word and mounts the symbolic chariot of deity (7.197–204) to accomplish his Father's will; and, again, both this triumphant charioteer and all those who accompany him are "infused" with God's transforming grace, the only truly transcendent force in Milton's meta-allegory, the inspired and spontaneous vehicles of faith in which "Spirit liv'd" (7.204). This transcendent grace is therefore represented in much the same way as God himself, as a figurative gap of meaning into which all others immanently converge, the space between opening and closing, as now

. . . Heav'n op'n'd wide
Her ever-during Gates, Harmonious sound
On golden Hinges moving, to let forth
The King of Glory in his powerful Word
And Spirit coming to create new Worlds.
(7.205–9)

Sin, we recall, could open the gates of hell, but not close them; the Son, however, can open the gates of heaven onto entirely new and unimaginably fertile worlds just as easily as he had closed the procreative opening of heaven to Satan and his rebel angels. This closure seals the anticreative "gap" that Satan produced there by creating an antithetical abyss into which the destructive energies of the malign may be poured,

. . . which op'ning wide,
Roll'd inward, and a spacious Gap disclos'd
Into the wasteful Deep; the monstrous sight
Struck them with horror backward, but far worse
Urg'd them behind; headlong themselves they threw
Down from the verge of Heav'n, Eternal wrath
Burn'd after them to the bottomless pit.
(*PL*, 6.860–66)

This punishment is warranted because the rebels neither could nor would heed the double sign of the Messiah, neither his emblematic banner unfurled in heaven, nor the literal and organic "sign" of his presence, the creative flowering of heaven's hills and valleys (6.781–84). As matter's most passive principle, Chaos is thus naturally more responsive than the self-blinded demons: it soon obeys his call much as heaven's chaotically devastated landscape had "heard his voice" (7.221). When the Son places his golden compasses on its "vast immeasurable Abyss / Outrageous as a Sea" (7.211–12) in order to "circumscribe / This Universe, and all created things" (7.226–27), the compasses, then at once synecdochally sign and metonymically or causally de-sign the meaning of God's "Eternal store." Although the "Celestial Equipage" (7.203) accompanying the Son again represents a largely incomprehensible force, his host of "numberless" (7.197) angels equipped with instruments from the "Armory of God" (7.200) witnesses a creation made comprehensible by the "process of speech" of the Word. Yet, rather than an authoritarian order, the Word establishes a creative gap within which "matter unform'd and void" (7.233) can achieve its own definition: a "just Circumference" (7.231) at once expressing its own immanent energies and refuting the more circumscribing designs of hell.

Nevertheless, as in the psychomachia, even the dialectical symmetries of destruction and creation soon become susceptible to metaallegorical critique, which once again proceeds by blocking or blinding the reader's direct access to God's incommensurable energies. Having imaginatively witnessed the Son's expulsion of the devils from Heaven with "ten thousand Thunders" (*PL,* 6.836) but also the eerie silence with which Chaos instantly hearkens to his voice, the reader can concretely interpret this paradoxical synthesis of competing forces only by focusing on the tangible and/or temporal signs emerging around this sublime aura. For, while life does indeed arise from death, the "native Element" of the living, like that of their language, consists in the experiential medium of matter's divine vitality, its spontaneous capacity to materialize concrete forms from the primal source of all energy and order. In tracing the reemergence of life from death, both the contrast and the isomorphism of satanic and divine energies are thus alternately revealed and dissolved in an organically evolving "procession" of differentiated species. Yet, at the outset, the inverse polarity of these energies is maintained as the Son's compass draws a circle over Chaos that silently enfolds and nourishes a potentiality whose natural disarray the demonic invasion had only painfully exacerbated:

> . . . confounded *Chaos* roar'd,
> And felt tenfold confusion in thir fall
> Through his wild Anarchy, so huge a rout
> Incumber'd him with ruin. . . .
> (6.871–74)

This contrast between the fall and the "resurrection" of matter is itself organic and spontaneous since it stems from the fact that hell is a mouth that eats its own—which "Yawning receiv'd them whole, and on them clos'd" (*PL,* 6.875)—while the painless circle of the "Omnific Word" draws on deeper resources of the abyss that do not cannibalize but engender life:

> His brooding wings the Spirit of God outspread,
> And vital virtue infus'd, and vital warmth

Throughout the fluid Mass, but downward purg'd
The black tartareous cold Infernal dregs
Adverse to life; then founded, then conglob'd
Like things to like, the rest to several place
Disparted, and between spun out the Air,
And Earth self-balanc't on her Centre hung.
(7.235–42)

Life in this account is destructive and constructive for both the divine and the satanic forces, but to opposite effect. Earth's creation is imaged as a peaceful and natural "delivery" of organic substance from a cosmic "womb," although not without violence: bounds must still be drawn, and materials "adverse to life" must be purged. Yet earlier, when Satan had "presided" over a similarly pregnant deep whose fiery "spume" rightly "tempered . . . shoot[s] forth / So beauteous, op'ning to the ambient light" (6.479–81), its violent birth had been converted into the still greater violence of cannon fire. As this example again illustrates, although the creative ends of the "spontaneous" as opposed to the self-hardened spirits differ, their creative means do not. As a result, the triumph of good must be understood as neither the mere defeat nor the extinction of evil but as an "opening" to life's "self-balanc't" search for its own natural center.

Thus, while an infinite distance ultimately separates Sin's snaky form from water's life-giving armies "with Serpent error wand'ring," their distance cannot be aligned with any objectively "clear and distinct" paths. In gently parodying the progress of the satanic troops, Milton's "serpent" waters illuminate their asymmetrical divergences as they are deployed over an unpredictable, unknown terrain under the command of a personified captain. This benign natural "army" then seeks out vitalistic currents that can have no other singular or "proper" meaning than their own innate potential to harmonize their own character with the landscape of their birth:[22]

. . . so the wat'ry throng,
Wave rolling after Wave, where way they found,
If steep, with torrent rapture, if through Plain,
Soft-ebbing; nor withstood them Rock or Hill,
But they, or under ground, or circuit wide
With Serpent error wand'ring, found thir way,
And on the washy Ooze deep Channels wore. . . .
(*PL*, 7.297–303)

The life-giving character of these channels suggests a half-sub-
merged allegory of motion as the twin of poetic creativity and the
antithesis of the rigid heroic clichés of the satanic legions. Not only
visual but auditory, earthly and watery freedom then gives birth to a
vastly discordant variety of joyous sound. Thus, as in heaven before
Satan's rebellion, on the new earth natural beauty is figured as a
mysteriously random harmony consistent both with life and with the
liberation of matter decreed by God.

Comically present even in Chaos, the domain of excessive freedom
without form, in paradise this dynamism finally directs the waters
to generate fluid forms more closely resembling heaven's "mazes
intricate":

> Forthwith the Sounds and Seas, each Creek and Bay
> With Fry innumerable swarm, and Shoals
> Of Fish that with thir Fins and shining Scales
> Glide under the green Wave, in Sculls that oft
> Bank the mid Sea: part single or with mate
> Graze the Seaweed thir pasture, and through Groves
> Of Coral stray, or sporting with quick glance
> Show to the Sun thir wav'd coats dropt with Gold,
> Or in thir Pearly shells at ease, attend
> Moist nutriment, or under Rocks thir food
> In jointed Armor watch: on smooth the Seal,
> And bended Dolphins play: part huge of bulk
> Wallowing unwieldy, enormous in thir Gait
> Tempest the Ocean: there Leviathan
> Hugest of living Creatures, on the Deep
> Stretcht like a Promontory sleeps or swims,
> And seems a moving Land, and at his Gills
> Draws in, and at his Trunk spouts out a Sea.
> (*PL*, 7.399–416)

Onomatopoeically as well as imagistically, paradise becomes a dance
of life in which the very separation of the elements leads to their
conjunction; fish "graze the Seaweed thir pasture," have "coats" that
reflect the Sun, "Armor" that aids in the contest of life, not death,
and so like the angels wear ornaments of pearl and gold. The fallen
scenes of books 1, 2, 5, and 6 now appear like mirages of the disor-
dered imagination dispelled by this reawakening. No longer a Satan

simile, Leviathan here turns comedian, imitating elephants and islands but pulling no unwary navigators under. Rupture itself is kindly beneath its sharp edge, its clangor signifying mating and maturation instead of mutual combat:

> Meanwhile the tepid Caves, and Fens and shores
> Thir Brood as numerous hatch, from th' Egg that soon
> Bursting with kindly rupture forth disclos'd
> Thir callow young, but feather'd soon and fledge
> They summ'd thir Pens, and soaring th' air sublime
> With clang despis'd the ground, under a cloud
> In prospect. . . .
> (7.417–23)

As in heaven, there is dark and light but no thunderclouds in this landscape, only cloudy shades. Large and small, finned or winged, create only a "grateful vicissitude" like that produced by the cave within the Mount of God, "where light and darkness in perpetual round / Lodge and dislodge" (*PL*, 6.4–8). The reader awakens from the evil spell of Satan's Realist allegory to find his terrifying disdain for the "lowly" ground recuperated in a vivid yet benign domesticity; the nightmare of his "despite," dissolving, restores the fluid dynamism of the actual, and the fertile life world conquers all-consuming death:

> . . . the Swan with Arched neck
> Between her white wings mantling proudly, Rows
> Her state with Oary feet: yet oft they quit
> The Dank, and rising on stiff Pennons, tow'r
> The mid Aereal Sky: Others on ground
> Walk'd firm; the crested Cock whose clarion sounds
> The silent hours, and th' other whose gay Train
> Adorns him, colored with the Florid hue
> Of Rainbows and Starry Eyes.
> (7.438–46)

In this animistic redemption, the "Proud fowls'" reminder of demonic destruction is colored in the lightest and most "florid" shades of baroque chiaroscuro, for now the "dank" pool and stiff wings of Satan's evil and ultimately inglorious strife give way to the "clarion sounds" of morning and mating beneath the "mid Aereal Sky."

The demons may darkly mimic but cannot "participate" in this more "rational delight" (*PL*, 8.390–91), the complement of "silent hours," nor can their dark trains regain the innocent pride of the swan's pure white majesty set among the living color of peacock plumes. All creations, even Satan, is beautiful; but this infinite parade of motion and freedom in which both serpent waters and the serpent himself are "not noxious" (7.498) is possible only where life has not turned against its source. These scenes thus demonstrate what the angels merely gloss: "to create / Is greater than created to destroy. / Who can impair thee, mighty King, or bound / Thy Empire?" (7.606–9). As they witness these dawning moments of unsullied life, we see rivalry and pride revealed as the natural components of a life-sustaining individuality corrupted only by demons, a rich tapestry within which the figure of the hierarchical God of Genesis appears only to disappear. In this fullest manifestation of his baroque immanence, matter obeys the Son to show that Son-like self-denial leads actually to greater self-expression, the destiny "imposed" by the Author of this Word through his most natural laws. As the medium of these laws, both the Son and the Spirit act as maternal aspects of creation, as vehicles of God's inseminating seed, sustainers of the blood and bone that allow all flesh to be born "limb'd and full grown," "each in their kind" (7.453–56).

Of course, in a more literal sense, these living souls are born and thrive as distinct conceptions of the earthly mother, "those rare and solitary, these in flocks / Pasturing at once," all sprung from the same womb, nurtured at the same breast, her "pasture" (*PL*, 7.461–62). Her children's continuities within difference are emphasized as the soft and peaceful flocks appear as plants, the stag's antlers thrusting up from the ground like tree branches. Behemoth heaves up from the earthy mold looking like the vast hillock from which he came, furrowed, huge; the "dungy" cattle too emerge from "grassy clods" of earth, which feeds them as they are fed: "the grassy Clods now Calv'd" (7.463). This dialectical representation of existence extends even to hippopotamus and crocodile, "ambiguous between Sea and Land," as well as to the insects who resemble the blooms they feed on, like them "deckt of Summer's pride / With spots of Gold and Purple, azure and green" (7.473, 478–79), all of which again inverts the demonic cannibalism of Satan's world of death. Yet the vitalism of these passages stems, not simply from the personification of the

earth, plants, seas, and land, but from the radical yoking of meton-
ymy with synecdoche that Milton reserves for unfallen or apocalyp-
tic realities, the temporal ground zero or infinity of his evolving
continuum. Thus, in the beginning, each creature not only takes on
the characteristics of his habitat but actually grows from and with it.
Because Mother Earth is here more than a metaphor, her powers are
not materially different from those of synecdoche or metonymy: she
is at once the material cause or "fertile Womb" of the living souls
she sustains, the effect or embryo of these causes, and the part of the
whole, the child of her own womb:

> The Earth was form'd, but in the Womb as yet
> Of Waters, Embryon immature involv'd,
> Appear'd not: over all the face of Earth
> Main Ocean flow'd, not idle, but with warm
> Prolific humor soft'ning all her Globe,
> Fermented the great Mother to conceive,
> Satiate with genial moisture, when God said,
> Be gather'd now ye Waters under Heav'n
> Into one place, and let dry Land appear.
> (7.276–84)

Yet, as in Eden's "vegetable gold," this circulation is ultimately too
dynamic and too temporal to conform to the emblematic stasis or the
ritual purity of allegory's eternal personae. Milton's hexameron sub-
verts these symmetrically fixed forms with the dialectical, evolution-
ary rhythm of the baroque by making the contained the container
and the sustainer of organisms that in turn recirculate into related
but highly individuated variations on the same process. The waters
ferment the embryonic Mother as her own "genial moisture" brings
forth life, first in reptiles and fish, then in the birds, their cousins
(a happy evolutionary intuition [*PL*, 7.387–94]), and all the beasts
of the field. This personification of Milton's Earth is as far from
Spenser's Venus as it is from his Charissa, both eternal mothers, not
sisters or fellow creatures who mature even in innocence. In this
continually evolving continuum, the paternal hierarchy of procrea-
tion is ultimately dissolved as earth produces the seminal substances
of her own evolution, and the Word is deferred onto its own fruition,
informing creation as prototype and brother rather than as lord and
master. As in books 5 and 6, this dialectic derives from a synthesis of

the deities of Job and Genesis: after the God of Genesis decrees, the God of Job informs, displays, and, hence, "corrects" the conventional schema. This arrangement collaterally revolutionizes the hexameral tradition in foregrounding not the invisible and ultimately incomprehensible Father but the visible Son and his humanly accommodated angel chorus, a heavenly fellowship that comes both to observe "the measures thereof" and communally/individually to bless the creation as these morning stars sing "together, and all the sons of God shouted with joy" (Job 38:7).[23]

Finally, then, the Job-like reader is also called on to witness this birth, as if in response to God's question, "Or *who* shut up the sea with doors, when it brake forth, *as if* it had issued out of the womb?" (Job 38:8). As we see the serpent waters of creation flow from their "womb" to the limits of their "crystal Wall" (*PL,* 7.293) and earth's dust once again "conglobing from the dry" (*PL,* 7.292; Job 38:38), it is difficult to forget Job's awe as the voice of the Almighty calls on him as on his angels to witness how "Great are thy works, *Jehovah,* infinite / Thy power; what thought can measure thee or tongue / Relate thee[?]" (*PL,* 7.602–4). If this Jehovah is to be adequately praised or comprehended by his spirit-infused or "deifi'd" creatures (8.431), then this praise would certainly seem to proceed through their awe before this organic, evolving creation rather than through the more emblematic or ritual symbols of battle and progress that have by now faded from view. In the end, the splendors of his chariot, golden compasses, and angelic armory have been contextualized and submerged in the rational/sublime of a particularized creation where individual accountability can best be accommodated on the "winding stair" of its evolutionary panorama. In anticipation of this end, Milton's epic psychomachia and ritual progress have been subjected to the destabilizing processes of baroque metareferentiality. Instead of allegorically objectifying virtues and vices as investments, instruments, or things, Milton's contrary practice of emphasizing verbal motion and exchange within a highly naturalized form of allegorical personification stands in stark opposition, not merely to Dante and Spenser, but to their common source in Ovid. Precisely because "the life of . . . [Milton's] verse largely resides in the verbs and adverbs, the words of motion," nearly always, as Joseph Summers observes, his " 'metamorphoses' concern movements from non-life to life, from the static to the mobile, from lower to higher forms." In thus inverting Ovid, Milton produces a meta-allegorical technique as far removed from medieval and early Renaissance allegory as its metatheatrical drama is from the morality play. In this de-ritualized psychomachia and its wake, the triumphal progress of life, formerly static symmetries have been reanimated as universally interactive motions differing only in degree, of kind the same.[24]

6

Demystifying Disguises

Gender, Hierarchy, and the Allegory of Desire

1

Milton's basic assumptions about the nature of the creative power in mind and nature are essentially dialectical, a point seldom disputed except in relation to his hierarchy of gender. For, in allegorizing the sexual powers of his universe, he also makes their dialectical nature seem more the vehicle rather than the tenor of this almost literalistic trope—as more sign than substance of full reciprocity, as Raphael hints. As this sociable spirit and Adam discuss the sexual power at the conclusion of the poem's "Dionysian" phase in book 8, the dialectic of "Male and Female Light, / Which two great Sexes animate the World" (*PL*, 8.150–51), seems to establish an epic norm that is also normatively weighted in favor of the male. Yet, in its "adventitious" extensions, such duality of creative power also ultimately renders any exclusive gendering uncertain. The case is similar in the early poems, where the dual male personae of "L'Allegro" and "Il Penseroso" somehow copulatively interact as a female and male pair that "engenders" within the attuned reader's mind that harmony of meet consorts Milton idealized, or, in "At A Solemn Music," where the *femininely* "mixt power" of the sister "Sirens" Voice and Verse form an equally mysterious procreative pair.[1] Nevertheless, the potential dialectical imparity is not thereby overcome since "the inane modulation" of sound, as the young Milton called it in *Ad patrem* (lines 51–52), is made fruitful by the dominating sense of the words or verse. If we cannot therefore accuse his poetics of logocentrism—which privileges the "full presence" of voice—then a comparable graphocentric privileging of the written or masculine sign seems to authorize Adam's preeminence over Eve: "Hee for God only, shee for God in Him" (*PL*, 4.299).

Yet, while such privileging is undoubtedly real, it is also as clearly unstable as the other baroque hierarchies and allegories of Milton's universe—of which the decentered psychomachia of good and evil explored in the previous chapter is a primary meta-allegorical "type." So too with Milton's theory of poetics in general, which as early as his Commonplace Book entry on the subject splits poetry's didactic function between two such relatively subordinate yet also reversibly coequal powers: "Basil tells us that poetry was taught by God to kindle in the minds of men a zeal for virtue. 'For when the Holy Spirit saw that mankind could be led with difficulty to virtue and that we are neglectful of upright living because of our proneness to pleasure, what did it do? It mixed with the doctrines the delight of melody so that we might unconsciously receive the benefit of the discourse through the charm and smoothness of the sounds'" (*CPW*, 1.382). Read above for *doctrine* the masculine sense of language or its "content" and for *delight* its melodic or feminine "voice," the totality of what is meant by *form*. Thus, in one sense, content or "virtuous" (male, strong) doctrine must be "superior" to melodic (feminine, weak) form or "delight"; yet, in another sense, it not only seems that "the benefit of the discourse" is fully reciprocal but even that "the charm and smoothness of the sound" may be more than the mere vehicle of the tenor, in fact an indispensable part of its essence. Given, then, the deeply ambiguous implications of these undoubtedly "graphocentric" assumptions it cannot be easy completely to agree either with those critics who argue for Milton's consistently antihierarchical impulses or with those who maintain that they end precisely where his allegory of gender begins.

Yet between Milton's allegory of gender and his meta-allegory of poetic form there is a seamless continuity, which means that hierarchies are displaced, not destroyed. Whatever meta-allegorical, iconoclastic, or readerly orientation is constructed by the Protestant poem's essentially fluid allegorical structure, its asymmetrical oppositions could not ultimately be so fluid as to constitute a formless or genderless subject of desire. Consequently, when as "Author of all" (*PL*, 8.317) God grants Adam a consort fit "to participate / All rational delight" (8.390–91) as a reward for his spontaneous protest— "Among unequals what society / Can sort, what harmonie or true delight?" (8.383–84)—the putatively free, guiltless, and mutual sexuality of Eden will not be absolutely equal, nor is such equality here assumed to be beneficial. Yet, in tune with the synthetic dialectic of content and form, voice and verse, the poem is inherently contradictory on this issue, for how otherwise are we to understand Adam's account of his creation and his dawning perception that he remains in "unity defective" (8.425) without an equal partner while we are also made to understand that "thir sex not equal seem'd" (4.296)? A number of readers attempt to explain away this second statement as a product of Satan's perception (as it is), although this defense of Milton's gender differentiation seems intrinsically flawed.[2] Satan's perception is by no means always faulty—nor does it seem so here, where it is corroborated by a wealth of narrative and symbolic detail. Qualifying his observation by pointing to the poet's use of the tentative verb *seeming* also fails to satisfy since he has Satan observe both how Adam and Eve are formed and how they seem: she for "softness" and "sweet attractive grace" but he "for contemplation . . . and valor form'd." Moreover, if we are to dispute his observations on this basis, then we must also doubt that Eve or Adam are "Lords of all" since to him they only *seem* worthy of this status or of the image of their maker—which in fact establishes their "true filial freedom."

Finally, then, because Satan arrives in Eden as a spy whose success depends on his accurate observations, and also because his gaze is mixed with unfeigned admiration, we should little doubt that he reliably perceives

> Two of far nobler shape erect and tall,
> Godlike erect, with native Honor clad
> In naked Majesty seem'd Lords of all,
> And worthy seem'd, for in thir looks Divine
> The image of thir glorious Maker shone,
> Truth, Wisdom, Sanctitude severe and pure,
> Severe, but in true filial freedom plac't;
> Whence true autority in men; though both
> Not equal, as thir sex not equal seem'd;
> For contemplation hee and valor form'd,
> For softness shee and sweet attractive Grace,
> He for God only, shee for God in him.
> (4.288–99)

This inherently contradictory portrait has thus generated a large number of disparate reactions: Milton is either the last great literary exponent of patriarchy, a moderately liberal proponent of gender equality within the context of seventeenth-century marriage manuals and Pauline doctrine, or "a radical and seminal revisionist" often divided against himself on the crucial issue of human freedom versus the stable economy of the Judeo-Christian family.[3] Given this extraordinarily wide range, it seems tempting to question whether Milton is pointedly contradictory on the subject of gender in precisely the terms dictated by his allegorical poetics: in tune with a technique that "baroquely" conserves the ruins of a tradition whose shortcomings he overstates to the point of parody, thereby once again implosively "correcting" its schemas. As we have seen, this technique neither rhetorically nor philosophically eliminates hierarchy, whether in theory or in practice; but it does subvert and modify its binary oppositions in ways that largely dissolve their symmetries. In this construction of Edenic allegory, its hierarchies would function neither normatively nor wholly deconstructively, as Stanley Fish has proposed, since the effect of baroque irony is not actually to "consume" the fluid panoramic landscapes thereby opened to metareferential critique but to broaden and naturalize them. For this reason, the poem continually achieves "effects of allegory," as G. K. Hunter remarks, although these are "either inextricably involved with other elements or else transposed into exemplary contexts."[4]

In order to pursue this alternative perspective, one in which Milton's synthetic dialectic at once cancels and upholds a multivalent and displaced form of symmetry, resolving the question of whether its "lords" differ in degree or in kind, or in what degree or kind, must first be subordinated to a more general consideration of Edenic allegory. Such an approach is not altogether novel since some of its functional elements are implicit in Kerrigan's psychoanalytic exploration of the antinomian aspects of Milton's monist universe. In essence, he proposes that the ritual exclusions and oppositions of Christianity's normative cosmos are here overturned by Milton's refusal to separate impure and dangerous implications from his concept of paradisal holiness. Setting aside Kerrigan's Freudian commitment to the "unconscious" operation of this process (which, if not impossible, cannot be proved, given the poem's strikingly rational organization), this hypothesis seems attuned both to the secularization that Benjamin finds fundamental to the baroque's antiritual tendencies and to much that seems paradoxical about Eden. Far from the primitive ritual systems that Mary Douglas describes as segregating purity from danger by anathematizing "contradictions between what seems and what is," Milton's Eden, like his *Areopagitica*, seems to make moral

danger the basis of freedom, not of contamination.[5] Here, once again
we encounter that familiar inversion of transcendence, that reversal
of the mystic's quest to surmount the material sphere and attain the
bodiless realms of light (a variant of the apocalyptic yearning to sur-
mount history and enter the all-consuming kingdom of God), that
forms the hallmark of Milton's meta-allegorical technique. More-
over, the very ambivalence attendant on masculine and feminine
genders seems similarly designed to guide his readers toward attain-
ing light in darkness, not by ascending, but by descending from
heaven to reclaim our "Native Element" (*PL,* 7.16).

The reader's entry into Eden in book 4 supplies an instructive
example of this aesthetic at work, for, like Raphael's later creation
narrative in book 7, the garden episode is framed by water metaphors
that serve to underscore the principle of concrete yet fluid exchange
and interpenetration as the foundation of birth, growth, and re-
generation. Eden's cool recesses, "umbrageous Grots and Caves"
(*PL,* 4.257) are inundated by streams, as

> murmuring waters fall
> Down the slope hills, disperst, or in a Lake,
> That to the fringed Bank with Myrtle crown'd,
> Her crystal mirror holds, unite thir streams.
> (*PL,* 4.260–63)

Here, in spite of initial appearances, neither wandering waters nor
mirroring lakes achieve hierarchical preeminence; rather, they min-
gle interchangeably. Further, although these dual forms of irrigation
may at first appear to represent disparate male and female principles,
roving waters "dispersing" while the placid lake "Her crystal mirror
holds," not even this gentle form of continuity in difference is left
undisturbed in Eden. The following simile disrupts this stable pas-
toral "mirroring" by emphasizing that Eden exists in a universe that
has never, in either mythical or historical time, included only static
reflections but that is always already subject to the entire spectrum of
dangerous moral forces:

> Not that fair field
> Of *Enna,* where Proserpine gath'ring flow'rs
> Herself fairer Flow'r by gloomy *Dis*
> Was gather'd, which cost *Ceres* all that pain
> To seek her through the world; nor that sweet

Grove Of *Daphne* by *Orontes,* and th'inspired
Castalian Spring might with this Paradise
Of *Eden* strive.
(4.268–75)

Because physical and moral rapine can neither metaphorically nor literally be excluded even from an Eden whose springs are "inspired" by choirs of birds and "vernal airs" more true than oracles (*PL,* 4.264), this simile serves as a reminder of the complete inability of pagan gods, human kings, or Yahweh himself to protect either their progeny (4.275–83) or the retreats invented to guard them.[6] Yet the simile's work is exemplary as well as ironic; since a greater Dis, Satan, who successfully led angels to rebel, here stands ready to seduce humans, the passage marks both Eden's potential and its prehistory as a site of purity necessarily inscribed within danger. Thus, Satan's threat represents only one of many possible histories, actual as well as fictive or mythical, partially or wholly unrealized. Because their common thread is potentiality itself, the simile's inclusion of Eden within the putatively excluded framework of danger and death serves the important aesthetic/philosophical positive purpose of canceling these exclusions in order to uphold the domain of "filial freedom" decreed by God, the ability to choose life or death and, with it, the course of history itself. Given this framework, the poem's sacred symbols necessarily blend pure and impure, light and dark, positive and negative: the binary oppositions that evolve out of the intertwined warp and woof of material possibility and individual accountability. Without wholly canceling Eden's apparently stable hierarchical structure, its boundaries thus take on a shape as open and as alterable as its artful balance of fair fields, caves, lakes, and streams. Canceling only the ritual idea that this lack of boundary is impure, the ambiguous landscape of paradise reformulates the very basis of purity by contextualizing the true, the false, and the redeemed within a continuous, historical "process of speech." Contamination exists, but not as the effect of divine curse, just as blessing exists, but not as the effect of ritual forms or prohibitions. Proceeding only from the inward and uncircumscribed motions of the heart, sin has definite physical consequences (such as those Michael reveals to Adam after the Fall) but no definite physical origins—most certainly not in the "female" complex of matter/mater.

Perhaps in part prompted, as Kerrigan suggests, by the undeserved yet, according to some, "damning" blindness inherited from his mother, Milton inverts this complex in ways that also reverse the conventional hierarchy of letter and spirit.[7] While both continue to signify, the spirit no longer transparently translates the letter as the *involucrum* or masculine "soul" of its feminine body or signature. Instead, the "verse" of the spirit now resides partly in the wholly immanent and invisible domain of its "voice" or will. Since these pairs evolve within a nontransparent physical continuum, they express the ultimate "spirit" of their combined reality only in organic time. Within that medium, as Adam informs Eve, "Evil into the mind of God or Man / May come and go, so unapprov'd, and leave / No spot or blame behind" (*PL*, 5.117–19). Thus, the potentially sinful letter is never necessarily sinful but, in becoming a positive site of contestation, frames the material medium of selfhood. No matter how threatening, words, signs, dreams, or any other external "marks" must not then be devalued but revalued, subjected to skeptical analysis and testing but not promoted into ritual symbols or (as the countervalent aspect of the same allegorizing process) demoted as mere dross. Instead, even in paradise, signs may not mean what they seem in any normative sense. As ambivalent vehicles of truth or falsehood incapable of being either purified or ignored, they must be used in their proper capacity as instruments but never as transparent vehicles of grace or sin—as Satan alone would urge. This Realist semiotic is in fact discredited by his intrusion into Eve's dream, an effect that can neither "magically" contaminate Eve nor be ritually dispelled by Ithuriel's spear—although it can be and is worked out through "process of speech."

This process also informs the emblematization of human and angelic authority, in both cases producing the decentered and unstable hierarchies characteristic of baroque allegory. Thus, while Raphael's initial "god-like" appearance (*PL*, 5.351) at first seems to indicate that his rank will require the reverence suitable "to a superior Nature" (5.360), these apparent distinctions seem to dissolve as he amiably accepts Adam's hospitality. Similarly, while at first Eve seems subordinately appointed to harvest and "concoct" the meal at which she later "minister'd naked" (5.444), her hospitable tasks seem to be performed as much on her own initiative as Adam's—whose "expertise" she corrects in the process (5.321–25). Eve's spontaneous assumption of the role of good hostess is further underscored by the angel's ceremonious "Ave Eva" salutation, after which they all equitably discourse together, "No fear lest Dinner cool" (5.395–96). Along with the allusion to Eve's naked or innocent ministry, her freedom from any domestic subjugation (even to hot meals), combined with her spontaneous desire to serve her guests, so forcefully associates Eve with the Son that the reader scarcely notices that only Adam poses narrative questions to Raphael. Yet, as the angel's greater wisdom and status also suggest, this cosmos is not without an ontological hierarchy of sorts, although it is so subject to subversion and dependent on individual choice that only the initial and ultimate— certainly not the intermediate—goodness of its material conditions can be regarded as predetermined.

Even Eden's single interdiction, that placed on the Tree of Knowledge, is thus carefully framed to condemn inauthentic rather than all forms of self-authorization, the meaning and worth of which can be determined only through a perpetual dialectic of challenge and self-discovery. Since the perfect application of universal law neither can nor should be fully understood by anyone but God alone, the solitary "Presence Divine" and "Author of all" (*PL*, 8.314, 317), the freedom of men and angels primarily consists in observing the necessity, responsibility, and divinity of interpretive choice. God clearly regards this act more highly than pure reason or any other form of abstract righteousness as evidence of sonship since it is Adam's "spirit within thee free" (8.440) that permits the dialogue between creator and creature. From this life-giving principle stems not only the garden's continuing purity but its very condition: the freedom extended to all creatures, even the animals themselves, who reason—and hence choose (3.108)—"not contemptibly" (8.374). Yet this system is also essentially paradoxical. On the one hand, it maintains hierarchy by apportioning different degrees of freedom among the angelic, human, and animal creation, while, on the other, it follows the principle of the "Vice-gerent" Son, who "reigns" only to engender greater fellowship among creatures "united as one individual Soul" (5.609–10), as the Latin root of his title implies.[8] Similarly, the Supreme Being removes himself from his ritual throne to model the processes of interpretive choice, processes in which his Son is given unique preeminence and exemplary authority without canceling the relatively equal aptitude of others successfully to imitate and be "deified" by their God (8.430–31). Nor do the other angels seem to be ranked beneath the Son according to degrees of intellectual eminence since the lesser angel Abdiel successfully resists not only a more sophisticated multitude but also the authority of his brilliant superior, Satan. Further, because only Eden's God can absolutely state that "Necessity and Chance / Approach not me" (7.172–73), on earth, as in heaven, all creaturely icons of power must be regarded as relative or liminal rather than absolute, as Abdiel perceives and Satan ignores to his peril, since the primary function of such signs is ambiguously to conceal/reveal the internal contradictions within which self-determination operates when conceived as the final but by no means the only cause of action.

In regard to man, the benefits and liabilities of divine detachment and creaturely interpretation are therefore equally ambiguous. While his ability to "retire" from positive foreknowledge or active goodness (*PL,* 3.117–18, 7.170) shields the Father from any legal accountability for Adam's fall, it also relieves his subjects of all but ultimate accountability to him. In informing Adam that "none I know / Second to mee or like, equal much less" (8.406–7), God implicitly institutes a doctrine of universal brotherhood and freedom since, in the great gap that stands between him and his creation, not even Satan has fallen so low that he cannot be used as a universal exemplum of the limits of creaturely knowledge, as he does in his entry into Eden. The mistaken "revenge" that he plots on the Tree of Life will backfire in self-destruction, in part because, like the rest of creation, he "little knows / . . . to value right / The good before him, but perverts best things / To worst abuse, or to thir meanest use" (4.201–4) but also in part because his inability to "value right" within shifting and ambiguous parameters stems from his insistence on maintaining the heavenly hierarchy at any cost, a price that includes foreclosing the dialectic of fellow inequals—including the productive internal disparities within an essentially androgynous self. Yet Satan remains an appropriate exemplum of the universal condition in that even this chief of demons has no unitary inner identity he can escape to or from. If the blindness of his choices has been deepened by his anterior acts, motives, and former eminence, similar influences as well as their antidotes surround all choices, including the "sinister" inclinations of "yet sinless" Adam and Eve. If Satan, like his victims, allows himself to be driven by the perverse misalliance of possessiveness, envy, and egoism that at once causes and exacerbates their falls, in the broader context of meta-allegory these emotions are merely one aspect of the general liability to error that inevitably accompanies universal freedom of choice. Inextricably linked with yet also "other" in comparison to the purity of God on his throne of unimaginable power, the Tree of Life, like the gates of Eden, thus becomes a comparable vanishing point: an authentic baroque symbol of potentially inauthentic signification, of self-creating choice relativized and demystified in relation to circumstance, time, and point of view, the inevitable corollary of mutability and freedom.

From this perspective, seemingly "ritual" instruments like Ithuriel's become aspects of a magical schema iconoclastically "corrected" by "Right Reason" within the course of narrative time. Yet, like the other bits and pieces of allegorical machinery that we find scattered throughout the poem, even initially these instruments function in an essentially different fashion from the supernatural "scales of justice, magic mirrors, crystal balls, signet rings and the like" that ornament more standard allegories. According to Fletcher, the surreal *kosmoi* of the standard mode are typically "placed on the picture plane without any clear location in depth. Their relative sizes often violate perspective (they are often out of proportion)" since "their extremely sharp-etched outlines" and "isolat[ed] imagery [follow] from the need to maintain daemonic efficacy."[9] But, in striking contrast to this surreal and magically "isolated" imagery, the gates of Eden lack their magical function even when they seem to possess their form, as portals

> Of Alabaster, pil'd up to the Clouds,
> Conspicuous far, winding with one ascent
> Accessible from Earth, one entrance high;
> The rest was craggy cliff, that overhung
> Still as it rose, impossible to climb.
> Betwixt these rocky Pillars *Gabriel* sat
> Chief of th' Angelic Guards, awaiting night;
> About him exercis'd Heroic Games
> Th' unarmed Youth of Heav'n, but nigh at hand
> Celestial Armory, Shields, Helms, and Spears
> Hung high with Diamond flaming, and with Gold.
> (*PL,* 4.544–54)

Inescapable as they are inefficacious, like Eden's other hyperbolic and apparently "sharp-etched" emblems, these huge towers perform no marvels of supernatural exclusion. While their steep ascent is said to be "impossible to climb," Satan simply leaps over them. Like Eden in comparison to the "fair field of Enna," which it is not, the only comparison between these gates and magical portals is the purely negative one that they have not more but less of that magical impermeability that would limit freedom as well as danger. Here, as everywhere in the poem, classical myth becomes a type or shadow of a reality plowed back into the material soil of its origins, its vision of nature revised. Not all the mythic guards emblematically "with Diamond flaming, and with Gold," can prevent the further "trial" of demonic assaults that had temporarily prevailed in heaven itself, for, as Gabriel sighs in response to Uriel's warning, "hard thou know'st it to exclude / Spiritual substance with corporeal bar" (*PL*, 4.584–85). While the "perfect sight" of this angel of the sun (4.577–78) does aid Gabriel in tracking down the disguised Satan and, with the aid of Ithuriel and Zephon, forcing him out of the toad in which he had concealed himself, on his own he has no power actually to rid Paradise of this pest. Unlike the magical instruments of normative allegory, neither Eden's gates nor its angelic panoply can exclude creatures bearing the spiritual danger that is freedom—ironically, the only danger in paradise.

These incidents, combined with Uriel's initial mistake in directing Satan's journey to earth, thus underscore the necessity *and* the purity of angelic fallibility as an ironic allegorical exemplum of the relativity of all divine hierarchies. Although, like Michael's sword, Ithuriel's spear has been tempered in the "Armory of God" (*PL*, 6.320–23), it neither defeats Satan nor drives him from the garden. Rather, as in Abdiel's rational but not physical victory over the fallen angel, the force of his spear merely "detects" his lies: for "no falsehood can endure / Touch of Celestial temper, but returns / Of force to its own likeness" (4.811–13). Yet this "celestial temper" also seems to allude to the Son's temper, the operation of his superhuman yet natural creaturely capacity to reflect by freely imitating the justice, mercy, and love of the Father (6.719–21). Of course, like the crystal ball or the enchanted ring, the spear does give Ithuriel a pseudoscientific advantage over Satan by instantly forcing him to return to his true likeness; but the broader context of the incident directly links his ability to separate true from false to his ability to obey under trial. This obedience to his own uncoerced image of the "spirit within" thus effectively determines his ability to wield this symbolic instrument of truth in much the same way that the posts assigned the rest of the heavenly host freely challenge them to test and (like Uriel) also to correct themselves. In this respect, the "Heroic games" of the angel guard hardly seem as "pointless" as critics like Fish claim; like the efforts of a blind poet who seems only passively to "stand and wait," their rewards pointedly contrast with the unheroic games of hell (2.530–46) in remaining independent of immediate success or failure.[10] As the War in Heaven also suggests, the service that God expects from his angelic troops is thus both as limited and as real as that expected of his human servants.

As in the case of Zephon and Ithuriel, they must fulfill their assignments not to support a God who can need none but to try, and thereby to sharpen, their own moral integrity and internal truth, a "trial" that progressively increases their ability to test the truth of others. Since these instruments "rightly temper'd are the very ingredients of vertu" (*CPW,* 2:527), when so tempered, virtue ultimately becomes its own reward, as appears even more plainly in the parallel incident of Satan's "evasion" of Uriel. Although "one of the sev'n / Who in God's presence . . . / Stand ready at command, and are his Eyes," Uriel "blindly" gives directions to the adversary, who appears as a "stripling Cherub" (*PL,* 3.636, 648–50),

> For neither Man nor Angel can discern
> Hypocrisy, the only evil that walks
> Invisible, except to God alone,
> By his permissive will, through Heav'n and Earth.
> (3.682–85)

Despite this incident's sinister foreshadowing of Satan's later, more successful dissimulation in serpent form, in this disguise, as in his appearance as a toad, Satan's success is neither fatal nor uninstructive to the faithful. Like any innocent interaction with unknown evil, this "trial" conveys no narrative destiny that cannot be corrected in time, as Uriel illustrates—not by exercising any special clairvoyance granted by his magical "Eyes," but through a form of long-range observation not unlike that performed by Galileo's telescope. Thus, here, as in *Areopagitica,* creaturely, accommodated truth is conceived as an exercise, a test or contest, but not as a supernatural path of ascent accompanied by ritual signs of confirmation. Even God's scales of justice execute his divine decrees primarily through mimetic means, acting as signs to the astute observer, or as snares to the unwary, but never as isolated, self-sufficient indices of good or evil that trap only the malign or reward only the benign servant of God. Satan may be more astute than Uriel, but his temporary triumph hardly prevents his immediate psychic disintegration into self-hatred and envy once he sees the beauties of earth—sights at last correctly coordinated by the angel of the sun.

In this demystified representation of purity, truth and error have thus become dialectical principles functioning in a shifting and infinitely correctable context of observation that alone conducts heroes and readers to their proper reward: to a rightly tempered virtue leading them away from a preestablished ladder of static signs and revelations and down into a variable course of history that they must interactively read, write, and revise. Just as Uriel's error cannot doom the earth, his correction cannot save it, for this duty rests ultimately with its rightful "lords" and guardians, Adam and Eve. Nevertheless, precisely because this angel of the sun cannot always see clearly, his acceptance of responsibility for reviewing his actions serves as a useful model not only of what they could but finally fail to do but also of what their heirs may yet succeed in doing. Reciprocally, then, the chief narrative "fate" imposed by God's "permissive will" involves the gradual liberation of Edenic emblems from their traditional isolation and stasis. This same fate also guarantees the eventual triumph of liberty and life, but no more than that: all intermediate means and ends rest in the hands of the creatures themselves. Whether Eden retains or returns to its purity, its fate ironically rests only partially on the all-powerful deity who can paradoxically decree the ultimate order but not the intermediate design of his creation.

As we have seen, similar paradoxes surround Milton's conception of liberty, which for the modern reader are intensified by his departure from contemporary notions of freedom, which generally begin by rejecting any comparable conception of underlying, innate order that for him serves as its final safeguard. Yet these paradoxes not only fuel but also invigorate many of the poem's emblematic inconsistencies, especially those surrounding the inability of Gabriel and his troops fully to profit from Uriel's warning by expelling their unmasked adversary, who instead stands "Like *Teneriff* or *Atlas* unremov'd" (*PL,* 4.987). The same "nonfate" attends God's own intervention, which, after "weighing" Satan in Libra and finding him wanting, enigmatically fails to prevent his subsequent success. Just as Satan at first easily entered Eden simply by leaping over its gates, later he will just as simply return by swimming up one of its streams and surfacing in the very fountain of life (9.71–75). These incidents illustrate both the complexities of Milton's concept of Christian liberty and some of its hidden continuities with more recent ideas of

self-determination. Since in Milton's cosmos even divine interven-
tion is ultimately an analogue of natural law, which, in dictating
natural survival, also prevents any unwarranted interference in its
processes, it must prohibit a "horrid fray" (4.996) between Gabriel
and Satan that would unnaturally and unjustly disrupt our Grand
Parents' "yet sinless" state. To prevent this disruption, God takes his
"golden Scales" and

> . . . now ponders all events,
> Battles and Realms: in these he puts two weights
> The sequel each of parting and of fight;
> The latter quick up flew, and kickt the beam.
> (4.997, 1001–4)

As earlier, an apparently traditional schema is corrected by invert-
ing both its biblical and its classical precedents.[11] Instead of deter-
mining the impending fate of the combatants as Zeus does in the
Iliad (8.69–72, 12.209), this God uses his scales merely to warn Satan
of the unfamiliar "lightness" he now experiences in verbal combat
and would experience in any physical assault on Gabriel. Although
Satan's self-accelerating hubris prevents him from observing how
much his rational and physical brightness has by now diminished—
as his debate with the archangel demonstrates to the reader, if not to
his own uncorrected self-image—God intervenes not to decree his
fate and perhaps not even to safeguard Eden's purity, which might in
theory be restored as effortlessly as heaven's had been by the Son.
Rather, he merely reminds him of the self-destructive nature of any
enterprise that flies in the face of inviolable natural laws, thereby
preventing a titanic collision uncalled for by earth's peaceful inhabi-
tants themselves. Because this reminder merely shifts Satan's heed-
less efforts to a different plane, the end result is "fated" only in
respect to the increasing impairment of his physical, rational, and
historical "vision," which of itself will dictate the "fitness" of his slow
self-annihilation.

None of these consequences are rationally avoidable: neither the
physical and moral deterioration Satan "earns" by dissociating him-
self from the unitary source of energy, light, and truth, nor his capac-
ity to propagate a fatally flawed "species" of like kind. Since Satan
chooses this alienation not once but several times during the epic, his
devolution again seems more mimetically than allegorically deter-
mined. At this juncture having cast out both conscience and pity

(*PL*, 4.23–26, 374–75), but without so far engendering like attitudes in any earthly creature, he must now simply leave, discredited and humiliated, his boasts of wisdom (4.904–5), leadership (4.947–49), loyalty (4.950–56), courage, and strength (4.957–67) needing no retort from God since Gabriel has already shown them to be as absurdly empty as his earlier and equally "dubious battle." Yet, as one of God's free creatures, Satan retains real power even in this devolution, as revealed through this need for divine intervention in his plans. In this respect, the scales of justice also reinforce the lesson first suggested by Satan's cynical misuse of the Tree of Life: although all are free to survey this landscape, only the Almighty can truly balance the original weight of "all things created" against their waxing or waning as choice, which is destiny, decides. Yet, in this weighing, the semiscrutable mind of God cancels neither the adversary's opportunities nor their potential consequences since, for Satan, as well as for Adam, Eve, and the angels, the exercise of choice knows no limits beyond those inherent in one's own self-canceling desires.

2

To outline the relative "weight" of Eve's gendered authority in this schema, we must then turn to her first interaction with Satan since it raises the related problems of her paradoxically "infected" "yet sinless" state at the time of her fall and those surrounding the nature of a divine justice that would prevent Satan from disrupting Eden's physical integrity but not from "tainting" her "animal spirits" with a sinister dream.[12] Why are corporeal barriers like gates and secret bowers quasi-ironically maintained when psychic ones are left open, or is there any meaningful distinction between them in a monist continuum? Adam's "sudden apprehension," which is able not only to name and understand the nature of the animals but also to postulate the processes of faculty psychology, suggests some answers later corroborated by Raphael's discourse on the processes of "one first matter." Because this first matter is interactively subject to internal and external codeterminants, the final cause of which consists in the consent or refusal of the will, like signs, spiritual states grow through but not from the material "letter" framing their apprehension and interpretation. In this respect, perceptual and physical states function essentially like the gates of Eden: they mark the portals or thresholds of choice, the liminal conditions but not the actual circumstance of "being in" a condition of purity or contamination. Thus, like its floral bower, the alabaster gates of Eden accurately bear the imprint of purity insofar as this state ordained by God is freely fulfilled by Adam and Eve, a status that the mere physical violation of its boundaries by contrary forces cannot alter. God can then permit indefinite experiential alterations in the psychomaterial space of his monistic universe because these alterations exist as mere temporal flux if unconfirmed by the will of spiritual beings—the only definitive determinant of their moral states. Matter both exercises and suffers the choices imposed on it by superior, more highly developed spiritual wills, but divine law guarantees that unasked for interventions into material freedom are not only transitory but even potentially benign phases in the ongoing process of growth through trial.

Because temporal experience is not temporal destiny, Adam can then confidently assert that "Evil into the mind of God or Man / May come and go, so unapprov'd, and leave / No spot or blame behind" (*PL*, 5.117–19). Just as Satan is temporarily free to misappropriate the Tree of Life, so he can temporally intervene in Eden's material and "animal" processes without unjustly coercing its free subjects to be "deprav'd from good." God may call a halt to further unwarranted interventions once an agent's freedom clearly infringes on that of others, as he does when he lifts his scales after Gabriel has already chosen to use his rational and spiritual freedom to defeat Satan in the trial of truth. Similarly, he may send Ithuriel to expel Satan after Eve has defeated him by rejecting the substance of his sinister dream. Yet neither victory can permanently "free" subjects from further trial, any more than any temporary vindication can make them permanently pure, for true purity is conceived as a process not only contingent on danger but heightened by it. In turn, danger is not a contamination that somehow "causes" Eve's fall, which her debate with Satan in fact nearly forestalls. Instead, only her newly awakened desire for unearned ascent, a preference that mirrors Satan's own, accomplishes that descent. Yet the dangerous threshold of trial and temptation that leads Eve to her fall can also eventually lead her out of it. This potential for redemption is equally implicit in her innocent rejection of the satanic dream's suggestions and in her fallen desire to take Adam's punishment on her own head, a spontaneous rejection of satanic selfishness that begins the process of repentance and renewal. While one act is sinless and the other sinfully flawed, in either case spontaneous apprehensions provide the only instrumental indices of a redemptive process that continues so long as the imagination refuses to reify them into magical "things," "spells" from which only restored freedom of conscience can truly liberate it.

As a result, Adam's apprehension is akin to, but actually more efficient than, Ithuriel's spear in dispelling the evil effects of satanic illusion on Eve. Although he recognizes her dream's sinister overtones, his "right reason" ensures the efficacy of their dialogue by synthetically acknowledging the indeterminacies of psychological, empirical, and theological conjecture:

> Yet evil whence? in thee can harbor none,
> Created pure. But know that in the Soul
> Are many lesser Faculties that serve
> Reason as chief; among these Fancy next
> Her office holds; of all external things,
> Which the five watchful Senses represent,
> She forms Imaginations, Aery shapes,
> Which Reason joining or disjoining, frames
> All what we affirm or what deny, and call
> Our knowledge or opinion; then retires
> Into her private Cell when Nature rests.
> Oft in her absence mimic Fancy wakes
> To imitate her; but misjoining shapes,
> Wild work produces oft, and most in dreams,
> Ill matching words and deeds long past or late.
> (*PL*, 5.99–113)

This explanation clearly reflects his own view as well as that of the narrative voice, especially the latter's implicit association of idolatry with traditional allegory. As true worship is the correction of false, so Adam's "correction" of erroneous causality recasts allegory's "symbolic logic" in its true form by rejecting sympathetic magic in favor of natural choice. Thus, in spite of the disturbances potentially produced "when Nature rests," Adam assures Eve that she should actually be encouraged by what "mimic Fancy" (even if satanic in origin) has brought to her attention. Since reason, the tool and vehicle of choice, rests while "Fancy wakes / To imitate her," dreams need have no permanent physical side effects but can be looked at as useful mental experiments. In the process of this explanation, Spenserian allegory, from which Milton seems to have drawn his dream sequence, is effectively turned on its head. Satan/Archimago's machinations enter the mind harmlessly when subject to rational discourse and dialogue, in themselves unable "daemonically" to pervert the imagination of Eve, who is no Redcrosse Knight so easily to be severed from from the powers of Una or Truth. Instead, by discussing these evil signs with Adam, Eve participates in a process of truth framed as a form of self-discovery—not a magical construct of pure, Una-like "oneness," but a reciprocal dialectic of moral construction.

Adam is thus enabled to "dissolve" Eve's unrest simply by proposing that, although her dream seems as sinister as any Archimagan illusion, its possible explanations, like its remedies, go far beyond the ritually contaminating or "guilty" mode of sacramental allegory. Since "mimic Fancy" misjoins sensations and "wild work produces oft, and most in dreams," Eve's fancy has probably concocted the dream from scraps of the prior evening's discourse, "but with addition strange" (*PL*, 5.110–16). After probing even more deeply and imaginatively into the matter, Adam then proposes that the disturbing addition (which only the reader and narrator can trace to Satan) may itself provide a helpful trial, a demonstration that "what in sleep thou didst abhor to dream, / Waking thou never wilt consent to do" (5.120–21). Although Adam is wrong in his final conjecture, the ways in which he is right are far more important. Satanic insinuations are not, in themselves, capable of contaminating anyone; only corrupt desires consciously carried out will "conceive" sin (James 1:14–15). Further, confronting these desires and then rejecting them can only strengthen their intended victims, which is in fact what happens here since Eve's innocence is not only vindicated but rewarded as her horror at this dreadful dream resides.

Although "cheer'd" by Adam's explanation, Eve weeps three tears; the first, as a more guiltless "type" of the woman who illustrates the folly of Pharisaical "righteousness" (Luke 7:37–50), she wipes with her own hair. Then

> Two other precious drops that ready stood,
> Each in thir crystal sluice, hee ere they fell
> Kiss'd as the gracious signs of sweet remorse
> And pious awe, that fear'd to have offended.
> (*PL*, 5.132–35)

Although external in form, this unprompted "evidence" of innocence clearly springs from Eve's heart so that, rather than proving her liability to contamination, the scene proves precisely the reverse: her self-sufficient capacity to resist it not only through rational dialogue with Adam but through her own "pious awe." Only when the dialogue between herself and Adam breaks down and this "pious awe" becomes wounded pride does she become susceptible to Satan's more insidious discourse. This more fateful temptation not only tests her spiritual and her fleshly "appetite" for power, as in the dream, but also her own interpretive apprehension of her experience of God's superior wisdom, goodness, and justice. Her fall thus consists in a failure of dialogue with herself, with Adam, and with Satan, to whom she wrongly cedes her own imaginative apprehension. But, because she can and does easily resist him here, even before her dialogue with Adam helped her digest the experience, this final challenge would have proved surmountable had she relied upon her own authentic experience of Eden rather than Satan's.

Yet, Satan's initial "seductions" of Eden and of Eve's imagination thus not only fail to deform their pure elements but also to provide anything other than a greater opportunity for moral growth and maturation during the course of an Edenic day. Since no one but the willing subject can activate the negative aspect of this opportunity, in the uncorrupted ebb and flow of the universe Satan's entry into Eve's dream, like his toad-like appearance at her ear and even his entry into Eden itself, is a physical event with no spiritual reality and hence no lasting physical duration in time. Only when angelic or human beings agree to pervert their true substance from natural good are external barriers anything but the vehicles of choice and the conditions of its possibility, and only in this case do ambiguous emblems harden into fateful punishments, for then the gates of Eden will exclude the human pair, and the serpent, unlike the still innocent toad, will become a permanent enemy to man.[13] The sins of the fathers are visited on the sons, or on forms of animal or vegetable life, only in a fallen world. Signs can pain and deceive in both worlds, but in paradise such deceptions are far more transient, their pain far more inconsequential. For now, like the righteous angels, the human pair remains susceptible to temporary defeat, or even to distress (like Eve, "discompos'd" and "unquiet" [*PL,* 5.10–11]), but not to vital transformation or anguish, their outer purity a result both of their danger and of their continuing integrity, like Eve's, temporarily "Virtue-proof" (*PL,* 5.384).

In paradise, as in any state of grace, hierarchical emblems thus temporally guide without governing the free interplay of all creation. When the human couple enters their holiest of holies, that "Bower / More sacred and sequester'd" than any in which "*Pan* or *Silvanus* never slept" (*PL,* 4.705–7), their innocent seclusion is maintained just as Eve's is: not by fixed laws but by the spontaneous "awe" in which beast, bird, insect, and worm hold human dignity. Responding much as Adam does at his first sight of Raphael, these creatures quite rationally retreat from the bower whose purity, like their own, is both a flowery metaphor and a literal expression of the free consent, fair intent, and divine sanction of the human pair. Their reaction is the more natural in that signs and referents coexist relatively unproblematically in paradise, for truth is here more naked than the "troublesome disguises which wee wear" (4.740), as the narrative voice laments. Yet, if its integrity within and beauty without together ensure its "sole propriety / In Paradise of all things common else" (4.751–52), the bower's claim on holiness has little to do with literal or even primal inviolability; strictly speaking, Satan himself can say of it, "et in arcadia ego."

Implicit in these meta-allegorical transformations of Eve and her Eden is the monist metaphysics in which the body has ceased to be a metonymy for the spirit, or even its synecdoche. As both and neither, body interacts with mind and mind with spirit at the boundaries of choice, the fluid and unstable thresholds of freer or more fatally circumscribed existence as the interaction of creaturely interpretation and desire alone determine. Yet, since choice is also material, here the pathetic fallacy is no fallacy but a natural reaction upheld by an organic continuum of matter, emotion, mind, and spirit common to all creation, including each gendered or androgynous individual. Yet, as this formulation suggests, Milton's paradise also seems to retain a gender-based hierarchy upwardly ranging from feminine to masculine and finally to the fully androgynous or indeterminate rank of angels. While desire here also becomes not only an essential and inalienable attribute of human perfection but actually a means of further ascent, what seems to be "free to all" (*PL,* 4.746–47) seems to remain inscribed within an essentially patriarchal hierarchy of ascending freedoms.[14] From this perspective, we must further question whether Eve's weaker attributes can be reconciled with her full reflection of God's image or whether her belatedness also implies a more static secondariness inconsistent with Eden's other continuities. For, if Eve is not merely "softer" but clearly subordinate ("He

for God only, Shee for God in Him"), what, if anything, can remain
of her "true filial freedom"? Does it not thereby become an empty
technicality or even a covert form of domination that, as Christine
Froula concludes, not only "transsexualizes" Eve's autonomous de-
sire but also serves as a means of "silencing and voiding . . . female
creativity"?[15]

Yet, like most either/or questions, this one fails fully to come to
terms with Eden's or the epic's radical ambiguity. Like a large number
of the "solutions" proposed by both Milton's detractors and his de-
fenders, Froula's account cancels its productive paradoxes by drawing
on inherited assumptions about the "orthodoxly" Puritan, patriarchal
poet and his "authoritarian" allegory of gender. Yet, just as surely as
Milton's Eden contrasts with the conventionally static paradise, his
portrayal of Edenic gender relations resists the traditional closure of
the normative mode. By using outmoded allegories of gendered sub-
jectivity and desire as schemas to be corrected, the poem subverts
them along with the ritual design of its normative machinery—the
gates and boundaries now subordinated to individual choice. Thus,
ironically, if Eve seems at first emblematically "destined" to serve as
the vine to Adam's elm, she later proves more of a quester, at least in
the physical, heroic sense, than he is, while he takes on the guiding
and corrective functions that Spenser would assign a feminine "con-
science" or soul like Una's.[16] In this way, not only are both sexes
"transsexualized," but the substitutions and transferences of this pro-
cess are never fully stabilized into a new hierarchy. "Impli'd" but not
coerced, even the most fundamental precept of Eve's submission—
that it be "requir'd with gentle sway" (*PL,* 4.307–8)—remains open to
her own as well as to Adam's interpretation. In fact, the multiple
meanings of *requir'd* underscore the ambiguity of Milton's interpreta-
tion of biblical headship (1 Cor. 11:3–10; Eph. 5:23) in ways that make
his verbal qualifications about this "sway" far more meaningful than
those surrounding satanic perspective from which they are viewed.
Since *to require* can mean either "to request" or "to exact," and since
the "yet sinless" Eve is not always "submiss," the former, not the
latter, sense predominates. By the same token, her emblematic role as
Adam's vine is itself qualified in ways that fail to limit her to a largely
passive or decorative role; while she may (and does) choose simply to
complement his "masculine" strength, she equally may (and does)
also choose to surpass or enthrall this "elm."

In their potential for both purity and danger, these paradoxes, like the poem's other vicissitudes, are no more "tainted" than Eve's dream. Even the apparently coy or flirtatious femininity condemned by more conventional critics suggests the "grateful" variety of her moods, which just as often take a serious turn. Like the various walks and seasons of Eden, her "sweet reluctant amorous delay" suggests a productive and not merely a teasing ambiguity, a paradoxical vicissitude fundamental not only to her own freedom but also to Adam's. The conditionality of Eve's responses and her complex individual "authority" either to accord with or withdraw from Adam's "sway" is thus the source and warrant of its independence as well as of its attractive grace, as even J. Hillis Miller reluctantly admits. Despite his objections to Eve's "wanton" admixture of "coy submission" and "modest pride" (*PL,* 4.305–10), he finds that these oxymorons place "her above Adam or outside his control . . . identif[ying] her with Milton's independent power of poetry. Eve's curly tendrils imply independence as well as subjection."[17] Of course, in a quite different sense, Froula also seems correct in complaining that "Eve is not a self, a subject at all; she is rather a substanceless image, a mere 'shadow' without object until the voice unites her to Adam."[18] While both humans receive "true autority" in reflecting their maker's "Truth, Wisdom, Sanctitude severe and pure," Adam seems the more exact copy, as the contemplation of "His fair large Front and Eye" declare. As noted above, Eve's gifts seem considerably less: softness, sweetness, attractiveness, and grace, even if the latter is taken to include spiritual as well as physical gifts. This subdivision seems to reinstate the relay system of sexual hierarchy whereby Adam is made for God and Eve for God in him since, if Eve need not interpret her creator only through Adam (a possibility unsettled by their equal worship), why does she so often need Adam's guidance, even in interpreting her own dream?

3

To answer these questions in a way that would comprehensively redefine the nature of Eve's "subjection" to the God in him as contingent on a series of continuities within difference that largely undermine it, we must then turn to the archetypal descriptions of awakening life to which Froula also returns: Eve's creation narrative in book 4 and Adam's parallel narrative in book 8. Only there and in

what follows can we fully discover the cumulative effect of compar-
ing Adam to Eve as curled "clusters" to viney "tendrils," contem-
plation to grace, truth to quest, and, finally, vision to re-vision—
comparisons that on at least three occasions relate them, not only to
each other, but to Raphael and, finally, to the whole heavenly order.
Although Eve relates the story of her awakening consciousness first,
this fact need not, as several feminist critics remind us, grant it any
kind of priority. First or last, "Great / Or Bright infers not Excel-
lence" (*PL,* 8.90–91), as Raphael is at some pains to teach Adam.
And, while Adam finally understands what Eve earlier had "sud-
denly apprehended," that "to know / That which before us lies in
daily life, / Is the prime Wisdom" (8.192–94), Raphael's implicit
approval of her reliance on experience over abstraction, like his mild
disapproval of Adam's more abstract "roving," fails wholly to elevate
her form of apprehension over his.[19] As book 9 will make abundantly
clear, not only do both modes have their dangers, but each is tied to
clear-cut sexual differences that Raphael's ritual hailing of the pair
reinforces. Playing on his name, Raphael greets Adam as more than
clay, as a creature fit to invite "Spirits of Heaven" (5.374–75). Eve, on
the other hand, is hailed as a type of Mary, "Mother of Mankind,
whose fruitful Womb / Shall fill the World" (5.388–89). The im-
plication here is that Adam is intrinsically closer to the Spirits of
Heaven and Eve to her nursery, for whose "tendance" she leaves the
discourse on astronomy (8.44–47). Hence, once again, the apparent
mutuality of gender roles appears to dissolve into what Froula terms
the "ontological hierarchy" of *Paradise Lost.*

This hierarchy is most specifically modified or "corrected" by
Raphael's narration of Satan's fall, which opposes the latter's rigid
"Orders and Degrees" (*PL,* 5.792) to Eden's "filial freedom," its ac-
ceptance of difference as an aspect of its equivocal equality. This ap-
parent mystification has become more difficult to justify owing to
the tremendous evolution in recent concepts of equality. As Joseph
Wittreich points out, earlier female readers were likely to interpret
gender differences as "evidence of distinction, not inequality"; early
feminists, too, generally supported a concept of male and female
mutuality in which "ideally their different qualities blend."[20] For
modern, post-Freudian feminists, however, difference signifies dom-
ination, which in part explains Froula's conclusion that Eve's birth
narration is subsumed in Adam's as a means of showing that "Eve
can only 'read' the world in one way, by making herself the mirror of

the patriarchal authority of Adam." Like her own reflected image, the mothering waters of the lake to which Eve is intuitively drawn are thus canceled by the "invisible voice" that leads her to Adam, the voice at once of God/Adam/Milton and Patriarchy.[21]

Yet a less tendentious reader might see that the mirroring process that vitally connects Eve to her lake just as vitally connects Adam to Eve, and through much the same process of recognition. In both cases, the perception of difference precedes that of continuity as a progressive series of subtle discriminations and corrections. More-over, Eve's awakening response is not in fact to her own reflection but, like Adam's, to the questions surrounding her existence: "what I was, when thither brought, and how" (*PL,* 4.452). Her next response is to a "murmuring sound / Of waters," which brings her to "a liquid Plain . . . / Pure as th' expanse of Heav'n" (4.453–56). Already aware of the existence of the heavens (which symbolize the mental orienta-tion of both human genders), Eve's fascination with their replication both beneath and above her then causes her to seek an answering existence. If, unlike Adam, she first finds this in the form of her own reflection, which Narcissus-like responds with "looks / Of sympathy and love" (4.464–65), Eve is actually an unfallen anti-Narcissus who, as she later acknowledges, is merely "unexperienc't" (4.457).[22] Unlike the conceited creature who prefers self-absorption to another's love, but like the child of Lacan's mirror stage, initially incapable of sepa-rating self (the form recumbent on the green bank) from Other (reflection, watery womb, or Mother), and like Adam, she needs an external stimulus, God's voice, to help her make this distinction and hail her into the symbolic order.[23]

In this respect, Eve provides an archetypal model of awakening consciousness fully as much as Adam does, for, like his, her "hailing" into the divine order initiates her dis- and re-union with a creature like herself ("whose image thou art" [*PL,* 4.472]), without any confu-sion or shadow barrier between them (4.470). Entering the landscape of names/language/difference, Eve thus gains a new title and posi-tion, "Mother of human Race" (4.475). This title, along with the acceptance and the renunciation it implies, exalts more than it limits her since it allies her with the Son. Like him, she becomes an exam-ple of the interdependence of growth and sacrifice, which can fully reflect the Father's creative design only by renouncing self-love. Both are thus appropriately rewarded by achieving the potential to pro-duce "Multitudes like thyself," not merely like the Father or Adam.

Just as the Son's descent "to assume / Man's Nature" neither lessens nor degrades his own (3.303–4) but instead grants him even greater equality with God, "equally enjoying / God-like fruition" (3.306–7), so Eve can enjoy "God-like fruition" only by quitting her virgin, self-mirroring independence.[24] In return, she, too, gains restoration and exaltation within an expanded mirroring process, the potential for limitless reflexivity in the space of Edenic marriage, an exchange of desire that is alone fecund.

Hence, the poet's striking revision—in fact reversal—of the Narcissus myth also illuminates his mutual exaltation of the "coy" Eve and the Adam who

> Smil'd with superior Love, as *Jupiter*
> On *Juno* smiles, when he impregns the Clouds
> That shed *May* Flowers; and press'd her Matron lip
> With kisses pure. . . .
> (*PL*, 4.499–502)

By personifying this exchange as that of "reformed" nature deities exchanging "kisses pure," Milton suggests that, like life itself, sexual love demands the alternation of similarity with difference—as when God "conglob'd / Like things to like, the rest to several place / Disparted" (7.239–41). Extending the metaphor, Adam and Eve may be understood as a primally innocent Jove and Juno "disparted" from all negative connotation, representatives of the masculine and feminine principles of sunbeam and cloud, male seed and female mist mingling in a flower-like, gentle form of "sway." The sun shines down on the cloud for purposes of propagation inseparable from sexual delight but inseparable also from the mysterious, asexual process of equality within difference imaged by Father and Son. Yet, here, we must once again address our recurrent problem; if Eve is represented as Son-Juno-cloud, the necessary principle of reception and nurture, then perhaps, as Mary Nyquist proposes, her desire is after all secondary: her-story actually a his-story of learning the "value of submitting desire to the paternal law."[25]

Continuing to weigh whether these stories blend into a kind of ur-story, we must next turn to Adam's reminiscences to Raphael in book 8 to see what actual limitations are imposed on Eve's desires by their different births. Unlike Eve's, Adam's first sensation is tactile (anticipating Adam's euphemistic identification of the primal effect of sexual contact or "touch" on his reason). Yet it seems natural enough for him first to feel the sunlight on his skin, given that he awakes in sunlight, Eve in shade (*PL,* 4.450–51, 8.254–55), although this contrast once again suggests that Adam is to Eve as strong "male" light of the Sun to shaded "female" light of the Moon. Nevertheless, the passage primarily serves to emphasize that, like Eve's, Adam's natural affiliation is with the heavens; the sun causes him to look upward much as the reflection of the heavenly expanse led her to gaze downward. In both cases, the stimulus of touch or sound first arouses their senses, then causes them to assume the "Godlike erect" inclination they share with the angels. This posture is thus the essence not of Adam's but of their kind, which "upright with Front Serene" displays a "Sanctity of Reason" (7.508–9) made "to correspond with Heav'n" (7.510–11).

Like the Son worshiping equally "with heart and voice and eyes" (*PL,* 7.513), the "upright" love they render the Father, like that they give each other, is then the exclusive prerogative of neither. Yet, as the contrast between their awakening in shade or sunlight and then gazing either upward or downward also suggests, the organs of "voice and eyes" are experienced differently by male and female. Eve is led on her awakening from sounds to sights and thence back again to the invisible voice. Adam, on the other hand, is led from tactile sensations to gaze at the "ample Sky" and finally to see a "shape Divine" in his dream (8.295). So marked is his preference for the organ of sight that he even represents the "liquid Lapse of murmuring Streams" as what he saw (8.261–63).[26] Yet, with an alternation characteristic of the poem, Adam's next impulse reasserts his analogy to Eve. Seeking a creature with an answering face, he searches among all

> Creatures that liv'd, and mov'd, and walk'd, or flew,
> Birds on the branches warbling: all things smil'd,
> With fragrance and with joy my heart o'erflow'd.
> Myself I then perus'd, and Limb by Limb
> Survey'd . . .
> . . . .
> But who I was, or where, or from what cause,
> Knew not. . . .
> (8.264–68, 270–71)

First stopping to survey himself, Adam's attempt to find an answering reflection of life does not then focus, as does Eve's, on his own image, although his motive seems the same: to find a living being who will return his gaze and fill his void.

Moreover, like Eve's, his attempts are at once enabling and impairing; although he immediately perceives his difference from the creatures who smile back at him and thus passes more spontaneously from the imaginary to the symbolic stage, his difficulty in locating the law's source—the Father himself—is actually greater than hers. Attempting to answer the questions that also trouble Eve, "who I was, or where, or from what cause," he appeals to the sun and earth: "ye that live and move, fair Creatures, tell / Tell, if ye saw, how came I thus, how here?" (*PL,* 8.276–77). Eve's affinity with both the sounds of creation and her own body is, taken as a whole, inadequate; but Adam's sense of difference and alienation is, if anything, more so. Yet the natural response of neither is sufficient to identify themselves or their creator; without direct revelation from God to Eve through his voice or to Adam through his vision, both would become idolaters either of Mother Goddess or Father Sun. These narratives thus show Adam and Eve erring in related but inverse directions. Adam attempts to "read" nature sheerly through tactile and visual stimuli and through analytic comparisons that allow him more rapidly to develop his symbolic consciousness. He questions his existence through rational contemplation, which allows him to conclude that his being is "Not of myself; by some great Maker then, / In Goodness and power preeminent" (8.278–79). Eve is also led to make comparisons, but she relies more on auditory sensations and on analogies rather than differences between inner and outer, higher and lower forms; her interest in the lake is prompted by the fact that it seems both a "liquid Plain" (4.455) and "another Sky" (4.459). Yet, if Adam is led by his sight, both physical and rational, into a more immediate entrance into the rational/symbolic order, Eve is equally adept at intuiting that her existence is alternately material and spiritual, just as the watery elements of earth and sky are alternately watery plain and fluid heavenly expanse.

Neither Adam nor Eve is thus able to perceive the Deity unaided; God must intercept both Adam's confused search ("thus I call'd, and stray'd I knew not whither" [*PL,* 8.283]) and Eve's pining with "vain desire." Adam is more dramatically depicted as seeking and conversing with his Maker, but only in a dream, and dream and voice are generally regarded as equivalent modes of prophetic knowledge. In any case, these modes reverse in books 11 and 12, where God speaks to

Eve in a dream, to Adam through the prophetic voice of Michael.[27] Since analogy as well as difference is stressed in these scenes, it is not surprising that the first decree of the "shape Divine" is strictly parallel, if gender specific. The Father names Eve "Mother of human Race" and Adam the "First Man, of Men innumerable ordain'd / First Father" (8.297–98). Following this, it is true, Adam is explicitly instructed in the uses and prohibitions of his garden, initiating a dialogue between Adam and his creator not later granted Eve. We must assume, however, that Adam instructs Eve in their joint authority over Eden since Eve unequivocally considers the garden her responsibility and since God declares both "authors to themselves in all" (3.122). Most significantly, neither Adam nor Eve knows God by any name more explicit than "Whom thou sought'st I am," an obvious variant of the Mosaic "I am that I am." Thus, Adam's question concerning intimate address, "O by what Name," "how may I / Adore thee" (8.357, 359–60), is never answered; Adam and Eve are to know the "author" through whom they become authors of mankind only through verbs of being: through spontaneous dialogue, listening, response, and vision, not through "naturalized" hierarchies of knowledge.

Thus, the Puritan poet carefully resists any suggestion of Adam's priestly functions in regard either to divine worship or to the ritual prohibitions this authority could sanction. Nor is God's fatherly instruction of Eve actually less than of Adam, even if it occurs offstage. As Adam describes his first sight of her to Raphael,

> . . . On she came,
> Led by her Heav'nly Maker, though unseen,
> And guided by his voice, nor uninform'd
> Of nuptial Sanctity and marriage Rites:
> Grace was in all her steps, Heav'n in her Eye,
> In every gesture dignity and love.
> (*PL*, 8.484–89)

With "Heav'n in her Eye," Adam must acknowledge Eve his sister as well as spouse, "one Flesh, one Heart, one Soul" (8.499). Far from subtracting from her female power, Eve's auditory response to God also performs a necessary complement to Adam's vision. Moreover, the name he gives her, "Woman," is her name not in the personal but only in the generic sense; Adam has wit enough to recognize his own species. For Eve's name is no more "Woman" than Adam's is "Man";

titles are hardly names. It is only by a considerable distortion of the text, then, that Froula claims that God "soothes Adam's fears of female power . . . by bestowing upon Adam 'Dominion' over the fruits of this creation through authorizing him to name the animals *and* Eve."[28] Nevertheless, even if we can assert that Adam lacks the complete authority over Eve that Froula claims he has, and if, by now, it is clear that their difference is one of degree, not of kind, a final charge of the feminist critique of the hierarchy of Edenic desire remains to be addressed.

Eve's more guided transition from the imaginary to the symbolic stage, her greater reliance on the intuitive, responsive ear as opposed to Adam's rational, active eye, appears in fact to suggest that, like Freud, Milton traces a "progress in spirituality" that places the female sex on a lower evolutionary rung.[29] And this objection could in fact be supported, did not the Christian poet set a much higher value than Freud on the primacy of the imagination, which for him performs an intuitive, holistic communion with the body of a universe that he insists is divine. Eve's greater access to this communion actually grants her a different source of authority fully equivalent—and hence potentially at times superior—to Adam's. Froula also concedes Eve's more than merely complementary role, for, as she notes, while "Adam's need to possess Eve is usually understood as complemented by her need for his guidance, . . . Milton's text suggests a more subtle and more compelling source for this need: Adam's sense of inadequacy in face of what he sees as Eve's perfection."[30] Yet Froula sees Adam's "alienation from his body" and even from God, not as parallel to the sense of inadequacy that Eve also feels, but as the direct cause of his subjugation of her. This view is challenged by the fact that Eve's ability to arrange thoughts and words, not merely domestic delights, clearly surpasses Adam's in a way that he finds both sustaining and inspiring. In highly cadenced and evocative blank verse, she turns her love for him into what James G. Turner calls an "aria," eighteen lines that have "the grace and recapitulative pattern of an Elizabethan sonnet." The author and not merely the singer of the piece, her voice is as authentic as her verse original. In claiming Adam as the demystified object of her own desire, she is no "coy mistress" forever eluding him on the banks of an Edenic Umber but an innovative sonneteer praising the exchange wherein "With thee conversing I forget all time" (*PL*, 4.629). Inverting Marvell's clever carpe diem to his lady, this lady seizes and returns the day and its times to the object of a desire to which she is also subject. Hierarchy is undermined by role reversal, which, as Turner also notes, blurs "the usual division of faculties into 'male' and 'female'; . . . [Milton's] Eve is more logocentric and intelligent than the conventional treatment, and his Adam, even in his prime, more emotionally susceptible."[31]

Yet the implications of Eve's "invention" are broader still. Concluding her aria with a question suggested by the theme of her composition, the course of an Edenic day, its "seasons and thir change" (*PL*, 4.640), she wonders what the purpose of the most mysterious of these changes, the procession of "glittering Star-light," might mean: "But wherefore all night long shine these, for whom / This glorious sight, when sleep hath shut all eyes?" (4.657–58). Adam is immediately aware both of the skill of her song and of the importance of this question; addressing her as "Daughter of God and Man, accomplisht *Eve*" (4.660), he replies with his own praise of divine Providence. Yet neither here nor elsewhere does his authority silence Eve; instead, it produces his own conjecture that these stars "shine not in vain" (4.675). The provisionality of this response is emphasized by the fact that it must be supplemented by a higher authority, who in outlining the two simultaneously competing and overlapping systems of the universe at once blends and elevates both male and female responses to creation. In cautioning that experiential knowledge may at times exceed abstract speculation and that all forms of knowledge, in fact all life, are ultimately relative, Raphael then advises them to avoid vainly seeking absolute truth ("Solicit not thy thoughts with matters hid" [8.167]) but to turn their united energies to affairs closer to hand. This cooperative merger at once depends on difference and eliminates it since, in "tract of time," the human couple may become as "softly" "Ethereal, as wee" (5.499), enjoying not only the intuitive understanding of the angels but also their fully unencumbered sexual freedom, which can "either Sex assume, or both" (1.424). Yet Raphael also acknowledges that their present state is not lacking in such perfection that they may prefer to continue their earthly, gendered existence (5.499–503); here, as throughout Milton's cosmos, no simple value can be attached to the process of "rising" in and for itself.[32]

However, Raphael's final, private discussion with Adam also affords the most problematic representation of the poem's hierarchy of desire. In appearing to agree with Adam's opinion of Eve as "resembling less / His Image who made both, and less expressing / The character of that Dominion giv'n / Oe'r other Creatures" (*PL,* 8.543–46), he adds that Adam's ambivalence as to whether Eve corresponds to this or to his other view of her "As one intended first, not after made / Occasionally" (8.555–56) lies in his own perceptions, not in Nature. Yet Raphael never precisely reveals what "Nature" dictates concerning Eve; he simply warns against "attributing overmuch to *things* / Less excellent" (8.565–66; emphasis added). Since these "things" can refer neither to Eve nor to her accomplishments but only to her "fair outside" (7.568), Raphael suggests that Adam can best appreciate and guide her by weighing her merits with his. Even this patriarchal-sounding advice must, however, be weighed in turn against its broader context, one in which the entire discussion between Adam and Raphael mirrors the previous conversations of Adam and Eve. Just as in the prelude to her sonnet Eve included a didactic statement of obedience, a brief summation of the Pauline doctrine of headship—"what thou bidd'st / Unargu'd I obey; so God ordains, / God is thy law, thou mine" (4.635–37)—so Adam now mimics her procedure in conversing with Raphael. A statement of submission is followed by a tribute to Raphael's sensory powers—a tribute that similarly bestows the powers of the subject on their desired object. Just as Eve had deferred to Adam by attributing her rich sensory experience of Eden, her "nursery," to his presence, by her example Adam now demonstrates his humility (which is also his authority) in granting Eve his firstborn prerogatives of wisdom, authority, and reason. The result of this exchange is simultaneously to exalt masculine and feminine dignity; Eve is its synthesis for him as he had been it for her. She now becomes a vision of masculine virtue in feminine form: "Greatness of mind and nobleness thir seat / Build in her loveliest" (8.557–58).

Still, like Raphael, the reader cannot immediately evaluate the full meaning of this transference, let alone how patriarchal, antipatriarchal, or even uxorious its assumptions may be, until it is tested against the background of Edenic gender relations as a whole. Here, for the third time, we have observed Adam and Eve performing a similar interchange, Eve responding, Adam recapitulating and interpreting her more spontaneous activity. She first questioned the purposes and motions of the stars, a query that Adam elaborates and poses to Raphael (*PL*, 8.15–31), while, a little earlier, she had narrated her experience of creation to Adam, a story that so delights him that he then adopts it as a means of entertaining the angel. On the third occasion, Eve set another pattern by first acknowledging the principle of marital headship, then giving Adam a verse account of the experiential value, greater than all of Eden, that she finds in his company, thus making her gifts, her perceptual and poetic skill, a supreme tribute to him. Later, Adam gives Raphael a similar acknowledgment of his "official" superiority, then adds an experiential account of the supreme value of his conversation, a "process of speech" that figuratively synthesizes and transcends "masculine" and "feminine" gender traits. His compliment in fact paraphrases the very words that Eve had used to express her love for him as he tells Raphael that

> For while I sit with thee, I seem in Heav'n
> And sweeter thy discourse is to my ear
> Than Fruits of Palm-tree pleasantest to thirst
> And hunger both. . . .
> (8.210–13)

While Adam recognizes Raphael's superior "Grace Divine" just as clearly as he sees that Eve's difference from himself also implies a relative difference in rank, at the same time he can do no better than follow her example. If for Eve "Nor grateful Ev'ning mild, nor silent Night / With this her solemn Bird, nor walk by Moon, / Or glittering Star-light mild, without thee is sweet" (4.654–56), for Adam no fruits of Eden can supply the sweetness of Raphael's words. Significantly, their theoretical affinities here reverse: Adam is more domestic in his metaphors, Eve more astronomical in hers.

Whatever this reversal may mean in the abstract, the concrete result is the same. As in the Father's relation to the Son, submission merits exaltation and, more importantly, reciprocity. Orders exist to be broken and transformed: as in the "one first matter" Raphael describes, energy and light flow both upward and downward. Anything more rigid or circumscribed would disturb the harmonious intercourse of the universe, as Raphael in response acknowledges:

> Nor are thy lips ungraceful, Sire of men,
> Nor tongue ineloquent; for God on thee
> Abundantly his gifts hath also pour'd

Inward and outward both, his image fair:
. . . .
Nor less think wee in Heav'n of thee on Earth
Than of our fellow servant, and inquire
Gladly into the ways of God with Man:
For God we see hath honor'd thee, and set
On Man his Equal Love. . . .
(*PL*, 8.218–21, 224–28)

In this exchange, the discourse of "rational delight" is made the simultaneous prop and leveler of hierarchies; Adam can scarcely be as superior to Eve as Raphael is to himself, yet his graceful deference merits acknowledgment of angel and man as "fellow servants" enjoying God's "Equal Love." In contrast, duplicitous self-promotion leads Satan, like Adam and Eve after the Fall, to bestiality. Yet, ironically, this descent has far less to do with their literal breaking of hierarchical boundaries than it does with their more immediate failure to follow Raphael's simple advice. Instead of skillfully weighing Eve's gifts with his—which would include balancing her more accurate interpretation of Raphael's warning alongside his equally accurate intuition of Satan's likeliest plan of attack—Adam is distracted by a temporary loss of face, which he fails to see has little or nothing to do either with his true authority or with Eve's true love for him.[33]

4

The separation scene that precedes the Fall of Adam and Eve is perhaps the most dramatic example of the logic of baroque allegory at work since its multiplanar perspective not only deludes each partner into believing in his or her own actually unbalanced self-vindication but engenders similar optical illusions in individual readers, often in accord with their gender sympathies. From one perspective, Eve's sense of responsibility toward her garden, her determination, and her well-reasoned (if overconfident) acceptance of trial as a concomitant of Edenic life undermines Adam's ability to direct and guide the admirable qualities that, unmodified, like both their garden and his own desire, "tend to wild." Yet, if this imbalance perhaps increases Eve's all-too-human liability to err, it cannot be said to produce her fall unless all we have seen of her, including God's pronouncement

that both were created "sufficient to have stood," is rendered mean-
ingless. Rather, Adam's failed conversation with Eve, his temporary
but not yet tragic loss of appreciation for their radical relativity,
becomes truly tragic only when Eve, like Adam overvaluing her
momentary victory, chooses to forsake successful conversation not
merely with Adam but also with herself and her God. Indulging in a
"process of speech" with the serpent that is actually a process of ra-
tionalization, she begins to dream of synthesizing and supplanting
Adam's abstract gifts with her own more empirical abilities—which
in turn leads to her failure to weigh her own experience against
Satan's fraudulent empiricism. Then and only then does she develop
a sinful appetite for what is properly neither hers nor Adam's, the
unearned and seemingly effortless but actually illusory ascent that
throughout the poem is shown to be the essence of all descent.

Yet the scene also produces a blurring of responsibility that ulti-
mately favors Eve, who is conventionally singled out as the culprit in
chief. Moreover, in the disagreement leading to their temporary
parting, Eve's arguments often carry a stronger weight of conviction,
especially when she rightly objects to a defensive strategy based on
mutual surveillance, a tactic that could result only in a prison-like
existence, a "narrow circuit strait'n'd by a Foe" (*PL*, 9.323). Perhaps
because he is still crestfallen after Raphael's warning against his own
potential bondage to Eve, or perhaps because he temporarily forgets
her "awful" acuity, Adam weakly replies that the mere fact of temp-
tation would prove contaminating—which, as Eve perceives, contra-
dicts everything they have learned of Eden from Raphael *and* God:

> How are we happy, still in fear of harm?
> But harm precedes not sin: only our Foe
> Tempting affronts us with his foul esteem
> Of our integrity: his foul esteem
> Sticks no dishonor on our Front, but turns
> Foul on himself; then wherefore shunn'd or fear'd
> By us? who rather double honor gain
> From his surmise prov'd false, find peace within,
> Favor from Heav'n, our witness from th' event.
> (9.326–34)

Eve's assessment seems fundamentally sound, particularly from the
perspective of the views stated in Milton's *Areopagitica*. Yet she also
errs in completely discounting Adam's perspective and glorifying the

trial of Abdiel-like individuals: "And what is Faith, Love, Virtue unassay'd / *Alone*, without exterior help sustain'd?" (9.335–36; emphasis added). The answer, of course, is not as she assumes, that these virtues are imperfect "unassay'd alone" since none of God's creation is truly self-sufficient, not even the Son. Adam senses that this is the correct response to her claims but also that his earlier exaggerations render it suspect. Humbled by this realization, he then wishes to seek Eve's approval, to save face rather than to weigh the merits of both arguments by synthetically insisting on their mutual obligation to a higher principle. Thus, in finally suggesting this obligation, Adam weakens his position by seeking to restore his amour propre rather than the principle of loving obedience alone:

> Seek not temptation then, which to avoid
> Were better[:] . . .
> . . . Trial will come unsought,
> Wouldst thou approve thy constancy, approve
> First thy obedience; th' other who can know,
> Not seeing thee attempted, who attest?
> (*PL*, 364–69)

Here, instead of linking love, obedience, trial, and constancy as tests that all God's servants must meet "unsought" but not truly alone, Adam self-righteously urges Eve to think that he is now the only valid witness of her trial despite the vast audience of "Millions of spiritual Creatures [who] walk the Earth / Unseen" (4.677–78). This contradiction of his own previous observation can only strengthen her desire to defend her "modest pride" through trial, therein supplying an additionally mistaken motive for wandering.

Nevertheless, Satan has chance on his side, just as Eve has the mischance of Adam's temporary lapse into egotistic defensiveness. Neither circumstance on its own is fatal, but the wandering mazes of their collusion, along with Eve's now heightened desire for experiential independence, create the critical temptation leading to her fall. Nevertheless, Eve is undone, not by a "femininely" vain desire for the universal adulation promised by Satan, but only by her relentless curiosity and desire for experimentation without recourse to the more careful checks of abstract reason. Although a desire for adulation follows fast upon her fall, its causes are far more broadly human than feminine. Satan's flattery itself only elicits her reiteration of God's commandment (*PL*, 9.659–63), while his exaggerated appeal to experience, the very "contest" in which she wants to be vindicated, at last sways her to follow the logic of his faulty empiricism, which is here also that of mystified or alchemical correspondences:

> O Sacred, Wise, and Wisdom-giving Plant,
> Mother of Science, Now I feel thy Power
> Within me clear, not only to discern
> Things in thir Causes, but to trace the ways
> Of highest Agents, deem'd however wise.
> Queen of this Universe, do not believe
> Those rigid threats of Death; ye shall not Die:
> . . . .
> . . . look on mee,
> Mee who have touch'd and tasted, yet both live,
> And life more perfet have attain'd than Fate
> Meant mee, by vent'ring higher than my Lot.
> (9.679–85, 687–90)

The issues Satan raises here far exceed those of gender: although he slyly praises the tree and its "science" as a "Mother," and although we have seen Eve inventing poetry and the culinary arts, his metaphor distorts rather than misrepresents these sciences by allegorically extending them beyond their proper domain—as does every ritual "idolatry" of signs.

Hence, Eve falls, not as a weak woman, but as an overzealous empiricist led on by poorly documented facts and the false apostle of a pseudoscience devoted only to destructive ends. Yet, in the meta-allegorical context of Eve's disagreement with Adam, no simple solution ever appears, as its problems are left open to readerly interpretation. Since her choices are more rash than irrational, and since both err in succumbing to the selfish desires that form the primary ingredient of satanic "logic," both male and female ironically seem to have been created precisely as God insists they are, "Sufficient to have stood, though free to fall" (*PL,* 3.99).[34] Thus, while the cause of Adam's fall is also different as well as more gender-specific, it is also equally selfish. If he easily sees through Eve's glorification of her twin goddesses, the Tree of Knowledge and the apple of "Experience," her "Best guide" (9.807–8), he also succumbs to his own most characteristic rational weakness, seeking to rationalize his possessive desire for Eve through a sophistic, abstract "logic" of cause and effect:

. . . if Death
Consort with thee, Death is to mee as Life;
So forcible within my heart I feel
The Bond of Nature draw me to my own,
My own in thee, for what thou art is mine;
Our State cannot be sever'd, we are one,
One Flesh; to lose thee were to lose myself.
(9.953–59)

Eve's response—"O glorious trial of exceeding Love" (9.961)—is thus rich with irony, for Adam's is not the kind of love manifested by the Son for the creation, any more than Eve's is the kind of trial victoriously faced by Abdiel. Their parallel mystifications of experience and science, or of the "mystic" bonds of natural love, in fact destroy true knowledge and love alike, replacing them with mutual recrimination, self-exoneration, hypocrisy, deceit, and, above all, the twinned faults of male misogyny and female manipulation.

Yet the first human pair eventually regain their love, significantly in ways that reverse these imbalances. Eve intuits the properly humble offices of healing love, and Adam rationally deduces the meaning of the protoevangelum (*PL*, 10.909–65, 1028–1055), a necessarily cooperative effort toward regeneration that reasserts their common humanity. At this point, the eternally procreative and not exclusively Edenic power of innocent love and desire is confirmed both because and in spite of the loss of Eden. Self-knowledge and recognition of difference, the basis of both growth and exchange, are reestablished as the proper and in fact only channels of true union and communion between spiritual beings. Yet, before as after the Fall, such conjunctions are necessarily temporary, ambiguous, and changing because they are inherently temporal, the result of free and rational choice in time. God alone can raise his creatures "deifi'd" by his communion to "what highth thou wilt" (8.430–31), but Adam can merit and Raphael bestow essentially the same benignly ephemeral exaltation channeled also through Eve's sincere repentance and magnanimous forgiveness. Through these Son-like qualities, the human genders alternately exalt one another, so that ideally each is equally fit both to initiate and "to participate / all rational delight" (8.390–91). Moreover, these human capacities follow directly from the fact that Eve is not the body to Adam's head or the senses to his intelligence, but, as experience, beauty, voice, Eve is directly analogous not merely to

Christ but to the poet himself. Milton can conceive her function in this way because he conceives both poetry and reason as necessary but not sufficient conditions of Grace. Its sufficient condition thus depends exclusively neither on Adam's more visual and analytic understanding nor on Eve's more auditory and empirical imagination but on a process of "weighing" and blending both. This process of harmonizing her gifts with his is what Raphael had recommended to Adam after showing him how to similarly manage his own conflicting motives; it is also what allows Eve to initiate their recuperation after the Fall. At this point, the role of marital headship is most completely exchanged, as she spontaneously intuits the necessity of accepting the responsibility for her fall, even while Adam's immodest pride leads him ever deeper into emotional ambivalence and endless rationalization. Yet their mutual and continuing imbalance is also partially corrected by their reciprocally alternate cycles of hope and despair, which finally rebalance their relationship in the "baroquely" synthetic image of the Son—their father, mother, judge, and brother.

Thus, the question of "whence true autority in men," one among many variants of the Miltonic question of "whence true autonomy," can be accurately resolved only by simultaneously refining and broadening our understanding of the universal basis of "Union or Communion" (*PL,* 8.431), that semimysterious conversation in which difference, including the ultimate difference between God and his creation, is resolved in a synthetic process of Other and self-reflection. Hence, true autonomy is imagined as a metonymy of male and female gifts and desires that, in perfect balance, generates the synecdoche of divine intercourse and human marriage alike. Raphael counsels Adam (and his heirs) not to upset the balance of this exchange, which, by resting on a reciprocal and unstable form of reflexivity, contains a liberating potential that is neither moderate nor conservative but extreme. Because this quasi-hierarchical balance depends on temporal interpretation and initiative, not on innate "natural dispositions," its inner harmonies are capable of both radical subversion and radical joy, the true analogue of the heavenly union revealed/concealed behind Raphael's rosy blush, "Love's proper hue" (8.619). For behind even this disguise are demystified glimpses—of an original sexual union without Original Sin, of the unencumbered embraces of the angels as a "Union of Pure with Pure / Desiring" (8.627–28), and of the mutual glorification of the Father and Son, whose balanced energies produce the spontaneous desire to exalt and multiply the Other, the basis of the universal desire that "to fulfill is all . . . bliss" (6.729).

This model of interchange between male and female, self and other, produces a modified allegorical hierarchy that is fluid to the point of collapse. As throughout Milton's gendered garden, the "reciprocity of tenor and vehicle has the effect of extending human sexuality rather than contracting it to a conceit," which according to Turner allows it to avoid the fate of the metaphysical and mystical allegorists whose visionary search for "'Authentick Drafts' of Adam and Eve . . . dissolved in the crisis of the mid-seventeenth century," leaving behind mere "personal hallucinations and *idees fixes.*" Looking backward, the ironically "open" dynamics of Milton's garden also stand in singular contrast to mere pastoral satire. Unlike even Donne, who, according to John Crowe Ransom, continues to find a "deep affinity between 'seeking secrets' and 'Poetiqueness,'"[35] Milton's baroque portrait of Adam and Eve attempts to unravel rather than to re-present such secrets. Informed instead by a mimetically balanced and unified conception of human motivation that culminates in the psychology of the novel, Milton's meta-allegory of desire does not wholly demystify the feminine gender, although through Eve it comes closest to Sidney's idealization of poesis as a plastic and prophetic form of making able to bind form to content, letter to spirit.

In much the same spirit, Adam describes his unfallen union with Eve as a form of music, a form of melodic "delight" in which male "verse" and female "voice" are most perfectly synthesized. In defending the "commotion strange" aroused by her sexual touch (*PL,* 8.530–31), he thus describes its "infusions" as continuous with the "delight" produced by all

> . . . those graceful acts,
> Those thousand decencies that daily flow
> From all her words and actions, mixt with Love
> And sweet compliance, which declare unfeign'd
> Union of Mind, or in us both one Soul;
> Harmony to behold in wedded pair
> More grateful than harmonious sound to the ear.
> Yet these subject not. . . .
> (8.600–607)

These musical analogies of course recall Milton's poetic theory of the aesthetic whole wherein, as voice, Eve completes the perfect "union of mind" that at once guarantees her independently "complete" and "absolute" powers and allows them when spontaneously "mixt with Love" to unite with Adam's "verse" as "one Soul." Adam can describe this ultimate harmony only as an unheard music beyond "harmonious sound": not the entangling spells of a siren or a Circe, but the truly liberating chords of demystified disguises that "subject not." Thus, like her arts, Eve possesses a musical comeliness or "decency" rooted, not in simple household husbandry, but in all her sensuous and inductive modes of apprehension. Never either a voiceless reflection of Adam or a plaything of the domestic sphere, she contributes to the human quest for truth in its highest formal and prophetic modes to a degree that made Northrop Frye see in her the dawning triumph of a mother-dominated salvation myth over a father-dominated cosmology.[36]

More recently, this recourse to a "naturalized" myth of gender may seem to constitute a renewed mystification that many feminists would find invalid: by opposing an Eve preeminently gifted with grace, audition, experience, intuition, and poetry to an Adam endowed with contemplation, sight, rational reflection, and analysis, this myth might seem too arbitrarily to divide the spheres of human competence that might be better understood as indivisible. But, indeed, there are genderable differences within the largely indivisible scale of human competence, and, as we have seen, not only does this allegory of desire represent all nature as ultimately indivisible, but it represents its gendered components as particularly so. In Milton's antitypical allegorical cosmos, the moon does not merely reflect the sun; both orbs reciprocally and individually emit "Male and Female Light." When applied to the fully animate sphere of human male and female, these genders overlap and unite in ways that more closely resemble the bisexual condition of the angels. That Milton regards this continuum as in place from the beginning of time is signaled by the heroic and poetic qualities granted Eve in paradise, qualities that are not, after the fashion of Shakespearian and Spenserian heroines, merely surrogate male values she will need to surrender once she marries. Already "matron" Eve, Milton's heroine possesses inherent strengths that are authentically and indivisibly hers, female versions of the "image divine" that her marriage with

Adam is meant to develop rather than to thwart. Avoiding magical or mythic dreams, desires, and interventions, *Paradise Lost* depicts a fundamentally unitary if also honorably distinct human psychology governed by complex causal chains that end only in individual freedom or its loss. Its vast monistic, meta-allegorical continuum thus equilibrates male and female roles through a constant rather than a foundational process of irony and role reversal that ultimately discredits the Elizabethan view of woman as an incomplete male and hence as a "naturally" disproportionate being.[37]

In avoiding along with the temptations of allegory the mystical or Platonic view of original androgyny, this representation of gender suggests some additional sources of the contrast between Spenser's more conventional allegory and Milton's "ruined" or baroque reworking of myth. Ultimately, when Eve falls victim to Satan's objectification of the powers of a single tree, she becomes the original "victim" of the mystical allegory that Milton's epic consistently critiques. Thus, while he adheres to the Pauline view that Eve alone falls "deceiv'd," his postlapsarian scenes overbalance this traditional "proof" of feminine weakness by making her far more self-reflexive, reasonable, empathetic, and even tragically heroic than Adam. As a result, Eve's proactive or Son-like humility distinguishes her from all the symbolic heroines of Spenserian myth—Belphoebe, Britomart, and all the rest of his Diana-like virgins—to form an idealized portrait informed by the real values of Protestant womanhood.[38] Yet, in collaterally exposing the temptations both of mechanistic science and of mystical allegory, Milton also prophetically anticipates the novelistic critiques of the liabilities of the Protestant ethic later explored by early feminists like Mary Shelley and late Puritans like Nathaniel Hawthorne. Measured against these standards, the fluid hierarchies of Milton's Arminian epic can therefore be described not only as post-Platonic and protofeminist but also as most emphatically "after" allegory.[39]

7

Realism, Nominalism, and the Politics of Reading *Adam's Journey from Orality to Literacy in Books 11 and 12*

1

The final books of *Paradise Lost* present a revised history of fallen language and human regeneration in which time continues to manifest the divine presence only through a new spatial "physics" where spiritual or mental motions have become corpuscular. In Michael's materialized vision of a wholly temporal "eternity," the static hierarchies of the older allegorical cosmos are then conclusively displaced onto the interiorized motions of the individual literate reader. This internalization of the word is complemented by the radical materiality of the graphocentric culture of the book, which is temporally projected onto the "space" of the prelapsarian state as the only basis for reconstituting anything like a Realist relation to God. Thus, the postlapsarian Adam must relearn his "original" graphocentric orientation toward signs, the ultimate horizon of which is Milton's own nominalist Protestant culture. Replacing the ritual reverence for God's hidden but coded name, this orientation identifies names with things or deeds, not coded letters—which is no doubt why God never reveals his name to Adam, even after his explicit questioning in paradise. As indicated by Adam's knowledge of him only as the fully transposable "I AM," not as a Hebrew Yahweh or Jehovah, here, as throughout Milton's concluding meta-allegory of history, signs are approached through a flexible and progressive nominalism that assumes that there is a real if also ambivalent power in names. This history's baroque remnants of sacramental signs are therefore byproducts of this ambivalence, for what sacramentalism understands as the memorialization of eternal grace here becomes an oscillational play between its ultimate realities and the arbitrary signs of a fully nominalist language. This oscillation also mediates between an oral or full "presence" of the word and its literate "absence," the opposing domains of the spoken and the interpreted sign that have become even more disparate as a consequence of Adam's fall.

Raphael had been in the habit—doubtless justifiable since the idiom of *Paradise Lost,* our transactional language, is continuous both with Adam's epic speech and with the revolutionary impact of print culture implicit in this narration of his history—of referring to the "book of Nature" or to heaven as a book. To regain this highly "literate" ground that Milton imagines as Adam's native condition, Michael's reeducation must pass from the recuperative oral mode of book 11 (the unregenerate Adam's "primer") to the restored literate mode of book 12. Through this revised paradigm of the Fall and the return to grace, Adam then recapitulates the progress of his race toward the dialectical literacy required by print culture. Oral culture is also dialectical, but in the quite different sense apparent from Plato's dialogues, which rehearse oral exchanges that would "ideally" be enacted, not limited to a silent reader able only partially to reenact the process of question and answer between himself and a wholly hypothetical author. The problems of internalization posed by the historical transformation effected by literacy and culminating, according to Walter Ong, in the seventeenth century are rehearsed in Adam's reeducation, which takes him as well as Michael's secondary audience on a symbolic journey through the continuities and discontinuities between the two modes. This journey, then, appropriately begins by proceeding in two contrary directions: forward to a history of linguistic progress and backward through the causes of Adam's linguistic regress, a pattern which will recur throughout human history. These twinned narrative themes structure the bulk of Michael's dialogue with Adam, achieving their synthesis as both Adam and his "true" heirs (his literate progeny) surmount the ritual mode still inherent in late classical orality and enter into the fully graphocentric mode of nominalist culture.

Of course, the irony here is that the prelapsarian Adam and Eve lacked the actual books of late classical or early chirographic culture, even though the complex discourse in which they participate with Raphael implicitly belongs to an advanced state of literacy in a number of important senses. Both the persistently skeptical attitudes toward signs displayed not only by Raphael but also by all of his narrative heroes (Abdiel, the Son or Word, and Michael himself) and their strongly objective/empirical orientation toward time contrast strikingly both with those of Platonic dialogue and with the predisposition for the eternal "now" of the speaking subject that it bequeathes to Neoplatonism and Augustinianism. The ritual, communal, and/or "homeostatic" attitudes implicit in these philosophies are thus fundamentally at odds with the methods that Michael requires to decipher the "untransmuted lump of futurity" of these final books. As C. S. Lewis's disparaging label implies, these methods presuppose the highly self-referential, introspective, and (in a narrower sense) "dissenting" attitudes of the Protestant individualist—attitudes he well understood but could not wholly admire.[1] But, from a Miltonic perspective, in this final foray the solitary, independent reader is meant to discover potentially liberating as well as newly "portable" reserves of inner spiritual strength as she finally redefines the meaning of "Patience and Heroic Martyrdom." Like the poet who sees himself as the fundamental composition and structure of a true poem, such readers no longer need to find any implicit concordance between the epistemic structure of the universe and its external "signatures" of grace.

Just as the old correspondences and hierarchies inherited from the lost worlds of Platonic and Pseudo-Dionysian cosmography have been finally "ruined" by the more material but also ironically more abstract realities of Galilean spatial mechanics, so the space of Christian history has been comparably dispersed in the obscurely coherent linear diagram underlying Michael's multiple time schemes. These "ruins" are more or less of a piece with the obsolescence of Augustinian cosmology and history, which had provided the underpinnings of the conventional sign system of the Christian oral/allegorical tradition.[2] Yet, since now neither the conventionally veiled but numinously "open" mysteries of allegory nor the rationally "plain" but spiritually "empty" calculus of nominalist signs is capable of justifying God's providential design, both Michael and his multiple readers (Adam, the dreaming Eve, and their absent audience) must wend a middle course between the Realist ruins and the nominalist "tables" of historical allegory to create a baroque synthesis in which an indefinitely incomplete "renovation of the just" (11.65) is more immediately completed by defining the hermeneutic stance appropriate to those worshiping in "Spirit and Truth" (*PL,* 12.533). Despite their indeterminacy, the signs of the "track Divine" (11.354) are thereby revealed as immensely superior to those of Hobbesian nominalism, "clear and distinct" human instruments unable to reveal divine grace, since they regard signs as "arbitrarily made by those that first of all imposed names upon things."[3]

The sense of historical transition embedded in the archangel's lessons also closely parallels that outlined in Ong's study of the transition between oral and literate cultures, since it explores how the progress from orality to full literacy fundamentally alters cultural models of epistemology and ontology, individual understanding and communal history. Even though both oral and literate cultures obviously need to preserve information, they do so in dramatically different ways: "Heavy patterning and communal fixed formulas in oral cultures serve some of the purposes of writing in chirographic cultures, but in doing so they of course determine the kind of thinking that can be done, the way experience is intellectually organized. In an oral culture, experience is intellectualized mnemonically. This is one reason why, for a St. Augustine of Hippo (AD 354–430), as for other savants living in a culture which knew some literacy but still carried an overwhelmingly massive oral residue, memory bulks so large when he treats of the powers of the mind."[4] Because a considerable "power of the mind" lies in its ability to preserve historical knowledge by constructing schemas for organizing, understanding, and memorizing it, heavy patterning demands mental habits that are "literately" unnecessary or even undesirable. These include the "agonistic" polarization of language into mutually exclusive types, traits, and formulas that guide the memory schemes later "translated" into the conventional *kosmoi* or types of fable, parable, and allegory.

Paradise Lost conserves this typologizing but, as Ong more generally acknowledges, also critiques it by reserving its normative form for the offspring of Satan and his demons, whose static psychic and rhetorical styles sharply contrast with the "grateful vicissitudes" of heaven and Eden. This critique is then explicitly extended by Michael into a correction of the "agonistic" or determinate style of allegory "naturally" preferred by the newly fallen Adam and the relapsed "types" of his historical offspring. Thus, as Michael gradually dispels the mental impairment that Adam suffers along with his lapse, he begins to return to the far more complex, ambiguous, and intuitive "apprehension" characteristic of his original state. This perceptual regeneration then allows Adam "literately" to embrace his savior, which, in the context of their dialogue, is accomplished only through a careful reassessment of his meaning—a process that Ong associates with the "back-scanning" technique of fully literate subjects. Since the Son's dialogues with the Father also consistently reveal this literate dialectic of subtle interpretation and ironic correction, in embracing them as his own Adam at last reclaims his "lapsed powers," which, along with God's "freely voutsaf't" grace (*PL*, 3.175–76), inform the proper dialectic of all his free servants. In teaching Adam to recapitulate these natural motions, Michael also appropriately prepares him to understand the allegorical progress of human history from "shadowy Types to Truth" (12.303).

This progress is structurally paralleled by Michael's abrupt shift from the typological, emblematic narrative of book 11 to the complex, open-ended lecture of book 12. The explicit advances of a literate, back-looping or -scanning sensibility over the oral, formulaic mindset thus at once accompany and conduct the progress of Adam's race, which he retraces as he leaves behind the antediluvian life world and advances toward the Reformed dispensation, proceeding

> . . . from Flesh to Spirit,
> From imposition of strict Laws, to free
> Acceptance of large Grace, from servile fear
> To filial, works of Law to works of Faith.
> (*PL*, 12.203–6)

In the process, the invisible, oral economy of hearing will gradually lose its precedence over sight, which at once verifies and redeems the maxim, "Sight isolates, sound incorporates."[5] Because, for Milton as for Protestants generally, salvation primarily depends not on the spoken but on the written word, the traditional Augustinian association between sight and sin is also thereby inverted. Print culture additionally reinforces this valorization of the eye over the ear, which is further reinforced by the Reformers' rejection of the *visibilia* of traditional Christian worship in favor of the less corporeal sight of the interpreted word. Since, like the mode of meta-allegory, that of the written word synthesizes the external or visual sign with the internally "heard" or silently apprehended sign of understanding, as in Milton's *Christian Doctrine*, it becomes the "image" by which we hear and see God.

This ideally synthetic apprehension of the "track divine" is therefore represented, not as a sudden "blinding" revelation that cancels sinful sight, but as a dialectical, even painful acquisition of back- and forward-scanning referentiality that mediates between oral or paratactic emblematics and the highly hypotactic or abstractly integrated mode typical of advanced print culture. Yet, because he is to recapitulate the entire semiotic progress of his fallen race, Adam is first initiated into the oral mode, which, as Ong details, requires a program of learning "by apprenticeship—by discipleship . . . by listening, by repeating what [he] hear[s], by mastering proverbs and ways of combining and recombining them and other formulary material—by participating in a kind of corporate retrospection—not by study in the strict sense."[6] In retracing this original economy of orality, the lapsed Adam thus appropriately experiences its limitations, although primarily to transcend them. As a result, his communal discussion with his angelic instructor emphasizes the elementary logic of orality: its copious, aggregate, paratactic, and often redundant language and its situational and empathetic rather than abstract or analytic presentation. Once these responses have been fully internalized, Adam will be ready to assimilate the complexly modulated lecture of book 12, which is only briefly interrupted by incisive questions on the part of his student. But, for now, Michael must repeatedly engage his pupil in the joint effort of "placing" the moral meaning of emblematic icons, and, since even these formulaic types have lost the relatively easy and natural meaning they might have possessed in paradise, his task is at becomes particularly painful. Later, when Adam has become more disciplined and less naive in his responses, Michael will no longer need to elicit such anguished responses as Adam now expresses upon seeing the fallen types of himself and Eve that Michael now turns into carefully polarized exemplums of his children. At that point, their communal dialogue will play a distinctly secondary role as he carefully solicits Adam's more thoughtful, readerly responses to his lectures. In experiencing both phases, Adam is thus also being acculturated in the progress from homeostatic types to hermeneutical truth.

Thus emblematic exercises of book 11 are thus less paradigmatic than preliminary or propaedeutic, although, like Michael's later discourse, they are framed by a gradually broadening moral or individual, typological or sociopolitical, and, finally, anagogic or spiritual understanding of the Fall. In this respect, the twinned narratives remain embedded in the multileveled form that they metareferentially critique—once again, a fundamental function of baroque allegory. At the same time, its characteristic expansion of these multiple planes of reference replaces the neatly "boxed" or stratified hierarchies characteristic of the oral mode with evolutionary and disjunctive historical perspectives.[7] Although divine Providence continues to intervene in this history's irregular and often bewilderingly erratic shape, the literate paradigm embedded in its historical agon provides the most fundamental link between the two modes. The end result is not a survey or "quick trip" through salvation history, as often claimed, but a sophisticated fusion of diverse exegetical traditions with a new emphasis on natural law, a theme proleptically developed in the opening of book II.[8]

Here, the reader encounters a "primitive," barely regenerate Adam who gives us a backward look into the oral life world that at the same time requires her own hypotactic or "back-scanning" synthesis of epic recapitulation and reevaluation. This synthesis is needed to reveal the enormous gap between Eden's primary or "readerly" and the Mount of Speculation's secondary or fallen mode of orality, a gap emphasized both by Adam's constant liability to childish interpretive errors and by his almost equally childish sentimentality regarding his lost home. However, neither disjunction nor continuity adequately summarizes his actual postlapsarian situation since Edenic "apprehension" exhibited a natural or intuitive synthesis of deduction and induction that can now only painstakingly be recovered through Michael's progressive lessons. Thus, in place of direct or "deifying" dialogue with God, Adam must undergo a dialectical experience of conflict, correction, and, finally (with Michael's aid), mature self-reflection. In the process, like the newly fallen angels, he now first experiences pain, which further complicates his already clouded vision. Now his unsuccessful attempts at grasping the angelic viewpoint no longer glance harmlessly aside but further exacerbate his guilt, grief, and susceptibility to emotional and ethical overstatement. These effects and their root causes in the kind of perceptual error already implicit in his fall are thus part of the hermeneutical problem to be solved. Unlike Satan, who externalizes his shame, Adam at first overly internalizes his personal responsibility for a postlapsarian situation that he must learn to overcome if he is to attain even a relatively accurate degree of corrected apprehension. At least initially, this attainment demands a relatively strict "homeostatic" apprenticeship to the authoritarian angel who has taken the place of the more amiable Raphael.

Among the most painful realities that Michael must inculcate is an understanding of the fallen conditions that inhibit or block Adam's native capacity. Since his self-reflexivity has been lost with his innocence, these conditions must be emphatically illustrated through a restricted and simplified curriculum. Yet his case is far from hopeless since, if Adam's "fall" from literacy is hardly fortunate, it also models the advantages of adhering to the ongoing task of "repair[ing] the ruins of our first parents by regaining to "Know God aright" (*CPW,* 2:366–67).⁹ Thus, like the true student in "Of Education" or the true wayfaring Christian of *Areopagitica,* Adam must learn that "The light we have gain'd, was giv'n us, not to be ever staring on, but by it to discover onward things more remote from our knowledge" (*CPW,* 2:550). If taking on this task initially requires accepting a childish method of instruction, the internalization of this discipline ultimately reaps the self-sufficient "harvest" of progressive revelation that begins by first "ploughing" this wilderness. In looking forward to this goal, the poet's twinned rationalizations of biblical myth and Christian history are thus already implicitly literate rather than "orally" mythic, legendary, or even typological, as the opening of book II suggests. There, Adam and Eve are expelled from Eden as if by the forces of natural law, by physical elements that naturally "eject" and "purge" mankind "off / As a distemper, gross to air as gross" (II.52–53). Accordingly, we are led to believe that their stay in paradise would be equally "unnatural" since the fruits of the Tree of Life would now only compound the delusive effects of the Tree of Knowledge. For already these "fruits" breed only the intoxicating "fancy that they feel / Divinity within them breeding wings / Wherewith to scorn the Earth," a fancy that, on awakening, is reduced to only so much vapor "bred of unkindly fumes, with conscious dreams / Encumber'd" (*PL,* 9.1009–11, 1050–51). Because such dreams do not vitally stimulate but only distract the creative imagination, the Almighty mercifully intervenes:

> . . . Lest therefore his now bolder hand
> Reach also of the Tree of Life, and eat,
> And live for ever, dream at least to live
> For ever, to remove him I decree,
> And send him from the Garden forth to Till
> The Ground whence he was taken, fitter soil.
> (II.93–98)

As this pronouncement suggests, the stuff of such dreams as Adam is prevented from being made of is that of which hellish allegory is made: vain desires, empty rationalizations, and sterile interventions into the otherwise naturally liberating resources of God's "immortal Elements."

Thus, in commissioning Michael to educate and solace Man by revealing "what shall come in future days" (*PL*, 11.113–14), the Father appoints a messenger and a message that will emphasize his role as the guardian of these natural/historical laws. Rightly to worship him, then, means rightly to read the dialectical cycles of material and social history, an aspect of God that becomes more pronounced as he retreats into abstractions ever more remote from the more transparent signs of Eden. At last largely an ironic effect or trace, after the fall God's presence is already largely transferred into those natural laws that now deliver mankind to its chosen kind, to "mortal food, as may dispose him best / For dissolution wrought by Sin, that first / Distemper'd all things, and of incorrupt / Corrupted" (11.54–57). Yet, in consigning Adam and Eve to the mortal elements they have chosen for themselves, God also announces a history of trial obliquely tempered by mercy:

> . . . I at first with two fair gifts
> Created him endow'd, with Happiness
> And Immortality; that fondly lost,
> This other serv'd but to eternize woe;
> Till I provided Death; so Death becomes
> His final remedy, and after Life
> Tri'd in sharp tribulation, and refin'd
> By Faith and faithful works, to second Life,
> Wak't in the renovation of the just
> Resigns him up with Heav'n and Earth renew'd.
> (11.57–66)

This enigmatic proclamation not only blurs and literalizes the conventionally redemptive feature of Christian history by vaguely deferring it onto a material "renovation of the just" but also replaces the homeostatic curse of Genesis with oblique irony, as God wryly announces to his angels, "O Sons, like one of us Man is become, / To know both Good and Evil" (*PL*, 11.84–85). Because in Milton's epic the Trees of Life and Knowledge no longer have any ritual or magical power, their stolen fruits can cause Adam to become "like" God only by learning what the deity would rather they not have known: without the "remedy" of death, man's tendency to indulge the illusion that such knowledge conveys power could but "eternize his woe."

Now a physician as much as a judge, God's removal of Adam from the temptation to eat of the still more fatal fruit of self-inflicted immortal woe mercifully "replants" him in the soil of providential history. Yet, like the fields he will now cultivate with the sweat of his brow, this soil well tilled will yield the rewards of self-deliverance through trial. Rather than a punishment, Adam's removal from Eden thus begins his education in the critical reevaluation of self-made and self-destructive icons, the signs of the wrong kind of allegory. By gradual correction and refinement, he will then be enabled to bear the fruits of a "second Life," which begin to bloom with his renewed understanding of the continuities within the new disparities between heaven and earth, the fruits of meta-allegory. By translating exile into reeducation, the myth of ritual punishment is then conclusively left behind, along with its oral parables and their emblems.

Moreover, because Adam's reeducation is meant to return him to the fundamental "realities" of his natural state, the Christian history of the final books stresses a postlapsarian epistemological continuity that strongly contrasts with the complete depravity of mind and will maintained in Calvin's reappropriation of the Augustinian tradition. Thus, as Balachandra Rajan observes, they transform what might have been a gloomy allegorical "pageant of the world's woes with the Messiah at the end" into a saga of gradual regeneration. Generally speaking, because in book 10 "Adam and Eve humble themselves instead of being humbled, the pageant of history is not a warning to the unrepentant but a means of enlightening those who have already repented."[10] Nevertheless, the gradual and precarious nature of their progress also stands as a warning to the self-deceptive, self-congratulatory tendency of individual interpretation to become its own kind of tyranny. This equally Protestant tendency, one only too apparent in Michael's outline of history, is immediately rebuked as we witness the repentant Adam's premature confidence in the power of prayer (*PL*, 11.148–58) and Eve's similarly naive expectation of the "infinite . . . pardon" of her Judge (11.167). Although neither is ultimately wrong, for now further discipline is needed since their idolatrous subjection to the tree and to each other leaves them much too liable to idolize the Word according to their fondest wishes. Moreover, while Adam can still accurately read the signs of nature (11.193–95), he can now no longer spontaneously reason out their higher significance, as he despondently admits: "Who knows, or more than this, that we are dust, / And thither must return and be no more"

(11.199–200). In their combined ignorance of the realities of their altered condition, both are once again mere children in the state of nature, grasping some aspects of its laws but ignorant of the telos designed by a God of just self-discipline as well as grace.

Dominated, moreover, by the mistaken hopes and carnal fears that "that day dimm'd *Adam's* eye" (*PL*, 11.212), their anxieties about their approaching exile only further augment their woe. Clinging to the mere tokens of their innocent state, Eve breaks into a lament for her first nurslings, the flowers that had decked her bower, while Adam laments the loss of the "bright appearances" (11.329) of the deity. Mistakenly identifying the holy with the mere places and images of God (11.315–22), both reveal habits of mind that it will become the goal of Michael's education to correct: a preference for viewing the literal "footsteps" of God (11.329) instead of intellectually grasping his ongoing presence within history. Since to grasp this presence is to replace mortal with immortal food, their progress ironically depends on their acceptance of loss and absence, including the aborted potential for an unfallen history of mankind, of a wholly benign social organization and a deathless dominion over the earth, where Eden, "perhaps thy Capital Seat" (11.343), would have extended its blessings to all future generations. Yet, for truly literate readers, the alternate and far gloomier history revealed by Michael still retains the wandering signs of the Father's goodness, love, and grace. As formerly, God will be present not so much in places as in motions and processes, as Michael "with regard benign" (11.334) assures them:

> Yet doubt not but in Valley and in Plain
> God is as here, and will be found alike
> Present, and of his presence many a sign
> Still following thee, still compassing thee round
> With goodness and paternal Love, his Face
> Express, and of his steps the track Divine.
> (11.349–54)

Yet, despite the comfort to be traced in the obscure yet also secure patterns of his "track divine," Adam and Eve must be prepared for an ambivalent mixture of "good with bad / . . . supernal Grace contending / With sinfulness of Men" (*PL*, 11.358–60), concerning which they so far have only the vaguest notions. Hence, Michael begins by giving Adam new eyes, "spectacles" here symbolized by the herbal aids that allow him to decipher the characters of his elementary primer. The film thereby removed is not that of original sin, which disappears only with the coming of the second Adam and the first Adam's acceptance of him as his Messiah. Propaedeutic rather than sacramental, the "Euphrasy and Rue" that Michael applies with water from the Well of Life (11.414–16) represent a reorientation rather than a purgation: they strengthen "the visual Nerve, for he had much to see" (11.415). Here, as in his oral education generally, the genuinely "rueful" Adam must first learn to detach himself from mere concrete places and things in order to master and then to overcome the coded language of types and allegories, from which he will proceed to the meta-allegory of signs. Preparing him to see Eden itself become an "Island salt and bare" (11.834), Michael thus removes him from his first home and from Eve to a hill like that "Whereon for different cause the Tempter set / Our second *Adam* in the Wilderness" (11.382–83). This prolepsis again stresses the hidden continuities between the two Adams as an aspect of the obscure but continuous metareferentiality of the historical track divine, which, in blending doubt with a cautiously hopeful attitude toward the progressive understanding of ambiguous signs, ultimately cancels the premature confidence of the Calvinist elect and its price: a subjection to a far more homeostatic and literal "track divine."

From the converse or "back-scanning" perspective on the courses of the intellectual and literary history being traced here, Milton's hill of contemplation even more sharply contrasts with the mount on which the Redcrosse Knight is sacramentally prepared to slay his dragon, for neither in this poem nor even in *Paradise Regain'd* is the dragon ever finally slain. Since "th' effects which thy original crime hath wrought" (*PL*, 11.424) not only bind Adam but separate him from Christ, his journey through the wilderness *he* "hath wrought" thus provides a far more interactive allegory of human salvation than the comparable episodes of Spenserian romance. Nevertheless, Adam will be initially inculcated in a more subtly "forward-scanning" version of this interpretive mode, learning to absorb its visual cues and emblematic paradigms until he can outgrow this oral "memory room." At that point, he will be able to detach himself from all figural types and all symbolic places and things. This detachment will then cause the "film" of false knowledge and early education to fall away because he will no longer be childishly inclined to misread the "Fruit that promis'd clearer sight" (11.413), "seeing" in its place only the God who planted it. This new "vision" is gained along with the analytic and literate skills that will return Adam to the Eden of the "paradise within," "happier far" in that it is closer to the deity's most accurately accommodated nature, which is more accessible through words than things and more through his complex providential history than through either.[11]

2

Appropriately, then, Adam's first oral lessons catechize him on the conditions of his intermediately altered nature, what he is and can expect to become, both of which have dramatically changed since he first received Raphael's painless lessons. He therefore homeostatically learns to accept, then to control his responses to the more rigorous dispensation his lack of faith has wrought. Having already witnessed the Son's self-sacrificial humility in his act of judging him, where he "disdain'd not to begin / Thenceforth the form of servant to assume" (*PL*, 10.213–14), Adam has already entered on an elementary form of discipleship. He is thus at least superficially able to grasp the significance of Michael's first emblem, the difference between Abel's humble and Cain's insincere sacrifice. Yet he still childishly misunderstands the more disturbing implications of the scene, and all that he can therefore infer from this type is that one of the brothers has behaved well and been rewarded poorly. Michael must then stress the deceptive appearances of rewards and the fact that even in this "oral" world God does not ritually dispense favors from a cloud, but bestows invisible if by no means wholly symbolic benefits. The faithful thus "lose no reward" even in an untimely death "rolling in dust and gore" (11.459–60), although this first correction merely allows Adam mistakenly to assume that he has "seen Death" (11.462), when he understands neither the full range of its disparate effects nor its unitary natural causes.

As a result, Michael must represent the literate "truth" that death is neither a merely ritual curse nor a physical fate through a simplified but gradually expanded process of emblematization. Since Adam has not grasped the role of envy in either the life or the death of Abel, the archangel now draws his attention to the role of desire turned to selfish "appetite." Formerly as perfect and whole as the human body, harmonizing with angelic tastes both in food and in love, appetite in the postlapsarian state takes on a significance as drastically altered as that of desire itself. Like Satan's own daughter, Adam's sister-wife and all her "fruits" will now be objectified by her brothers as external temptations rather than as a synthesis of her physical and spiritual graces. For even now the sins of Adam and Eve, their choices and their effects in time, have already become so ingrained in their consciousness that they "naturally" tend to separate this synthesis by creating an Other within as well as without. Because Adam cannot "see" these effects in himself until he views their consequences in Michael's simplified primer, he fails to see how Cain's self-righteous envy recapitulates the double source of his own fall: self-righteous attachment to "his" Eve and selfish doubt of God's goodness and mercy, both of which implicitly recapitulate the fall of Satan. The coda that Michael attaches to this scene ("th' just the unjust hath slain / For envy" [*PL*, 11.455–56]) then suggests that the cause of the first murder is not unlike Adam, Eve, and Satan's competing appetites for divine fruit, and divine favor, which, when unjustly pursued, ultimately draws all sin toward death.

Even here anticipating a far more internalized education in the "onward" pattern of remoter things, Adam's initial, situational responses to Michael's instruction act as a sort of screen through which the reader glimpses that his abstract relationship to Providence is actually "written" and "seen" rather than heard even when he is least aware of it. The germs of this insight can be found in the human form itself, which, both before and after the Fall, illustrates the continuous, evolutionary operation of natural law. If at first Adam can no longer grasp these laws, by mastering the subtext of Michael's initiatory scenes he begins to refamiliarize himself not only with their physical and moral but also their historical operations. Yet, precisely because they are designed to rehabilitate a virtually illiterate Adam, Michael's simplified emblems still fail to compare with Raphael's complexly subordinated and plotted language. At this point, his rhetoric thus seems closer to the style of primary epic, where theme and subtext are reinforced through verbal repetition, episodic structure, and circular design. Paratactic rather than hypotactic, at both micro and macro levels this style (as Cedric Whitman notes in his work on the *Iliad*) relies on "boxes within boxes created by thematic recurrences, not Freytag's pyramid."[12] Unlike the sophisticated, ironic, and baroquely inflated dramatic narration of the War in Heaven, Michael's discourse thus constructs building blocks of meaning rather than the subtle subversions and substitutions of more complex forms of accommodation. Having lost his ontologically "primary" but in fact highly literate orality, the newly "naive" Adam must now progress by assimilating a set of loosely overlapping episodes reinforced by "heavy" moral types before he can post-Homerically proceed to Socratic dialogue and, thence, to silent reading.

In preparing for these later stages, Michael next instructs Adam in the art of unpacking a typical Homeric catalog. His list of the Lazar house with its "diseases dire" (*PL*, 11.474) consists of "boxes within boxes" meant both to reinforce and to supplement the connections left incomplete in Michael's first account of appetite, envy, murder, and death, the consequences directly contingent on the "inabstinence of *Eve*" (11.476), but indirectly also on Adam's own appetite. Hence, the harsh, dogmatic lessons of this catalog are inculcated in order to be mitigated later on, when Adam will be better able to assimilate the complex complementarity between the causes and the effects of his and Eve's sin. Stressing that the causes of these defects must be confronted if they are to be controlled, Michael then imparts a classical oral catechism of rules and precepts to which Adam must adhere in his newly vulnerable mortal state, which at first permits little immediate scope for free interpretation. By applying the "rule of not too much, by temperance taught" (11.531), Michael assures him that he can avoid many of the pains of his new condition, although not the "melancholy damp of cold and dry" old age and death (11.544) to which he is now subject. In dealing with the latter, Adam must merely accept Michael's stoic advice: "Nor love thy Life, nor hate; but what thou liv'st / Live well, how long or short permit to Heav'n" (11.553–54). Yet not until book 12 will he be ready to absorb the truth that even these "permanent" ravages of Original Sin will be partly remedied by his Messiah's advent and wholly by his return.

From this more holistic historical perspective, even the radically simplified education appropriate to earth's fallen inhabitants ultimately reveals the constant laws of God's evolving universe. Throughout the fallen world, material choices continue to produce commensurable material if also moral consequences, which can and ultimately will be temporally and organically reversed or maintained, largely depending on the creature's individual will. Thus, whether they accept or reject "God's Image" (*PL*, 11.525), his creatures remain subject to the laws of his physical creation. Further, although "inductive mainly to the sin of *Eve*" (11.519), the narcissistic sensuality here emblematized in female form is actually made the responsibility of both genders; by giving themselves over to "ungovern'd appetite," all Adam's children, male and female, inherit the same propensity to take "His Image whom *they* served" (11.517–18; emphasis added). Because such satanic service can occur only at the expense of God's physical or external as well as of his spiritual or internal image, it "naturally" produces, not the promotion Satan promises, but the double demotion, spiritual and material, that attends his seduction of the human pair. Neither a ritual curse nor a compulsory insignia per se, the fruits of their service to this perverse image become a *habit* in the modern sense, a choice made in response to external stimuli that, repeated over time, becomes an organic reflex. That sin creates the addictive habits is the "literate" meaning concealed in the emblem of the Lazar house, which teaches Adam that its inhabitants suffer from

> Disfiguring not God's likeness, but thir own,
> Or if his likeness, by themselves defac't
> While they pervert pure Nature's healthful rules
> To loathsome sickness, worthily, since they God's
> Image did not reverence in themselves.
> (*PL*, 11.521–25)

With this stoic if also commonsense reminder of the benefits of temperance, Michael thus forms the oral "habits" of a sensibility that he will later internalize in exploring the more complex sociohistorical pathology of sin. In the end, instead of a standard typological or incarnational allegory, this pilgrim's progress models no predetermined path to grace but a gradually individualized interpretation of and interaction with history. Yet, in preparation for this end, Adam must continue to rely on "heavy figures" while he progresses through a phase of fallen history in which both the incarnate and the written Word of God remain distant.

After inculcating the dangers of "appetite" in the narrower, more individual sense, that of inordinate desire, Michael thus anticipates this end by reaching for the broader "box" that frames its social consequences. As its contents are emptied, Adam can perceive how improperly resolving the struggle between pursuing "ungovern'd appetite" and the "track Divine" produces a violent perversion of Edenic harmony. Those swayed from true worship by selfishly seeking only the sensual gifts bestowed on "accomplish't Eve" then neglect

To worship God aright, and know his works
Not hid, nor those things last which might preserve
Freedom and Peace to men. . . .
(*PL*, 11.578–80)

Their sons thus inherit not only the fallen rectitude of the fathers but the selfish sensuality of their mothers, the daughters of Cain. To Adam's untrained eye, however, these women resemble, not the "Rib / Crooked by nature, [and] bent . . . / More to the part sinister from me drawn" (10.884–86) on whom he had unjustly blamed his fall, but the sinless bride of his wedding day. Like appetite in the former scene, delight is the appearance that now must be unpacked and resynthesized, its dangers anatomized as Adam's bent is untangled as one still unthinkingly "inclin'd to admit delight / The bent of Nature" (11.596–97).

As Michael explains, the revised course of human history will henceforth demand Adam's attention to the fact that not all bents of nature and not all delights will prove as innocuous as the innocent pleasures of Eden. The just who "all thir study bent / To worship God" (*PL*, 11.577–78) can now be (re)bent by God-given, womanly arts, which, when misused, construct an ensnaring "amorous Net" (11.586) of originally innocent pleasure and amorous delight. The accomplishments of those "Bred only and completed to the taste / Of lustful appetence" (11.618–19) thus impart to "Love's disport" the same side effects as the wine of the "fallacious Fruit" (9.1042–46): not only a bitter aftertaste, but a state of human affairs that a whole "*world* of tears must weep" (11.627; emphasis added). Once Adam's descendants yield "all thir virtue, all thir fame / Ignobly" (11.623–24) to sexual idolatry, "Man's effeminate slackness" (11.634) again breeds monstrous fruits, but on a much larger scale. Now an entire race of giants will compound the faults of both prototypical "male and female" ancestral stocks without inheriting the virtues of either. In this simplified fable, the miscegenation of the valley dwellers ("Inventors rare, / Unmindful of thir Maker" [*PL*, 11.610–11]) with the studious "just men" of the neighboring hills (11.577) produces sons studious only to invent tyranny, rapine, and war. They thus improve on Cain, their maternal grandsire, only in the terrible scale of their "slaughter and gigantic deeds" (11.659).

For one with little experience in the laws of historical cause and effect, this scene demands the strong sense of communal identification elicited by Michael. Using his listener's errors to instill both humility and empathy for his offspring, he underscores the salient situational aspects of false delight. Adam's first reaction to this scene also reciprocally underscores the necessity of this approach, since he again simplistically sees only his own "deception" by Eve:

> O pity and shame, that they who to live well
> Enter'd so fair, should turn aside to tread
> Paths indirect, or in the mid way faint!
> But still I see the tenor of Man's woe
> Holds on the same, from Woman to begin.
> (*PL*, 11.629–33)

Here Michael must reprimand Adam for self-righteously oversimplifying the polarities between the "heavy figures" that he socratically sets up only to demolish. He then asks his pupil to break down and recontextualize the essence/appearance, male/female oppositions he is using, for Adam must learn accurately to correlate characterological types with moral truths before he can finally be weaned away from them. As Ong observes, this same process of oral patterning is recapitulated in the early childhood education of literate societies through the heavy figures of folk- and fairy tale, where "Colorless personalities cannot survive. To assure weight and memorability, heroic figures tend to be type figures."[13]

Like the semiliterate child, Adam is being inducted into the experience of orality not merely to recapitulate but to transcend it. As a result, Michael's focuses not merely on identifying the heroes and villains of the piece but also on teaching him that authentic heroism stems not from a simple refusal of colorful feminine wiles but from the internal strength of the one who can "hold his place / By wisdom" (*PL*, 11.635–36). However, this simple moral tag only slightly shifts the ground of what remains a communal interpretive enterprise that internalizes even as it polarizes virtue as due to "superior gifts receiv'd" (11.636), for it now begins to redirect Adam's attention to the more complex patterns of historical vice exemplified by the disastrous decline of "that sober Race of Men, whose lives / Religious titl'd them the Sons of God" (11.621–22). Building on the broader and more analytic aspects of this history, Michael's next scene expands its application well beyond the emblematic snares of "appetite" or "delight," for, like other quasipersonifications, these soon prove inadequate to the maturer representation of the evolutionary saga of tyranny, exploitation, decadence, and self-destruction that must now be told in subtler or later "Homeric" shadings of character and scene. Pastoral peace, the last remnant of Eden before the Flood, is at this point finally ruined by the legendary epic of human warfare that rounds out Michael's myth. Here, Adam sees his giant sons

> With cruel Tournament the Squadrons join;
> Where Cattle pastur'd late, now scatter'd lies
> With Carcasses and Arms th'ensanguin'd Field
> Deserted: Others to a City strong
> Lay Siege, encampt; by Battery, Scale, and Mine,
> Assaulting; others from the wall defend
> With Dart and Jav'lin, Stones and sulphurous Fire;
> On each hand slaughter and gigantic deeds.
> (11.652–59)

At this juncture Adam must learn to see these sons of "ill-mated Marriages" (*PL*, 11.684), not merely as symbols of moral good or evil, but as historical forces carrying out their own manifest destiny as "Death's Ministers, not Men, who thus deal Death / Inhumanly to men, and multiply / Ten thousandfold the sin of him who slew / His Brother" (11.676–79). In this context, there are no longer any villains or heroes per se, only the relentless recurrence of a form of human error that can be countered, not by physical combat, but only, Enoch-like, through integrity and faith or, Adam-like, through a thorough understanding of Michael's historical perspective. To gain this perspective, the legendary notions of military glory demystified throughout the epic—but especially in the invocation introducing the theme of the Fall—must be decisively rooted out. If "To overcome in Battle, and subdue / Nations, and bring home spoils with infinite / Man-slaughter, shall be held the highest pitch / Of human Glory," entitling its victors to be regarded as "Conquerors, / Patrons of Mankind, Gods, and Sons of Gods," the forefather of such "heroes" at least recognizes them as "Destroyers rightlier call'd and Plagues of men" (11.691–97). At this historical turning point leading up to the great deluge of Noah's day, Michael and his pupil will have completed the primary phase of their course in the history of human corruption, whose culminating moment occurs when the "name" of virtue has become utterly meaningless except as an absent sign: "Thus Fame shall be achiev'd, renown on Earth, / And what most merits fame in silence hid" (11.698–99). At this point, emblems fail

because all appearances, even linguistic ones, have become so hope-
lessly entangled with the laws of false desire that human worth or
value can no longer be known even from its fruits. Here, peace itself
becomes a misleading appearance instead of a blessing, an interlude
that merely gives broader scope to "luxury and riot, feast and dance, /
Marrying or prostituting, as befell, / Rape or Adultery" (II.715–17).

In this stage of human decline, any simple polarity between the
sons of God and the daughters of Cain becomes pointless; God may
intermittently intervene to rescue individuals like Enoch or Noah,
but the social pathology of sin overcomes the rest in epidemic pro-
portions. Yet Adam's response to the Noatic Flood reveals that,
while he has learned not to accept signs at their face value, he has not
yet been fully weaned away from assessing "heavy types" in the sim-
pler sense. As he sees all of his seed apparently lost in the Flood, he
despairs not only of their "Birth / Abortive" (*PL*, II.768–69) but also
of his own ability ever to distinguish good from evil:

> . . . I had hope
> When violence was ceas't, and War on Earth,
> All would have then gone well, peace would have crown'd
> With length of happy days the race of man;
> But I was far deceiv'd' for now I see
> Peace to corrupt no less than War to waste.
> (II.779–84)

While he clearly recalls that Michael has shown that both the con-
querors and "The conquer'd also, and enslav'd by War / Shall with
thir freedom lost all virtue lose" (II.797–98), he forgets his initial
lesson about the deceptive appearances of divine reward. In insisting
that, if black is white, white must be black, he thus despairs of divine
Providence itself, which he wrongly assumes has abandoned the
small family "Wand'ring that watr'y Desert" (II.779).

At this point, Adam has gained the ability to examine and care-
fully weigh the surface meaning of emblems against their broader
context, but he has yet to learn the shortcomings of a purely empa-
thetic orality. As a result, he has completely missed Michael's point
that the conquered are partly overcome by their own loss of faith in
virtue, which then produces God's refusal to reward mere "piety
feign'd" (*PL*, II.799). In allegorical terms, he inhabits a primitive
phase of divine accommodation where signs remain impenetrable
mysteries rather than enigmas to be probed by a baroque or literate

back looping that would uncover their semieffaced connections in time. To prompt him in this direction, the angel suggests that, when situational and polarizing logic prove mutually ineffective, they must be supplemented with more, not less, analysis. He then reminds Adam of his first, still imperfectly understood lesson, "that God attributes to place / No sanctity, if none be thither brought / By Men who there frequent, or therein dwell" (11.836–38). Fully to assimilate this lesson is to leave Michael's picture book behind, to part with a childish reliance on pictorial types and exempla, and thus ultimately to synthesize rather than merely to separate appearance and reality. To do this requires more than a visual "memory room" in which false and true, good and evil, are first opposed and then more diagrammatically realigned; it requires an analysis of motivation, history, and its providential design that at once accepts things as what they seem to be and as far more than they seem: as at once proper names, their first causes and etymologies, and their invisible but calculable destinations in time.

Once Adam grasps these points, the waters of the Flood recede under the spell of a poetic kinesthesia reminiscent of the creation episodes. Participating in this linguistic form of fertility, the natural vitality of sun, earth, air, and water is imagistically re-created in the midst of the Flood's destruction. Life again miraculously proceeds from death; as the spirit of the dove had purged "the black tartareous cold Infernal dregs / Adverse to life" (*PL,* 7.238–39), so the north wind now cleanses and wrinkles "the face of the Deluge, as decay'd" (11.843). From its depths, the aged sea produces a wrinkled infant earth, the rhythmic intercourse of life breathing and ingesting through its combined winds and waters in a new heavenly "rest":

And the clear Sun on his wide wat'ry Glass
Gaz'd hot, and of the fresh Wave largely drew,
As after thirst, which made thir flowing shrink
From standing lake to tripping ebb, that stole
With soft foot towards the deep, who now had stopt
His Sluices, as the Heav'n his windows shut.
(11.844–49)

Although the vibrant personification of this passage has, like many another, too often been generally slighted in favor of its doctrinal content, it is difficult not to see its vitalistic interchanges again reviving the male and female figures of "voice and verse" as the sun gazes on the deep and as their "tripping ebb" or "dance" produces the motion and change restoring life to earth as repetition gives way to difference, difference to repetition.

The fact that Adam, too, participates in this transformation is signaled by his "sudden apprehension" of the meaning of the sign of Noah: "A dewy Cloud, and in the Cloud a Bow / Conspicuous with three listed colors gay, / Betok'ning peace from God, and Cov'nant new" (*PL*, 11.865–67). This response at once reprises the joy, praise, and renewed faith that the angels experience at the creation (7.602–16) and reaffirms the continuing reliability of God's word and grace, the almost but not actually ineffable signs of his "track Divine" traceable in the benign mutability of the postlapsarian universe. At the same time, Adam's response signals a new stage in human experience, a new covenant that parallels the resumption of God's dialogue with men, and a parallel "re-creation" of literate sensibility. His apprenticeship to the oral life world now complete, mankind's prototypical parent demonstrates the advantages of a synthetic inductive/deductive assessment by correctly associating the physical appearance of the rainbow ("three listed colors gay") with its material and final causes. Avoiding the errors of a merely deductive orality, he literately grasps that, while its immediate appearance of salvation can rightly be linked to its redemptive telos, its final meaning must be associated with neither exclusively. The rainbow can accurately be "seen" as a sign of life, which in turn signifies both God and his covenant, because it at once represents and enacts the material processes that at last allow Noah to set forth on a misty world of water, air, and earth's "flow'ry verge" of vegetation, to encounter a new life tree "rooted" in primally purified light and water. Praising how "Dext'rously thou aim'st" (11.884), Michael validates Adam's holistic perception of the rainbow, his ability to see through it not only "the Brow of God appeas'd" (11.880) but also the synthetically material/symbolic processes of evaporation in which sun interacts with wave to produce regular rainfall, earthly vegetation, and human regeneration. Adam's insight into how the "bloom" of this "flow'ry verge" binds "The fluid skirts of that same wat'ry Cloud, / Lest it again dissolve" (11.881–83) thus organically accommodates his vision to that of the angelic spirits who glimpse their creator through his baroquely receding skirts, "dark with excessive bright."

Michael's response to Adam's accurate "aiming" also foreshadows the former's retreat from the tedious, heavy figures of his previous narration and his awareness that a more complex form of dialogic interaction is now possible. His painful, agonistic dialogue having fulfilled its purpose, he is able to leave behind the face-to-face medium of late orality, where, as Ong suggests, oral forms of discourse persist alongside chirographic media, as they do in Platonic dialogue. While this abrupt shift in pedagogy has been variously described as a typological ascent "from shadowy types to Truth," from primary to late allegory, or from Renaissance Neoplatonism to Ramist individualism, these disparate descriptions also suggest a synthetic foundation: a prototypical Adam who has been weaned away from a simplistic understanding of signs that would ultimately (if more spontaneously) have been superseded even in Paradise.[14] By now initiated into the exegetical practice of Reformed readers fully confronting the ambiguities of evolutionary history, Adam has attained the pinnacle of instruction in an oral mode where pictorial emblems and their superscriptions reinforce communal attitudes toward roles and responses. Having mastered and then outgrown them, this primer is no longer useful; therefore, in book 12, he must proceed from secondary to advanced hermeneutics.

3

Adam's departure from the oral mode is heralded at once as a release from allegorical mystery—since "objects divine / Must needs impair and weary human sense" (*PL,* 12.9–10)—yet also, nostalgically, as a loss of the immediacy of childhood. Michael now demands Adam's fullest attention (12.12) since it has become clear that, if the discipline of his former visions would now only "impair" his hermeneutical progress, his more advanced education will require a different kind of rigor. If laboring at his primer had caused frustration of one sort, learning to "scan" history literately is potentially even more wearisome, as the final book of *Paradise Lost* proves by documenting the painful and unresolved contests behind both the Reformation and the Puritan revolutions: the struggle to define and achieve Christian liberty and the accompanying debate over the authority and interpretation of the written word.[15] Yet, while acknowledging the toil involved in leaving the oral life world behind, its final book also records benefits far outweighing its disadvantages. Adam thus begins the second phase of his education like the other survivors of the

Flood, hopefully poised "Betwixt the world destroy'd and the world restor'd" (12.3), a witness to the triumphant new order in which "Man as from a second stock proceed[s]" (12.7).

This new order also authorizes a whole new curriculum, a comparative study of religious and political history not unlike that attempted by the self-proclaimed "inventor" of modern historiography, Jean-Jacques Rousseau. While in a great many respects book 12 significantly differs from Rousseau's *Discourse on the Origins of Inequality*, both accounts trace the destruction of primitive equality to human greed and aristocratic ambition.[16] Thus, if in Rousseau's schema all forms of pastoralism represent a departure from the state of nature while Milton's account locates "natural" equality in peaceful agrarian groups united "under paternal rule" (*PL*, 12.24), Milton just as clearly condemns those

> Of proud ambitious heart, who not content
> With fair equality, fraternal state
> Will arrogate Dominion undeserv'd
> Over his brethren, and quite dispossess
> Concord and law of Nature from the Earth.
> (12.25–29)

If he defends rather than blames private property for the loss of the "fraternal state," Milton also parellels Rousseau in tracing society's evils to aristocratic usurpers, for whom the hunting of "Men not Beasts shall be his game" (12.30). Here, inequality evolves through city and empire building, which end the random violence of the first state of nature only to replace it with a more organized form of plunder. Hence, if Milton's "natural man" is a pastoral nomad or farmer and Rousseau's a hunter/gather, both idealize a natural system of individual or family rights that takes precedence over the Hobbesian laws of the sovereign state. In one case, the "natural" norm consists of individualists resisting aristocratic violence, and, in the other, it consists of God-fearing republicans gathered into "Families and Tribes" (12.23) who have "some regard to what is just and right" (12.16). For Milton, this just order is disrupted by the first human tyrant, who "from Heav'n claim[s] second Sovranty" (12.35), a personification of kingship that in the form of Nimrod implicitly continues his defense of the people's right to resist the unjust tenure of kings and magistrates.

Thus, for both Milton and Rousseau, "man is born free, and everywhere he is in chains"[17] forged by the mystified power of aristocratic and priestly ambition. Although the differences between these two revolutionaries are equally real, they should not be exaggerated by overlooking the internal ambiguities of the philosophe's own political program. Because he is generally regarded as the "father" of the French Revolution, readers too easily forget that, as a litterateur, Rousseau was far more a moral idealist and an a priori thinker than a systematic political theorist. Like Milton an adherent of the early natural law school of political thought, Rousseau similarly conflates the "general will" with that of an abstract "moral person." The result in either case is closer to ethical theory than modern political science (which stems rather from Hobbes): a "defense" of liberty that, as Ernest Barker observes, emphasizes the "*quality* of the 'object' sought, and not the *quantity* of the 'subjects' by whom it is sought."[18] In Milton's case, this "moral person" is ideologically continuous with the individualistic, antitypical hero who regularly reappears in Michael's historical outline, where he serves as at once the source, engine, and goal of human history. His interrelated prototypes begin with the abstract "types" of the Sons of God and extend through all the Enochs, Noahs, Abrahams, and Moses of the faith, culminating in Michael's abstract ideal of the literate reader, the other natural "enemy" of the patriarchal theory of kingship.

Although Milton's libertarian ideals are complicated by his adherence to the spiritual ideal of the invisible church, to a certain extent (as Barker notes) they parallel Rousseau's belief "in the miracle of the true State, rationally constructed and continuing to act by rational self-control—the miracle that turns a stupid and limited animal into an intelligent being. The State which he attacks . . . is only the perverted or despotic State, irrational because it is not the expression and organ of a free rational will."[19] Needless to say, the quite different socioeconomic conditions to which Rousseau and Milton are responding should also not be overlooked, although their similarities remain instructive. Concerned throughout their lives with the elementary and advanced education of readers as the proper foundation of a just society, both Milton and Rousseau regard the "fall" of man from an original pastoral freedom as at least partially capable of being restored by reexamining the conditions inherent in the original state of nature. In Milton's account, a fall from these conditions occurs not once but three times: first, when Adam loses his primary, preliterate, yet "discursive" orality in Eden; next, when the Sons of God are seduced from their freedom and spawn a race of tyrannous militarists; and, finally, when all of Noah's successors fall away from the covenants designed to safeguard "the peace and freedom" that both he and Rousseau regard as the natural heritage of man.[20]

The main focus of Milton's epic finale is thus on surveying the covenants prefigured in the Noatic rainbow and the underlying reasons why the first like the final covenant is subject to constant subversion, misinterpretation, and aristocratic appropriation. Once these reasons are understood, then the invisible church/state's "living Temples, built by Faith to stand" (*PL,* 12.527)—at once the invisible reader and the regenerate Christian symbolized by Adam—can survive the tyrannous attacks of the symbolic Nimrods and Pharaohs who will continue to use Adam's free dominion to justify their unjust subjugation of their fellow men. Yet Milton's Adam himself denounces the first in this line indignantly, pronouncing him

> O execrable son so to aspire
> Above his Brethren, to himself assuming
> Authority usurpt, from God not giv'n:
> He gave us only over Beast, Fish, Fowl
> Dominion absolute; that right we hold
> By his donation; but Man over men
> He made not Lord; such title to himself
> Reserving, human left from human free.
> (12.64–71)

This excoriation of the doctrine of Robert Filmer and other royalist apologists by the very "king" supposedly supplying their precedent also links political to spiritual tyranny in a number of meta-allegorically significant ways, for, in this scenario, the "invention" of tyranny is accompanied by the related misrule of confusing and contradictory signs, a babbling discord of mutually alien tongues that can later be deciphered only by a laborious and literate investigation of language.[21]

Thus, as with satanic tyranny in general, God makes Nimrod's punishment fit his crime. Just as Satan's triumphal march through hell ends in the universal hiss compulsively cast from the demons' mouths, so now Nimrod's tower is greeted wth "a jangling noise of words unknown" ending in a "work Confusion nam'd" (*PL,* 12.55, 62). Yet, once again, the causes of tyranny are to be identified, not with Babel itself, but with its simultaneously psychic, social, and semiotic causes, since with Adam's "original lapse," the ability of reason correctly to determine the means most likely to preserve its natural "twin," liberty, has been radically undermined. Therefore, "Tyranny must be, though to the tyrant thereby no excuse" (12.95–96), for now "upstart Passions" too easily "catch the Government / From Reason, and to servitude reduce / Man till then free" (12.88–90). Since this usurpation occurs at both the micro and the macro levels of human government—both in individuals like Adam or Cain and in corporate bodies like Nimrod's—what the exemplary literate subject most needs to understand is how these twin forms of corruption can be withstood at all.

Ironically, the ultimate solution to this question is implicit in Adam's own situation upon the baroquely winding course of human history itself. As he soon learns, while God's providential design is not always immediately evident, the astute reader can trace its patterns in the rise and fall of nations. While unjust rulers are "naturally" allowed to tyrannize over peoples who have either individually or collectively forfeited the inner freedom whose loss subjects them "from without to violent Lords" (*PL,* 12.93), these times too must have a natural stop:

> Yet sometimes Nations will decline so low
> From virtue, which is reason, that no wrong,
> But Justice, and some fatal curse annext
> Deprives them of thir outward liberty.
> (12.97–100)

While this deistic conception of Justice "automatically" carrying out the naturalized processes of historical cursing and blessing at first seems to offer little hope, it also implies a solution that ingeniously fuses the advantages of an interventionist view of history with those of a more remote or "cool" literate approach. Because the mysterious ways of divine Providence guide the natural "laws" of virtue and liberty, these can be understood as functioning through a feedback mechanism in which individual initiative and collective will mediate the relatively unpredictable but also humanly comprehensible dialectic of tyranny, reaction, partial reform, and backsliding. When these cycles bottom out, this dialectic becomes recuperative, as the naturalistic recoil of divine justice intervenes; but, in the meantime, the subject trapped in the decadent phases or "loops" of this history can correctly "read" them in ways that not only relieve him of direct responsibility for its debacles but also direct him toward the enduring refuge of those "living Temples, built by Faith to stand" (12.527).

The task of historical reading thus supplements and directs faith and implicitly redemption itself, which will not be wholly fulfilled until the final "renovation of the just." Traditionally Stoic but also proto-Hegelian, this account of Christian history is nothing if not "back looping" in its formal and narrative drive, for its immanent progressions depend not only on a complex interaction between natural or divine justice and the free interpretation and response of its subjects but also on the reversibility inherent in these processes. As in Hegelian history, the last phases of each historical cycle build on the first in the ceaseless if also erratic upward spiral of civilization, until the telos of the regained Eden justifies the whole. Yet, in part because each new reversal of progress occurs at a higher point of critical or cultural "mass," Milton's version of these historical cycles is also less communal and more individualistic: Since unlike Noah the literate individual cannot expect to determine the whole, integrity in the face of defeat becomes paramount over social action or change itself. Thus, when all else fails, the subject of history can simply "stand and wait," in his secure faith experiencing the "paradise within." Yet the chief tool and supplement of that paradise becomes the literate insight that through the back looping process itself surmounts the mazes and treadmills of history. For that reason, the sifting and refining process begun with Adam's expulsion from Eden now continues in reverse. Although still removing pure from impure, the process of individual refinement is at last reestablished as the norm from which all tyrannous desires, internal and external, are mere temporary impurities.

Hence, God's servants achieve outward liberty only in some phases of history, the literate attainment of inner freedom is always available to his truly inquiring servants. The same understanding that preserves pre-Christian believers like Enoch from sinking into religious or political idolatry, the besetting sin of the oral and precovenantal life world, thus also preserves Abraham from the "Idol-worship" in which he was "bred up." Scorning the ritual worship of man's "own work in Wood and Stone," Abraham's "visions" of invisible "living God" (*PL*, 12.115–19) make both his literal and his figurative seed the people of the living book. Yet, in rejecting his "kindred and false Gods," Abraham avoids the perils of mental and spiritual tyranny rather than any literal pollution or curse transmitted through idols. As Adam's true heir, he thus produces the lineage leading to the Messiah in part by becoming the model "type" of the literate reader, who is also the truly heroic patron of liberty. This aspect of his blessing on "all Nations of the Earth" (12.147) is fulfilled as his seed establish a protorepublican state: "In the wide Wilderness, there they shall found / Thir government, and thir great Senate choose / Through the twelve Tribes, to rule by Laws ordain'd" (12.224–26). Recovering the original, pastoral freedom of the Sons of God outside the promised land, they are further rewarded by receiving the rule of law, the only proper form of government for faithful, free men. Yet this law itself must be progressively internalized, interpreted, and refined, never worshiped. In contrast, Abraham's earthly enemies espouse the idols of ritual allegory and of "magical" or priestly orality that also sustain the idols of political tyranny. Hence, Pharaoh refuses Abraham's "God, or message to regard," precisely because he is a "lawless Tyrant" who understands only fixed "Signs and Judgments dire" (12.173–75). Like Nimrod, this misreading places him in the moral line of Satan, a ruler whose "stubborn heart" causes his own "palpable darkness" to be spread throughout the land of this "River-dragon" (12.188, 191–93).

In this typology, Milton's revolutionary emphasis is clear since, like Rousseau, he carefully demonstrates how law itself can circumscribe freedom when it is considered sacred and inalterable, an error into which the Hebrew, like the English, kings ultimately fall. As these kings gradually lapse from the faith of Abraham, they then retreat into the oral, communal sensibilities that undervalue individual responsibility. This lapse brings in its wake an attachment to fetishized signs and symbols, ironically recreating the sin of Adam. In making their law king, the people begin to long for the rule of actual kings, who bring with them the additional fetishes of ritualized worship and royal ceremony. Instead of freeing, the law then enslaves, shrinking the scope of its subjects to the confines of their weaker natures. The spirit of orality returns, but not to Adam, who has literately perceived the contradictions inherent in the overvaluation of law. Thus, as he queries,

This yet I apprehend not, why to those
Among whom God will deign to dwell on Earth

So many and so various Laws are giv'n;
So many Laws argue so many sins
Among them; how can God with such reside?
(*PL,* 12.280–84)

Without denying that the law of Moses assumes the "natural prav-
ity" (*PL,* 12.288) to which Adam objects, Michael explains that, like
Adam's own primary education, this law is a propaedeutic intended
so that

. . . they may conclude
Some blood more precious must be paid for Man,
Just for unjust, that in such righteousness
To them by Faith imputed, they may find
Justification toward God, and peace
Of Conscience, which the Law by Ceremonies
Cannot appease, nor Man the moral part
Perform, and not performing cannot live.
(*PL,* 12.292–99)

Mosaic or ritual law thus becomes another exemplary "type" that
must be superseded, a shadow not only of a greater fulfillment but of
its own inadequacy. While it serves as an instructive discipline for
those still suffering from Adam's sin (12.285–86), its primary pur-
pose is to be replaced by a more sufficient "justification toward God."
This release can be achieved only through a ransom sacrifice of "just
for unjust," for then the faith and integrity now imputed to believers
by fixed signs can be freed from shallow homology and transformed
into the fluid forms of individual reception and response. Written
law will then at last accord with its original purpose, that of syn-
thesizing the discipline of faith with the freedom of grace, as its
readers progress

From shadowy Types to Truth, from Flesh to Spirit,
From imposition of strict Laws, to free
Acceptance of large Grace, from servile fear
To filial, works of Law to works of Faith.
(12.303–6)

In this "better Cov'nant," the original "fraternal state" of nature is
again restored, along with human peace and freedom. Now, always
as intermittently before, among the "Sons of God," among Noah's

children before Nimrod, and among the Hebrews in the wilderness, the spirit of the unwritten law of reason and justice supersedes the letter. Despite its ongoing incompletion, this ultimate and eternal return of the fraternal state at the Messiah's coming once and for all establishes the principles of earthly government maintained in Milton's political treatises, which argue that laws were invented to restrain, not to entitle, monarchs, "so man, of whose failings they had proof, might no more rule over them, but law and reason, abstracted as much as might be from personal errors and frailties" (*CPW*, 3:200). Moreover, even these laws are contingent, not absolute, for, "if any law or custom be contrary to the law of God, or nature, or of reason, it ought to be looked upon as null and void."[22] As Michael's narrative similarly implies, the irrational and oppressive propensities of "strict Laws" must not be allowed to invalidate the last, best covenant of the Second Adam, even though tyrants will continually attempt to "force the Spirit of Grace itself, and bind / His consort Liberty" (*PL*, 12.525–26). Thus, ironically, the initial conflicts between the city of Nimrod and the wilderness of Abraham will continue until the return of Eden, an inscrutable event whose delay is compensated only by the rational "covenant" of the literate reader. This covenant serves as a check both on those who would backslide into the "shadowy expiations weak" (12.291) of ritual law and on those who would "worship" the divine right of hereditary kings, who even in Judah were "Part good, part bad, of bad the longer scroll" (12.336). Like the luxury and corruption of the priests, whose "strife pollution brings / Upon the Temple itself" (12.355–56), these mystified rulers and their laws are belied by the true king who ushers in the rule of grace (12.416–17).

Through the "satisfaction" paid by the Son, the entire world thus enters the literate community along with Adam, its human model; having surpassed token sacrifices and emblematic laws, it receives the gift of free interpretation through faith and historical understanding. The bruising of Satan then inflicts no "local wounds / Of head or heal" (*PL*, 12.387–88) on evil itself but instead delivers the deathblow to semiotic literalism and its static allegories of history. As Michael informs Adam, since Christ's sacrifice "annuls thy doom" (12.428) by smashing the tyranny of Sin and Death (12.431) over his faithful offspring, they "over him no power / Shall long usurp" (12.420–21). Thus, like both model readers, Adam and the Son, the literate reader is also freed from the power of literalism in all its forms, from mistaking interpretive choice for the one plain sense of things. At all stages of history, this logic threatens individual apprehension with the consensual tyranny of "clear and distinct" ideas, much as the "deliberation" of Hobbesian nominalism would once again put an end to individual liberty by banning all "unscientific" speculation, which for Hobbes includes the free interpretation of the Christian rule of liberty or grace.[23] Yet, for Milton, the validity of such doctrines is forever canceled by the Messiah when

> . . . to the Cross he nails thy Enemies,
> The Law that is against thee, and the sins
> Of all mankind, with him there crucifi'd,
> *Never to hurt them more who rightly trust*
> *In this his satisfaction.*
> (12.415–19; emphasis added)

From this point, literate apprehension and teaching (12.440) proceed like human life itself, as from another and final dividing of the waters, washing their beneficiaries "from guilt of sin to Life" (12.443) and hence from oral mystification to the filial covenant of the readerly word.

Although in its broadest dimensions a concrete social force, this literate "baptism" thus conveys largely internal and individual blessings. For those who "offer'd Life / Neglect not" (*PL*, 12.425–26) to choose freedom over slavery and death, death is no longer a hideous monster with an allegorical dart but "A gentle wafting to immortal Life" (12.435). Choice thus returns to what it was in Eden, a question of the "mind prepar'd" (12.444). Yet, even within this horizon of freedom, both Christian literacy and political "independency" are so unstably constituted that church and state remain potential "arms" of mystification even after the demise of Satan's "two main arms," Sin and Death (12.431). If the end of history will declare the triumph of "*Abraham's* faith" (12.449), returning all earth to paradise (12.463–64), this end is not yet. The fundamental opposition between the city of God and the city of mankind is not so soon resolved, not least of all because God no longer has a temple in any earthly city, only an invisible church. Thus, once Christ reascends, a new cycle of corruption sets in, leaving his true followers to "cruelties" recompensed chiefly with "inward consolations" (12.494–95). After joyfully exclaiming on what appears to be his fortunate fall ("Light out of darkness!" [12.473]), Adam then more literately reconsiders the darkness still surrounding the faithful:

> But say, if our deliverer up to Heav'n
> Must reascend, what will betide the few
> His faithful left among th' unfaithful herd,
> The enemies of truth; who then shall guide
> His people, who defend? will they not deal
> Worse with his followers than with him they dealt?
> (12.479–84)

In conformity with the rest of his narration, Michael's answer to this extremely pertinent historical question is complexly modulated and qualified, for the faithful do retain one assured temple on earth, the one the poet began his epic by invoking, the spiritual temple of "the upright heart and pure" (*PL,* 1.17–18). Its Spirit will thus descend when the Messiah reascends, ever present to strengthen and guide the faithful:

> . . . from Heav'n
> Hee to his own a Comforter will send,
> The promise of the Father, who shall dwell
> His Spirit within them, and the Law of Faith
> Working through love, upon thir hearts shall write,
> To guide them in all truth, and also arm
> With spiritual Armor, able to resist
> *Satan's* assaults, and quench his fiery darts.
> (12.485–92)

The Spirit thus "writes" a nonformulaic "Law of Faith" in the hearts of believers, which is externally manifest in their ability to resist tyrannic assault. Possessing this inward "code," true believers will not need the aggregate communal support of orality or its homeostatic organization; their individual armor will be "supported so as shall amaze / Thir proudest persecutors" (12.496–97). Yet, for many, the immediate force of the Spirit will lapse along with apostolic miracles (12.498–507), thereby allowing a renewed onslaught of idolatrous "wolves" who will again afflict the faithful by perverting "all the sacred mysteries of Heav'n / To thir own vile advantages" (12.508–10). Superstition and corrupt tradition will once again triumph, although the truth will remain in "written Records pure" (12.512–13) even when no spiritually literate eye understands the word waiting to be rediscovered in the process of human interpretation and time.

The spiritual struggle to rerecord these truths at once concludes the epic and brings it into the present tense of the reader. As for the future and final tense of the vindication awaiting the restoration of Eden, it remains like eternity itself, an "end no eye can reach" (*PL,* 12.556), a vanishing point "visible" only to the inner eye and ear. The poem's final lines thus suggest a synthesis of resignation and hope appropriate to the sacrifices of both literate subjects and failed revolutionaries. Promising "New Heav'ns, new Earth, Ages of endless date / Founded in righteousness and peace and love" (12.549–50), Michael nevertheless fails to contextualize these in a world where "Truth shall retire / Bestruck with sland'rous darts, and works of Faith / Rarely be found" (12.535–37). While he is left "not disconsolate," Adam now inherits the melancholy "exile" of literate subjectivity, the baroque "homelessness" of decentered speakers and listeners who must always uncertainly waver between the poles of textual space and readerly time. In historical terms, this also means that they must subjectively mediate between what Andrew Milner calls their "*particular* defeats and the epic victory of the *historical-universal,*" which, broadly understood, requires overcoming a dualist or reifying nominalism with a more organic or synthetic dialectic.[24] For, as in the case of royalists like Hobbes, spiritual, political, and linguistic battles amount to much the same thing; determinists of his empiricist stripe are to Milton akin to political and spiritual tyrants in their effort to enslave the Spirit to the thing:

> Then shall they seek to avail themselves of names,
> Places and titles, and with these to join
> Secular power, though feigning still to act
> By spiritual, to themselves appropriating
> The Spirit of God, promis'd alike and giv'n
> To all Believers; and from that pretense,
> Spiritual Laws by carnal power shall force
> On every conscience. . . .
> (12.515–22)

The inner temple of freedom and grace must therefore ceaselessly oppose these "carnal powers," enslaving social forces activated through the censorship of central authority, fixed interpretation, communal judgments, and hierarchical codes.[25] Michael's objection to every form and aspect of this system speaks also for Adam's literate apprehension as well as that of the narrator and his "fit audience" of readers as he questions

> . . . What will they then
> But force the Spirit of Grace itself, and bind
> His consort Liberty; what, but unbuild
> His living Temples, built by Faith to stand,
> Thir own Faith not another's: for on Earth
> Who against Faith and Conscience can be heard
> Infallible? yet many will presume. . . .
> (*PL*, 12.524–30)

In contrast to these "presumers," the "living Temples" of the faithful will reject all reifying forms of interpretation since they understand that the word can be fully internalized and "read" only on the shifting screen of Michael's revisionary history, the spiritual path obliquely linking paradise to wilderness, liberty to law. As a result, Adam's final words meta-allegorically waver between assertion and denial, between otherworldly confidence in God's providence and mercy and his own internalized accommodation of them, which is all "this Vessel can contain" (12.559). His final "sum / Of wisdom" (*PL*, 12.575–76) is thus itself a model of clausal subordination, temporal back scanning, and hermeneutical balance—the qualities demanded of a competent reader or believer in the literate life world:

> Henceforth I learn, that to obey is best,
> And love with fear the only God, to walk
> As in his presence, ever to observe
> His providence, and on him sole depend,
> Merciful over all his works, with good
> Still overcoming evil, and by small
> Accomplishing great things, by things deem'd weak
> Subverting worldly strong, and worldly wise
> By simply meek; that suffering for Truth's sake
> Is fortitude to highest victory
> And to the faithful Death the Gate of Life.
> (12.561–71)

Here, Milton's "attentive reader," like the one addressed in the conclusion to Rousseau's *Discourse on the Origin of Inequality*, might find a view of history in which the same force that maintains Milton's

"worldly strong" despot also overthrows him, since "all things hap-
pen according to the natural order. As a result, no man can complain
of the injustice of another, but only of his own imprudence or his
misfortune," for as both Rousseau and Milton agree, humankind
only degenerates when it becomes enslaved to words like *power* and
reputation. Then, the "worldly wise" and "worldly strong" produce
"honour without virtue, reason without widom, and pleasure with-
out happiness. . . . [T]his is not at all the original state of men, . . .
only the spirit of society together with the inequality that society
engenders which changes and corrupts in this way all our natural
inclinations." Thus, "by the light of reason alone," Rousseau urges
his fit audience to set aside "the sacred dogmas which give to sov-
ereign authority the sanction of divine right" and dwell according
to the laws of our natural state, where each individual was defined
by the abilities apportioned by Providence. In this way, "by things
deem'd weak"—the self-reflexive light of ordinary mortals that Paul
calls the "foolish things of the world"—the "worldly strong" can
be subverted and "highest victory" attained, either in this world
or for Milton later, in the renovation of the just.[26] Thus, despite
political failure, the victory of the literate revolution embodied in
Adam ultimately guarantees that the great will succumb to the small,
strength to weakness, and worldly wisdom to Christian humility—
the essence of readerly freedom and its fine but hardly insignificant
discriminations. Overcoming the "carnal power" of hierarchical au-
thority, Adam and Eve then enter the "subjected Plain" (*PL*, 12.640)
of a purely internal Eden. Forsaking the proud dreams and enslaving
illusions of fixed signs, they must also shed "some natural tears"
in taking "thir solitary way" (12.645–49) through a wilderness of
conflicting signals. Yet, in contextualizing these signs with the real
things of their world, they also represent the Reformed reader's lib-
eration from the condescending language of accommodation inher-
ited from the oral life world.[27] In place of priestly or patriarchal
rituals or sacraments, they are empowered by Michael's highly flexi-
ble and portable interpreter's Bible. This baroque descent into nature
and time also allows their reascent into a liberated language, an
"esemplastic" organ of the human tongue, mind, and spirit—the
synthetic organ in which Milton discovers the ruined remnant of
Edenic allegory, the immanently expanded "meta" medium in which
its natural language lives again.

Conclusion: The Track Divine

Protestant Ethics, Skeptical Rationalism,

and Ruined Allegory

Two excesses: to exclude reason, to admit nothing but reason.

PASCAL, *Pensées*

One way or another, I have been proposing throughout this study that the universe of Milton's great Protestant epic should be contextualized, not only within the modernity that came into being during the seventeenth century, but also within a postmodern frame of reference defined by the "uncertainties" that we now must find endemic in all correlations of words, things, and thought. To that end, we must situate Milton's poetry, not in the closed or Realist cosmos of "ritual" correspondences that still informed the theory and practice of Renaissance allegory, but in the transitional cosmos of baroque poetics. From this perspective, the difficulties posed by reading Milton's poem can be traced to his redoubled critique of the mystified "essences" and signatures by which God's "track Divine" had been traditionally accommodated, on the one hand, and, on the other, of the new "certitudes" posed by the implicitly godless Cartesian mechanics in what Foucault defines as the Classic Age of Western rationalism.

Thus, while the repeated references in *Paradise Lost* to Galileo and the new astronomy, to an early type of "chaos theory," and to the material monism of the infinite universe (to name but a few) are signposts that clearly situate the epic within the modernity ushered in by the new science, the poem's theodicy is itself ultimately grounded in the transitional indeterminacies of a "rational" grace whose paradoxes may be compared to those of Pascal's *Pensées*. This comparison is especially fruitful since the Newtonian age, which includes much, if not all, of the twentieth century, viewed the idea of rational grace as largely a contradiction in terms: a paradox unworthy of scientific or philosophical consideration, a mystification suitable only to metaphysics, theology, or the other traditional "sciences" banished by the Classic Age. Yet not only did these disciplines remain rationally and empirically viable in Milton's era, but they were often synthesized with advanced natural philosophy and mathematics—as they are by Pascal, the inventor of probability theory in mathematics and, in science, of an empirical demonstration of the vacuum. Yet even profound and innovative intellectual historians like Foucault have tended to mislead literary historians and critics by imposing an overly abrupt and absolute paradigm shift on the seventeenth century, a period whose epistemic break was marked by the uneven and often bewildering transitions reflected in the baroque art form itself. In this period, some, but not all, influential thinkers had accepted the binary logic that was beginning to systematize its empirical "tables of signs" in order to produce the nominalists' true, rational, and transparent order of things—a paradigm that would become fully ascendant in the eighteenth century.

The postmodern critic thus has a decided advantage in approaching Milton's poem, if only because, where once contradiction and indeterminacy (to which Milton's *Logic* refers as "paralogisms") were surrounded either with suspicion or with nostalgia, they can now be recontextualized as alternate aspects of rationalism. As Heisenberg's indeterminacy principle, Gödel's theorems, and modern chaos theory have begun to establish, contradiction, not consistency, seems to lie at the basis of human systems of thought and natural evolution alike. That both Milton and Pascal foresaw at least the dim and general outlines of this post-Newtonian paradigm shift is suggested both by the epigraph above and by the double nature that both ascribe to their semi-paralogical God. Pascal's deity is at once deductively apparent in the double infinities of ever larger and smaller extension—the limitless mathematical vanishing points of macrocosmic and microcosmic space—and intuitively apparent in our apprehension that only a benign deity could coordinate such vast extensions of life. However, since his existence is only probable, not certain, the human subject must make a hyperrational "leap of faith" if he is to access the "higher" certitudes supplied by our intuitions of divine grace. Milton presents a similar conception of the deity both in his *Christian Doctrine* and in *Paradise Lost.* On the one hand, his epic God is not only deductively defensible but even logically defends himself. Yet, on the other hand, his accommodated truths can be fully "known" only in the paradoxically dark light of his historical design. His theological treatise presents a similar dichotomy, for, while it spends considerable effort in logically demonstrating the unitary (as opposed to the more mysterious threefold) nature of God, it concludes that his "wonderful" nature is also ultimately "incomprehensible" (*CD* 14:43, 61)—as do the angelic hymns of his epic.[1]

But to interpret these contradictions as simply mystical ruins of the theological tradition is also to ignore the role of probability in all human calculation, particularly in the infinite reaches of space and time, which Pascal describes as divinely "incommensurable." In this context, the idea of an incommensurable God coordinating its vanishing points is no more *conventionally* mystical than the concept of the big bang or the black hole, the perspective from which Stephen Hawking suggests we might apprehend the "mind of God."[2] As noted in the introductory chapters of this study, Milton made God similarly "calculable" but unknowable when he concluded, "The hidden wayes of his providence we adore & search not; but the law is his reveled wil, his complete, his evident, and certain will; herein he appears to us as it were in human shape, enters into cov'nant with us, swears to keep it, binds himself like a just lawgiver to his own prescriptions, gives himself to be understood by men, judges and is judg'd, measures and is commensurat to right reason" (*CPW,* 2:292). The paradoxes inherent in this understanding of man's relation to God are perhaps best summarized by Adam, who acknowledges to the Almighty that

> Thou in thy secrecy although alone,
> Best with thyself accompanied, seek'st not
> Social communication, yet so pleas'd,
> Canst raise thy Creature to what highth thou wilt
> Of Union or Communion, deifi'd.
> (*PL,* 8.427–31)

This tactic of ironically uniting man to God by distancing him from the infinite deity constitutes the fundamental modus operandi of Milton's baroque allegory, the core content of its form, with all the attendant consequences pointed out by Benjamin. Such works exhibit the melancholy aura of the mysterious grace that had formerly anchored the hermeneutic certitudes of Renaissance theology, unities that later fall victim to the either/or of grace and reason not only introduced by Cartesian skepticism but also implicit in Lutheranism and Calvinism themselves.

In Calvinism particularly, "irresistible grace" is an a priori condition of salvation in eternity, which in this life is to be demonstrated primarily by sober and rational conduct, not sacramental affirmations. Together, these segregations of works and grace produce the characteristic tendencies recorded by Benjamin: denying works "any special miraculous spiritual effect, making the soul dependent on grace through faith, and making the secular-political sphere a testing ground for a life which was only indirectly religious."[3] This tendency to deny the miraculous in daily life was felt most directly in allegorical literature, a traditional form of spiritual narrative in which consistent or discontinuous eruptions of the marvelous or fantastic guide the reader through a ritual journey, the goal of which is to outline the structure of the divine universe—or at least some of its fundamental aspects. Tracing the "track Divine" in an infinite universe where the "eruptions" of the sacred both in the sacrament and in the transcendence of divine space and time have largely disappeared thus calls for a radical readjustment. When a Galilean universe of number, motion, and relative direction no longer provides a ladder of ascent to divine truth, nothing—neither its center, the human observer, nor God, its pinnacle—has a "natural" place that can now reveal its meaning. All that then remains is the vaguely intuited "godlikeness" that both the narrator of the *Pensées* and Milton's Adam can define only in terms of disparity. In dissolving yet also retracing the traditional relationship between God and man, such seekers also require a reaccommodated symbolic language somehow "commensurable" with the relative dimensions of this expanding space. In the new scientific age, the only legitimate language has become the Cartesian analysis or calculus of signs, which as Foucault observes "is to thought and to signs what algebra is to geometry: it replaces the simultaneous comparison of parts (or magnitudes) with an order whose degrees must be traversed one after another. It is in this strict sense that language is an *analysis* of thought: not a simple patterning, but a profound establishment of order in space."[4] Since allegory is not necessarily precluded from this analytic language, it usually responds either by restricting allegorical patterning to a humbler comparison of "magnitudes," with the result that, as in neoclassicism, it becomes a mere ornament or metaphoric commonplace, or, alternatively, by rationally expanding its large-scale comparisons to the point of ironic rupture or "incommensurability." The latter technique, that of baroque allegory, uses this rupture to locate its rational/irrational "certitude" in the beyond: in the inaccessibly higher but relatively *calculable* logic of infinite truth, which is also the vanishing point where its numinous aura reemerges.

Thus, the underlying assumption of the present work (one that can be fully demonstrated only through further investigations of the seventeenth-century context) is that allegories of this and later periods will tend to adopt neoclassical techniques when their animating plot, idea, or argument (here understood as different aspects of the allegorical design) is grounded in the new certitudes established by rational empiricism and its banishment of incalculable mysteries. In contrast, baroque allegory conserves these uncertainties by pushing the rationalist program to its own logical breaking point. Borrowing the trajectory of Pascal's "double infinities," Milton's paradoxical "Union or Communion" with the divine begins within the commonplace space/time of earthly computation but ends in an immanent "union" with the infinite space/time where God dwells in his "secrecy alone." This union therefore represents an imaginative, not an ecstatic, transcendence. The summit of its paradoxical "progress" is then imaged, not as the top of a vertical ladder, but, as Hugh Davidson remarks of the *Pensées,* as some infinitely displaced point attained through the ladderless force of inspiration. This irregular vanishing point therefore "ruins" the processes of normative allegory, where "Battles and victories, inventions and productions, inclinations and insights, kinds of brilliance and greatness all vary according to the [predestined] order, each being knowable to or accessible to a particular human faculty." Yet here, "When intellectual problems must be solved, sparks that bridge the gaps between the orders make explanations possible."[5]

While Milton was hardly a mathematician let alone a systematic philosopher to the same extent as Pascal, his work in theology, logic, rhetoric, and poetry would have made him aware of the radical ambiguity and ultimately unknowable or "indecidable" order inherent in language itself.[6] Moreover, as his slighting of neoclassical in favor of baroque allegory suggests, he regards these ambiguities as "benignly" incapable of being concealed, restrained, or exaggerated. Since irony represents the most extreme degree of ambiguity, it then seems safe to say that the poetics of incertitude (of which baroque allegory is a primary instance) will feature a far greater incidence of ironic paradoxes and equivocations than either the neoclassical or normative form, where they will be either restrained or concealed as mystical adumbrations of a ritually accessible sense of the divine. From this observation follows a second and less obvious corollary, that the undecidability of this mode does not make the mode in itself undecidable. In other words, "ruined allegory" should not be taken as ruining the enterprise of literary interpretation, the proper concern of which is primarily to ascertain the scope, limits, and design of a work's metaphoric range, much as I have attempted to do here. Because *Paradise Lost* cannot be consistent with itself does not mean that it cannot be made generally consistent with a mode featuring the uses of irony outlined above, nor do these ironies fail to support certain conjectures about the poet's intentions. This last point leads to my final and by now I would hope obvious corollary, that neither his intentionals nor his irony indicate that this paradigm of seventeenth-century style promotes the creation of "self-consuming" literary artifacts, a form that (contra Fish) is much better identified with the mystical and transcendental poetics of the Augustinian "now." Instead, its infinitely receding vanishing points attempt to conserve a unified and at least liminally sacred cosmos through a radically temporalized form of poetic and historical accommodation.

Yet, as Milton's poetic invocations and the stated ambitions of his prose alike suggest, this project involves both deconstruction and reconstruction, beginning with a decentering of earlier sacred and heroic "types" that (much like its critique of Cartesian rationalism) proceeds from within their very midst. In order to write a work "doctrinal to a nation" that would "repair the ruines of our first parents" (*CPW,* 1:810–15, 2:366–67), like his own Samson the poet must pull the pillars of the old temples down in ruins around his own head—as Marvell's dedicatory verse ironically yet prophetically suggests. In the epic itself, the climactic moment of this agon is reached in the jarring invocation to book 9, which gloomily rehearses Milton's earlier doubts about the future of English epic, considering the "advers climat, or the fate of this age" (*CPW,* 1:814). From here, just as ironically, he will denounce the entire tradition of heroic poetry in which he writes—and whose conclusion he prophetically announces. Because the "Races and Games" (*PL,* 9.33) of Virgil have become as outmoded as the "gorgeous Knights" (9.36) of Spenser, he attempts a new "Subject for Heroic Song" whose continuities with the past nonetheless remain apparent both in its "long choosing" (9.25–26) and in its careful recasting in classical twelve-book form. Yet this potentially "ruinous" "attempt" (words thereafter heavily freighted with satanic connotations) declared in the first invocation marks a point of rupture in which these old songs must be sung in a new key, from an ultimately ladderless point of inspiration that burns the old bridges behind them. As demonstrated in the preceding chapter, this highly iconoclastic and self-reflexive literate sensibility is in one sense liberating; but it is also conducive to a melancholy ambivalence about the sacrifices inherent in such liberation. Through Michael's lessons, Adam gains a fuller apprehension of the signs of the "track Divine," yet at the same time loses the full presence of God's "blest count'nance" (11.316–17). These liabilities parallel those surrounding the poet's own struggle to identify himself with a nameless and potentially dangerous muse—should she or he prove "erroneous."[7]

Even more sobering is the poem's replacement of synchrony with diachrony, which demands "True patience, and to temper joy with fear / And pious sorrow, equally inur'd / By moderation either state to bear" (*PL*, 11.361–63). While Adam and Eve thus achieve a self-determination that, like Samson's, is capable of bearing "either state" that history may impose, such gains proceed from the loss of Edenic synchrony, tranquil growth, and effortless interpretive advance. In this sense, *Paradise Lost* is also an allegory of orality lost, a saga detailing the journey whereby the concrete communal hierarchies and fixed symbols of traditional allegory are replaced with an allegory of reading in a "wand'ring" world situated somewhere indeterminately between the demands of reason and grace. Here, a dimension of divine truth and reality remains, but not one immediately accessible to Adam, Eve, or the narrative voice. When in the poem's final simile the Cherubim assume "thir fixt Station" in obedience to the divine command, they appear to the human couple obliquely, as agents of a baroquely disappearing place and time. "Gliding metereous, as Ev'ning Mist," they are ambiguously poised between a river and its "marish" ground, which appropriately threatens to confuse the footsteps of a symbolic "Laborer" seeking but not yet finding his home (12.626–32). Thus, if Adam and Eve are dismissed from Eden "not disconsolate" (11.113), theirs is a strikingly qualified kind of consolation.

While Pascal's response to the exigencies of reading the signs of a radically random universe is more explicitly pessimistic than Milton's, it also reveals a similarly ambiguous affirmation of potential recuperation. As suggested earlier, the differences between the two are those of degree, not kind: if Milton's affirmation of rational grace

is tenuously couched in less negative terms than Pascal's, both con-
struct a dialectical synthesis of negation/affirmation that grounds
faith in doubt and presence in absence. In this synthesis, reason is at
once accepted and rejected as a means of Christian certitude. The
Miltonic form of this skeptical rationalism regards reason as poten-
tially impure except when informed by the intuition of free grace,
while, in the Pascalian version, its ultimate, although by no means
only, "strength" lies in succumbing to its own weakness in the leap of
faith. As in the case of Adam and Eve, this renunciation of certitude
requires a compensatory embrace of the temporal cycle, which in
turn implies a loss of spatial or sacramental "centering." Yet both
theodicies manage to extract victory from defeat by foregrounding a
man/God dichotomy that supplies the paradoxical basis of a re-
newed form of human/ divine accommodation. This common strat-
egy is best illustrated in the section of the *Pensées* appropriately
entitled "Contradiction":

A good portrait can only be made by reconciling all our contradictory
features, and it is not enough to follow through a series of mutually com-
patible qualities without reconciling their opposites; to understand an
author's meaning all contradictory passages must be reconciled. Thus to
understand Scripture a meaning must be found which reconciles all contra-
dictory passages; it is not enough to have one that fits a number of compat-
ible passages, but one which reconciles even contradictory ones. . . . If we
take the law, the sacrifices and the kingdom for realities, these passages
cannot all be reconciled; it necessarily follows that they are only figurative.[8]

Milton's consideration of God's figurative physiognomy or "por-
trait" is stated in reverse order but produces essentially the same
result. At first insisting that the features of the divine face described
in his revealed Word are not contradictory when taken literally, he
also argues that this very literalism suggests a radical dichotomy
between our perceptions and divine realities, for, "when we talk about
knowing God, it must be understood in terms of man's limited pow-
ers of comprehension. God as he really is, is far beyond man's imagi-
nation, let alone his understanding." Yet later he concludes that the
divine being is best understood synthetically—as a being whose literal
and figurative levels of representation at least relatively or probably
correspond. Thus, we ought "to form an image of God in our minds
which corresponds to his representation such a conception of him, as
he, in condescending to accommodate himself to our capacities, has

shown that he desires we should conceive." We can only accomplish this through a rationalist approach to the Scriptures, considering that they "contain nothing unsuitable to the character or dignity of God, and that God should say nothing of himself which could derogate from his own majesty" (*CD,* 14:31–33). Yet this theological accommodation produces only a nominally concrete, not a real, assessment of God's nature, for "since [given that] it has no causes, we cannot define the 'divine nature'" (*CPW,* 6:137). At this point, Milton turns to a discursive sifting of God's nominal features, a process that closely parallels Pascal's tactic of opposing literal to figurative meaning. While he ultimately concludes that Truth and Spirit are the essential divine attributes, his reversal of their scriptural order in John 4:24 suggests that, like Pascal, he regards the quality of Truth in a sufficiently naturalistic and affirmative sense that it needs no qualification or even explanation. In contrast, Spirit becomes a concept capable only of negative definition: "What a spirit is, or rather what it is not, is shown Isa. xxxi.3. 'flesh, and not spirit.' Luke xxiv. 39. 'a spirit does not have flesh and bones'" (*CPW,* 6:140).

Milton thus seems to regard God's truth as unproblematically analogous to rational human figuration but his Spirit as approachable only through rational defiguration. These two attributes, Truth and Spirit, then become paradigmatic for all the rest, which fall into two categories: those that are described in an affirmative and those described in a negative sense. The latter are necessary in that they show that God is not imperfect as created things are, the former in that they "show his divine power and excellence under the ideas of VITALITY, INTELLIGENCE, and WILL" (*CD* 14:53–55). Like truth, these latter qualities present no problem for the human interpreter, who shares them in a parallel if lesser sense, so at this point Milton produces only a catalog of scriptural citations. This procedure of implicitly, if not overtly, setting literal against figurative and affirmative against synthetically negative/affirmative statements about God can thus be seen to be in substantial harmony with Pascal's more cryptic but scarcely less dialectical strategy of accommodation. In each case, the solution attests to the continuity of the problem: now, the observer, not an allegory of nature, bears witness to the existence of a God who can at once be discovered inside and outside the human subject but who is at last incommensurably absent and present to himself alone. In the relativistic universe, reason thus produces the contradictory "benefit" of secure calculation only within an uncertain, underlying disparity, which in turn calls for a redefinition of how the human subject acts as the imago dei. Although both reason and rational freedom continue to identify man as the godlike not-God, now this identification is additionally based on the mutual alienation of man and deity from an infinite creation that can properly "contain" neither. Where even the trace of the track divine has in its infinite wisdom also become infinitely incommensurable, the task of the subject is similarly "Other": at once to calculate the precise figurative and literal boundaries of representation and to transcend them by approximating the incalculable coordination of the Spirit whose calculus this is.

Indeterminacies paralleling those of spiritual interpretation also define the limits of human representation, which, to achieve the most reliable approximations, depends on similar incommensurabilities, as Milton's multiple invocations of the "nameless" Urania attest. Thus, following the logic of Pascal's *Dieu caché*, her unfolding of his hidden ways ultimately becomes accessible only through an admission of the weakness of reason and representation alike. Yet, ironically, this experience of loss and gain also demands the most rigorous exercise of rational freedom, for only through this exercise is poet or philosopher able to enter the ruptured realm where man, Pascal's "thinking reed" or Milton's "suddenly apprehending" Adam, encounters God. Since his providential ways are to be adored and searched not only after they have been rationally researched, as Adam's dialogues with God illustrate, this dialectical inquiry leads finally to an obscure apprehension of his reflection of God's infinitely secret "aloneness," the process wherein he is "deifi'd." Immanent means thus become more important than transcendent ends, which are now projected beyond the vanishing point of human vision. Since they now occupy no place or pinnacle but only an empty space within a universe composed of motion, time, and relativity, the necessary and unavoidable calculus of the double infinities outlines but cannot even obscurely translate a divine hermeneutics. As Pascal observes, this means that, on the one hand, "it is on thought which we must depend for our recovery" (200) and, on the other, that this recovery lies outside: "Be comforted; it is not from yourself that you must expect it, but on the contrary you must expect it by expecting nothing from yourself" (202).

In this respect, Pascal's "disproportionate" man closely parallels the fallen and semiredeemed Adam of *Paradise Lost*, who similarly has cause to be both comforted and humbled by his partially restored dialogue with God. Yet, initially, his ability to approach God's understanding of the true dimensions of nature serves only to distance him from both since, as Pascal observes, in the newly trackless wilderness of the world, he is both more and less than a mere dot, a point finally impossible to fix once "nature is an infinite sphere whose center is everywhere and circumference nowhere." This ironic echo of Nicholas of Cusa also establishes our distance from all earlier conceptions of infinity once rationalization and alienation increase in geometric proportion to one another: "Anyone who considers himself in this way will be terrified at himself, and, seeing his mass, as given him by nature, supporting him between these two abysses of infinity and nothingness, will tremble at these marvels." Yet, while Pascal argues that the proper attitude toward this limitless extension is silence, he himself is not silent since he immediately proposes a standpoint from which the subject may view himself, so long as he contents himself with balancing deductive negations against inductive affirmations: "For, after all, what is man in nature? A nothing compared to the infinite, a whole compared to the nothing, a middle point between all and nothing, infinitely remote from an understanding of the extremes; the end of things and their principles are unattainably hidden from him in impenetrable secrecy" (199).

Viewed from the perspective of the "nothing," the midpoint who is man is ignorant, lost, terrified by the incomprehensibility of infinite spaces. Yet, when viewed from the perspective of the whole, he becomes the ground of the rational reintegration the narrator himself demonstrates, arriving at a positive, if ironic, recognition of his "place" in the disintegration of an infinite, as opposed to a finite, chain of being. Although man is trapped in this eternal circulation of space and time, his knowledge of the infinite creation of atoms from nothingness and their infinite retreat into the future still allows him "mathematically" to project the formal whole that must underlie their functioning, the equation that "fixes" the predictable infinitude of their permutations in the incomprehensible unity of the hidden God. Thus, Pascal remarks that just as Euclidean geometry has been made obsolete by the discoveries of the new mechanics, this mechanics, too, will become obsolete once a truly "adequate" geometry of infinity. This conjecture allows him to conclude that an adequate calculus must lie neither in Aristotelian realism nor in Cartesian nominalism but in the displacement and reconstruction of each.

The chief feature of this reconstruction is the heterogeneous, self-canceling element of endless disproportion, the element of zero. It is the element that puts into play the dialectical process in which, as de Man observes, "the homogeneity of the universe is recovered, and the principle of infinitesimal symmetry is well established. But this has happened at a price: the coherence of the system is now seen to be entirely dependent on the introduction of an element—the zero and its equivalences in time and motion—that is itself entirely heterogeneous with regard to the system and is nowhere part of it."[9]

Yet, if nominalism produces a chart of signs and of their infinite reproduction without either a terminus or (in Realist terms) a meaning, in contrast, Pascal's skeptical rationalism proves that "real" meaning, understood as knowledge of true proportions and limits, is the negation of the partial meanings generated by whole numbers and their linguistic equivalent, determinate signs. A solution to the crisis of signs is thereby achieved, but only outside a binary sign system based on regular divisibility and replication. Since infinitely divisible signs and numbers are alike incalculable as wholes, all that remains calculable is the juncture between their endless permutations and the unity of real wholes or essences. Somewhere (but also nowhere) in this juncture stands man, in his duality conceivable to himself only as the inverse of that point where these dichotomies are healed, in God. By deriving "infinite" but also godlike incertitude from certitude, Pascal stands the Cartesian cogito on its head; here, rational dialectic is what allows man to analyze the universe but also what sets him apart from it and God, who now becomes central rather than peripheral to the whole (as he is in Descartes).[10] Yet, in this respect, man's thought in some way also "centers" creation, even if, from the standpoint of his own disparity, it produces only a negative assurance: "Man is to himself the greatest prodigy in nature, for he cannot conceive what body is, and still less what mind is, and least of all how a body can be joined to a mind." Thus, his knowledge must be regarded as a series of empty metaphors in pursuit of what is at once a *cosmos,* a *deus* and a *cogito absconditus:* "For it is impossible for the part of us which reasons to be anything but spiritual, and even if it were claimed that we are simply corporeal, that would still more preclude us from knowing things, since there is nothing so inconceivable as the idea that matter knows itself. We cannot possibly know how it could know itself" (199). The human condition, then, contains an infinitely double disparity at its center: an incapacity to attain real knowledge of the "two abysses of infinity and nothing-ness," which parallels the infinity and nothingness of its spiritual and material elements, God and man or soul and body.

Yet this mournful perception ultimately pits dualism against itself in order to reconceive the mind as its own incommensurable yet very real "place," like God chiefly in knowing that it has no place and, further, that places themselves have no necessary limits—that nature, for instance, does not abhor a zero or a vacuum. The similarity of Pascal's critique of the fundamental binarism of the Classic Age to the epistemological decentering at work in Milton's prose theology is thus once again strong but not absolute. Pascal similarly regards reason as the necessary but not sufficient condition of salvation since it is at once free and bound, caused and uncaused, material and immaterial. In poetic terms, as J. B. Savage points out, these sim-ilarly paradoxes become "the crux of the [epic] poem" since there is no unitary possibility of resolving them. Although Savage criticizes Milton for making us "swallow the notion that, in one sense he [Adam] is 'free' to sin or not to sin, but in another, not 'free' should he sin," this defining disproportion is precisely what situates his freedom between infinity and nothingness or, more concretely, be-tween the "incommensurable good" of God and the more "commen-surate" finitude of creation for him embodied in Eve. The contradic-tion to which Savage's "Cartesian" logic objects can then be seen as a productively tautological definition of Adam's existence, for "what 'seems' real about Adam himself . . . comes to constitute his real, existential nature, even if it is not his *essential* nature as determined by God. . . . Likewise, his freedom, which was possible only in ad-herence to God, which was metaphysical in that it was conferred in proportion to his transcendence of a world of appearances, becomes theoretical, incapable of realization." Yet this insuperable contra-diction between the laws of time (or choice) and physical necessity (or causality) creates the very horizon in which decentered human agency not only consists but in which it is also realigned with the "absent" trace of the "track divine."[11] Here, as Milton warns, "not only is it impossible to know God with nature or reason," but *even with the assistance of his word* it is impossible to comprehend accu-rately *under any form* of definition the 'divine nature'" (*CD*, 14:31).

Like Pascal's, Milton's reason is thus ultimately a "figure," a hu-man analytic or discursive calculus that can darkly shadow but not illumine its displaced reflection of the divine. In this portrait, "Figure includes absence and presence, pleasant and unpleasant. Cipher with a double meaning, of which one is clear and says that the meaning is hidden" (265). Yet Pascal's God also remains humanly knowable as the distant corollary or cipher of the human condition, an answering echo of its absence, a vanishing point at the juncture of the incommensurable oppositions where the double infinities meet or, as the *Christian Doctrine* postulates, where "the singular and plural of this word [God] both mean the same thing" (*CD*, 14:53). Not surprisingly, then, both Pascal and Milton accommodate God to man in the baroque language of wandering, evanescence, and trace, evident not only in Adam's final "wandring steps and slow" (*PL*, 12.648) but in the parallel allusions that the *Pensées* (here given in French to preserve the qualitative nature of its "figures") makes to man as

un étrange monstre, et un égarement bien visible. Le voilà tombé de sa place. . . . (131)

L'homme ne sait à quel rang se mettre. Il est visiblement égaré, et tombé de son vrai lieu sans le pouvoir retrouver. (312)

En voyant . . . l'homme sans lumière, abandonné à lui-même et comme égaré dans ce recoin de l'univers. . . . (389)[12]

In also drawing on the same dark/bright vocabulary that permeates Milton's epic, Pascal's contradictory light figures—*lumière, éclat, clarté, ténèbre,* and *obscurité*—employ the same oxymoronic rhetoric that finally counterpoises Satan's monstrous "darkness visible" to God's "dark with excessive bright," the double vanishing points that we establish the incommensurable poles of the Miltonic universe.

In the revised allegory of interpretation that these images construct, God no more fills man's emptiness than does nature itself. While natural revelation is necessary, it is also necessarily inadequate since, as Pascal remarks, "There are perfections in nature to show that she is the image of God and imperfections to show that she is no more than his image" (934). No longer reflecting so much as refracting a God whose very existence is situated in the gap between necessity and freedom, justice and mercy, or damnation and election, nature tells us only that, "if there is a God, he is infinitely beyond our comprehension since, being indivisible and without limits, he bears no relation to us." Yet, as observed above, these negations do not preclude but reorient the subject's traditional quest for God as a path or progress no longer guided by mystical symbols and analogies. Now a largely self-guided, virtually "blind" pilgrimage without clearly definable means or ends, the search for divine truth here becomes less a positive attainment than an exercise and the narrative hero of this search less its vehicle than its potentially "erroneous" victim. As Pascal exclaims, "If my words please you and seem cogent, you must know that they come from a man who went down upon his knees before and after to pray this infinite and indivisible being, to whom he submits his own, that he might bring your being also to submit to him for your own good and for his glory: and that strength might thus be reconciled with lowliness" (*Pensées*, "The Wager," 418). This dialectical process replaces a stable ladder or grid of signs with a perspectival field centered on the subject's own standpoint. As Sara Melzer explains, here the subject instead experiences a "blank" echo of truth within which "the [narrator's] shifts in perspective play out the movement of a fall from truth into error. The readers seek to locate a perspective of truth in order to arrange the parts in a hier-archical structure that will provide an interpretative key. No sooner do the readers posit a hierarchical model, however, than it rotates on its own axis, undoing the old one, illuminating its error, and forming a new one. In this way, the text thwarts the attempts of reason to grasp its essential meaning, thus subverting the order of reason."[13] Caught in these multiple rotations, like Milton, Pascal cannot cele-brate the mortal consequences of the Fall as "fortunate" even in the highly paradoxical sense outlined in the previous chapter, although both ultimately find it obscurely enabling.

For much the same reasons, both mystical withdrawal and empiri-cal euphoria are framed as invalid or inauthentic responses to the human condition.[14] Like Milton's Adam, Pascal's man has been plunged into a blinding darkness ("les ténèbres qui l'aveuglent, . . . la mortalité et . . . les misères qui l'affligent" [149]). In these circum-stances, his partial vision can be retained only by strenuously scan-ning the elusive ground of truth that will at times utterly fail him unless supplemented by the spirit. Yet, even in Pascal's most gloomy fragment, where the "voice" of man is humbled by the muse-like voice of wisdom (in Milton's epic, the "sister" of Urania), the slender thread leading from nature to truth is never wholly severed since men "retain some feeble instinct from the happiness of their first nature," even when "plunged into the wretchedness of their blindness and concupiscence, which has become their second nature" (149). Hence, by going beyond himself, by seeking the trace that leads from fallen nature back to this remaining "feeble instinct," man can regain the "beyond" of his other nature. Not all will choose this path, but it is there for any who wish to see it: "There is enough light for those who desire only to see, and enough darkness for those of a contrary disposition." Yet, instead of a Calvinist doctrine of election, this "light" implies salvation by choice and rational endeavor as much as by grace, although by neither alone. Milton's *Christian Doctrine* records a very similar if somewhat more optimistically or "Arminianly" inflected viewpoint: "The unwritten law is the law of nature given to the first man. A kind of gleam or glimmering of it still remains in the hearts of all mankind. In the regenerate this is daily brought nearer to a renewal of its original perfection by the operation of the Holy Spirit" (*CPW,* 6:516). Called not outside but within human time, and implicated in a ceaseless dialectic of truth and error, the freedom of the elect is thus maintained within a particularly opaque version of revelation history.

As the site of a "baroque" struggle within and without, semi-ignorant, alone, but still mysteriously participating in the divine will, the seeker must test himself in every sphere of action, his attention directed exclusively neither to spiritual nor to secular things. In order to demonstrate that the truth has set him free, like Milton himself he must therefore strive to "become a true poem, that is, a composition and patterne of the best and honorablest things—not presuming to sing high praises of heroick men or famous Cities, unless he have in himselfe the experience and the practice of all that is praiseworthy" (*An Apology, CPW,* 1:890). Once again, we find a similar ethic in Milton's Adam, who, in awakening to life, spontaneously realizes the theomorphism or godlikeness of his shape and nature, which all but immediately leads him to recognize that he must have come there, "Not of myself; by some great Maker then" (*PL,* 8.278). This height of self-knowing is largely analogical and commensurate with God's great analogizing Idea of him as magnanimous in his rational correspondence with heaven, which even in its disparity is dialogically realized by the mysteriously deifying potential of the "spirit within" (8.440). Yet at the other end of self-knowledge lies Adam's embarrassed mention to Raphael that the sexual "touch" of Eve, who embodies both his likeness and God's, "somehow" disorders and subordinates his reason to passion if not concupiscence. This discreet but accurate displacement of the sexual act onto that universal component of all language, the press of a signifying thing on its signified, constitutes a physical metonymy that delicately conveys the negative touchstone of what humanly it means to be endowed with godlike reason within an intransigently material/figural condition.

So considered, *touch* supplies a characteristically indeterminate correlative of the capacity of language for divine accommodation, for Raphael cannot discredit this power that he would have the unfallen Adam subordinate to his higher reason—which effectively and essentially turns out to be the power of displaced analogizing. Here, we are presented with a circular but not therefore despairing cycle. If touch is in every sense the fundamental apperceptive sensation giving rise to figure, its linguistic movement can take place only self-referentially, that is, through the analogizing of something like metonymy itself—the signifying by contiguity or causal process. If touch is metonymy, and the metonymic is the diachronic, then touch is the grounding metonymy of a history inexplicable or meaningless except in relation to the absent "presence" that Adam is inevitably drawn to seek, the temporal presence of God's trace in the invisible voice or in Eve. Yet, if after the Fall "meaningfulness" emerges at the other side of this process, from the metonymic depth of a lost Eden, it can do so only by virtue of the language of self-reference (as in Descartes's master analogy) in this case (or in this revision of the Cartesian cogito) supplemented by grace. In the final books of *Paradise Lost*, this figure of grace appears in the "impressions" mediated by "one who is like God," which both literally and figuratively is the archangel Michael, here both the meaning and the name the poet summons. Yet, insofar as it tends toward globalizing constructions, all such "theomorphizing" language is inescapably entrammeled in a type of self-referentiality that we now know cannot be free from self-contradiction.

The larger aspects of this matter will be considered in later work on the canonical function of the "zerocentric" paradigm, but here it must be added that the inherent constraints of self-reference alike exploited both by Gödel's postmodern theorems and by baroque allegory are also evident in the signifying axiomatics of "poetic" touch itself. If allegorical narration is seen—as it ought to be—as an extension of analogy, then it is as limited and as free as the displacement of the multiple senses of touch (impression, trace, sign, or—in the sexual sense—ultimate identity), for in this sense it is confined by the inherent limitations of similitudinous language to perform a simultaneous comparison of disparate parts or magnitudes. But, if as a symbolic language, allegory may be used to analyze comparisons "whose degrees must be traversed one after another" (as Foucault's study of the Classic Age suggests it now must), then it can also be made to function as a logical language demonstrating the fact that extended analogies cannot be pushed too far before their coherence and intelligibility, qua analogy, break down. In normative allegory, this problem is avoided through a sequence of interchanges that constantly relay their comparisons yet they are finally deferred onto a projected center of static closure or transcendence. But, in ruined or baroque allegory, the strategy is precisely the opposite: by pushing the analogy until it does break down into a form of meta-allegorical or self-referential irony, the reader finally descends into an immanent but also semierased presence. Thus, for both Milton and Pascal, the incommensurabilities generated by this process are godlike since they at once ascend to an elevation of divine power as intuitive apprehension or pure poesis and a descent into the deductive figurations necessary to morphic man. "Making a creation like to Gods" (*Animadversions, CPW*, 1:721) is how Milton describes the effects of embracing these poles, which makes his role as poet possessed of an *ad extra* grace, a poetics creatively accessible to us by way of his succession of implied, stated, and incommensurable similitudes.

If it is true that poetry is written best out of its own constraining limits, then Milton's poem "succeeds" because its allegory transcends the limits of an extended theomorphic analogy that would have lost its original way had not the analogy of the poet as godlike creator been extended beyond the logical limits that it probes. By descending back into the primacy of metonymy as the formal basis of analogy, the poem's metaphoric basis is also analogically enlarged. It achieves this enlargement by deriving the coherence, intelligibility, and power of its gropings by touch or tact from a history of things conceived as continuous with God's providence as the internal form of matter: an *ex deo* pattern or design secretly encoded within the innermost level of reality's resemblances. At that level, the level at which Milton submits his allegory to the apparent incoherence and unintelligibility of reality, he has indeed created his new and "advent'rous song," something hitherto unattempted in prose or rhyme. In thereby foreseeing the end of the culture that produced it, Milton's poem also proleptically foreshadows its own ruin, the ruin of a theological meaning that could still survive as a species of aesthetic meaningfulness, its form as much as its content carrying a weight of significance that transforms its original intentionality. Thus, one consequence of its loss of certainty is an access of richness in the possibilities of its reading—to which the richness of commentary we have reviewed testifies. Yet the epic "catalog" of a culture of modernity to which Milton's poem testifies in Wittgenstein's sense, in its own sense fulfills the obscure prophecy of "Lycidas." Fusing the pagan gods and the "old bards" of the "famous *Druids*" (line 53) who are being left behind with "Lycidas," the victim both of the failure of church reformation and of ritual depletion, the swain "gathers up" their culture with a "twitch" of "his mantle blue," synthesizing it into a new "Genius of the shore," then, like Adam and Eve, departing in search of "fresh Woods, and Pastures new" (line 183, 192–93).

It is not true, however, that on these terms *Paradise Lost* is comprehensible to very few, as Wittgenstein imagined such a poem would be. As a sort of elegiac valediction to certainty itself (now only the trace of that elusive presence), Milton's poem is probably the last of the great allegorical epics born at the dawn of our civilization and the first of an entirely new genre, of which Joyce's *Ulysses* and *Finnegan's Wake*—or even the poetry of Wallace Stevens, considered as a whole—are later examples. These are all works that look backward to archaic patterns for a formal meaningfulness that can be projected forward into an entropic void somehow capable of "negentropically" recovering a lost order out of chaos, as if any such ordering were a sign of cultural redemption. Unless we assume that such poetry, and *Paradise Lost* preeminently, serves only the light industrial purposes of ingrown academic communities dedicated to the survival of archaic artifacts brought forth from museum cases and aired at conferences without any real concern for the actual functions they persist in serving (as once they did when we read them as works of love), it may well be that only on such terms can we justify the increasingly Sphinx-like capacity of such poetry to survive. Survival is, as Auden said, a matter of speaking, becoming an alien mouth enigmatically and self-referentially uttering the future in the terms of the past. Yet Milton is not a Shakespeare and will never surprise us with the heartbreaking passion of a Lear or with the volatile nausea of a Troilus. He has his moments, to be sure—as when the natural sublime aura of the baroque most spectacularly shines. Here, he offers probably the most colossal literary example of the ultimate self-referentiality of our conceptions of God or, for that matter, of Satan as well. No culture can end and at the same time be reborn without reference to such monumental conceits or their surrogates, which fundamentally derive from the arrogance of the human mind patiently submitting the universe, both its beginnings and its ends, to its own self-justifying means.

Notes

Introduction

1 Thus, Marx argues that, *after* Milton sells his epic, he joins the world of alienated merchant capital (see Karl Marx, *Capital*, trans. Ben Fowkes [New York: Vintage, 1977], 1:1044). For a reading of "L'Allegro" and "Il Penseroso" along roughly these lines—as anticipating "the future of which they are at once the ground and product"—see Marshall Grossman, "The Fruits of One's Labor in Miltonic Practice and Marxian Theory," *ELH* 59 (1992): 98.

2 *Complete Prose Works of John Milton* (hereafter *CPW*), ed. Don M. Wolfe, 8 vols. (New Haven, Conn.: Yale University Press, 1953–82), 2:273. Unless otherwise noted, all quotations from the prose works are from this edition; citations to the *CPW* will hereafter be given in the text.

3 Walter Benjamin, *The Origin of German Tragic Drama*, trans. John Osborne (London: New Left, 1977), 178.

4 Claude Shannon's *Mathematical Theory of Communication* (Urbana: University of Illinois Press, 1959) defines anything that interferes with univocal meaning as "noise," but also makes it intrinsic to the feedback process of communication. Thus, as William Paulson explains, "To exclude noise from a closed communication system would be equivalent to excluding molecular movement from a closed system . . . ; it would be equivalent to excluding time" (*The Noise of Culture: Literary Texts in a World of Information* [Ithaca, N.Y.: Cornell University Press, 1988], 68)—or, one might add, the diachronic processes of meaningful speech.

5 *John Milton: Complete Poems and Major Prose*, ed. Merritt Y. Hughes (Indianapolis: Odyssey, 1957), *Paradise Lost*, 6.859–61. Unless otherwise noted, all quotations from the poetry are from this edition; citations will hereafter be given in the text (*PL* = *Paradise Lost; PR* = *Paradise Regained; SA* = *Samson Agonistes*).

6 On Spenser's typical technique of deferral and displacement, see Harry Berger Jr., *The Allegorical Temper: Vision and Reality in Book II of Spenser's "Faerie Queene"* (Hamden, Conn.: Archon, 1967). On allegory's debt to ritual and its construction of upwardly spiraling patterns of ascent without reintegration in normative allegory, see Angus Fletcher, *Allegory: The Theory of a Symbolic Mode* (Ithaca, N.Y.: Cornell University Press, 1964), esp. 151–80, and also his *The Prophetic Moment* (Chicago: University of Chicago Press, 1971).

7 In *The Order of Things*, Foucault also retraces some of the same intellectual/historical ground covered by Benjamin, although with a more ex-

tended discussion of the role played by resemblance and correspondence in the "triangular" hermeneutics of the Renaissance and the contrast of this hermeneutics with the binary system of resemblances dominating the Cartesian "Classic Age" of the seventeenth century. However, his neglect of the "intervention" of baroque allegory during this period renders his own history rather *too* cataclysmic, as a number of critics have complained. See, however, *The Order of Things: An Archaeology of the Human Sciences* (New York: Random House, 1970), 17–124.

8 See Ernest Sirluck's note to the passage (*CPW,* 2:549), noting that Milton seems to distinguish between Plutarch's allegory "On Isis and Osiris" and his own much more sharply than Sirluck does.

9 For an examination of Milton's epic theodicy, see Dennis R. Danielson, *Milton's Good God: A Study in Literary Theodicy* (Cambridge: Cambridge University Press, 1982). For studies of its place in the Cartesian revolution from a somewhat different (although not fundamentally incompatible) perspective from that provided here, see Stephen Fallon, *Milton among the Philosophers: Poetry and Materialism in Seventeeth-Century England* (Ithaca, N.Y.: Cornell University Press, 1991); and Harinder Singh Marjara, *Contemplation of Created Things: Science in "Paradise Lost"* (Toronto: University of Toronto Press, 1992).

10 The passage is self-referential in that Michael's indignation with "strict Laws" and ceremonies rather broadly hints at the Milton of the antiprelatical tracts; a similar interjection memorably occurs in the midst of *Lycidas*. For a similar reading of Milton's departure from mainline Christian Neoplatonism, see William G. Madsen's seminal study *From Shadowy Types to Truth: Studies in Milton's Symbolism* (New Haven, Conn.: Yale University Press, 1968). However, Madsen's view of Milton's anti-Platonism seems overstated, especially since in different form it was one of the guiding forces behind his Ramist logic (see chap. 1 below).

11 See John Carey and Alastair Fowler's edition both for a reproduction of the Trinity manuscript in which the full outline of this schema appears and for some pertinent remarks on how the contrast should encourage us to see *Paradise Lost* as "a tragical epic rather than a pure epic" (*The Poems of John Milton* [London: Longmans, Green, 1968], 419–22).

12 John Calvin, *Institutes of the Christian Religion,* ed. John T. McNeill, 2 vols. (Philadelphia: Westminster Press, 1960), 1.5.1, pp. 52–53; 1.5.14, p. 68.

13 On the centrally structuring roles played by the "daemons" of normative allegory, see Fletcher, *Allegory*. On the mythic origin of concepts of evil, see Paul Ricoeur, *The Symbolism of Evil,* trans. Emerson Buchanan (New York: Harper & Row, 1967).

14 See Mindele Anne Treip, *Allegorical Poetics and the Epic: The Renaissance Tradition to "Paradise Lost"* (Lexington: University of Kentucky Press, 1994), 126–28.

15 *Objectivist* here is a much more accurate term than the *rationalism* often associated with the Enlightenment, for there are many kinds of rational-

isms, although the *dominant* standard of the seventeenth century also proved to be that of the eighteenth: that set by Cartesian objectivism, mechanism, and/or positivism. For a good summary of the influence of Eliot and Leavis and their politics on the great "Milton controversy" as well as the political implications of neoclassicism itself, see David Norbrook, *Poetry and Politics in the English Renaissance* (London: Routledge & Kegan Paul, 1984), 1–17. For a reading of Milton's *Samson Agonistes* as a rejection or an "overthrow" of the standards of Hobbes's Cartesian calculus, see my essay "The Phoenix and the Crocodile: The Dialectic of Hobbesian Contract and Miltonic Covenant in *Samson Agonistes*," in *The Literature of the English Civil Wars*, ed. Claude Summers and Ted-Larry Pebworth (Columbia: University of Missouri Press, 1998).

16 See esp. Paul de Man, "The Rhetoric of Temporality," in *Blindness and Insight* (Minneapolis: University of Minnesota Press, 1983); and Fredric Jameson, "Magical Narratives," in *The Political Unconscious* (Ithaca, N.Y.: Cornell University Press, 1981). On the seventeenth-century discrimination between emblem and impresa, see Barbara K. Lewalski, *Protestant Poetics and the Seventeenth-Century Religious Lyric* (Princeton, N.J.: Princeton University Press, 1979), 182–83.

17 However, the Romantic and neoclassical approaches often overlap, as they do in Anne Davidson Ferry's seminal study *Milton's Epic Voice: The Narrator in "Paradise Lost"* (Cambridge, Mass.: Harvard University Press, 1963). Here, "fallen" allegory self-implodes in favor of "sacred symbols," an approach more recently echoed in the work of Stephen Fallon (in *Milton among the Philosophers*) and Maureen Quilligan (in *Milton's Spenser: The Politics of Reading* [Ithaca, N.Y.: Cornell University Press, 1983]). C. S. Lewis's approach is also obviously indebted to both traditions, i.e., to a Coleridgean emphasis on Milton's symbolic poetics as well as to a reinvigoration of the "privative" or "self-consuming" allegory of Augustinian tradition (*A Preface to "Paradise Lost"* [London: Oxford University Press, 1942]). The latter approach has been adopted to better effect by Stanley Fish (in *Surprised by Sin: The Reader in "Paradise Lost"* [Berkeley: University of California Press, 1971]) since he at least allows Milton to remain a Puritan, while Lewis was notoriously in danger of "converting" him into a high Anglican—something with which Coleridge has also been rightly charged. On this aspect of Coleridge's criticism, see Mary Ann Radzinowicz, "The Politics of *Paradise Lost*," in *Politics of Discourse: The Literature and History of Seventeenth Century England*, ed. Kevin Sharpe and Stephen Zwicker (Berkeley and Los Angeles: University of California Press, 1987).

18 For a contrary view, see Fallon, *Milton among the Philosophers*, 172–80, who argues that allegory necessarily declines with the waning of the tradition of philosophical realism and the rise of neoclassicism. However, as Treip points out in *Allegorical Poetics and the Epic*, 106–8, the neoclassical objections to personified abstractions seems chiefly to have influenced such unsuccessful epic productions such as those of Davenant and Cowley.

19 Note that here, as throughout the following work, *Realism*, like *Independency*, refers to a proper noun, respectively a philosophical and political movement or faction. For a useful overview of the various contemporary theological positions on style (ranging from the high Anglican's affirmation of classical learning to the radical Puritan's rejection of it, with moderate Puritans and Independents midway between—although usually closer to the "low church" position), see Lewalski, *Protestant Poetics*, 219–26. For a more detailed overview of this shift, see Debora Shuger, *Habits of Thought in the English Renaissance* (Berkeley and Los Angeles: University of California Press, 1990). For a contemporary appropriation of a Lucretian "entropos," see Michel Serres, "Lucretius: Science and Religion," in *Hermes: Literature, Science, Philosophy*, ed. and trans. Josué Harrari and David F. Bell (Baltimore: Johns Hopkins University Press, 1982), 98–124.

20 The problem is essentially referable to the implications for semiotics and critical theory of Kurt Gödel's "undecidability" and "incompleteness" theorems of 1931, the most relevant reading for literary study being an essay by David Wayne Thomas, "Gödel's Theorem and Postmodern Theory," *PMLA* 110 (1995): 248–61.

21 Quoted from the prefatory verse included in Hughes, ed., *Complete Poems*, 209.

22 Gordon Teskey, *Allegory and Violence* (Ithaca, N.Y.: Cornell University Press, 1996), 8–11. See also his "Irony, Allegory, and Metaphysical Decay," *PMLA* 109 (1994): 397–408.

23 Fletcher, *Allegory*, 230.

24 See Northrop Frye, *Anatomy of Criticism: Four Essays* (Princeton, N.J.: Princeton University Press, 1957), esp. 90–92; and also Teskey's remarks, cited above. On the issue of authorial "instructions" as crucial to allegory, Teskey clearly sides with Frye (see chap. 1 below). The only "anatomy" of *Paradise Lost* so far produced is Barbara K. Lewalski's *"Paradise Lost" and the Rhetoric of Literary Forms* (Princeton, N.J. Princeton University Press, 1985), which is, in fact, a relatively unsystematic catalog of the poem's genres—and one that for its own idiosyncratic reasons (detailed below) eliminates allegory altogether.

25 William Empson, *The Structure of Complex Words* (London: New Directions, 1951), 346. One well-known application of this "double-plot" theory to *Paradise Lost* can be found in Geoffrey Hartman's "Milton's Counterplot," in *Beyond Formalism* (New Haven, Conn.: Yale University Press, 1970). On the ways in which the fourfold paradigm is both altered and conserved, see Shuger, *Habits of Thought in the English Renaissance*.

26 As to the first point, see Robert Scholes and Robert Kellogg, who argue that "typological significance precedes . . . moral (or 'tropological') significance" and inevitably shades into it (*The Nature of Narrative* [New York: Oxford University Press, 1966], 124). This point has been more recently substantiated in Jon Whitman's *Allegory: The Dynamics of an Ancient and*

Medieval Technique (Cambridge, Mass.: Harvard University Press, 1987); see chap. 1 below.

27 This example is not, however, unique to Milton since the image of the apocalypse and a "coelestiall Theater" also appears in Joseph Mede's *Key of the Revelation*, trans. Richard More (London, 1643).

28 See D. P. Walker, *The Decline of Hell: Seventeenth Century Discussions of Eternal Torment* (Chicago: University of Chicago Press, 1964); and Erich Auerbach, "Figura," reprinted in *Scenes from the Drama of Western Literature*, trans. Ralph Manheim (New York: Meridian, 1959).

29 See William Whitaker, *A Disputation on Sacred Scripture*, trans. William Fitzgerald (Cambridge: Parker Society, 1849), 405–8. On this historical sense of inwardness, Barbara Lewalski's conclusions support my own (see *Protestant Poetics*, 125–31); but, more generally, they support a far more restrictively typological reading of Protestant poetry than that maintained here. On the spirit of iconic fetishism that had flourished in England before Henry's break with the Church of Rome, see Eamon Duffy, *The Stripping of the Altars* (New Haven, Conn.: Yale University Press, 1992).

30 Thomas S. Kuhn, *The Structure of Scientific Revolutions* (Chicago: University of Chicago Press, 1962).

31 For some "prophetic" remarks, see Edwin A. Burtt, *The Metaphysical Foundations of Modern Physical Science* (London: Routledge & Kegan Paul, 1924), 80; and also chap. 2 below.

32 On the inspirational paradigm and its reliance on an *ad extra* grace, see Courtland Baker, "Certain Religious Elements in the Doctrine of the Inspired Poet," *ELH* 6 (1939): 309–10. On the principle of "emergent revelation" in the hermeneutical and political practices of Milton and his party, see Michael Fixler, *Milton and the Kingdoms of God* (Evanston, Ill.: Northwestern University Press, 1964), 119–21.

33 Marshall Grossman explores this aspect of *Paradise Lost* in *"Authors to Themselves": Milton and the Revelation of History* (Cambridge: Cambridge University Press, 1987).

34 See Jameson's "On Interpretation," in *The Political Unconscious*.

35 See Michael Fixler's suggestive studies of the inspirational invocations of *Paradise Lost* and the narrative segments each keys in "Plato's Four Furors and the Real Structure of *Paradise Lost*," *PMLA* 92 (1977): 952–62, "Milton's Passionate Epic," in *Milton Studies*, vol. 1, ed. James Simmonds (Pittsburgh: Pittsburgh University Press, 1969), 167–92, and "The Apocalypse within *Paradise Lost*," in *New Essays on "Paradise Lost*," ed. Thomas Kranidas (Berkeley: University of California Press, 1969).

36 See Angus Fletcher, *The Transcendental Masque: An Essay on Milton's "Comus"* (Ithaca, N.Y.: Cornell University Press, 1971), esp. 143–45, where Fletcher explores Milton's stylistic, structural, and allegorical debt to Shakespeare (a point that implicitly links his theory to Benjamin's baroque allegory).

37 For a discussion of the temporal orientation away from eternity in the Romantic genre, see my "On the Persistence of Quest-Romance in the Romantic Genre: The Strange Case of *Pamela,*" *Poetics Today* 12, no. 1 (1991): 87–109.

38 For the dominance of the "similarity thesis" (the Cartesian approach to objects) in the period before "agency theory" is philosophically revived by Kant, see Edward Craig, *The Mind of God and the Works of Man* (Oxford: Clarendon, 1987). For an examination of this strand of Neoplatonic thought, see D. P. Walker, *Spiritual and Demonic Magic from Ficino to Campanella* (London: Warburg and Courtauld Institute, 1958).

39 On Milton's "ethos of composition," see Thomas O. Sloane, "Rhetoric, 'Logic' and Poetry: The Formal Cause," in *The Age of Milton: Backgrounds to Seventeenth Century Literature,* ed. C. A. Patrides and Raymond B. Waddington (Totowa, N.J.: Barnes & Noble Books, 1980).

40 For an insightful treatment of sin as repetition, see R. A. Shoaf, *Milton, Poet of Duality: A Study of Semiosis in the Poetry and the Prose* (New Haven, Conn.: Yale University Press, 1985). On Milton's "literate style," see Walter J. Ong, *Interfaces of the Word: Studies in the Evolution of Consciousness and Culture* (Ithaca, N.Y.: Cornell University Press, 1977), 195–203.

1 Milton's Metamorphosis of Allegory

1 On Puritan "emergent revelation" as trace of God's Spirit in events, see the discussion of the claims for it by the Dissenting Brethren (with whom Milton was aligned) in the Westminster Assembly, in Fixler, *Milton and the Kingdoms of God,* 119–21. As I have argued elsewhere, this "covenantal" stance is even more obvious in *Samson Agonistes* (lines 1381–83), which most overtly fuses all four forms; see n. 15 of the introduction above and also chap. 2 below.

2 On Milton's choice of narrative, see Fallon, *Milton among the Philosophers,* 183. However, Fallon unfortunately overlooks how almost by definition this choice would demand some response to or revision of a standard epic-allegorical tradition. Thus, in following Addison's view of this tradition as favoring only a "dull moral" (p. 178), he projects an anachronistic neoclassical criterion on Milton's epic projects, which, as in the invocation to *Paradise Regained,* proclaim their moralizing intent to sing a new heroic ethic "worthy t'have not remain'd so long unsung" (line 17).

3 Fletcher, *Allegory,* 130. On *kosmoi,* a Greek spelling that Fletcher conserves to emphasize the original, double sense of the word as "world" and "ornament," see ibid., 125–33. On Milton's place in the "new subjectivism" casting the narrator as hero, see ibid., 243.

4 See Gordon Worth O'Brien, *Renaissance Poetics and the Problem of Power* (Chicago: Institute of Elizabethan Studies, 1956), 73–77. My interpretation of Nicholas makes him a somewhat more transitional figure than

O'Brien's, although, as I argue throughout, this transition anticipates the cataclysmic seventeenth-century paradigm shift that also irrevocably divides Milton from these forebears, including Spenser (see below).

5 Thus, rather than a dissection of abstract virtues in the manner of Spenser, the masque effectively pits the cosmic forces of Plato's Eros against Anteros or Empedocles' Love against Strife, although with their ordinary values dialectically synthesized since here personal strife provides the basis of authentic love of self and, in turn, of others. A similar transformation underlies Milton's allegorization of Eros and Anteros or plenitude and penury in the *Doctrine and Discipline of Divorce* (*CPW*, 2:254–58).

6 Sir Francis Bacon, *The Advancement of Learning*, in vol. 3 of *Works*, ed. James Spedding, Robert Ellis, and Douglas Heath, 14 vols. (London: Longman, 1858), 2.10.2.

7 See ibid., 3:485; and also O'Brien, *The Problem of Power*, chap. 1; and Fletcher, *Allegory*, 187–90.

8 William Righter, introduction to Gay Clifford, *The Transformation of Allegory* (London: Routledge & Kegan Paul, 1974), v. On the secular horizon of Milton's epic, see Keith F. W. Stavely, *Puritan Legacies: "Paradise Lost" and the New England Tradition, 1630–1890* (Ithaca, N.Y.: Cornell University Press, 1987). Although gradually waning, the old intellectual-historical tendency to regard the new science as producing a cultural crisis *toute court* (a misunderstanding and/or exaggeration of Donne's famous lament that the "New Philosophy calls all in doubt") is still too much with us. However, for a more balanced and innovative approach, see Alastair Fowler, *Time's Purple Masquers: Stars and the Afterlife in Renaissance English Literature* (New York: Oxford University Press, 1996).

9 See Foucault, *The Order of Things*, sec. 1.

10 See Joseph Hall, *The Invisible World* (1652; reprint, London: William Pickering, 1847), 59.

11 On the "participatory consciousness" that had earlier produced a habit of mind in which "firm boundaries and distinctions consistently blur into a semi-differentiated connectedness," see Shuger, *Habits of Thought in the English Renaissance*, 61. Her discussion of Lancelot Andrewes provides another excellent example of how this system was employed as well as of its incipient breakdown (see esp. 46–68). See also Walker, *Spiritual and Demonic Magic*. On the effects of the "I know not what," see Owen Felltham, "Of the Worship of Admiration" and "Of Poets and Poetry," both from *Resolves, Divine, Moral, and Political* (1623?) and reprinted in *Seventeenth Century Prose and Poetry*, ed. Alexander M. Witherspoon and Frank J. Warnke, 2d ed. (New York: Harcourt Brace, 1963), 320–21, 329–31. On Chomsky and the seventeenth-century quest for linguistic universals, see *History of Linguistic Thought and Contemporary Linguistics*, ed. Herman Parret (Berlin: Walter de Gruyter, 1976), 2–102, passim.

12 I am here making some concessions to modern usage; in more technical terms, Galilean method involved a process of resolving motion into its

component parts, which would then be recomposed by means of mathematical equations. As most historians of science agree, this method is crucial to the evolution of scientific method and modern philosophy alike; see esp. Ernest Cassirer, *The Individual and the Cosmos in Renaissance Philosophy*, trans. Mario Domandi (New York: Barnes & Noble, 1963).

13 John Rogers examines the formative role of this vitalism in *The Matter of Revolution* (Ithaca, N.Y.: Cornell University Press, 1996) in a much more univocal sense than that explored here. In general, he concludes that seventeenth-century vitalism inherently fosters the Republican goals and ideals of the age, even when adopted by such apparently opposing political thinkers as Milton, Hobbes, and Harvey. This would seem to apply the functionalist error that vitiates Talcott Parsons's understanding of the "Protestant ethic" (a pseudoentity no longer accepted by most modern sociologists as a meaningful unit) to the equally diverse conceptual resources and ramifications of vitalism. On the inherent instability of complex terms like *Protestantism* and *Puritanism* themselves, see Shuger's suggestive introduction to *Habits of Thought in the English Renaissance*. On the ambiguities surrounding Protestant ethic, see my "Self-Raised Sinners and the Spirit of Capitalism: *Paradise Lost* and the Critique of Protestant Meliorism," in *Milton Studies*, vol. 30, ed. Albert C. Labriola (Pittsburgh: University of Pittsburgh Press, 1994), 109–33.

14 See Treip, *Allegorical Poetics and the Epic*, 19–21, quoting from the *Epistolario di Coluccio Salutati*, ed. Francesco Novati, 4 vols. in 5 (Rome: Forzani e C. Tiografi del Senato, 1891–1911), vol. 4, pt. 1, 235, 238.

15 See Jurij Lotman, "Numerical Semantics and Cultural Types," in *Soviet Semiotics*, ed. David P. Lucid (Baltimore: Johns Hopkins University Press, 1977), 227–31.

16 See the title of chap. 16 in Heidegger, *Nietzsche*, vol. 1, ed. and trans. David Krell (San Francisco: Harper & Row, 1987).

17 For a historical overview of the conflict between representation ("similarity") and enactment ("agency") models of epistemology, see Craig, *The Mind of God*; and also the introduction above. For an extended discussion of the role of mathesis in the Cartesian revolution, see Foucault, *The Order of Things*. For a discussion of the icastic imagination, see Paul Stevens, who points out that, for Milton, the "imagination at its highest potential is not simply a necessary evil. . . . It is a God-given faculty which has a specific purpose in assisting man toward knowledge of his Maker. . . . [T]he *educated* imagination is the peculiar instrument of grace" ("Milton and the Icastic Imagination," in *Milton Studies*, vol. 20, ed. James Simmonds [Pittsburgh: Pittsburgh University Press, 1984], 44).

18 As I mean to indicate, Fletcher is here (*Allegory*, 125–33, as throughout his chapter "The Cosmic Image") particularly suggestive, although his work largely omits any extended consideration of the allegorical process in modern linguistic terms, notably either the Wittgensteinian modalities of saying and showing or their Heideggerian variants as enactment and

representation—the latter being particularly important to distinctions between different forms of the allegorical mode. This may be why he only impressionistically differentiates Milton from Spenser. For a more linguistically informed application of these dichotomies to the theory of allegory, see Teskey's *Allegory and Violence*, esp. chap. 1, which discusses the allegorical dialectic between "personification" (representation) and "capture" (enactment) (see p. 8).

19 On Benjamin's essential approach to baroque allegory, see *The Origin of German Tragic Drama*, 178; the introduction above; and also Teskey, *Allegory and Violence*, 4–5.

20 On Milton's continuing faith in these emergent revelations, as well as on his rejection of revolutionary apocalypticism, see Fixler, *Milton and the Kingdoms of God*.

21 Benjamin, *On the Origin of German Tragic Drama*, 138.

22 Frank Kermode brilliantly captures this aspect of *Paradise Lost* in "Adam Unparadised," in *The Living Milton* (London: Routledge & Kegan Paul, 1960).

23 See the *OED*, 14:335; and also Michael Fixler's entry on *ecclesiology* in the *Milton Encyclopedia*, ed. William B. Hunter (London: Associated University Presses, 1978), 190–203.

24 Although William B. Hunter ("The Provenance of the *Christian Doctrine*," *Studies in English Literature, 1500–1900* 32 [1992]: 129–42) has recently argued for the questionable authorship of the posthumously published *Christian Doctrine*, these questions seem somewhat irrelevant here since nearly all its positions can be found in other well-established prose works—in this case, *The Doctrine and Discipline of Divorce* (*CPW*, 2:325) and the *Art of Logic* (1672; *CPW*, 2:144)—or in Milton's epic itself. However, in its own right, Hunter's argument is unconvincing, as suggested by the responses published with his essay (see Barbara Lewalski and John Shawcross, "Forum: Milton's *Christian Doctrine*," *Studies in English Literature, 1500–1900* 32 [1992]: 143–54, 155–62).

25 Milton's more or less arbitrary use of such emblems as Isis or Osiris as tropes rather than hieroglyphs is suggested by his antithetical treatment of Isis and Osiris in his "Nativity Ode," a point Sirluck also underscores in his note on the passage (*CPW*, 2:549).

26 For Ficino, see Benjamin, who quotes him in *The Origin of German Tragic Drama*, 169. Above, he quotes Konrad Burdach, 180. As the following quotation from Benjamin suggests, he traces the form of the conflict between the Renaissance and the Reformation and Counter-Reformation to "the allegorical outlook[, which] has its origin in the conflict between the guilt-laden physis, held up as an example by Christianity and a purer *natura deorum* [nature of the gods], embodied in the pantheon" (226).

27 See Frances Yates, *The French Academies of the Sixteenth Century* (London: Warburg and Courtauld Institute, 1947). Both Milton's early academic prolusions and his first prose treatise, *Of Reformation*, are overtly engaged

with overthrowing the false traditions of inherited wisdom, which for him includes everything from conventional Aristotelianism and prelatism to the idea that the world reflects the remnants of an eternal, gradually decaying order that must be shored up until Christ's return (on the later, see esp. *Natura non pati senum;* on the former, "At a Vacation Exercise"). For a historical overview of Milton's scientific and philosophical debts and contributions to this revolutionary mode of thought, see Richard Jones, *Ancients and Moderns: A Study of the Rise of the Scientific Movement in Seventeenth Century England* (Berkeley: University of California Press, 1965).

28 William Kerrigan, *The Sacred Complex: On the Psychogenesis of "Paradise Lost"* (Cambridge, Mass.: Harvard University Press, 1983), 237.

29 See Kevin Hart, *The Trespass of the Sign: Deconstruction, Theology, and Philosophy* (Cambridge: Cambridge University Press, 1989), 3–8.

30 See Foucault, see *The Order of Things,* 25–35. As he remarks, in this view of language, "The great metaphor of the book that one opens, that one pores over and reads in order to know nature, is merely the reverse and visible side of another transference, and a much deeper one, which forces language to reside in the world, among the plants, the herbs, the stones, and the animals" (35).

31 Benjamin, *The Origin of German Tragic Drama,* 180–83.

32 For these observations on Benjamin's attitude, see *The Essential Frankfurt School Reader,* ed. Andrew Arato and Eike Gebhardt (New York: Urizen, 1978), 208.

33 The term *earthly individualism* is of course borrowed from Max Weber's classic work on Calvinist psychology in *The Protestant Ethic and the Spirit of Capitalism* (trans. Talcott Parsons [New York: Charles Scribner's Sons, 1958]), a model to which Benjamin is also indebted (see esp. 87–88).

34 Friedrich Creuzer's *Symbolik und Mythologie der Alten Völker* is quoted in Benjamin, *The Origin of German Tragic Drama,* 165. For a similar view of Marvell's "prophetic" insight that Milton's poem would bring Truth down to fable "rather than fable in its ruin leading up to Truth," see Patricia Parker, *Inescapable Romance: Studies in the Poetics of a Mode* (Princeton, N.J.: Princeton University Press, 1979), 13.

35 Madsen, *From Shadowy Types to Truth,* 86. Madsen presents an interesting analysis of typology as allegorical correlative, vitiated by its presumption of a sharp dichotomy between the two, particularly in its misreading of Milton's "Platonism," which he reads into nonexistence—really a classic case of the baby vanishing with the bathwater.

36 See esp. Paul de Man, "The Rhetoric of Temporality," in *Blindness and Insight.*

37 See Lewis, *A Preface to "Paradise Lost,"* esp. 59, 78; Isabel Gambel MacCaffrey, *"Paradise Lost" as "Myth"* (Cambridge, Mass.: Harvard University Press, 1959); Jackson I. Cope, *The Metaphoric Structure of "Paradise Lost"* (Baltimore: Johns Hopkins Press, 1962); and Ferry, *Milton's Epic Voice.*

38 Scholes and Kellogg, *The Nature of Narrative,* 124.

39 Whitman, *Allegory,* 125–26.

40 Benjamin, *The Origin of German Tragic Drama,* 183.

41 In an able discussion of Coleridge's confusions, John Hodgson demonstrates that, in attempting absolutely to distinguish allegory from symbol as synecdoche from metonymy, Coleridge's "transcendent" symbols end up acting more like a double metonymy or "overdetermined metaphor," thereby causing his great rhetorical oppositions ultimately to "resolve into a common figure" ("Transcendental Tropes: Coleridge's Rhetoric of Allegory and Symbol," in *Allegory, Myth, and Symbol,* ed. Morton Bloomfield [Cambridge, Mass.: Harvard University Press, 1981], 280, 291).

42 Benjamin, *The Origin of German Tragic Drama,* 165–66.

43 See Fletcher, *Allegory,* 8, who not only comments on Frye's observation (*Anatomy,* 89) but also notes that, while all commentary is essentially allegorical, "no 'pure' allegory will ever be found."

44 See Teskey, "Irony, Allegory, and Metaphysical Decay," 398, 400. However, Teskey's views on Milton are in many respects quite close to those presented here, except for one crucial difference: he would place Milton outside the "violent" allegorical tradition altogether (see his "From Allegory to Dialectic: Imagining Error in Spenser and Milton," *PMLA* 101 [1986]: 9–23). His position thus considerably exaggerates that of Frye, who on a "sliding scale" situates Milton directly below continuous (Spenserian) and "free-style" allegory (*Anatomy,* 91), which in a certain sense can be taken as a "naive" version of Milton's ironic allegory.

45 Fletcher, *Allegory,* 240–41.

46 Teskey, *Allegory and Violence,* 3–5, 6–7. Tesky further stresses two points underlying my argument: not only the "microcosm-macrocosm analogy is more than a purely formal structure, allegory's *most comprehensive imaginative form"* (p. 7; emphasis added), but further, by expanding our horizons "beyond the limits of poetics, we see how allegory does not simply refer upwards, anagogically," but "oscillates" between different "projects" or levels (p. 8).

47 Benjamin, *The Origin of German Tragic Drama,* 166.

48 In Milton's sense, which is also that adopted by Tasso and the major allegorists of his period, the argument is an "assert[ion]" (*PL,* 1.25), which means not merely persuading but "'observing, acknowledging, and/or experiencing the existence'" of the central elements of his epic "Idea," which "are in turn organised, set forth and 'proved' by the poem's form" (see Sloane, "Rhetoric, 'Logic' and Poetry," 308; on the broader Renaissance context of the epic "Idea," see Treip, *Allegorical Poetics and the Epic,* 42–49, 150–67).

49 Fletcher, *Allegory,* 180, where he also cites Bacon.

50 See Ricoeur, *The Symbolism of Evil,* 12, 25. On p. 25, Ricoeur also quotes Pettazzoni's *La confession des péchés* (Bologna, 1929–36).

51 See, e.g., Regina Schwartz, *Remembering and Repeating: Biblical Cre-*

ation in *"Paradise Lost"* (Cambridge: Cambridge University Press, 1988); and also Michael Lieb, *Poetics of the Holy: A Reading of "Paradise Lost"* (Chapel Hill: University of North Carolina Press, 1981). The latter work especially undercuts its own claim that, in Milton's oeuvre, "the residue of the archaic concept of holiness . . . continues to linger with not a little of its original force" (35) by creating a decontextualized tissue of misleading citations too vast to detail here. So far as the current study is concerned, Lieb's earlier work on *The Dialectics of Creation: Patterns of Birth and Regeneration in "Paradise Lost"* (Amherst: University of Massachusetts Press, 1970) would seem to lead in a quite different and ultimately more satisfying critical direction.

52 See Teskey on Benjamin in *Allegory and Violence,* 13. On the characteristic figure of death in baroque art, see also Erwin Panofsky's seminal essay on the subject, "Et in Arcadia Ego: Poussin and the Elegiac Tradition," in *Meaning in the Visual Arts: Papers in and on Art History* (New York: Doubleday, 1955), 295–320.

53 These paradoxes also characterize the *Christian Doctrine,* which, while arguing for as nearly literal an understanding of God as possible, makes this possibility fundamentally ambiguous by concluding that he is ultimately "WONDERFUL and INCOMPREHENSIBLE . . . *since . . . there is no finding out his greatness; Isa.* xl. 28; *his powers of foresight are beyond discovery"* (*CPW,* 6:152). On these points, also see my conclusion below.

54 Ricoeur, *The Symbolism of Evil,* 98 n. 46 (quoting G. von Rad, *Theologie des alten Testaments* [1948], himself quoting [in part] Öhler).

55 *The Faerie Queene* (hereafter *FQ*), 3.6.40, quoted from *The Complete Poetical Works of Spenser,* ed. R. E. Neil Dodge (Boston: Houghton Mifflin, 1908). Citations are hereafter given in the text.

56 As Paul Tillich further says, "Christ gives immortal knowledge, the knowledge which gives immortality. . . . He gives both the knowledge of immortality and the drug of immortality, which is the sacrament. Ignatius called the Lord's Supper the remedy against our having to die, the *antidoton to me apothanein.* There is a very profound meaning in this idea that the sacramental materials of the Lord's Supper are, so to speak, drugs or remedies which produce immortality. First of all, it shows that the apostolic fathers did not believe in the immortality of the soul. . . . otherwise it would be meaningless for them to speak about immortal life which Christ offers. They believed that man is naturally mortal, just as the Old Testament held that in paradise man was able to eat from the food of the gods, called the 'tree of life', and to keep alive by participating in this divine power. Similarly the apostolic fathers taught that with the coming of Christ the situation of paradise has been re-established. Again we may participate in the food of eternity, which is the body and the blood of Christ" (Paul Tillich, *A History of Christian Thought: From Its Judaic and Hellenistic Origins to Existentialism,* ed. Carl E. Braaten [New York: Simon & Schuster, 1967], 23–24).

57 For the ways in which the Adamic myth combines with both the Orphic myth of exile and the Platonic myths of the soul in the mainline Christian tradition, see Ricoeur's central discussion in *The Symbolism of Evil*, 330–46. On the workings of a spirit contemporaneously conceived as an "ideal fiction of pure will," see Sloane, "Rhetoric, 'Logic,' and Poetry," 333.

58 For the "beautiful form of the Tree" (and implicitly Raphael's) as a traditional embodiment of the divine, see Fletcher, *Allegory*, 134. For its connection (through the image of the golden chain, discussed below) to earlier forms of materialism, see Robert Lamberton, *Homer the Theologian: Neoplatonist Allegorical Reading and the Growth of the Epic Tradition* (Berkeley: University of California Press, 1986).

59 On Milton's "free will" theodicy and his rationalization of myth (including the mythic Chaos), see Danielson, *Milton's Good God;* and also chap. 4 below.

60 Jacques Derrida deconstructs Plato's use of this primitive "complex word" in *Disseminations,* trans. Barbara Johnson (Chicago: University of Chicago Press, 1981). However, it should also be kept in mind that most modern medicines are also quite literally poisons.

61 The fact that Sin springs from the "left side" (*PL,* 2.755) of Satan's head suggests that, in some peculiarly literal sense, creatures can choose to compose motives from either the "sinister" or left-brained or the "dextrous" or right-brained aspects of their consciousness—although how precisely these internalized choices interact is one of those paradoxes Milton neither would nor could resolve.

62 Thus, it also seems significant that Milton wrote no poem on the circumcision, a traditional seventeenth-century topos and a rite that more conservative theologians made analogous to the cleansing power of the sacrament in general—a view that Milton explicitly rejects (*CPW,* 6:547–49).

63 Frances A. Yates, *The Art of Memory* (Chicago: University of Chicago Press, 1966), 284.

64 Pan, of course, is specifically the all-god in Milton's hymn "On the Morning of Christ's Nativity," stanza 8.

65 Yates, *The Art of Memory,* 156, 368, 234–40.

66 This is the Benjamin described in his friend Gershom Scholem's dedicatory valediction, which praises him for uniting "the insight of the Metaphysician, the interpretative power of the Critic and the erudition of the Scholar. [And] DIES AT PORT BOU (SPAIN) ON HIS WAY INTO FREEDOM" (in *Major Trends in Jewish Mysticism* [Jerusalem: Schoken, 1954]). See also Gershom Scholem, *Kabbalah and Its Symbolism* (1960), trans. Ralph Manheim (New York: Shocken, 1965), 1–2.

67 In Genesis, Chaos is present in the "deep" or Tehom that God must silence, Tehom being a transformation of the sea monster Tiamat of the Babylonian *Enuma Elish* (see chap. 3 below). Here, too, it may be recalled

that Denis Saurat long ago associated both Milton's materialism and his doctrine of the godhead with elements of cabalism—in *Milton, Man and Thinker* (1925; reprint, London: Dent, 1946) and *Milton et le materialisme chrétien en Angleterre* (Paris: Rieder, 1928). Although Saurat made some telling connections, it seems most unlikely that any claims for a direct indebtedness on Milton's parts to cabalistic doctrine can be sustained.

68 Scholem, *Kabbalah and Its Symbolism*, 117. See also ibid., 110–16.

69 On this aspect of the poem, see Michael Fixler, "All-Interpreting Love: God's Name in Scripture and in *Paradise Lost*," in *Milton and Scriptural Tradition: The Bible into Poetry*, ed. James H. Sims and Leland Ryken (Columbia: University of Missouri Press, 1984), 128–29.

2 Between the Visible and the Invisible

1 See Giovanni Pico della Mirandola, "Oration on the Dignity of Man," in *The Renaissance Philosophy of Man*, ed. Ernst Cassirer, Paul O. Kristeller, and John H. Randall Jr. (Chicago: University of Chicago Press, 1956), 229, 225. However, in terms of imagery alone, Pico's influence on Milton seems unquestionable; his introductory passages contain a version of the Osiris allegory that seems a far more likely source of Milton's famous extended analogy in *Areopagitica* than Plutarch's "On Isis and Osiris," as Sirluck claims (*CPW*, 2:549).

2 Cassirer, *The Individual and the Cosmos*, 182, 178.

3 On Henry More's attempt to counter Hobbes by arguing for the non-material "extension" of spirit, see Samuel I. Mintz, *The Hunting of Leviathan: Seventeenth-Century Reactions to the Materialism and Moral Philosophy of Thomas Hobbes* (Cambridge: Cambridge University Press, 1962), 84–91. Within their own historical context, none of these "interim" solutions can be considered completely idiosyncratic, including Milton's. Versions of his materialist vitalism were shared by other important seventeenth-century thinkers, notably William Harvey—although not, interestingly enough, Robert Boyle, who in theological and political spirit is far closer to Milton. For this reason alone, we need to be wary of John Rogers's conclusion that, in this period, vitalism is always inherently revolutionary in function, if not intention (see, however, Rogers, *The Matter of Revolution*).

4 Compare, e.g., the eternal transcendence of mutable nature projected by Spenser's *Mutabilitie Cantos* with Milton's description of the state of the blessed "in Paradise . . . [as] not to be conceiv'd . . . [as] confin'd and cloy'd with repetition of that which is prescrib'd, but that our happinesse may orbe it selfe into thousand vagancies of glory and delight, and with a kind of eccentrical equation be as it were an invariable Planet of joy and felicity" (*CPW*, 1:752). For a discussion of Milton's free will theology in the context of this evolving universe, see Danielson, *Milton's Good God*.

5 As Mintz explains in *The Hunting of Leviathan*, Hobbesian reason is *only* logical thinking, not the " 'Right Reason' of the Cambridge Platonists, or of Puritan thinkers such as Milton. . . . It is not an inward illumination, 'the candle of the Lord', an intuitive apprehension of external reality" (p. 25). On Hobbes's extreme "materialistic-nominalist outlook," see also ibid., 93–94; and my "The Phoenix and the Crocodile." On More's own contributions to later theories of absolute space and time, see Mintz, *The Hunting of Leviathan,* 91.

6 See Daniel C. Dennett, *Darwin's Dangerous Idea: Evolution and the Meanings of Life* (New York: Simon & Schuster, 1995).

7 See Michael Fixler, "Plato's Four Furors and the Real Structure of *Paradise Lost*," 959. On the subordinate status of the image in normative allegory, see Michael Murrin, *The Veil of Allegory: Some Notes toward a Theory of Allegorical Rhetoric in the English Renaissance* (Chicago: University of Chicago Press, 1969). On the vitalism and animism of the Miltonic universe, see Marjara, *Contemplation of Created Things,* 210–19.

8 Compare John Leonard, *Naming in Paradise: Milton and the Language of Adam and Eve* (Oxford: Clarendon, 1990); and Parker, *Inescapable Romance.* As Parker notes, "Milton simultaneously builds the lofty rhyme and undermines the potential Babel of figures, and this movement of construction and deconstruction becomes in *Paradise Lost* part of a poetic *Aufhebung* which suggests how the same poet might be at once image-maker and iconoclast" (p. 127). The problematic structure of Milton's physical cosmos is by now virtually a cliché of Milton studies, equally well attested to by Walter Clyde Curry's *Milton's Ontology, Cosmogony and Physics* (Lexington: University of Kentucky Press, 1957) and by Marjara's much more recent *Contemplation of Created Things.*

9 Fletcher, *Allegory,* 242; emphasis added. Fletcher's view here provides a useful correction to Stephen Fallon's mistaken assumption that, in the seventeenth century, "an intellectual environment fostering a supple and organic response to allegory disappeared along with confidence in the reality of universals, or at least with consensus on their nature" (*Milton among the Philosophers,* 182).

10 On the overlapping ambitions and ideals of Puritanism and empiricism, see Jones, *Ancients and Moderns.* On the relations of Milton's Chaos to this broader context, see my "Fire, Ice, and Epic Entropy: The Physics and Metaphysics of Milton's Reformed Chaos," in *Milton Studies,* vol. 35, ed. Albert C. Labriola (Pittsburgh: University of Pittsburgh Press, 1998).

11 Michael Fixler, "Presence and Paradigm Shift in *Paradise Lost*" (Tufts University [emeritus], typescript), 4–5 (initial emphasis added).

12 On More, see Mintz, *The Hunting of Leviathan,* 86–90. On Milton's material or "esemplastic" imagination, see Coleridge, *Bibliographia Literaria,* chap. 13, the seminal discussion of Raphael's "one first matter."

13 Georgia Christopher, *Milton and the Science of the Saints* (Princeton, N.J.: Princeton University Press, 1982), 74. As Christopher also observes, in this displacement Milton is wholly unlike the traditional "Catholic poet

[who] could appropriate, according to the Analogy of Being, any sensuous object from real or imagined Nature to symbolize God" (ibid.). On Aristotle, see Marjara, *Contemplation of Created Things*, 68–75 which also observes that "Milton denies Aristotelian dualism not merely by de-emphasizing the mutability of the sublunary world, but even more by postulating the changeability of the superlunary world, an unthinkable proposition in Aristotelian science" (ibid., 72).

14   Andrew Milner, *John Milton and the English Revolution: A Study in the Sociology of Literature* (London: Macmillan, 1981), 156–57.

15   Here, it might be added that the genre of this "episode" is precisely that of discontinuous allegory. All the stones (which correspond to those on the priestly *ephod* of Aaron) glow with a radiant but still natural light (that is to say, with the light of the fourth day rather than the supernal light of the first day of creation), the "natural" light also of an Old Testament figure (which is to say, brilliant but shadowed). To these stones is added one not on the *ephod*, the true philosopher's stone, which Milton ambiguously affirms exists nowhere else but here on the vital sun. The alchemical quest for the philosopher's stone had represented the quest for the transformative power inherent in *vis rerum*, its occulted power deriving, like the Son's own power, from the Etherial Stream of God's supernal light, the light of Creation's first day identified by the evangelist John with the Word as the embodiment of the Paraclete or the living presence that in some sense makes the historical Jesus for John secondary. Thus the stone now represents the living or ongoing illuminative power of God, which in the context of Satan's malignantly inspired presence means also the power above all to transmute evil into good. In vain philosophers call up volatile Hermes (whose temple was also a temple of the sun) when the ultimate transformational power, providential and moral, represented by the revitalized force of the philosopher's stone, is God's, whose temple is the Son. And, in the celestial sun, secretly dominated by God's power, run rivers of potable gold and pure elixir, which Thomas Vaughan the alchemist called "the wise men's Mercury," a holy light, the light of God's crystalline court (*Aula Lucis, Works*, ed. A. E. Waite [London, 1919], 317–18).

16   For a similar interpretation of this situation, see Fallon, *Milton among the Philosophers*, 79.

17   Although philosophical in orientation, Craig's hypothesis in *The Mind of God* illuminates a similar dialectic in literary history, as, e.g., why Pope, a classic proponent of the similarity thesis, would mount such a heroic attack on Milton's conception of human agency in his *Essay on Man*.

18   See Thomas Hobbes, *Leviathan* (1651), ed. C. B. Macpherson (Hammondsworth: Penguin, 1968), 99, 401, 405–6. For an illuminating commentary on the socioempirical effect of Hobbes's "modern constitution," see Bruno Latour, *We Have Never Been Modern* (Cambridge, Mass.: Harvard University Press, 1993).

19 Burtt, *Metaphysical Foundations*, 80.

20 On the importance of Milton's rejection of the idea of the deity's necessity to create, see Stephen Fallon's important "'To Act or Not': Milton's Conception of Divine Freedom," *Journal of the History of Ideas* 49 (1988): 425–49. For a fuller treatment of Milton's rejection of Calvinism's antinomian tendencies, see Stavely, *Puritan Legacies*, 62–97; and my "Self-Raised Sinners." For a similar critique of the antinomian implications of Hobbesian ethics and its ironic parallels with Calvinism, see Mintz, *The Hunting of Leviathan*, 134–46; and Christopher Hill, *Puritanism and Revolution: Studies in Interpretation of the English Revolution of the 17th Century* (New York: Schocken, 1958), 288, 296–98.

21 Danielson, *Milton's Good God*, 46, 38.

22 Fallon, *Milton among the Philosophers*, 134–35.

23 Milton's view of this "true Liberty / [which] is lost" (*PL*, 12.83–84) after the Fall is complex; just as in innocence it may be "obscur'd, or not obey'd" (12.86) in Eve, so afterward it remains even less constant but still recuperable, especially after Adam's Saviour "shall recure" (12.393) Satan's works in him and his seed, which restores inward, if not always outward, liberty (12.524–33). See also the passages from the *Christian Doctrine* cited above, esp. *CPW*, 6:397.

24 Marshall Grossman's assessment is similar in many respects: "Historical experience is a necessary moment in the dialectic of revision and redefinition that leads man to this reunification with God. . . . Milton's narrative articulates its mimesis of this dialectical process. Possessed of the Gospel, Milton's readers are enjoined to follow a path through the wilderness that has already been prepared for them, a path through history to eternity, through death to life. Milton's text . . . thus becomes . . . the word that makes history a sacrament." However, as the previous chapter outlines, any application of sacramentalism to Milton's poetics must be more carefully qualified than it is here, where the concept may seem too closely assimilated to normative allegory's transformation of time "into space . . . [,] an allegorical landscape in which all times and places signify God's divine order" (*"Authors to Themselves,"* 195, 22). Yet, as Grossman notes, this kind of "transubstantiation" is more characteristic of Spenser than Milton.

25 See also Irene Samuel (*Dante and Milton: The "Commedia" and "Paradise Lost"* [Ithaca, N.Y.: Cornell University Press, 1966]), who comments on the equally grim irony implied by St. Peter's "Wicket," to which might be added another buried pun on the "balance" that only weighs down its vainly unbalanced and abortive seekers (456, 465, 474). However, while Samuel may be right that corresponding passages in Dante can be read as making the punishment fit the crime, a more contextual reading must account for Milton's contentious Puritan relation to this source—which, however sympathetic to some of Dante's anticlericalism, goes far beyond a

mere "independent rereading of *Inferno*" (87). A similar contentiousness is apparent in Milton's rejection of Ariosto's limbo (459; see also 85–93).

26   See Arthur O. Lovejoy, "Milton's Dialogue on Astronomy," in *Reason and the Imagination: Studies in the History of Ideas, 1600–1800*, ed. Joseph A. Mazzeo (New York: Columbia University Press, 1962).

27   See the notes to the relevant passages (*PL*, 8.117–22, 137) in Carey and Fowler, eds., *The Poems of John Milton*. And cf. Marjorie Hope Nicolson, who long ago remarked, "No matter what the lesson of the dialogue on astronomy, Milton again gave himself away. Why introduce the passage [*PL*, 8.25–29] at all at this important point in the argument unless the new astronomy *was* important to man, whatever he decided about it? And why develop it in so much detail? Would the Angel have permitted man to discourse at such length, unless Adam's creator, too, had felt the fascination of cosmology? . . . [Here, as earlier,] he elevated both sources to poetry which, taken from its context, might well make its author seem one of the 'soaring souls' who felt the spell of a new vast cosmic nature" (*The Breaking of the Circle* [New York: Columbia University Press, 1962], 184).

28   In common with members of the Hartlib circle, Milton characteristically rejects the "tyrannous aphorismes" of Scholastic law, science, and especially divinity, all of which he would replace with practical experts who could impart "a reall tincture of naturall knowledge" (*CPW*, 2:394) to learning. Metaphorically, he envisions these reforms as leading humankind to the top of a "strait . . . hill side" (*CPW*, 2:376) of knowledge—a figure borrowed from George Hakewill's *Apologie*, but a hallmark of this faction as a whole. This metaphor pervades Milton's early prose and poetical works (as, e.g., sonnet 9) to much the same extent that the scientifically charged images of the telescope and microscope pervade in his mature epics. On the former points, see Jones, *Ancients and Moderns*. The centrality of the telescope image in *Paradise Lost* and its relation to the microscope image in *Paradise Regain'd* was long ago pointed out by Marjorie Hope Nicolson in "Milton and the Telescope," *ELH* 2 (1935): 1–32.

29   See Arthur O. Lovejoy, *The Great Chain of Being: A Study in the History of an Idea* (Cambridge, Mass.: Harvard University Press, 1936), 126–30, 161, 212.

30   On the baroque aspects of Milton's art and its architectural and/or pictorial use of vanishing points, see Roy Daniells, *Milton, Mannerism and Baroque* (Toronto: University of Toronto Press, 1963); and Murray Roston, *Milton and the Baroque* (Pittsburgh: University of Pittsburgh Press, 1980).

31   Brian Rotman, *Signifying Nothing: The Semiotics of Zero* (New York: St. Martin's, 1987), 72.

32   The term is borrowed from Paul de Man's "Pascal's Allegory of Persuasion," in *Allegory and Representation*, ed. Stephen J. Greenblatt (Baltimore: Johns Hopkins University Press, 1981), 1–25.

33   Rotman, *Signifying Nothing*, 55.

34 For an overview of the reintroduction of probability theory and its place within the holistic monism of information theory, see Jeremy Campbell, *Grammatical Man: Information, Entropy, Language and Life* (New York: Simon & Schuster, 1982), esp. 53–66. As Campbell shows, "The fruitless debate over subjective versus objective interpretations of probability . . . is made obsolete by an understanding of the deep relationship which exists between probability and information" (64). For Foucault's thesis concerning the absolute "epistemic break" produced during the Classic Age (and his significant exclusion of Pascal), see *The Order of Things*.

35 See Lucien Goldmann, *The Hidden God* (London: Routledge & Kegan Paul, 1964), 31 ff.

36 De Man, "Pascal's Allegory of Persuasion," 11–12.

37 As de Man points out (ibid., 8), the only scripture quoted in Pascal's *Réflexions* is "Deus fecit omnia in pondere, in numero, et mensura."

38 Rotman, *Signifying Nothing*, 32.

39 E. H. Gombrich, in *Art and Illusion*, quoted by Wolfgang Iser, who additionally suggests that "the functional fecundity of the Gombrich model . . . [lies in the fact that] the schema embodies a reference which is then transcended by the correction. While the schema enables the world to be represented, the correction evokes the observer's reactions to that represented world" (*The Act of Reading* [Baltimore: Johns Hopkins University Press, 1978], 91).

40 See James Whaler, "The Miltonic Simile," *PMLA* 46 (1931): 1034–74. Specifically, Whaler remarks of prolepsis that, "as a definite narrative device, this function of anticipating event in the fable by means of simile seems to be distinctive with Milton" (1036).

41 See also Geoffrey Hartman's suggestive sketch "Adam on the Grass with Balsamum" in *Beyond Formalism* (New Haven, Conn.: Yale University Press, 1970), esp. 138–40.

3 From the Allegorical Kosmos to Miltonic Space

1 See Samuel Johnson, *Works*, ed. Arthur Murphy (London: Nichols & Son, 1801), 2:44. On neoclassicism's "sensuous analogisms," see de Man, "The Rhetoric of Temporality," in *Blindness and Insight*, 205.

2 On allegory's relation to the pun, especially in terms of Spenserian allegory, see Maureen Quilligan, *The Language of Allegory: Defining the Genre* (Ithaca, N.Y.: Cornell University Press, 1979). For the digressively connective or "wandering" aspect of allegorical imagery, see Berger, *The Allegorical Temper*.

3 For a very different reading both of Milton's use of puns and of his relation to Spenser, see Quilligan, *Milton's Spenser*.

4 See Alberto Pérez-Gómez, "Chora: The Space of Architectural Repre-

sentation," in *Chora: Intervals in the Philosophy of Architecture* (Montreal: McGill-Queen's University Press, 1994), 1:22–24.

5 The passage has by now a long history contemporarily stemming from Christopher Ricks's seminal discussion in *Milton's Grand Style* (London: Oxford University Press, 1963). Once again, Quilligan's "revisionist" understanding of his interpretation (in which there seems to be considerable slippage of terms) is diametrically opposed to the one presented here (see, however, *Milton's Spenser*).

6 Marshall's punning sermon, *Meroz Cursed* (1641), and its immediate political significance is discussed by Fixler, *Milton and the Kingdoms of God*, 87–88.

7 The *Apologeticall Narration*, cited by Fixler in ibid., 120.

8 As Robert E. Stillman observes, Hobbes "makes precise what etymologically might signify a 'wandering' from the truth by specifying the term's application to 'an *absurdity*, or senseless speech' " ("Hobbes's *Leviathan*: Monsters, Metaphors, and Magic," *ELH* 62 [1995]: 792, 800).

9 Once again, Spenser's contrast with Milton is most evident in the first book of *The Faerie Queene*, when after Archimago's tampering with the Redcross Knight's dreams he is led ever deeper into the illusions of an enchanted forest under the spell of Duessa, the daemon of falsehood and antithesis of Una. Only after being sacramentally "purged" of these illusory "dreams" can his real quest be resumed. In striking contrast, Satan's fallen imaginations actively create the bulk of the realities common to hell and earth and, for a while, even heaven.

10 On the importance of the "agency theory" of mind in Romantic thought, see Craig, *The Mind of God*. On the nominalist "algebra" characteristic of the latter half of the seventeenth century (which Craig would refer to the theomorphic mind's implicit adoption of a "similarity thesis"), see Stillman, "Hobbes's *Leviathan*," 797–98. On the philosophical tendency of earlier Neoplatonism to make its adept into cosmic "patients," see O'Brien, *The Problem of Power*, 73–77, discussed in chap. 1 above.

11 See Fletcher, *Allegory*, 107–10, 180.

12 De Man, "The Dead-End of Formalist Criticism," in *Blindness and Insight*, 235.

13 Susan Handelman, *The Slayers of Moses: The Emergence of Rabbinic Interpretation in Modern Literary Theory* (Albany: State University of New York Press, 1982), 22. Although Handelman is concerned with the visual bias of Judaic culture, she also substantially agrees with Walter J. Ong's view of the oral bias of Greek culture: here the beauty of visual form is meant to lead to the perception of abstract (or mathematical) forms of truth, which ultimately (like the spoken word) represent invisible relations (see Ong's *Orality and Literacy* [London: Methuen, 1984]).

14 See Douglas Bush, *"Paradise Lost" in Our Time* (Ithaca, N.Y.: Cornell University Press, 1945), 97; but also Dennis Danielson's more recent assertion that the poem's profoundly "open-ended" and "organic" form of repre-

sentation encourages the view that both metaphor and model are by nature multilayered and irreducible" (*Milton's Good God*, 23).

15 See Fish, *Surprised by Sin*, esp. 351–52. A more extreme version of Ferry's still current view (considered below) is expressed by Leland Ryken, who argues that "in passage after passage the visual image is not simply blurred and vague but wholly denied, with the images which describe the apocalyptic state naming qualities which have no sensory object as their referent" (*The Apocalyptic Vision in "Paradise Lost"* [Ithaca, N.Y.: Cornell University Press, 1970], 198). Besides those already named, other more influential exponents include T. S. Eliot (*Of Poetry and Poets* [London: Faber & Faber, 1957], 13–14) and F. R. Leavis, who objected to "vegetable gold" in almost identical terms as "incompatible with sharp, concrete realization" (*Reevaluation: Tradition and Development in English Poetry* [London, 1936], 50). See also Lewis, *A Preface to "Paradise Lost."*

16 Ferry, *Milton's Epic Voice*, 131–32, 113, 104.

17 Fletcher, *Allegory*, 85–87. On *Comus*, see his *Transcendental Masque*, also cited in the introduction above.

18 According to Fletcher, the chief characteristics of allegorical style are the "emblematic, isolated, mosaic imagery; the paratactic order; the ritual that accompanies the religious observance; . . . the lack of that perspective which would create a mimetic world; [and] the microcosmic character of the imagery" (*Allegory*, 171; cf. also 86–87, 109).

19 See Quilligan, *The Language of Allegory*, 119–20.

20 See Madsen, *From Shadowy Types to Truth*, 140.

21 Stavely, *Puritan Legacies*, 20–21.

22 On the psychology and linguistics of "authoritarian language games," see Carlo Levi, *Of Fear and Freedom* (New York, 1950). Fletcher (*Allegory*, 170–71) cites this model as an accurate measure of the presence of allegorical rhetoric.

23 For a convenient summary of the commentary on this passage, including Ryken's very similar treatment of the "apocalyptic function of . . . enameled imagery" (*Apocalyptic Vision*, 76), see Roland Mushat Frye, *Milton's Imagery and the Visual Arts: Iconographic Tradition in the Epic Poems* (Princeton, N.J.: Princeton University Press, 1978), 251–52.

24 See J. B. Broadbent, *Some Graver Subject: An Essay on "Paradise Lost"* (New York: Barnes & Noble, 1960), 176.

25 Fixler, "The Apocalypse within *Paradise Lost*," 143–44.

26 Stavely, *Puritan Legacies*, 28–32.

27 Jacques Derrida, "Khora," in *On the Name*, ed. Thomas Wood, trans. Thomas Dutoit (Stanford, Calif.: Stanford University Press, 1995); and *The Cambridge Platonists*, ed. Gerald R. Cragg (Oxford, 1968). In the latter, see especially the introduction (27–28) on Henry More and plastic substance and selections from Ralph Cudworth (253–577) and John Smith (111). Thus, even without reference to Derrida, the objection holds—especially since Don Wolfe annotates Milton's allusions both to Heraclitus and to alchemy

(citing a by now dated text by Dorothy M. Fisk, *Modern Alchemy* [New York: Appleton-Century, 1936]) in his edited volume of Milton's prose (*CPW*, 1:795–96 n. 11).

28 Robert L. Entzminger, *Divine Word: Milton and the Redemption of Language* (Pittsburgh: Duquesne University Press, 1985), 28. See also Calvin, *Institutes of the Christian Religion*, 1.5.1, pp. 52–53; and 1.5.14, p. 68 (discussed in my introduction above).

29 Christopher Hill, *Milton and the English Revolution* (London: Faber & Faber, 1977), 386.

30 Murrin, *The Veil of Allegory*, 84.

31 Fletcher, *Allegory*, 284–85, 290. Of course, as Fletcher warns, even in "typical" examples of the mode, "allegory is never present as a pure modality" (p. 312). Compare Teskey, "Irony, Allegory, and Metaphysical Decay," 400.

32 Thus, according to Whaler, the concrete, historical effects of Milton's simile are the result of its departure from the typical medieval or early Renaissance practice of blending it with eternal moral exempla ("The Miltonic Simile," esp. 1070–71). For more recent studies along these lines, see Linda Gregerson, "The Limbs of Truth: Milton's Use of Simile in *Paradise Lost*," *Milton Studies* 14 (1980): 135–52; and John C. Ulreich Jr., "The Typological Structure of Milton's Imagery," in *Milton Studies*, vol. 5, ed. James Simmonds (Pittsburgh: Pittsburgh University Press, 1973).

33 See Harold Fisch, "Hebrew Style and Motifs in *Paradise Lost*," in *Language and Style in Milton*, ed. Ronald David Emma and John T. Shawcross (New York: Frederick Ungar, 1967), 47–49. On the self-reflexivity of Milton's similes, see also Linda Gregerson, who remarks that Milton creates a form of epic simile in which "the projections of human intentionality and imagination have become the subject" ("The Limbs of Truth," 140). On baroque perspective, see Pérez-Gómez, "Chora."

34 These terms, originally drawn from Schiller's *Naive and Sentimental Poetry*, broadly allude to the distinctions between primary, secondary, and tertiary epic, discussed by, among others, Harold Bloom in *A Map of Misreading* (New York: Oxford University Press, 1975). See also chap. 7 below.

35 For Augustine's *horror vacui* and that of the early Christian tradition generally, see Rotman, *Signifying Nothing*, 61–66. For opposing (i.e., Augustinian) interpretations of Milton's conception of evil, see Fallon's summary in *Milton among the Philosophers*, 168–93; on this point, Fallon follows both Quilligan and Ferry.

36 Erich Auerbach, "Odysseus' Scar," in *Mimesis: The Representation of Reality in Western Literature*, trans. Willard Trask (New York: Doubleday, 1957), 17, 19.

37 Teskey, "From Allegory to Dialectic," 16. In part, however, the disagreement is terminological since some of Teskey's conclusions are similar to those presented here. Thus, he also concludes that in this period "allegory . . . augments its power to lay hold the temporal, objectifying what it

makes as belonging to the very substance of history rather than to the realm of ideas" ("Irony, Allegory, and Metaphysical Decay," esp. 401–3).

38 Compare Lieb, who finds that Satan's primary role is to act as the uncreator of God's creation, debasing "that which has already been divinely created into the aboriginal 'dark materials' from which creation came" (*The Dialectics of Creation*, 17).

39 Similar analyses, although more Lacanian in orientation, have been applied to the satanic condition by Shoaf (*Poet of Duality*, 14–15) and Grossman ("*Authors to Themselves,*" 29, 206–07 n. 6).

40 Hughes traces the passage to *Inferno*, 3.112–14, but fails to see the allusion to the Twenty-third Psalm in Vallombrosa's "valley of the shadow."

41 Compare Arnold Stein's observation that "Milton's imagination maintains a distinctive control of the perspective of distance and of space. In detail it is physical, remarkably so; in concept it is intellectual, with space, it seems to me, an aspect of time. He presents the immediacy of the moment in the conscious perspective of time." Recalling the *Timaeus*, Stein then adds that, in *Paradise Lost*, "things are held at an epic distance; if they approach close they are nevertheless always seen in the perspective of that distance, in the dimension of God's announced Idea of time . . . [, so that] by . . . the constant outward thrust of the imagery, by countless structural references [, it creates] 'a moving likeness of eternity'" (*Answerable Style* [Minneapolis: University of Minnesota Press, 1953], 155).

4 Some Versions of Allegory

1 The most recent exponent of this view is Stephen Fallon, who also cites Maureen Quilligan's *Milton's Spenser,* Anne Davidson Ferry's *Milton's Epic Voice,* and Arnold Stein's *Answerable Style* as supporting the same general thesis (see Fallon's *Milton among the Philosophers,* 180–93). Objections to Ferry are detailed in the previous chapter, to Quilligan below. With some important differences, the argument advanced here follows the "minority" position advanced by Philip J. Gallagher, "Real or Allegoric: The Ontology of Sin and Death in *Paradise Lost,*" *ELR* 6 (1976): 317–33; and John Rumrich, "Milton's God and the Matter of Chaos," *PMLA* 110 (1995): 1035–46, although the latter is potentially misleading. Certainly, as Rumrich suggests, "For Milton nothing can exist without indeterminacy" (1044); but for Milton not all indeterminacies are equal. Chaos's passive and randomly mutable entropy is thus fundamentally distinct from the hermaphroditic deity whom Rumrich regards as "espousing" it. Here, Teskey seems more right in urging that Milton's allegory should not be "read in any sense but the literal" ("From Allegory to Dialectic," 19)—although he unfortunately opposes dialectic to allegory, where I would "baroquely" synthesize them.

2 Here, as throughout the chapter, *Chaos* refers to Milton's epic persona,

chaos to the state, phase, or theory of chaos. For a suggestive study of Milton's dualities (as opposed to his *dualism*) along semiotic lines, see Shoaf, *Milton, Poet of Duality.*

3   See John Ray, *Three Physico-Theological Discourses* (London, 1693), 6.

4   Fletcher, *Allegory*, 60.

5   Samuel Johnson, "Life of Milton," in *Johnson's Lives of the English Poets: A Selection*, ed. J. P. Hardy (Oxford: Oxford University Press, 1971), 108.

6   See also Kenneth Borris, "Allegory in *Paradise Lost:* Satan's Cosmic Journey," in *Milton Studies*, vol. 26, ed. Albert C. Labriola (Pittsburgh: University of Pittsburgh Press, 1990), 101–33.

7   See Burtt, *Metaphysical Foundations*, who points out that unlike medieval science—which was primarily interested in teleological rather than efficient causes (5)—seventeenth-century science had already begun to separate final and efficient causes as discrete branches of study (17–19). On the intellectual reaction against Hobbes and the suspicion of Descartes, see Mintz, *The Hunting of Leviathan.*

8   Milton retains the fourfold Aristotelian system of causality in both the *Christian Doctrine* (1.7) and *The Art of Logic* (1.9), but, as we will see, he also registers the general reorientation of the period.

9   John S. Tanner, " 'Say First What Cause': Ricoeur and the Etiology of Evil in *Paradise Lost,*" *PMLA* 103 (1988): 49.

10   J. A. K. Thomson, ed., *The Ethics of Aristotle* (Harmondsworth: Penguin, 1958), 87.

11   Madsen, *Shadowy Types to Truth*, 122.

12   This irony is most apparent in the portrait of a Devil who not only is nominally heroic but actually advocates some of the positions expressed in Milton's political treatises (see Radzinowicz, "The Politics of *Paradise Lost,*" 221–23).

13   G. K. Hunter, *"Paradise Lost"* (London: George Allen & Unwin, 1980), 24.

14   Kerrigan, *Sacred Complex*, 227, 201 (quoting Bruno, *Cause, Principle, and Unity*).

15   Thus, as described by Harry Berger Jr.: "The emphasis on the dense-to-rare continuum as the criterion of rank and diversity produces a corresponding emphasis on a unity ('one first matter all') which is more than analogical and which is attributed to Being, not merely to Thought" (*"Paradise Lost* Evolving: Books I–VI," *Centennial Review* 11 [1967]: 519). Similarly, Jonathan Goldberg observes that, although a structural "analogy between . . . planes [moving around fixed points] falls well within the normative hierarchical scheme. . . . Milton introduces a further movement, which, instead of maintaining motion at a single level of the cosmos (horizontal motion) allows for the possibility of vertical motion. To complicate matters even further, no principle of simultaneity is described with respect to these vertical movements, since the tree's growth does not seem

linked to the possibility of man's growth (ascent), which depends on his obedience. Thus, at once, we have four different kinds of motion which are being compared: the movement around a central point on a single plane (the 'active Spheres assign'd,' 477); the Neoplatonic cosmic movement of the *circuitus spiritualis;* the natural growth of the tree; the possibility of man's ascent (its reflection of Raphael's descent constitutes a mirror for man's ultimate freedom of movement). The reconciliation of these various motions passes beyond the limits of hierarchical analogy, just as Milton's cosmology represents a shift from the so-called Elizabethan world picture" (*"Virga Iesse:* Analogy, Typology, and Anagogy in a Miltonic Simile," in *Milton Studies,* vol. 5, 181–82).

16 William B. Hunter, "Milton's Power of Matter," *Journal of the History of Ideas* 13 (1952): 551–62.

17 See Pérez-Gómez, "Chora," 8–9. On Milton's relation to the "occulted substances" of Platonic tradition, see the introduction and first chapter above.

18 See Serres, "Lucretius," 98–124. The important new scientific model shared by modern biology and information theory and its contrast with classical or Newtonian mechanics is outlined in Ilya Prigogine and Isabelle Stengers, *Order out of Chaos: Man's New Dialogue with Nature* (Toronto: Bantam, 1984), esp. 29, 68, and 76.

19 On reintegrative flux in modern theory, see Prigogine and Stengers, *Order out of Chaos,* 131–76.

20 See Quilligan, *Milton's Spenser,* 126–27. As noted above, Fallon endorses essentially the same position in *Milton among the Philosophers.*

21 For an extended analysis, see chap. 1, sec. 4 above.

22 See Michael Lieb, "Milton's 'Dramatick Constitution': The Celestial Dialogue in *Paradise Lost,* Book III," *Milton Studies,* vol. 23, ed. James Simmonds (Pittsburgh: University of Pittsburgh Press, 1987), 215–40.

23 Bacon, *Works,* 4:92.

24 See also Samuel S. Stollman, "Satan, Sin, and Death: A Mosaic Trio in *Paradise Lost,*" in *Milton Studies,* vol. 22, ed. James D. Simmonds (Pittsburgh: University of Pittsburgh Press, 1986), 101–20. According to Stollman, "Sin and Death and their encounters with Satan act out one of Milton's major doctrines, namely, his . . . antinomian view of the Mosaic Law and of the Law's impediment of the attainment of Christian liberty" (101). For the opposing view, see Quilligan, who argues that "Sin (like Satan) makes her decision with a rhetorical question, to which the respondent is not meant to respond, the speaker having answered in the very framing of the question, forestalling and therefore paralyzing further free choice. Such rendering passive the auditor's will is the core of Sin's rhetoric of irresponsibility . . . her very slavish willessness, . . . [and her] snakily undulating parody of true obedience, a parody of the rights due proper and original authority" (*Milton's Spenser,* 89).

25   For a persuasive argument concerning Satan's real ability to repent, see Keith W. F. Stavely, "Satan and Arminianism in *Paradise Lost*," *Milton Studies*, vol. 25, ed. James D. Simmonds (Pittsburgh: University of Pittsburgh Press, 1989), 125–39.

26   For a fuller consideration of the Hesiodic and other traditions on which Milton draws, see my "Fire, Ice, and Epic Entropy: The Physics and Metaphysics of Milton's Reformed Chaos."

27   *The Presocratic Philosophers: A Critical History with a Selection of Texts,* ed. G. S. Kirk, J. E. Raven, and M. Schofield (Cambridge: Cambridge University Press, 1983), 191. The wording here is that of the editorial gloss on the passage, not an exact translation.

28   Marjara, *Contemplation of Created Things,* 234.

29   John Carey and Alastair Fowler trace these hybrid symbols to an allegory of Raban Maur's (Migne cxi 342) but also note that the "legend of the 'gold-guarding griffins' in Scythia, from whom the one-eyed Arimaspi steal, was often retold out of Herodotus (iii 116) and Pliny (*Nat. hist* vii 10)" (*The Poems of John Milton,* p. 552). Yet one might further note that, as an embodiment of the original Golden Age, Eden abounds with organic forms of gold (the more memorable of which is its "vegetable gold" [*PL,* 4:420]). Equally rich in symbolic significance, the golden floor of heaven is usually understood as representing the free righteousness of the Son, the "ground" of his being literally "misconceived" and misappropriated by demons like Mammon and Satan.

30   See John T. Shawcross, *The Complete Poetry of John Milton* (New York: Random House, 1970), 289 n. 36. On Milton's proleptic similes, see chap. 3 above.

31   As Victoria Kahn remarks, Milton's allegory dramatizes the actual "indifference" of his mode, i.e., the essential continuity of a pre- and postlapsarian language in which "signs, including prohibitions and laws, are not simply a consequence of the fall, but the precondition of any genuine ethical choice: language itself is a thing that can be used well or badly" ("Allegory, the Sublime, and the Rhetoric of Things Indifferent in *Paradise Lost,*" in *Creative Imitation: New Essays on Renaissance Literature in Honor of Thomas M. Greene,* ed. David Quint, Margaret W. Ferguson, G. W. Pigman II, and Wayne A. Rebhorn [Binghamton, N.Y.: Medieval and Renaissance Texts and Studies, 1992], 150). By pushing allegory to this limit, she suggests that Milton approaches the sublime—or (as my argument implies) the indeterminate or "ruined" dimension of a form "adventitiously" extended by its own implosion.

32   For a suggestive consideration of how satanic or sinful narcissism causes *copia* to degenerate into a "mere copy," see Shoaf, *Milton, Poet of Duality,* 27–29.

33   For the most recent version of this old view of Chaos as evil or "hostile to God," see Schwartz, *Remembering and Repeating,* 8–24. For a more balanced view, see Rumrich, "Milton's God."

34 The speciousness of this liberation becomes especially apparent later, when Sin looks forward eagerly to the "Monarchie" in which she shall "divide / Of all things" (10.379–80) with Death and Satan, when in fact their bridge (or *pontifex*) to earth will allow them to "share" their new world only in the most negative sense of division, that of segregating, despoiling, exploiting, and reducing the richness of its potential.

35 Anna K. Nardo, *Milton's Sonnets and the Ideal Community* (Lincoln: University of Nebraska Press, 1979), 13. Nardo gives a convenient summary of this paradigm shift on pp. 4–26.

5 Milton's Meta-Allegory of Action

1 Roston, *Milton and the Baroque,* 119; Hunter, *"Paradise Lost,"* 131.

2 For an influential mock-heroic reading of the War in Heaven, see Stein, *Answerable Style.*

3 Mary Ann Radzinowicz, *Toward "Samson Agonistes": The Growth of Milton's Mind* (Princeton, N.J.: Princeton University Press, 1978), 133. For another important discussion of Milton's rejection of apocalyptic literalism, see Fixler, *Milton and the Kingdoms of God.* For Milton's critique of traditional heroism, see John Steadman, *Milton and the Renaissance Hero* (Oxford: Clarendon, 1967).

4 For a discussion of this historical paradigm, see Ernst Troeltsch, *The Social Teachings of the Christian Churches,* trans. Olive Wyon (New York: Macmillan, 1931), vol. 2, esp. p. 817.

5 Lee A. Jacobus, *Sudden Apprehension: Aspects of Knowledge in "Paradise Lost"* (The Hague: Mouton, 1976), 97.

6 Fletcher, *Allegory,* 162.

7 See Clifford, *The Transformations of Allegory,* 37.

8 These principles form the foundation of Milton's *Defence of the English People,* where he argues that, if "any law or custom conflict with divine law *or with reason,* it is not to be considered . . . valid" (*CPW,* 5, pt. 1:486; emphasis added). For a more extensive consideration of Milton's "debate" with Hobbes, see my "The Phoenix and the Crocodile."

9 Kester Svendsen, *Milton and Science* (Cambridge, Mass.: Harvard University Press, 1956), 121.

10 Stella Purce Revard, *The War in Heaven: "Paradise Lost" and the Tradition of Satan's Rebellion* (Ithaca, N.Y.: Cornell University Press, 1980), 189–90.

11 Quilligan presents one of the more recent revivals of this view; for her, "Satan is not only the father of Sin, he is also the father of corrupting wordplay" (*Milton's Spenser,* 93).

12 The pun on "Jehoviality" is in this case G. K. Hunter's, not mine—therefore releasing me from the necessity of making unnecessary apologies. See his cogent discussion in *"Paradise Lost,"* 131.

13   Revard, *The War in Heaven*, 196–97.
14   Hugh G. Evelyn-White, ed. and trans., *Hesiod: The Homeric Hymns and Homerica*, Loeb Classical Library no. 57 (Cambridge, Mass.: Harvard University Press, 1982), lines 656–57, p. 127.
15   For a discussion of *Paradise Lost* as a tertiary epic, see Bloom, *A Map of Misreading*.
16   Fletcher, *Allegory*, 190.
17   I refer only to the more obvious symbolism of these lines: the "eagle-wing'd" Victory refers to the Greek personification of this force as Nike, the Son's quiver suggests the arrows of Apollo, and the quiver's contents, its "three-bolted Thunder," refer to Zeus.
18   Murrin, *The Veil of Allegory*, 30.
19   Although noting the poetic symbolism of the devils as a "Herd of Goats" (*PL*, 6.856–57), interpreters generally fail to notice the similarity of their expulsion to that performed by Jesus in sending evil spirits into the herd of swine that then drowns itself in another "wasteful Deep" (6.862), the oceanic counterpart of hell. In substituting goats for the swine of the original passage (Matt. 8:32), Milton complicates the allusion by conflating two typological references: the goats that are separated from the sheep depict the general category of the damned, which is here conflated with the specific case of the swinish devils.
20   Radzinowicz makes the related observation that Milton "rejects the Son's hereditary right for a much more political reason than the theological question of the Father's unique unbegottenness, however. He rejects it in order to instate the Son as Son on the grounds of merit." As a result, "it is impossible to argue that this concept of merited 'sonship' is a necessary part of the subordinationism so familiar to theology, or that its grounds in God's desire to augment the quantum of freedom and fraternity in the universe is a necessary aspect of that perfectly unheretical doctrine, *let alone that either proposition is particularly biblical*" ("The Politics of *Paradise Lost*," 209–10; emphasis added).
21   Steadman makes a similar observation in *Milton and the Renaissance Hero:* "As Milton presents it, charity—*verus amor*—is the 'soul' of all the other virtues. In the Son it is coupled with wisdom and fortitude and the responsibilities of the leader; out of love towards humanity and obedience towards God, he risks death to save 'a whole race lost.' . . . It is linked with zeal for God's glory, for it is to 'glorify' the Father that the Son humbles himself to the 'form' of a servant" (129–30).
22   As Wayne Shumaker observes, "Like everything else in the poem, concrete or abstract, insensate or conscious, the very materials out of which creation was accomplished are given quasi-personal status" (*Unpremeditated Verse: Feeling and Perception in Paradise Lost* [Princeton, N.J.: Princeton University Press, 1967], 85–86).
23   On Milton's departure from the mainline structure of Christian myth, see Kerrigan, *The Sacred Complex*, 270; and also chaps. 6 and 7 below.

24 Joseph H. Summers, *The Muse's Method: An Introduction to "Paradise Lost"* (Cambridge, Mass.: Harvard University Press, 1962), 139.

6 Demystifying Disguises

1 See Michael Fixler, "The Orphic Technique of 'L'Allegro' and 'Il Penseroso,'" *ELR* 1 (1971): 165–77.

2 For examples of apologetic in this vein, see James Grantham Turner, *One Flesh: Paradisal Marriage and Sexual Relations in the Age of Milton* (Oxford: Clarendon, 1987), 266–67; and David Aers and Bob Hodge, "'Rational Burning': Milton on Sex and Marriage," in *Literature, Language and Society in England, 1580–1680* (Dublin: Gill & McMillan, 1981), 143–46.

3 Milton's patriarchalism and misogyny is most emphatically stated in the work of Sandra Gilbert and Susan Gubar (*The Madwoman in the Attic: The Woman Writer and the Nineteenth-Century Imagination* [New Haven, Conn.: Yale University Press, 1979]), as against the moderately conventional patriarchalist view of Barbara Lewalski's "Milton on Women—yet Once More" (in *Milton Studies*, vol. 6, ed. James D. Simmonds [Pittsburgh: Pittsburgh University Press, 1974], 3–20). Jean Hagstrum, however, sees Milton self-divided on this issue (*Sex and Sensibility: Ideal and Erotic Love from Milton to Mozart* [Chicago: University of Chicago Press, 1980], 29).

4 Hunter, *"Paradise Lost,"* 129.

5 William Kerrigan (*The Sacred Complex,* 151–53) also calls attention to Victor Turner's concept of "ritual liminality" as a suitable description of the situation of Milton's moral cosmos. See also Mary Douglas, *Purity and Danger* (London: Routledge & Kegan Paul, 1966), 53–54. For a sense of how Miltonic sexuality overturns the systems Douglas describes, see Turner, *One Flesh,* 252. For a fuller exposition of the antiritual impulses of baroque allegory, see chap. 1 above.

6 See Kerrigan's discussion of how, like other of Milton's innovations, the revised role of Satan contradicts his avowed intention to render a "literal" account of biblical creation (*The Sacred Complex,* 100–101, 129–32).

7 In essence, Kerrigan argues that "the theology of his blindness elevates, to the point of heresy, the dignity of the physical world" (ibid., 133), which seems exactly right in regard to Milton's extensive reliance on Matt. 15:17–18, both here and elsewhere.

8 Milton seems to use this title to suggest that the Son is a coruler or manager in the sense of *gerens,* one who "bears" as well as conducts, not merely a *regent,* a word derived from a different root, *regere,* which means simply "to rule." On the maternal associations of the Son with Eve and vice versa, see Summers, *The Muse's Method.*

9 Fletcher, *Allegory,* 87.

10   See Fish, *Surprised by Sin,* 171.

11   The biblical precedent for this incident seems to lie in its oblique allusion to God's condemnation of Balshazzar, "Thou art weighed in the balance and art found wanting" (Dan. 5:27)—which is here applied to Satan.

12   A fairly thorough overview of the "Adam and Eve question" can be found in Stavely, *Puritan Legacies,* 34–61. As Stavely points out (37, n. 2), the problem has been greatly complicated by the feminist debates of the 1970s and 1980s. However, one of its more fruitful results is Diane McColley's fine study of *Milton's Eve* (Urbana: University of Illinois Press, 1983), which also mentions the allusion to Luke noted below (103); it does not, however, register the more recent aspects of the debate considered here. See also McColley's recent *A Gust for Paradise: Milton's Eden and the Visual Arts* (Urbana: University of Illinois Press, 1993).

13   Biblically, toads typically represent the signs but not the form of the accursed, as does the serpent (see Rev. 16:13–14).

14   For this view, see Gilbert and Gubar, *The Madwoman in the Attic,* esp. 187–247.

15   Christine Froula, "When Eve Reads Milton: Undoing the Canonical Economy," *Critical Inquiry* 10 (1983): 338.

16   See McColley, *Milton's Eve,* esp. 110–86. McColley extols Eve for the seriousness of her vocation, sense of responsibility, and commitment to liberty even in the context of the separation scene (154). For Eve's more explicitly "masculine" characteristics as well as her transcendence of them in becoming Christ-like, see Aers and Hodge, "'Rational Burning,'" 141.

17   J. Hillis Miller, "How Deconstruction Works: *Paradise Lost,* IV, 304–8," *New York Times Magazine,* 9 February 1986, 25. Critics of this and related passages are, as this suggests, legion, although William Empson somewhat characteristically regarded Milton's depiction of Edenic sexuality as "a splendid bit of nerve." For an overview of this and of other less enthusiastic responses, see Edward Le Comte, *Milton and Sex* (New York: Columbia University Press, 1978), esp. 92. For another positive view of Milton's paradise as "depend[ing] upon a wise management of temptation," see William Kerrigan and Gordon Braden, "Milton's Coy Eve: *Paradise Lost* and Renaissance Love Poetry," *ELH* 53 (1986): 42.

18   Froula, "When Eve Reads Milton," 328.

19   Mary Nyquist stresses this point in "Gynesis, Genesis, Exegesis, and the Formation of Milton's Eve," in *Cannibals, Witches, and Divorce: Estranging the Renaissance,* ed. Marjorie Garber (Baltimore: Johns Hopkins University Press, 1987), 147–209. Yet, in the sense noted by William Shullenberger, "Eve *is* Eden, and the poetry of pristine astonishment appropriate to that paradisal place is hers" ("Wrestling with the Angel: *Paradise Lost* and Feminist Criticism," *Milton Quarterly* 23, no. 3 [1986]: 73–74).

20   Joseph Wittreich, *Feminist Milton* (Ithaca, N.Y.: Cornell University Press, 1987), 84.

21 Froula, "When Eve Reads Milton," 330.

22 For a detailed description of the ways in which Milton reworks the Narcissus myth, see Kenneth J. Knoespel, "The Limits of Allegory: Textual Expansion of Narcissus in *Paradise Lost*," in *Milton Studies*, vol. 22, 79–99.

23 Both Kerrigan (*The Sacred Complex*) and Nyquist ("Gynesis, Genesis, Exegesis") find prototypes of Freudian psychology in *Paradise Lost*; the poem was, after all, on the list of Freud's ten favorite books (*The Standard Edition of the Complete Psychological Works of Sigmund Freud*, ed. James Strachey, 24 vols. [London: Hogarth, 1953–74], 11:245). Nyquist also argues (albeit in a less favorable sense than Kerrigan) that the epic can be read within the terms of both Freudian and Lacanian psychoanalysis (201–2). Shullenberger more imaginatively contrasts Eve's constructive use of the mirror stage with Satan's destructive "amnesia" about his own origins ("Wrestling with the Angel," 81).

24 Thus, as Kerrigan remarks, "Femininity symbolizes the something 'more' in Christ, the epistrophe of voluntary love that makes him exceed a mere echo of his creator. For Christ, as for angels and men, femininity constitutes the sphere of freedom" (*The Sacred Complex*, 187–88). Kerrigan's insights into gender as well as into the monist continuum of the poem are at times brilliant, but too often his work seems to suffer from the assumptions of a somewhat dated Freudian ego psychology. As I suggest, a Lacanian model seems more immediately applicable to this dimension of the poem.

25 Nyquist, "Gynesis, Genesis, Exegesis," 203.

26 Here, Adam transfers what might have begun as a preeminently auditory experience, as stressed by the alliteration of "liquid Lapse" and its association with "murmuring," back into the visual field of seeing the lapsing current.

27 For an important commentary on the mythic significance of this reversal, see Northrop Frye, "The Revelation to Eve," in *"Paradise Lost": A Tercentenary Tribute*, ed. Balachandra Rajan (Toronto: University of Toronto Press, 1969).

28 Froula, "When Eve Reads Milton," 332.

29 Froula observes that Milton's "silencing and voiding of female creativity" recalls "all the elements of Freud's 'progress in spirituality'" (ibid., 338).

30 Ibid., 331.

31 Turner, *One Flesh*, 237.

32 In "'Rational Burning,'" Aers and Hodge find true equality of desire only in the angelic state; yet, if angels are Milton's "chief means of conceiving satisfactory sexual relations," they hardly seem to be his only means, as Aers and Hodge assert (142–43). Sandra Gilbert ("Patriarchal Poetry and Women Readers: Reflections on Milton's Bogey," *PMLA* 93 [1978]: 368–82) even more radically misinterprets the nature of angelic bisexuality in claiming that the female gender is excluded from heaven, a view dismissed by Joan M. Webber, "The Politics of Poetry: Feminism and *Paradise Lost*,"

in *Milton Studies,* vol. 14, ed. James D. Simmonds (Pittsburgh: Pittsburgh University Press, 1980), 3–24. Gilbert's misreading is also trenchantly critiqued—particularly in terms of her validation of a narcissistic Satan-hero who exalts rising at the expense of others—by Shullenberger, "Wrestling with the Angel," 79.

33   See Diana Benet's exemplary treatment of this source of Adam's failure in "Abdiel and the Son in the Separation Scene," in *Milton Studies,* vol. 18, ed. James D. Simmonds (Pittsburgh: Pittsburgh University Press, 1983), 129–43, esp. 138–39.

34   Thus, although the Father says that he "made *him* just and right" (*PL,* 3.98; emphasis added), he is obviously referring back to "Man" (3.93) in the generic sense of "mankind." This inference is warranted by the fact that, immediately afterward, he shifts to *they* and remains in the plural until his concluding statement. Thus, even when he refers to "Man" in a sense that seems to exclude Eve—"Man falls deceiv'd / By th' other first: Man therefore shall find grace" (3.130–31)—it actually refers especially to her deception and to her status as the primary recipient and vehicle of grace.

35   Turner, *One Flesh,* 241, 141; and John Crowe Ransom, "Poetry: A Note in Ontology," in *Critical Theory since Plato,* ed. Hazard Adams (San Diego: Harcourt Brace Jovanovich, 1971), 880.

36   See Frye, "The Revelation to Eve." For a related view of the poem's final books as "an Eviad," see Earl Miner, "The Reign of Narrative in *Paradise Lost,*" in *Milton Studies,* vol. 17, ed. James D. Simmonds (Pittsburgh: Pittsburgh University Press, 1983), 20. On Eve's unique relation to grace, see also n. 34 above.

37   For the masculine biases inherent in the androgynous, Neoplatonic view of sexuality, see Stephen Orgel, "Nobody's Perfect: Or Why Did the English Stage Take Boys for Women?" *South Atlantic Quarterly* 88 (1989): esp. 26–28; Mary Nyquist, "Gynesis, Genesis, Exegesis"; and Marilyn R. Farwell, "Eve, the Separation Scene, and the Renaissance Idea of Androgyny," in *Milton Studies,* vol. 16, ed. James D. Simmonds (Pittsburgh: University of Pittsburgh Press, 1982), 3–21.

38   As Hagstrum notes: "Spenser is drawn to what Milton sharply rejects, the Platonic imagery of androgyny. . . . To Milton such mythologizing is not congenial: he keeps his sexes sharply distinct and will have no traffic with the Platonic wit about the *ur-* sex or any kind of union that blurs the sharp contrast necessary for productive sexual alchemy" (*Sex and Sensibility,* 32).

39 On the implicitly male gendering of seventeenth-century empiricism, see Catherine Belsey, *The Subject of Tragedy: Identity and Difference in Renaissance Drama* (London: Methuen, 1985). Belsey's model of female exclusion makes a particularly good "grid" against which to measure Milton's inclusiveness, which then seems to merit the *protofeminist* label that I suggest.

7 Realism, Nominalism, and the Politics of Reading

1 Lewis, *A Preface to "Paradise Lost,"* 129. Lewis's nostalgia for ritual culture is almost a commonplace, as is his dislike for the narrower techniques of scholarship in which he often excelled.

2 For Murrin's remarks on the role of oral memory in allegory, see *The Veil of Allegory,* 70, 75–97.

3 Thomas Hobbes, *De corpore: The Elements of Philosophy concerning Body,* 1.2, in *The English Works of Thomas Hobbes,* ed. William Molesworth, 11 vols. (London: John Bohn, 1839–45), 1:36.

4 Ong, *Orality and Literacy,* 36.

5 Ibid., 72. On "back scanning" in literacy, see ibid., 104.

6 Ibid., 9.

7 On the evolutionary and rationalizing aspects of this history, see John Rogers, "Milton and the Mysterious Terms of History," *ELH* 57 (1990): 281–305.

8 See, e.g., H. R. MacCallum, "Milton and Sacred History: Books XI and XII of *Paradise Lost,*" in *English Literature from the Renaissance to the Victorian Age: Presented to A. S. P. Woodhouse,* ed. Millar MacLure and F. W. Watt (Toronto: University of Toronto Press, 1964), which presents an informative critique of the problems associated with this view derived from C. S. Lewis.

9 For a thorough examination of the ways in which *Paradise Lost* refutes the medieval doctrine of the fortunate Fall, see my "Self-Raised Sinners."

10 See Balachandra Rajan, *"Paradise Lost:* The Hill of History," *Huntington Library Quarterly* 31 (1967): 47–48.

11 Walter R. Davis puts the case somewhat differently, arguing that "the orientation of Book XI is visual," while that of book 12 "moves Adam and the reader from the difficult interpretation of visual events to the easier and more harmonious auditory style of faith." While it is hard to see what is easier about Michael's "literate" style or his "three-pronged" lecture, certainly this style calls for "emotional response and tonal adjustments," interpretation, and final unification of the voices of "man, angel and God" ("The Languages of Accommodation and the Styles of *Paradise Lost,*" in *Milton Studies,* vol. 18, 107–8).

12 See Ong's comments on Whitman in *Orality and Literacy,* 144.

13 Ibid., 70.

14 On Plato, see ibid., 117–23. For contrasting views of the poem's conclusion, see Stephen M. Fallon, "Milton's Sin and Death: The Ontology of Allegory in *Paradise Lost,*" *ELR* 17, no. 3 (1987): 335–39; Murrin, *The Veil of Allegory,* 167–98; and Kathleen M. Swaim, *Before and after the Fall: Contrasting Modes in Paradise Lost* (Amherst: University of Massachusetts Press, 1986).

15   For Ong's discussion of the poem in these terms, see *Interfaces of the Word*. For the relation of Christian liberty to that authority to interpret the Word reserved even by established Protestantism to church and communal authority—and its role as the very dynamic of Puritanism's revolutionary processes—see Fixler, *Milton and the Kingdoms of God,* passim.

16   See Jean-Jacques Rousseau, *A Discourse on Inequality,* trans. Maurice Cranston (Harmondsworth: Penguin, 1984), pt. 1, 81–107.

17   Jean-Jacques Rousseau, "The Social Contract," in *The Social Contract: Essays by Locke, Hume, Rousseau,* ed. Sir Ernest Barker (London: Oxford University Press, 1962), bk. 1, 169.

18   Sir Ernest Barker, introduction to *The Social Contract,* xxxiii. On Rousseau as "inventor" or history, see also Fredric Jameson, *Postmodernism, or the Logic of Late Capitalism* (Durham, N.C.: Duke University Press, 1992), 219 ff.

19   Ibid., xxxii. Here, Barker also notes that Rousseau's opposition to the patriarchal state stems from many of the same sources (primarily in Plato) as Milton's opposition to the patriarchal state/church.

20   See Rousseau, *A Discourse on Inequality,* 136.

21   This defense of the "divine right" of kings can be found, not only in Robert Filmer, but also in James I. Filmer's *Patriarcha* (ed. Peter Laslett [Oxford: Basil Blackwell, 1949]), which makes Adam not merely the model but the actual ancestor of kings. For an extended survey of the ideological effects of this interpretation, see Jonathan Goldberg, *James I and the Politics of Literature: Jonson, Shakespeare, Donne and Their Contemporaries* (Baltimore: Johns Hopkins University Press, 1983), 85–112.

22   The actual Latin of this quotation is taken from *The Prose Works of John Milton* (London: Henry G. Bohn, 1848), 1:168–69. The Yale edition is unfortunately "flatter": "Should any law or custom conflict with divine law or with reason, it is not to be considered a valid law" (*CPW,* 4, pt. 1: 456).

23   On Hobbes's polemical and (false) etymological uses of this literal sense of *de-liberation,* see George Shelton, *Morality and Sovereignty in the Philosophy of Thomas Hobbes* (New York: St. Martin's, 1992), 8.

24   Milner, *John Milton and the English Revolution,* 59.

25   Thus, it goes without saying that I fail to see Michael's account presenting a quietistic or conventional Christian history wherein God's role as true "auctor" makes man a mere "spectator." Nor do I see it wholly lacking in "the emphasis on energetic social confrontation and conflict" of the earlier political tracts, a "tragic" testimony to a Milton irremediably torn between the impulses of engagement and retreat (although its greater melancholy is obvious), as does David Loewenstein (*Milton and the Drama of History: Historical Vision, Iconoclasm, and the Literary Imagination* [Cambridge: Cambridge University Press, 1990], 96, 98, 118–20). For a similar view, see also Thomas Amorose, "Milton the Apocalyptic Historian: Competing Genres in *Paradise Lost,* Books XI–XII," in *Milton Studies,* vol. 17, 141–62.

26 Rousseau, *A Discourse on Inequality*, 135, 135–37.

27 As Victoria Kahn similarly notes, "In *Paradise Lost* the reader is called upon to make ethical decisions in the act of reading rather than to accept the 'implicit faith' (*Areopagitica*, 739) of episcopacy" ("The Rhetoric of Things Indifferent," 151), which ultimately means that he or she learns to practice a rhetoric authorizing both religious and political dissent.

Conclusion

1 *Christian Doctrine*, in *The Works of John Milton*, ed. Frank Allen Patterson (New York: Columbia University Press, 1933), 4:43, 61; hereafter cited as *CD*, by volume and page number. The Latin translation contained in this edition is used here because its style most strongly conveys the flavor of Milton's sense. Some citations in this chapter, as noted, are also taken from the Yale edition (*CPW*).

2 Stephen Hawking, *A Brief History of Time: From the Big Bang to Black Holes* (Toronto: Bantam, 1988), 175.

3 Benjamin, *The Origin of German Tragic Drama*, 138.

4 Foucault, *The Order of Things*, 83.

5 Hugh M. Davidson, *The Origins of Certainty: Means and Meanings in Pascal's "Pensées"* (Chicago: University of Chicago Press, 1979), 56–57.

6 For a modern philosophical exploration of this aspect of language, see Max Black, *Models and Metaphors: Studies in Language and Philosophy* (Ithaca, N.Y.: Cornell University Press, 1962).

7 Thus, while with Urania's help the poet may attempt things yet unattempted "in prose or rhyme" (*PL*, 1.16), it seems highly significant that every other use of the word *attempt* in *A Concordance to Milton's Poetry* (ed. William Ingram and Kathleen Swaim [Oxford: Clarendon, 1972]) is overtly satanic (eighteen in the singular) or (generally in reference to Samson) fallen (eight in the plural, past, and participial tenses). Milton is thus highly aware of the ironic "temptation" embedded in the word *attempt*, although that no more makes it wholly impure than the similarly ambiguous sense attached to *erroneous*. See the discussions of Urania in chap. 5 and of "mazy error" in chap. 3 above.

8 This and all subsequent translations of the *Pensées* are taken from A. J. Krailsheimer's version of the text (Harmondsworth: Penguin, 1966), which is based on the order of the text followed in the four editions of M. Louis Lafuma; the French quotations also follow the Lafuma order, which unless otherwise stated are listed by fragment, not page number. (This particular quotation is taken from p. 257.) It is not possible to consider the problems generated by the fragmentary nature of Pascal's text in the scope of the present study; see, however, Krailsheimer's summary on pp. 27–29; and also Sara E. Melzer, *Discourses of the Fall: A Study of Pascal's Pensées* (Berkeley: University of California Press, 1986), 128–35.

9 De Man, "Pascal's Allegory of Persuasion," 10.

10 Of course, Descartes's *Meditations* technically foreground the deity as the "necessary" anchor of a system of "clear and distinct" signs otherwise threatened with disruption by an imaginary "evil genius." Yet, since this godhead is merely the logical anchor of a system whose essential orderliness was being mathematically demonstrated by the new science, this deity effectively becomes a logical fiction, both in Descartes's own time (for radical Cartesians like Hobbes) and especially during the Enlightenment.

11 J. B. Savage, "Freedom and Necessity in *Paradise Lost,*" *ELH* 44 (1977): 297, 301–5.

12 Patricia Topliss, from whose study I draw these passages of Pascal in the original, goes on to point out that "égarement" or wandering leads man directly to his emptiness or void, "son néant, son abandon, son insuffisance, sa dépendance, son impuissance, son vide" (160), which she interprets as indicating Pascal's place in the psychological tradition of Augustinian apologetics—a somewhat disappointing interpretation since it tends to collapse the importance of the void in his system and thus underestimate the indeterminacy of his theology. Just as his oppositions refuse to be resolved into the positive antitheses of conventional theology, so his use of the void cannot be reduced to the Augustinian theme of the "emptiness" or "nothingness" of man. As de Man notes ("Pascal's Allegory of Persuasion," 11 ff.) "nothing" for Pascal is as inherently unstable as the One that God no longer is: although the "néant" surrounds the void, it is never equivalent to it. For Pascal, "nothing" is self-cancellation, but, in dramatic contrast to the "vide" in Bérulle's Augustinian apologetics, the zero, void, or gap is a placeholder that exists precisely not "d'être rempli." See, however, Topliss, *The Rhetoric of Pascal: A Study of His Art of Persuasion in the "Provinciales" and the "Pensées"* (Amsterdam: Leicester University Press, 1966), 266–67.

13 Melzer, *Discourses of the Fall,* 56.

14 Hence, Lucien Goldmann finds that, where a Jansenist like Barcos typically "gives an absolute *no* to the world, Pascal gives a paradoxical *yes* and *no*" (*The Hidden God,* 169).

Index

Catherine Gimelli Martin

is Associate Professor of English at

the University of Memphis.

Library of Congress Cataloging-in-Publication Data

Martin, Catherine Gimelli.

The ruins of allegory : Paradise lost and the metamorphosis

of epic convention / Catherine Gimelli Martin.

p.   cm.

Includes index.

ISBN 0-8223-1980-2 (cloth : alk. paper). —

ISBN 0-8223-1989-6 (pbk. : alk. paper)

1. Milton, John, 1608–1674.   Paradise lost.   2. Literature

and history—England—History—17th century.

3. Christian poetry, English—History and criticism.

4. Epic poetry, English—History and criticism.

5. Metamorphosis in literature.   6. Prophecies in literature.

7. Monism in literature.   8. Allegory.   I. Title.

PR3562.M287   1998

821'.4—dc21   97-42591